SAP PRESS Books: Always on hand

Print or e-book, Kindle or iPad, workplace or airplane: Choose where and how to read your SAP PRESS books! You can now get all our titles as e-books, too:

- ▶ By download and online access
- ▶ For all popular devices
- ▶ And, of course, DRM-free

Convinced? Then go to **www.sap-press.com** and get your e-book today.

Procurement with SAP® MM—Practical Guide

 **PRESS**

SAP PRESS is a joint initiative of SAP and Galileo Press. The know-how offered by SAP specialists combined with the expertise of the Galileo Press publishing house offers the reader expert books in the field. SAP PRESS features first-hand information and expert advice, and provides useful skills for professional decision-making.

SAP PRESS offers a variety of books on technical and business-related topics for the SAP user. For further information, please visit our website: *www.sap-press.com*.

Martin Murray
100 Things You Should Know About
Materials Management in SAP ERP
2013, 316 pp., paperback
ISBN 978-1-59229-438-1

Jawad Akhtar
Production Planning and Control with SAP ERP
2013, 1033 pp., hardcover
ISBN 978-1-59229-868-6

Sandeep Pradhan
Demand and Supply Planning with SAP APO
2013, 797 pp., hardcover
ISBN 978-1-59229-423-7

Martin Murray
Materials Management with SAP ERP:
Functionality and Technical Configuration (3rd Edition)
2011, 666 pp., hardcover
ISBN 978-1-59229-358-2

Matt Chudy and Luis Castedo

Procurement with SAP® MM—
Practical Guide

Galileo Press

Bonn • Boston

Galileo Press is named after the Italian physicist, mathematician, and philosopher Galileo Galilei (1564–1642). He is known as one of the founders of modern science and an advocate of our contemporary, heliocentric worldview. His words *Eppur si muove* (And yet it moves) have become legendary. The Galileo Press logo depicts Jupiter orbited by the four Galilean moons, which were discovered by Galileo in 1610.

Editor Laura Korslund
Acquisitions Editor Katy Spencer
Copyeditor Julie McNamee
Cover Design Graham Geary
Photo Credit iStockphoto.com: 14788270/© Crisma, 183681/© Digiphoto, 11306163/© Sarahneal
Layout Design Vera Brauner
Production Graham Geary
Typesetting Publishers' Design and Production Services, Inc.
Printed and bound in the United States of America, on paper from sustainable sources

ISBN 978-1-59229-840-2

© 2014 by Galileo Press Inc., Boston (MA)
1st edition 2014

Library of Congress Cataloging-in-Publication Data
Chudy, Matt.
Procurement with SAP MM : practical guide / Matt Chudy and Luis Castedo. — 1st edition.
pages cm
ISBN-13: 978-1-59229-840-2 (print)
ISBN-10: 1-59229-840-0 (print)
ISBN-13: 978-1-59229-841-9 (e-book)
ISBN-13: 978-1-59229-842-6 (print and e-book) 1. SAP ERP. 2. Industrial procurement—Data processing.
3. Purchasing—Data processing. 4. Materials management—Data processing. 5. Management information systems.
I. Castedo, Luis. II. Title.
HD39.5.C48 2014
658.7'2028553—dc23
2013040750

Contents at a Glance

Dear Reader,

Above the surface, procurement seems like a walk in the park. Need something? Call or email, ask for it, and it's yours! But wait—things can't really be that simple, can they? After working on this manuscript, I have the greatest appreciation that in fact no, procurement is much more complex than what appears on the surface. Lurking in the depths, just waiting to confuse you are tricky little activities such as taxes, invoicing, and stock management, oh my!

But never fear: veteran authors Matt Chudy and Luis Castedo know the ropes and will help guide you safely as they delve into the daily activities you'll encounter when working with the procurement of materials and products. I'm confident that this book will help you get to know the functions in Materials Management that are available, and the necessary tasks you'll encounter.

Your comments and suggestions are the most useful tools to help us improve our books. We encourage you to visit our website at *www.sap-press.com* and share your feedback about *Procurement with SAP MM—Practical Guide*.

Thank you for purchasing a book from SAP PRESS!

Laura Korslund
Editor, SAP PRESS

Galileo Press
Boston, MA

laura.korslund@galileo-press.com
www.sap-press.com

Contents

Appendices 453

Introduction

When deciding to write this book, we started by reviewing the basics. First, any company that procures products or services must be able to efficiently place, track, and receive orders for products and services. Second, SAP has an integrated Materials Management system, which includes sophisticated procurement processes that enable companies to create contracts and agreements, acknowledge order receipts, and process incoming invoices. In today's competitive environment, a tool that can effectively handle the cost of these processes is vital. Procurement in the Materials Management (MM) component of SAP ERP is such a tool. Furthermore, MM is one of the most important and most often implemented SAP logistics functionalities for managing the different stages of the procure-to-pay process, making the information more manageable and accessible.

This book is a practical guide to the key processes in procurement; it provides you with practical, detailed guidance for the day-to-day use of procurement in MM, including troubleshooting and problem-solving information. It covers typical functionality such as master data, sourcing, purchasing, material requirements planning (MRP) and forecasting, special procurement functions (e.g., third-party, subcontracting, cross-company), inbound logistics, inventory management, warehouse management, and invoice processing. This book will help you make use of SAP ERP MM more effectively.

Who This Book Is For

There are many books on the market that cover a lot of SAP ground, from the basics to technical details, configuration, optimization, and more. This book addresses the needs of a wide spectrum of users—from end users learning to crawl in SAP, to a group of firmly walking procurement team members already using SAP transactions, to the runners at the front lines supporting the systems and implementing new processes and functionality.

New SAP family members getting their implementation projects started can use this book as a guide bringing a wealth of knowledge to the table from the start. Experienced SAP professionals will find it handy as a memory refresher when needed. This book will also be useful for the SAP business user community craving to learn what SAP can offer and stretch its capabilities to the limit. The IT side of the world can use the book as a guide to close the gap between process and SAP functionality. Although it's never easy to address so many different readers at once, we hope to bring as much interesting material as possible to satisfy the hungriest of appetites for procurement knowledge in SAP.

Chapter Breakdown

The book begins by providing an overview of the SAP components and organizational structures that build a foundation for procurement activities. We briefly talk about other tools in the SAP arsenal that can help build further on the core. In a chapter on master data that covers the building blocks needed to perform the procurement functions, we touch on material masters, service masters, business partners, sourcing master data, pricing, taxes, routes, batch records, and manufacturer part numbers, just to mention a few major ones.

We then move to a planning and forecasting chapter that describes the beginning steps of procurement—identification of requirements—where we focus on MRP, forecasting, planning, and evaluation methods.

Chapter 1 introduces the SAP ERP system and the organizational structure as it applies to the MM component, an overview of the same MM component, and a brief description of other procurement tools within the SAP Business Suite.

Chapter 2 covers the master data used in procurement by explaining the different master catalogs (e.g., material master and the vendor master) and all of the specific purchasing master data (e.g., info records and source lists).

Chapter 3 is all about planning, how the MRP subsystem generates requirements, the relationship with the master data, and how to evaluate the data produced by MRP.

Chapter 4 covers how purchasing documents are created and maintained, including requisitions, purchase orders, RFQs, and outline agreements. We also discuss vendor evaluation, including how it is structured and executed.

Chapter 5 covers special procurement functions. We step outside of common procurement functionality and talk about subcontracting, third-party procurement, cross-company transactions, Kanban, and retail-specific load builder transactions.

Chapter 6 discusses the procurement of external services, including processing service requirements and service agreements, purchasing services, recording service entries, and integrating with other processes.

Chapter 7 dives into inbound logistics, inbound shipments, appointments, and shipment cost document processing, along with its integration with purchasing and reporting.

Chapter 8 covers Inventory Management, including receiving, managing of special stocks such as sales order stock and consignment, transfer postings, and stock transfers.

Chapter 9 talks about Logistics Invoice Verification, along with how to handle taxes and delivery costs; how to block and park invoices; how to handle progress payments, down payments, and reversals; and how to use accounts payable everyday reports.

And finally in the **appendices**, additional charts and tips are provided that cover everything from the most-used MM tables to some quick tricks and tips that can save you a few minutes when performing day-to-day procurement tasks.

We'll start off with the overview of SAP ERP components and the system's integrated architecture. We'll review the foundations that procurement is built on—organizational structures—and how they influence the functionality of your organization and material master overview, which we'll discuss in detail in the next chapter. As we mentioned at the beginning,

SAP's offering does not stop with the core SAP ERP. We'll introduce you to some of the other tools from the SAP Business Suite that are available if your organization needs to close some gaps between standard SAP ERP and your business processes. We'll also briefly focus on SAP HANA, a new SAP initiative. Let's begin our introduction journey through SAP ERP procurement with an overview of SAP ERP components and integration.

Enterprise resource planning systems have revolutionized how businesses are run today. Procurement has been there from day one, and it has been getting better ever since.

1 Introduction to SAP ERP and the SAP Business Suite

It seems like more and better SAP products are being released every day, and what used to be the original purpose of having a complete and integrated enterprise resource planning (ERP) system has evolved. Now, the SAP ERP system is contained in one such product: the SAP ERP Enterprise Central Components (ECC) system.

SAP ECC is the integrated piece of software that is used to execute the everyday operations of a company. A company can plan and execute the entire collection of steps involved in its supply chain—from the sales forecasts, master production scheduling, production planning, production scheduling, purchasing, inventory management, to warehousing—along with the logistics chain that is involved in the distribution of the company's products, shipping, transportation planning, and yard management.

SAP ECC

Procurement plays an important role in most of these activities; it includes all activities and processes related to acquiring goods and services. This includes defining the requirements for goods and services, establishing a source of supply, negotiating contracts, performing vendor evaluations, and purchasing, which crowns these activities with purchase orders, brings the goods into the warehouse, and finishes with payment to the supplier.

Procurement

Most top-tier ERP applications include procurement, and SAP AG has provided this capability as one of its key functionalities since the company's inception in 1972. As SAP's software evolved from R/1 through R/3 into a better and more robust product with each new release, procurement needs have been addressed along the way, bringing additional functionalities and new tools to help companies with planning, forecasting, processing purchase requisitions, assigning sources of supply, creating purchase orders, receiving, and paying the incoming invoices.

This chapter helps you understand the structure of SAP ERP software, in which Materials Management (MM) plays a central role. We'll help you understand how the SAP Purchasing component (which is often referred to interchangeably with Procurement) integrates into the SAP architecture, and then provide a brief overview of the SAP Business Suite. Many of these suite components provide functionality that integrates with the procurement functionality, which we'll discuss throughout the book.

1.1   SAP ERP Components

In this section, we'll provide an overview of the different areas, or components, that make up the whole of SAP ERP.

The SAP ERP system is divided into functional pieces called modules or *components*. Each functional area of a company might use one or more components, but many times, a person's work won't involve more than one. All of the components are tightly integrated, and they all update financial information, and depending on the process, share master data such as vendors, customers, materials, and employees. This tight integration, along with the ability to operate in multiple currencies and in multiple languages, is the key to SAP ERP's success.

In the following subsections, we'll go over the components that are included in the SAP ERP system.

1.1.1   Financial Accounting (FI)

Business transactions

Financial Accounting (FI) captures the organization's business transactions. Integration with Sales and Distribution (SD), Purchasing, and MM components allows you to select any financial transaction and drill down to the originating transaction, whether it's a purchase order, sales order, or material movement—all while satisfying external reporting requirements. Local legal considerations are predelivered with the system, and the ability to manage and report on multiple companies in multiple countries with multiple currencies is part of the standard functionality.

In its heart is the SAP General Ledger; like a hub and spokes, it touches every other component. Every time you sell, buy, pay, collect, or manufacture, the accounting system is updated. Values are posted to an account in the ledger to show a customer's balance, changes in inventory value, payables that need to be covered with your vendors, and so on.

G/L

But while accountants are probably the happiest customers after SAP ERP is implemented in a company, it's the integration between processes and its ability to run in different languages and in a multicurrency environment that make it so advantageous.

FI components include the General Ledger, Accounts Payable, Accounts Receivable, Bank Accounting, Asset Accounting, Funds Management, and Travel Management submodules.

1.1.2 Controlling (CO)

Controlling (CO) provides organizations with a method of analyzing costs from a management perspective and provides a view of profitability beyond that of basic financial reporting. It allows cost planning and tracking, activity-based costing, product costing, and profitability analysis.

Cost analysis

1.1.3 SAP Project System (PS)

SAP Project System (SAP PS) provides tools to track project milestones, costs, and resources. Its tight integration to the CO, Human Resources (HR), and Logistics components, allows SAP PS to use personnel records from HR, roll costs into CO, link to materials and customers, or trigger purchases in Logistics.

1.1.4 Sales and Distribution (SD)

Sales and Distribution (SD) provides a comprehensive tool to support the sales cycle of a company from following sales leads and preparing quotes, to firming orders, including individual orders, contracts, and scheduling agreements. It also covers the warehousing activities of picking, packing, and shipping customer orders.

1.1.5   Materials Management (MM)

MM takes care of the material requirements planning (MRP), purchasing, material valuation, and inventory control. It manages the orders to vendors, including individual orders, contracts, and scheduling agreements. The topics discussed in this book reside in this component under the Purchasing, or Procurement, subcomponent.

1.1.6   Logistics Execution (LE)

Logistics Execution (LE) has a little overlap with the SD component. It takes care of all of the inbound and outbound flow of materials from vendors and to customers. It executes the shipping control as well.

1.1.7   Quality Management (QM)

Quality Management manages and facilitates the processes related to sampling materials purchased from vendors or manufactured in house. It handles all of the sampling, testing, and quarantine procedures and documentation.

1.1.8   Plant Maintenance (PM)

Through the use of technical objects, Plant Maintenance (PM) registers the installation and maintenance of the company's equipment. This component plans and executes preventive and corrective maintenance, while keeping a complete record of all work done on each piece of machinery.

1.1.9   Production Planning and Control (PP)

The Production Planning and Control (PP) component provides the functionality to store bills of materials (BOMs), recipes, and routings for the products that a company manufactures. It works with the MRP component to create planned or firm production orders to supply the product that customers demand.

1.1.10   Human Resources (HR)

The Human Resources (HR) component provides tools to manage employees, work centers, training and development plans, benefits, and, in some countries, even payroll.

1.2   Materials Management Organizational Structures

SAP ERP installation requires an enterprise structure that can be molded to reflect your own organization for basic business transactions to take place. These structures can be grouped together to serve specific functional areas such as finance, materials management, logistics, sales, and so on.

None of the procurement transactions can be executed in the SAP system without a foundation built by organizational structures. Procurement functions require finance, materials management, and logistics structures to be defined. Figure 1.1 provides an overview of the enterprise components we'll be discussing, which are described in the following sections.

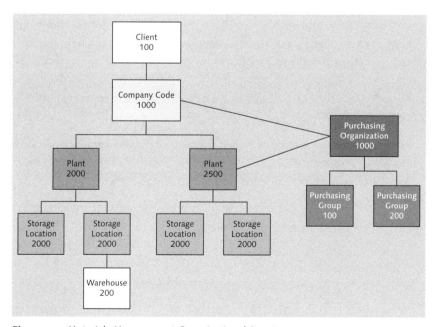

Figure 1.1   Materials Management Organizational Structures

1.2.1 Client

The client number is the SAP instance in which we'll be working. You have to enter this number in the logon screen along with your user ID and password. This number is used to differentiate between development, quality, and production systems within your SAP ERP installation. It also provides users with common database tables and master data files. Cross-client objects are an exception to this rule.

1.2.2 Company Code

Company's legal entity

The company code represents a company's legal entity. This is the first functional level, and it belongs to finance. If your company is made up of a conglomerate of companies, then your SAP instance probably has more than one company code. Each company code has a General Ledger.

1.2.3 Plant

Company structure

The logistics structure reflects the operational structure of a company, and the plant stands at the top of this pyramid. The plant is the element where a company's operations are executed (i.e., purchasing, production, inventory, and sales). The plant should reflect a physical location within the company structure. In other words, it's the SAP tool to reflect a manufacturing plant or a distribution center. In some cases, when the operations within a facility are too different from one another due to the unique materials and procedures used, you can define separate plants in SAP ERP as well.

A plant has its own material master data, address, tax jurisdiction code, and factory calendar. It can also have its own account determination. Your stock inventories are also valuated at the plant level.

Below the plant, there are several levels from different functional areas in SAP ERP, which we discuss in the following subsections.

Storage Location

Stock

This organizational structure belongs to a plant and represents places where stock is kept. In the SAP ERP system, the storage locations keep the quantity of every material a company uses. Every time a material is received from a vendor, used in a production order, or sold to a customer, the storage location reflects these changes in the stock levels, and, at the same time, it updates the accounting General Ledger at the plant level.

Warehouse

The warehouse number represents the physical warehouse complex, including the collection of all racks, bins, cages, and crates that are used to store the product. While the storage location tells you how many units of a certain product you have and how much they are worth, the warehouse number tells you where in the warehouse to find them.

Physical location

1.2.4 Purchasing Organization

This organizational structure is responsible for the procurement of goods and services for your company. Purchasing organizations can be molded to fit many different forms of procurement, which we'll discuss in the following subsections.

Procurement

Centralized Purchasing

This form of procurement is best for organizations dealing with large volumes of raw materials, consolidating demand from multiple organizations, and where purchasing activities are directed from a single buying office. The SAP corporate-wide model allows for purchasing for multiple organizations with a single purchasing organization assigned to multiple plants of different company codes (see Figure 1.2 for examples).

Raw materials

Decentralized/Localized Purchasing

This form of purchasing is best suited for companies where requirements from different organizations can't be consolidated and where volumes of raw materials are relatively small. Localized purchasing organizations offer local controls with more efficient communication and shorter delivery times due to local sources of supply. You can pick from two SAP models: company-specific purchasing or plant-specific purchasing.

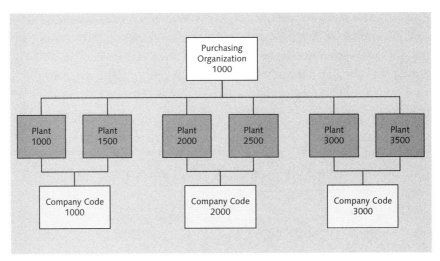

Figure 1.2 Corporate-Wide Purchasing

Company-specific purchasing In the multi-company code situation, purchasing organizations are defined for individual company codes (see Figure 1.3). Each company code purchasing organization maintains its own master data.

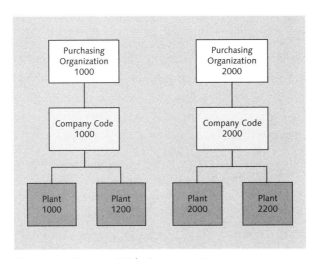

Figure 1.3 Company-Wide Procurement

You can define purchasing organizations that serve individual plants. This form of distributed purchasing offers local control of procurement and local master data maintenance. Corporate-level reporting can be cumbersome (see Figure 1.4 for an example).

Plant-specific purchasing

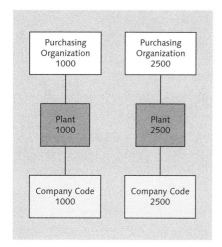

Figure 1.4 Plant-Specific Purchasing

Hybrid Purchasing Organizations

SAP enables you to combine different forms of purchasing organizations, which allows centralized and localized forms of procurement to co-exist and offers the best of both worlds.

If you're sharing common contracts and want to take advantage of the buying power of multiple organizations, you can maintain a *reference purchasing organization,* which is linked to multiple purchasing organizations and allows for cross-company contracts and pricing. This type of organizational structures guarantees the same level of control, quality of goods and services, flexibility to manage purchasing activities globally and/or locally and improved authorizations maintenance, better reporting and visibility to cross-company activities, and economy of scale. All master data, however, needs to be maintained in the reference organization. See Figure 1.5 for a reference purchasing organization sample layout.

Reference purchasing organization

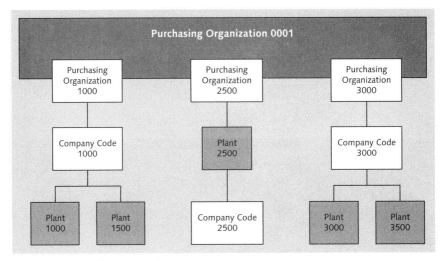

Figure 1.5 Reference Purchasing Organization

Standard purchasing organization

If several purchasing organizations procure different types of products and services for a single plant location, or multiple plants of different company codes, you can choose one of them to serve as a standard purchasing organization for pipeline procurement, consignment, and stock transfers. The standard purchasing organization is automatically determined with transactions for these types of stock (see Figure 1.6).

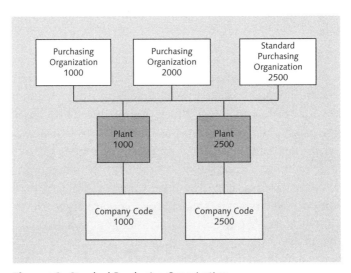

Figure 1.6 Standard Purchasing Organization

1.2.5 Purchasing Groups

Each purchasing group is assigned to one purchasing organization. The purchasing groups represent a buyer or groups of buyers procuring specific product groups or services. Each purchasing group can have a name, telephone number, fax number, and e-mail address. All of this information is added to a purchase order when it's printed or sent to the vendor so the vendor has a way of contacting the buyer.

1.3 Materials Management Overview

Materials Management (MM) is the SAP ERP component that contains most of the purchasing, or procurement, activities. This very important part of the Logistics components of the SAP ERP system executes several different processes within a company including materials planning, purchasing, inventory control, and inventory valuation.

> **Note**
>
> In this book we often use the terms *purchasing* and *procurement* interchangeably.
>
> To differentiate procurement from purchasing, the term *procurement* is the function that describes the activities and processes to acquire goods and services. This includes all of the activities involved in establishing fundamental requirements, sourcing activities such as market research and vendor evaluation, and negotiation of contracts. The term *purchasing* refers to the process of ordering and receiving goods and services. It is a subset of the wider procurement process.

To support these processes, the MM component has several tools, including the following:

Procurement tools

- A very robust MRP system

- Several different procurement tools that allow companies to choose a variety of different ways in which they can interact with their vendors

- An inventory control system that is based on movement types that allow a different accounting treatment depending on whether the material came in as a result of a purchase order, a production order, or an inventory adjustment; or if the materials are taken out of the warehouse for consumption, for production, for order fulfillment, to supply consignment stores, or other movements that may affect the count of materials inside the warehouse and thus the valuation of that inventory in accounting

Functionally, MM can be divided into the following: MRP, Purchasing, and Inventory Valuation and Control (see Figure 1.7). We'll discuss each of these in the following sections.

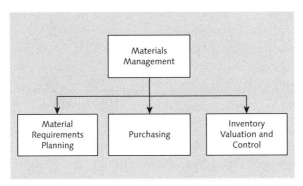

Figure 1.7 Materials Management: MRP, Purchasing, and Inventory Valuation and Control

1.3.1 Material Requirements Planning

Material
monitoring

Material Requirements Planning (MRP) is the submodule that monitors all of the needs of the different materials that the company buys and sells. It can start off with the Planned Independent Requirements (PIRs) or the sales forecast for the finished goods, and from there explode the bill of materials (BOM) and generate the pegged or inherited requirements for each of the components that form that finished good. Planned production orders are generated for manufacturing depending on the lead times for making or assembling the product and also on the purchasing lead times of each of the components.

1.3.2 Purchasing

Linked to the MRP results, and along with triggering or planning production orders, SAP ERP can also create or plan purchase requisitions for those components that are either missing or that have to be replenished after consuming the quantities taken by manufacturing.

To execute those purchases, SAP ERP can either create individual purchase orders or have agreements with the vendors that help a company secure lower prices, have quantities of materials available on certain dates, or both. These agreements also serve as a way to communicate to the vendors the consumption forecast for some materials and to arrange deliveries of smaller quantities more often to reduce the inventory to a manageable minimum. We'll discuss the different documents available to you in Procurement in more detail in Chapter 4, and how they fit in the overall procurement process. Figure 1.8 shows where these documents belong in SAP ERP, from a functionality point of view.

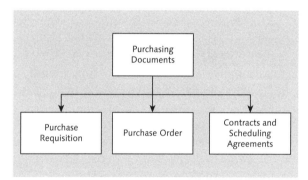

Figure 1.8 Purchasing System's Document Types: Requisitions, Orders, Contracts, and Scheduling Agreements

1.3.3 Inventory Valuation and Control

The SAP ERP system acts as the system of record to keep track of all of the receipts and all of the issues of materials. At the same time, it maintains the real-time stock quantity for each material and, if necessary, of each batch. These stock quantities are valued based on the individual value set in the material master.

1.3.4 Master Data

Within MM, a collection of master data is also maintained: The material master contains all of the information about all materials the company buys, sells, or manufactures. It includes basic information about the

Material master

material, including descriptions, codes, weight, and measurements, as well as how the material is purchased, sold, planned, stored, and valued.

Vendor master The second kind of master data that needs to be maintained is the vendor master, which is a collection of the company's supplier information, from name and address, to accounting rules and bank information. Both master catalogs are the heart of the MM component.

1.4   SAP Business Suite: Other Procurement Tools

Throughout the years, SAP has been adding packages to improve specific functionalities that the core component doesn't address or that would require massive development or customization effort to the available functionality. To close the gaps, several additional tools are available for you to make your portfolio complete, while still being supported by a single software company. In the following sections, we'll explain some of the most important applications that address procurement needs.

1.4.1   SAP Sourcing

SAP Sourcing is part of a web-based applications portfolio designed to process procurement sourcing functions that include project management, online bidding, contract negotiation, and compliance monitoring.

SAP E-Sourcing With SAP E-Sourcing, you can support the sourcing component of the procurement process with the following functionality:

▸ Expenditure analysis

▸ Supplier identification

▸ Negotiation events that include the following:

▹ Request for proposal

▹ Reverse auctions

▸ Supplier management

▸ Contract management

This solution helps you eliminate manual processes, brings visibility and real-time compliance monitoring, and provides the holistic approach to the sourcing process. Although this holistic approach to the sourcing process is available in SAP ERP and SAP Supplier Relationship Management (SAP SRM), it's not as well integrated as in the SAP E-Sourcing package. The collaborative approach allows you to bring your selected pool of suppliers to the negotiating table early, reducing the sourcing cycle drastically. This tool definitely helps free up your procurement resources to focus on more complex strategic initiatives.

1.4.2 SAP Supplier Lifecycle Management

SAP Supplier Lifecycle Management is another SAP application that helps you manage suppliers in a holistic approach, from selected vendor onboarding (registration, qualification, classification) through ongoing maintenance and evaluation. You can also connect supplier relationship management to SAP Supplier Relationship Management (SAP SRM) or to SAP ERP Enterprise Core Component (ECC).

The basic functionality that this component delivers includes the following:

▶ Registering suppliers

▶ Maintaining supplier data

▶ Qualifying suppliers

▶ Managing the supplier portfolio

▶ Evaluating suppliers

Figure 1.9 shows the high-level architecture components and how they are connected for deployment; specifically, it shows the option of connecting to SAP SRM and SAP ERP systems.

SLM deployment options

SAP Supplier Lifecycle Management is divided into the sell side—representing suppliers—and the buy side, which is your company's purchasing organization.

The sell side can be deployed on Supplier Self-Services (SUS), which is part of SAP SRM. Companies can perform the following tasks:

Sell side

▶ Register as the supplier.

▶ Maintain supplier company data.

▶ Qualify suppliers to take part in qualifying activities that your purchasing organization defines.

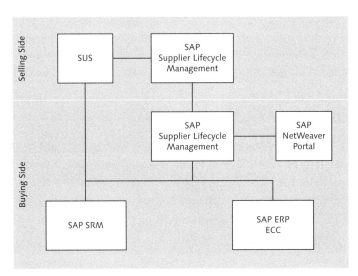

Figure 1.9 Supplier Lifecycle Management: Deployment Options

Buy side

On the buying side—that is, the purchasing organization side—you can perform the following activities:

▶ Manage purchasing categories such as product and service types.

▶ Manage supplier portfolio information such as vendor master data, qualifications, and business relationships.

▶ Qualify existing and new suppliers for new requirements based on the answers to the information you request.

▶ Evaluate suppliers/vendors by using questionnaires and scorecards manually either on a periodic basis or automatically where information is collected based on activities in the backend system (e.g., SAP SRM or SAP ERP) via event-driven processes.

1.4.3 SAP Supplier Relationship Management

Procure-to-pay

SAP SRM is designed to automate, simplify, and accelerate procure-to-pay processes for goods and services with a very important focus on web-based operations and e-commerce. Some of the functions included in this application are the following:

▶ E-sourcing (spend analysis; category and project management; requests for proposal, information, and quotation; forward and reverse auctions; contract generation and management; and supplier management)

▶ On-demand e-sourcing

▶ SAP Contract Lifecycle Management

▶ SAP BusinessObjects Spend Performance Management

SAP SRM provides multiple deployment scenarios to choose from, along with different levels of integration with SAP or other applications. Your choice of deployment scenario will impact the complete solution delivery. Although hybrid scenarios are possible, the available main options include what we discuss in the following subsections.

Indirect Procurement

This flavor of procurement is for consumption and requires account assignment. At the time of receipt, purchased goods aren't stocked because they are immediately consumed by the reference cost object. The following deployment options are possible for this form of procurement.

Classic Scenario

This scenario offers shopping cart functionality, but all follow-on documents—such as purchase requisitions and purchase orders—are created in the backend system. External requirements are transferred to SAP SRM because the shopping cart will be created in sourcing. There is no ability to release or approve; only approved requisitions can be transferred from the backend systems. All purchase orders are generated, and changes can be made in the core system. Users can post confirmations in SAP SRM, which posts goods receipt or a service entry in the SAP ERP core, and also accounts payable (AP) invoices can be entered either on the SAP SRM side or the SAP ERP core. This scenario is best for organizations using SAP ERP already that have a solid purchasing organization and interfaces to suppliers maintained on the SAP ERP side and SUS linked to MM.

Shopping cart functionality

Extended Classic

The extended classic functionality also offers shopping cart functionality. Only approved purchase requisitions are transferred from SAP ERP to SAP SRM because the shopping cart will be created in sourcing. As in the classic scenario, there is no ability to release or approve. All purchase orders are generated, and changes can be made in SAP SRM only and then transferred to SAP ERP where they can be accessed in display mode only. Users can post confirmations in SAP SRM that can translate to either a goods receipt or a service entry in the SAP ERP core. Generally, however, they are posted directly in the backend system. Similarly, AP invoices can be entered either on the SAP SRM side or the SAP ERP core.

Primary work space

This scenario is best for organizations that want SAP SRM to be the primary work space for the purchasing organization and want to take advantage of integrated sourcing capabilities without legacy interfaces. Organizations that don't want to use SAP requisitions or reservations in the procurement process will also find this scenario useful. SUS usage is not fully supported; consult the SAP SRM implementation guide for information on enabling SUS functionality in this scenario.

Standalone Scenario

The majority of all procurement activities are performed in SAP SRM in the standalone scenario. No external requirements are transferred from backend systems, and confirmations posted in SAP SRM don't create corresponding goods receipts or service entries. Additionally, invoices are created in SAP SRM and translated to an accounting document on the SAP ERP core side. SUS is supported and available. This scenario is best for organizations that don't currently use the MM component of SAP ERP or that want to carve out the purchasing activities off the core system.

Direct Procurement

Opposite to the previous scenario, direct procurement refers to purchases of materials to stock. At the time of receipt, the procured materials show up on the balance sheet of the valuation area requesting the goods. Although the standalone scenario is not supported, the following scenarios are available for direct procurement.

Classic/Extended Classic Scenarios

These scenarios are pretty much one and the same with no noticeable differences. Both offer shopping carts that represent external require- ments (purchase requisitions) that are transferred to SAP SRM. There is no ability to release or approve, and only approved requisitions can be transferred from the backend systems. All purchase orders are generated, and changes can be made in SAP SRM only. Users can post confirma- tions in SAP SRM, which posts goods receipts or a service entries in the SAP ERP core. AP invoices can be entered either on the SAP SRM side or the SAP ERP core. This scenario is best for organizations already using SAP ERP with a solid purchasing organization and interfaces to suppli- ers maintained on the SAP ERP side. SUS usage is not fully supported; consult the SAP SRM implementation guide for information on enabling SUS functionality in this scenario.

Service Procurement

For purchasing organizations that use MM and external services manage- ment functionality, only the classic scenario is available in SAP SRM (see the "Indirect Procurement" section earlier in this chapter for details).

1.4.4 SAP Supply Chain Management

The SAP Supply Chain Management (SAP SCM) application is probably one of the most complex applications interfacing to SAP ERP. It helps integrate multi-instance, complex supply chains into a single planning, execution, and monitoring system.

SAP SCM is capable of rapidly sharing information with your company's partners and enhancing collaboration capabilities. SAP SCM evolved into a package that now includes SAP Advanced Planning and Optimization (SAP APO), which is a very robust and popular planning system. Further integration of the new collaboration and execution components made it a very powerful tool. Now it helps you deal with multi-plant capacity planning and scheduling, global ATP, distribution planning, and other very complex functions that in many cases used to be executed outside of SAP ERP systems. The latest releases of SAP SCM include SAP Event Management (SAP EM) and a completely redesigned new warehouse management application designed to compete with best of breed—SAP

Planning and scheduling

Extended Warehouse Management (SAP EWM). The following are some of the functions supported by the SAP SCM application:

Functions

- ▶ Planning (demand planning and forecasting, safety stock planning, supply network planning, distribution planning, strategic supply chain design)

- ▶ Execution (order fulfillment, procurement, transportation, warehousing, manufacturing)

- ▶ Supplier collaboration (access to supply chain information for demand and supply synchronization)

- ▶ Customer collaboration (replenishment management, vendor-managed inventory [VMI])

- ▶ Contract manufacturer collaboration (extending the visibility of the manufacturing process)

1.4.5   SAP Transportation Management

SAP Transportation Management (SAP TM) helps you manage your need for inbound and outbound transportation by redesigning what SAP SCM's Transportation Planning and Vehicle Scheduling has to offer. Following are some of the available functions:

- ▶ Maintenance of forwarding orders
- ▶ Integration with the core SAP ERP system
- ▶ Freight bookings
- ▶ Transportation planning, tendering, carrier selection
- ▶ Integration with foreign trade services

1.4.6   SAP HANA

SAP HANA is a new and revolutionary in-memory computing concept that takes advantage of the low cost of hardware, such as RAM memory and solid-state drives, and offers significant improvements in performance. Its multi-query language helps in large database environments used for analytics and optimization. Although this engine doesn't impact procurement functions directly, this platform is applied to SAP NetWeaver

Business Warehouse as well as SAP CRM and SAP SCM. SAP HANA will definitely be on top of the charts for the next few years and will also be applied as a base for SAP ERP in the near future.

1.5   Summary

In this first chapter, we gave you an overview of the components of the SAP ERP system and how they are integrated to exchange information and create a flow that follows the different enterprise processes. We also described the organizational structures that are used in MM and provided an overview of all the functions that can be executed in MM.

These are the building blocks that we'll describe in detail in this book. It's very important that you have a good understanding of the different pieces that integrate purchasing in SAP, so you can use them to get better results from the system and to avoid manual processing as much as possible.

So, let's get started with Chapter 2, which introduces master data needed for procurement processes.

The materials you buy, the vendors you buy them from, and the prices your company gets from each vendor, are all part of the master data in the SAP ERP system.

2   Master Data

The versatile SAP ERP system provides many ways to buy, stock, sell, and value materials. A lot of those options are set on an individual material basis. Those settings are entered in the central material catalog or material master. In the same way that you store information and settings for the materials your company buys, manufactures, and sells, you can also store information and settings for the vendors you source the materials and services from in the vendor master. Further master data for procurement is created when you detail prices, discounts, and terms of payment for each material when you buy it from each different vendor in purchasing info records in SAP ERP.

In this chapter, we'll explain the main components of each of these pieces of master data and the importance they have in the procurement process. You'll learn why and how each field affects the outcome in a purchasing document so you can more efficiently maintain your master data to yield better results when executing purchasing activities.

2.1   Importance of Master Data in Procurement

Master data in SAP ERP and specifically in Materials Management (MM) procurement is the foundation on which transactions are executed. When you create a purchase order in the SAP ERP system, for example, you have to enter the vendor number for the party you're buying from, the material number of the product you're buying, the quantity you're ordering, and the place where you want it delivered.

Based partially on this information, the system determines the price and discounts that you can get from this vendor, the shipping address, the place where the vendor is shipping the materials to, the shipping conditions, and the shipping methods. It also determines what kind of information needs to be passed on to the warehouse so that the warehouse employees can start putting away the product when they receive it. The system also tells them if a quality inspection of the goods is required.

As you can see, when you create transactional data, the system makes many determinations for the execution of that business process that are based on business rules and on the master data involved in that transaction.

If you want accurate results, you need to make sure that the master data is accurate. The more time you invest in making sure that the master data is correct and complete, the better the transactional results will be, thus substantially reducing the time required to correct or complete incomplete or incorrect transactions; which, in the end, results in better order fulfillment, fewer missing parts, and thus higher quality in your company.

Pricing is another important element. You need to make sure that the relevant pricing condition records, including list price, volume discounts, shipping surcharges, and other price variables, are included. This avoids errors in the value of the purchase orders. Pricing will be discussed in detail in later chapters.

Master data isn't static, and it's very important that it's maintained constantly and accurately. Your SAP experience will be much more productive and much less stressful if you make sure your master data is of the highest quality possible. Now that you understand why master data plays such an important role in procurement activities, let's move on to discuss the different types of master data that need to be maintained.

2.2 Material Master

The material master is the central repository of data about everything your company sells, buys, or transforms. The SAP ERP system treats materials differently according to their purpose in your company. To differentiate them, materials are classified into material types:

▶ **Raw materials**

These materials will be either transformed or assembled in your company's production processes. Each has to be set up in the material master.

▶ **Trading goods**

These are products that your company buys and then resells without any transformation. For example, a wholesaler or a sales company acquires manufactured goods from other companies in the same corporation and then sells them to retailers or end consumers.

▶ **Non-stock materials**

These materials aren't kept in a warehouse. For example, software is downloaded from a digital stream instead of a CD being shipped from a warehouse.

▶ **Services**

All the services your company buys from other companies, such as maintenance, consulting, auditing, and others, must be set up in the material master. You should also set up those services your company sells.

▶ **Packaging materials**

These are the materials that will contain or wrap the products when shipped from the warehouse. Examples of packaging materials are boxes, crates, containers, and so on.

▶ **Finished goods**

The result of the manufacturing or assembly process is a finished good that will be sold to clients. In some cases, finished goods are also bought or transferred from other subsidiaries of your company.

▶ **Competitive products**

Some companies decide to keep material master records for products from their competitors. The intention is to keep track of the product characteristics and notes about how they compare to your company's own products.

In the material master, you keep generic information such as the SKU number, a brief description of the item, the dimensions, the weight, the unit of measure. You also classify the item by assigning it a material group and a place in the product hierarchy. This is the place where you also assign different EAN codes for different product presentations or packaging, such as single items, six-packs, and so on.

Views   Each material type requires a different type of data, and the SAP ERP system uses what in SAP terms is known as *views* to organize the sets of data for each material type. We'll discuss the different views that are available in the material master (as shown in Figure 2.1) in the following subsection.

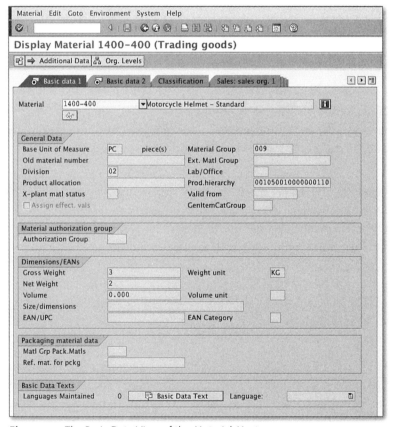

Figure 2.1 The Basic Data View of the Material Master

2.2.1 Basic Data View

This view contains information that is central to the material, which denotes that all the departments in a company use the information. In the following subsections, we introduce you to some of the most important fields in the BASIC DATA views.

Material Number

This number uniquely identifies an item in the system. In the SAP ERP system, the number can either be assigned automatically by the system through the use of internal number ranges, or it can be assigned by the user via external number ranges. In your company, you'll have either internally or externally assigned numbers depending on your own needs and business definitions. So depending on your system setup, you'll either enter an external material number or leave the field blank so the system can assign a number from the pool of number ranges.

Cross Plant Material Status

The X-PLANT MATL STATUS field is used to communicate the stage in the product's lifecycle where the product is. These statuses are maintained during the configuration of the system and can tell you that the material is, for example, in development, or has been released for sales, if it's blocked, or even if it's discontinued. This field isn't only for informative purposes; it drives specific functionality based on the configuration of the system, allowing or blocking certain business functions such as buying or selling. You have to select the right value for each material, depending on its status, to determine which functions are available.

Base Unit of Measure

Every material is handled differently; for example if you work in the chemical industry, you might be buying raw materials or selling your finished products by either weight or volume. So the unit of measure for your material is either kilograms/pounds or liters/fluid ounces. This allows you to know how much stock is available in the warehouse, as well as how much you order from your vendors. In the consumer product industry, you likely buy and sell your products by the piece, so piece (PC) is the base unit of measure. Make sure you select the right unit of measure because after you create transactions, have stock, or add this material to other master data, the system won't let you change it.

Net Weight, Gross Weight, and Volume

These fields are very important for storage, shipping, and transportation activities. If these values are inaccurate, your company might overpay on shipments or overload trucks, which in both cases will result in stopped shipments and ultimately in unsatisfied customers. Make sure you enter the right information in these fields; one way to get the correct weight and dimensions is to run each material through a machine such as a CubiScan™.

Product Hierarchy and Material Group

These two fields help you classify and give a hierarchy to the products. If your company sells sporting goods, for example, then you might have material groups that segregate golf products from clothing, from baseball products, and so on. The hierarchy provides a similar classification but can be more granular. You can have several levels that allow you to build a product family tree.

Other important features of the material group and the product hierarchy are that they are used by the financial modules to derive special postings and profitability analysis. Always make sure you discuss the values to be entered in these fields with your engineering, sales, and controlling peers.

2.2.2 Purchasing View

The PURCHASING view, shown in Figure 2.2, contains data that is relevant only to a specific purchasing organization and plant. This allows different areas of the same company to buy the same material or product in different manners, according to their processes or geographic location. Different areas may buy the same product differently.

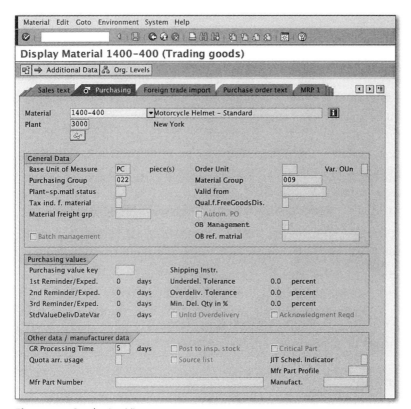

Figure 2.2 Purchasing View

We'll go over the important fields in the following subsections.

Purchasing Group

This field indicates which group or person is in charge of buying this material when it's required. Enter the value that reflects who buys each material.

Order Unit

When you buy a material in a unit of measure different from the base unit of measure, you indicate it in the ORDER UNIT field. You have to indicate a conversion factor between the two units of measure so that the system can calculate the quantities and prices correctly. If you enter a unit here, it applies for all vendors; you may choose to use this information in the specific purchasing info record for each vendor. Enter the value that better reflects the way you purchase your material: boxes, bags, pallets, and so on.

Plant-Specific Material Status

The plant-specific material status field (PLANT-SP.MATL STATUS) restricts the usability of the material for the plant concerned; that is, it defines whether a warning or error message is displayed if you include the material in a particular function in Purchasing, Inventory Management, Warehouse Management, Production Planning, Plant Maintenance, or Costing. For each material, depending on its status, you have to select the right value to determine which functions are available.

Valid From

When a status is managed, a validity date until when that specific status is valid must be entered. Here you normally enter the current date.

Tax Indicator

The TAX IND. F. MATERIAL field helps the system during tax determination. This indicator is used along with other system settings to determine the tax code that applies for specific purchases. Check with your finance peers on the correct values that you need to enter here.

Automatic PO

The AUTOM. PO indicator used with other vendor information, allows the system to automatically create purchase orders from purchase requisitions. When this indicator isn't set, you have to manually convert requisitions into purchase orders. Fill this field only if you want to allow the creation of automatic POs. Leave it blank if you'll convert them manually.

Purchasing Value Key

This field drives several things in the system: reminders to the vendor for expediting the shipments, tolerance limits for receipts of material into the warehouse, minimum receipt quantity, and whether acknowledgements are required. It also includes the shipping instructions that apply for each material. All these values guide the functionality of the purchase orders. Check the available values offered by your system configuration, and select the one that best suits each material. If you need different values, they can only be created by the functional analyst configuring them for you.

Goods Receipt Processing Time

This value tells the system that this material isn't received into stock as soon as it's delivered at the warehouse. The warehouse processes may delay the receipt for a few days, and that time is taken into consideration in the delivery lead time to ensure timely availability of the materials. Check with your warehouse and quality groups on the time it takes them to put the material into stock from the moment it's received through the dock door.

Quota Arrangement Usage

A material can be included in a quota arrangement if the QUOTA ARR. USAGE field is used. Quota arrangements are discussed in later chapters. Enter the right value for the different purchasing documents where quota arrangements are going to be used for each material.

Post into Inspection

A material is put into inspection stock upon receipt at the warehouse when the POST TO INSP. STOCK field is set. This triggers the Quality Management (QM) functionality. Check this field only if you're using the QM component in your company because it triggers specific functionality and affects the stock category where the material is received.

Source List

A material requires a source list if this field is used. Source lists are discussed in later chapters. Check this field only if a source list is mandatory.

Manufacturer Part Number

You can keep the number your vendor identifies a material with in this field, and you can also use it in purchase orders. Enter the manufacturer part number if you need it to appear in the PO when you purchase this material.

Manufacturer

The MANUFACT. field indicates which manufacturer makes this part. In this field, you select the manufacturer from the vendor master. So if you're going to use this field, you need to create it as a vendor.

Critical Part

When you use this field, the system tells the QM component that a full count needs to be done on this material upon receipt at the warehouse.

Look at Table 2.1 for a list of transactions for material master maintenance.

Transaction	Menu Path
MM01: Create Immediately	LOGISTICS • MATERIALS MANAGEMENT • MATERIAL MASTER • MATERIAL • CREATE GENERAL • IMMEDIATELY
MM02: Change (any material type)	LOGISTICS • MATERIALS MANAGEMENT • MATERIAL MASTER • MATERIAL • CHANGE • IMMEDIATELY
MM03: Display (any material type)	LOGISTICS • MATERIALS MANAGEMENT • MATERIAL MASTER • MATERIAL • DISPLAY • CURRENT
MMH1: Create Trading Goods	LOGISTICS • MATERIALS MANAGEMENT • MATERIAL MASTER • MATERIAL • CREATE SPECIAL • TRADING GOODS
MMN1: Create Non-Stock	LOGISTICS • MATERIALS MANAGEMENT • MATERIAL MASTER • MATERIAL • CREATE SPECIAL • NON-STOCK
MMS1: Services	LOGISTICS • MATERIALS MANAGEMENT • MATERIAL MASTER • MATERIAL • CREATE SPECIAL • SERVICE(S)

Table 2.1 Material Master Transactions via the Materials Management Menu

Transaction	Menu Path
MMV1: Create Packaging Materials	LOGISTICS • MATERIALS MANAGEMENT • MATERIAL MASTER • MATERIAL • CREATE SPECIAL • PACKAGING
MMH1: Competitor Product	LOGISTICS • MATERIALS MANAGEMENT • MATERIAL MASTER • MATERIAL • CREATE SPECIAL • COMPETITOR PRODUCT

Table 2.1 Material Master Transactions via the Materials Management Menu (Cont.)

2.3 Service Master

We've already mentioned that you can create services in the material master and that you can then buy them for your company as if they were any other part or component. And sometimes that is just fine, but it's not enough for some services, such as consulting or construction projects that take a very long time and in which you have to account for hours of services rendered, or for progress in a deliverable, or any other partial delivery.

Services created in the material master, being non-stock materials, can't be received, so the only function in MM is the invoice receipt, in which you enter the billed amount into accounts payable.

Non-stock materials

The SAP ERP system includes the ability to track this kind of service through the Purchasing component with the use of the service master. Any services created in this master catalog receive special attention and can be received or verified by an employee who is tasked with this responsibility. Usually, this is the manager of the area that requested the service or a project manager in charge of a specific project.

You can purchase, for example, the total number of consulting hours that a project requires, and receive, or verify, the partial hours rendered every week. Receiving a service in the SAP ERP system consists of completing a service entry sheet, which is to services what a goods receipt is to materials. A sample purchase order for a service is shown in Figure 2.3; note the account assignment K and item category D for the service.

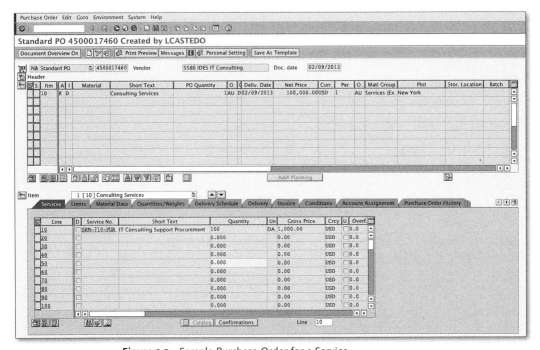

Figure 2.3 Sample Purchase Order for a Service

Three-way match This way, you can match the deliverables requested in the purchase order with the services rendered and verified in the service entry sheet, and then also with the invoice in the Invoice Verification process—giving you a three-way match.

Additionally, the service master allows you to standardize communication with your vendors so that both refer to the same entry or work breakdown structure (WBS) in a project plan. You can also make reference to a higher level service when you're specifying subservices. You can see an example as shown in Figure 2.4.

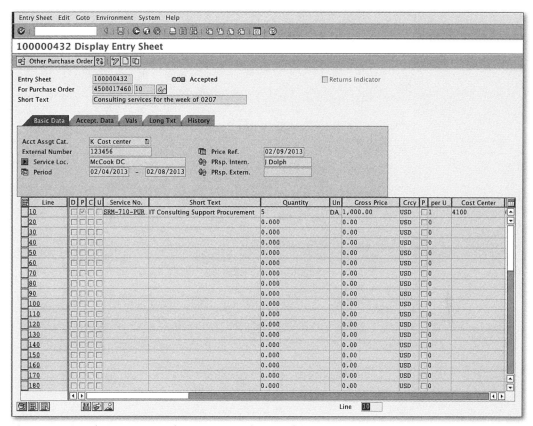

Figure 2.4 Sample Service Entry Sheet: Service Delivery and Progress

2.3.1 Service Master Sections

The following subsections describe some of the most important fields in the service master shown in Figure 2.5. The service master doesn't have views, but instead has different data sections.

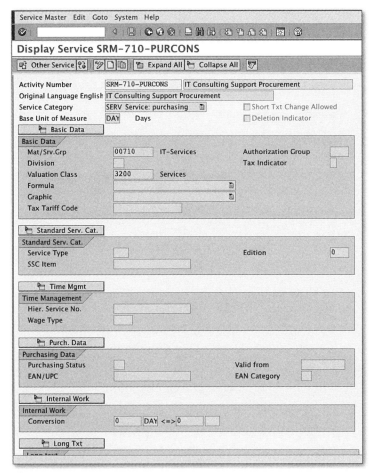

Figure 2.5 Service Master Data Sections

General Data

The upper section of the service master includes the following:

▶ ACTIVITY NUMBER
This number *uniquely* identifies a service in the system. This number is externally assigned. The text box next to the number is the service short text where you enter the description of the service.

▶ SERVICE CATEGORY
This field is use to categorize the different services your company buys. These categories are classifications of the services, equivalent to the

material type in the material master that determines the valuation class for the service. The available values are set in configuration and can't be changed by users.

▶ BASE UNIT OF MEASURE
The base unit of measure is the unit in which the service will be bought from the vendor.

▶ DELETION INDICATOR
Unlike the material master, in the service master, you can set the deletion indicator directly in each service.

Basic Data

The BASIC DATA section includes the following:

▶ MAT/SRV.GRP
The material group helps group together services that belong to the same service hierarchy. It also helps finance derive special postings and profitability analysis. The available values for this field are also set in configuration and can't be changed by the user.

▶ DIVISION
The division is another value that helps you group services for sales. This field isn't relevant for purchasing services.

▶ VALUATION CLASS
This is the key used to derive accounting postings in conjunction with material movement types used during service confirmation.

Standard Service Category

The STANDARD SERV. CAT. section includes the following:

▶ SERVICE TYPE
The service type is used to standardize texts that are used to identify services in communication with the vendors. For example, if a service is part of a project, you can define types that tie to mutually agreed on codes such as a WBS number.

▶ SSC ITEM
This number comes from the Service Catalog, and helps standardize service descriptions to help eliminate data redundancy. It is also used

to link services in the SAP system with the number assigned by the partner rendering it; for example, a WBS number such as 1.1.3.

Purchasing Data

The PURCH. DATA section includes the following:

▶ PURCHASING STATUS
The purchasing status controls the usability of the service in purchasing activities. By assigning a status, you can, for example, quote a service, requisition a service, purchase a service, or do nothing at all.

▶ VALID FROM
When a status is managed, a validity date until when that status is valid must be entered.

Internal Work

The INTERNAL WORK section includes the CONVERSION fields that allow you to include conversion factors for the service's base unit of measure, such as days to hours.

Long Text

The LONG TEXT free format text field can hold a very long description of the service—as long as several pages.

2.3.2 Creating a New Service

To create a new service, go to Transaction AC03 or follow the path LOGISTICS • MATERIALS MANAGEMENT • SERVICE MASTER • SERVICE • SERVICE MASTER. Once there, enter a short text that describes the services, a service category (usually you'll choose SERV for service purchasing), and the base unit of measure.

In the BASIC DATA view, enter a material group and a valuation class. This is the minimum information that you need to provide to create a service, depending on the kind of services you're creating. You can take a look at the fields described earlier and then decide if you can use specific fields for your own purposes.

Table 2.2 includes a list of transactions to maintain and list services and standard service catalogs (SSC).

Transaction	Menu Path
AC03: Service Master	LOGISTICS • MATERIALS MANAGEMENT • SERVICE MASTER • SERVICE • SERVICE MASTER
AC06: Service List	LOGISTICS • MATERIALS MANAGEMENT • SERVICE MASTER • SERVICE • SERVICE LIST
ML01: Create	LOGISTICS • MATERIALS MANAGEMENT • SERVICE MASTER • SERVICE • STANDARD SERVICE CATALOG • CREATE
ML02: Change	LOGISTICS • MATERIALS MANAGEMENT • SERVICE MASTER • SERVICE • STANDARD SERVICE CATALOG • CHANGE
ML03: Display	LOGISTICS • MATERIALS MANAGEMENT • SERVICE MASTER • SERVICE • STANDARD SERVICE CATALOG • DISPLAY
MLS6: List Display	LOGISTICS • MATERIALS MANAGEMENT • SERVICE MASTER • SERVICE • STANDARD SERVICE CATALOG • LIST DISPLAY

Table 2.2   Transactions for Service Master Maintenance

2.4   Business Partners

To initiate any transaction in any enterprise resource planning systems, including SAP ERP, such as creating a purchase order, receive incoming delivery, and issuing payment, you must have master data objects defined. This includes your business partners. In SAP ERP, you can clearly divide these business partners depending on the business transaction and the role this partner plays. Business partners can be defined as the following:

▶ **Vendors**

Partner types

A vendor is a primary business partner that deals in procurement purchasing functions; that is, vendors provide your company, affiliates, or external customers with goods and services directly. Vendors can also be both internal and external, such as your distribution warehouses or other affiliates procuring goods within your organization.

Also, if your vendor is buying goods and services from your organization, you can link the vendor master record to the customer master.

▶ **Customers**
A customer is a business partner to whom you're providing goods or services. Customers can be external or internal, and if that customer is also providing you with goods and services, you can link the customer master record to a vendor master. Individual customer master records can be defined for specific partner functions and can be linked together.

▶ **Other partners**
This partner category includes a mix of things such as site data, contact person, sales personnel, and competitors. Some of these objects can also be linked to other business partner master records.

In the following sections, we'll explain how to work with business partners.

2.4.1 Number Ranges, Account Group, and Field Status

Before you can create any vendor-related transactions, you need an account—a vendor master—for a business partner, and you have to assign an account group that defines the type of vendor. Depending on the configuration setting, you may need to specify the account number using an external number range, or let the system assign the internal number range for you. The following objects help in defining and managing the business partner data:

Define/
maintain data
▶ **Number ranges**
The NR field contains the number range used to define the business partner account; the entry can be all numbers or alpha-numeric. Every business partner requires an account number. You define the number ranges in configuration and assign the interval to account group. This assignment will then be proposed when the account is created—either internally by the system or externally were you can manually type it in during account creation.

▶ **Account groups**
The account groups serve as templates for business partner accounts that should have the same properties such as number range and data screen layouts and fields that are captured. The account group

manages display screens, their sequence, and fields for entering data. Some examples of different account groups are shown in Figure 2.6.

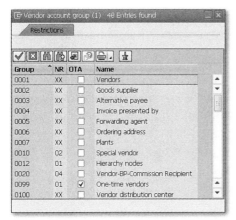

Figure 2.6 Account Groups

▶ **Field status**

The field status allows you to suppress or require certain data fields. Each of your account groups can have different data requirements; for example, standard vendor accounts won't have the same fields as one-time suppliers. A one-time vendor won't require banking information, for example. You can define field statuses based on the transaction used or make them company code-specific—but these settings should only be made as an exception.

Tips & Tricks

When you create new account groups, always maintain the field status. If you don't mark a status for a field group, all relevant fields will be set to optional and will be displayed during vendor account creation or changes. Also bear in mind that if you're changing settings for an existing account group with existing vendor master records in the database and you suppress a certain field, its content will be considered when the transactions are processed.

2.4.2 Vendor Master Data Structure

Vendor master records are generated using the previously discussed template data defined in the account groups. Vendor data presented to you is organized and grouped based on the level of detail, from the most generic to most specific. Vendor master data stores the information that is relevant for the different uses within procurement and other functionalities, and it's broken down to general data, company code, purchasing organization, and sales and distribution data for accounts linked to the customer master.

Transaction XK03

To understand the data structure, we'll walk through the vendor master display transaction. You can access it via Transaction XK03 (Display Vendor) or by using menu path LOGISTICS • MATERIALS MANAGEMENT • PURCHASING • MASTER DATA • VENDOR • CENTRAL • XK03 – DISPLAY. Several different data tabs are available. The following subsections provide more explanation of each data group.

General Data

General data applies globally to one unique business partner for all of your business organizational structures. This section includes the following:

▸ ADDRESS
This is where you store the name of the vendor, search terms for fast entry, physical address, and if needed, the PO box information and communication information, such as phone numbers, fax, and email address.

▸ CONTROL
This is where you can link your vendor with the customer master records and reference data further defining the industry, location, transportation zone, tax, and VAT information.

▸ PAYMENT TRANSACTIONS
This data tab stores the vendor's bank information and alternative payer data.

▸ CONTACT PERSON
This field holds the miscellaneous master data object that allows you to create a detailed contact list of people working for your vendor that you're communicating with. You can keep record of their home address, personal data, and visiting hours.

Company Code Data

The company code data is the next segment of the vendor master, and applies to one unique company code, storing information relevant to Financial Accounting (FI). If you have multiple company codes, you will have multiple records created. The following data sections are maintained:

▶ ACCOUNT MANAGEMENT
This field stores accounting data, including reconciliation accounts, interest calculations, and reference data, such as the previous account number, personnel number, and buying group.

▶ PAYMENT TRANSACTIONS
This field records the terms of payment and tolerance group, and allows you to enable payment history recording and set the time for the deposited checks to clear for monitoring purposes. You can also maintain information for automatic payment transactions.

▶ CORRESPONDENCE
In this field, you can maintain data related to dunning procedures, accounting clerk data responsible for communication with the customer, and set payment notices to be sent to your customer after the payments clear.

▶ INSURANCE
This field records the insurance policy number, provider, and amount insured, as well as the validity dates of the export credit insurance.

▶ WITHHOLDING TAX
In this field, you can maintain the tax withholding data by selecting the tax types, tax codes, and validity periods applicable to them.

Note

Extended tax withholding functionality must be active for the company code selected to maintain this data.

Purchasing Organization Data

In this portion of the vendor master, you can maintain data that's driving purchasing transactions. See Figure 2.7 for an example of the DISPLAY

VENDOR: PURCHASING DATA screen. These settings are purchasing organization-specific so if you've implemented a decentralized form of your organization, you'll have an option to create multiple different records for the same supplier.

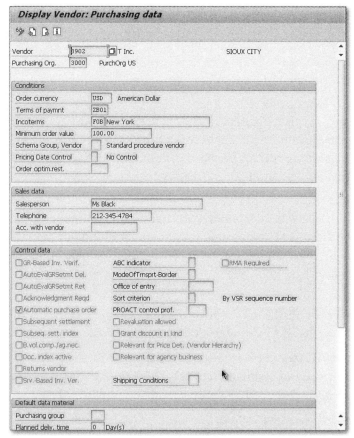

Figure 2.7 Vendor Master: Purchasing Data

The following data sections can be set up here:

▸ CONDITIONS
This section is used to influence pricing, pricing schema determination, order currency, and Incoterms.

▶ Sales data

If you have a specific person that is identified as a salesperson as your primary contact, and if you have an account with this vendor, you can store it here.

▶ Control data

This section of the purchasing organization data stores a lot of different controls related to PO acknowledgement requirements, invoice receipt processing, evaluation receipt settlement (ERS) settings, and settlement controls. You can also set the return vendor assignment by linking your vendor to a customer master ship-to account, set the shipping conditions default, set the ABC indicator where A indicates the greatest share of your business annual spend in dollars and cents, and finally set the foreign trade data defaults.

▶ Default data material

This section allows you to preset data that will be copied into the purchasing documents during transactions. You can set the purchasing group (buyer) tied to the vendor account, the planned delivery time, and the confirmation control key that controls if advance shipping notification is required to process your purchase orders for a specific supplier. You can also set up a default units of measure group for grouping several allowed units of measure used in rounding profiles.

▶ Service Data

This section houses additional controls for vendor-managed inventory (VMI) scenarios and automatic load builder transactions.

Partner Functions

In real-world purchasing scenarios, you place an order with a supplier that receives your purchase order, another party sends the goods, you get an invoice from the vendor's headquarters, and you send your payment to yet another location by another partner a different location where their accounts receivables are processed. SAP allows you to define this complex structure by maintaining all relevant or even mandatory partner functions via partner roles. *Partner roles* are define in Customizing, and allowed role combinations are assigned to account groups. Here is a list of some of the commonly used partner roles:

Roles

Commonly used roles

- AZ: Alternative payee
- DP: Delivering site
- GS: Goods supplier
- FA: Forwarding agent
- IP: Invoice presented by
- OA: Ordering address
- VN: Vendor

For example, you want your vendors to have multiple ordering address partners, but you don't want the ordering address to be defined as a plant or invoicing party. See Figure 2.8 for examples of permissible partner role relationships to account groups.

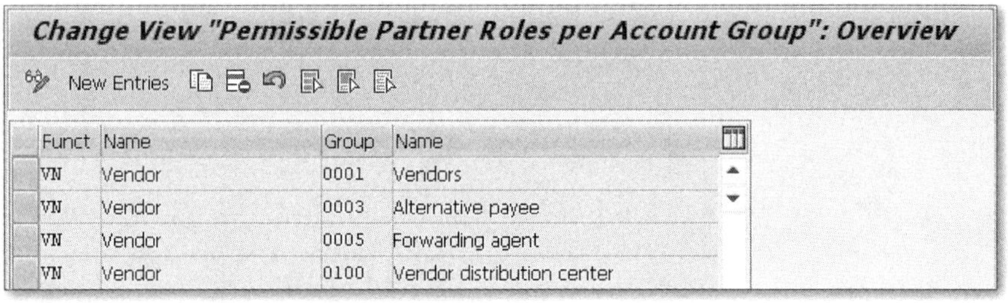

Funct	Name	Group	Name
VN	Vendor	0001	Vendors
VN	Vendor	0003	Alternative payee
VN	Vendor	0005	Forwarding agent
VN	Vendor	0100	Vendor distribution center

Figure 2.8 Permissible Partner Role Definitions

Uses

Some of the most common uses for the partner functions include the following:

- **Ordering address**
  Usually used for output processing.
- **Goods suppliers**
  Used for tax purposes and foreign trade.
- **Invoice presented by**
  Used to identify a party that will produce the invoice for your order.

You can also define allowed partner combinations in a form of partner function determination schema, which is a kind of template that can be applied repeatedly to speed up your data maintenance. The partner function determination schema—defined in Customizing—sets the required partner functions, which are then assigned to the account group, purchasing documents, and rebate agreements. You can make certain partners mandatory and control whether changes are allowed after a record is created. These schemas are used when you define the vendor master record, create purchasing documents, or create rebate agreements.

The PARTNER FUNCTIONS data screen, shown in Figure 2.9, allows you to maintain permissible partners and their account numbers. You can also display partner addresses and remove the entry if needed using the DELETE LINE button.

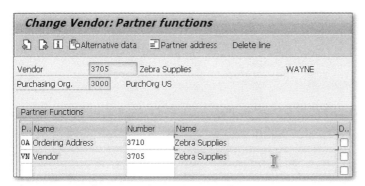

Figure 2.9 Vendor Master: Partner Function Data

When setting up your vendors and partner roles, try to make them as simple as possible to make your vendor master data maintenance easier and cleaner, especially if your organization spans multiple environments and other legacy applications. Keeping it simple

Alternative Purchasing Data

If you have detailed procurement requirements and your MRP also requires a lot of information to maintain multiple plants in a geographically distributed organization and supply chain, you can use alternative purchasing data.

This extended data maintenance feature allows you to capture separate purchasing organization and partner function details using individual plants and/or vendor subranges. Access the subrange data maintenance Vendor subrange from the PURCHASING ORGANIZATION DATA maintenance screen by using the SUB-RANGES button shown in Figure 2.10.

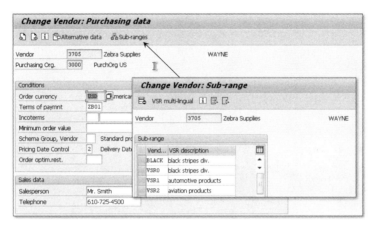

Figure 2.10 Vendor Master: Subrange Maintenance

Vendor subranges can represent groups of your vendor product offerings, such as fasteners, abrasives, oils, and so on. Each of these subrange groups is then assigned to a purchasing info record (see Section 2.8 for details). Purchasing info records help determine the data during PO creation; the vendor information, including partner functions, and data such as planned delivery time for the material being purchased automatically populate the fields.

Group-specific data   Vendor subrange master data allows you to maintain product group-specific data, which can be used in combination with your destination plants. You can have a different planned delivery time, Incoterms, and currency for a specific plant/subrange combination, and also different partner function combinations; see Figure 2.11 for examples. In the screen, you can locate the VENDOR SUB-RANGE entry for AUTOMOTIVE PRODUCTS and PLANT NEW YORK combination with "X" in the PURC. (purchasing) and PARTNER columns. When you double-click on that X or click on the PURCHASING or PARTNERS buttons, you'll get to the detailed screens where you maintain the data. For each subrange line shown, you can have different data applied.

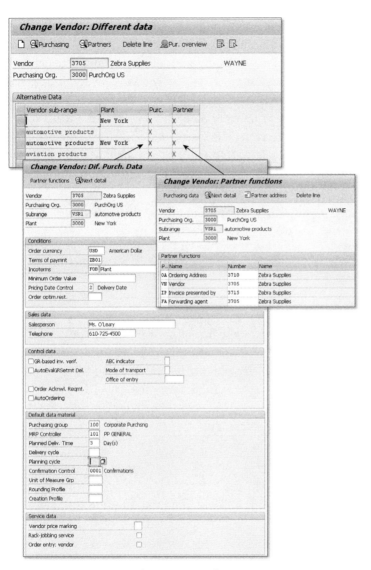

Figure 2.11 Alternative Purchasing Data and Partner Functions

Note

The DEFAULT DATA MATERIAL section has additional fields compared to the regular vendor master purchasing data view and includes the cycles discussed in the following subsections.

Delivery Cycle

You can assign a planning calendar that specifies the days your vendor delivery should be planned for; that is, basically establishing the delivery cycle. Imagine you want your vendor to deliver goods every Friday, and the planned delivery time is three days. All POs created before Wednesday will get this week's Friday delivery date. Any PO created after that will be scheduled to be delivered next Friday. Other controls on the planning calendar allow you to make the system react to holidays falling on the Friday and shifting the delivery dates accordingly (covered in Chapter 3).

> **Note**
>
> Before a material can be planned using this method, make sure the MRP setting allows time-phased planning. Check the lot sizing assignment and definition in Customizing for full effect.

Planning Cycle

You can assign a planning calendar that defines the day on which the material purchase order has to be placed. The procedure works similar to the delivery cycle; however, in this case, you create a PO on the established day of the week. So, for example, your weekly orders are placed on Tuesday for Friday delivery and a planned delivery time of three days. Any requirements that are within this planned delivery time are included in the PO created Tuesday.

> **Note**
>
> If you're using purchasing load builder functionality, don't maintain these fields at the vendor subrange (VSR) level. The plant level is the lowest possible level for additional purchasing and partner data.

Creation Profile

Timing control The creation profile controls the timing of scheduling agreement delivery releases and transmission to the vendor. This profile is assigned to the scheduling agreement items. SAP recommends that if you haven't specified a time in the schedule lines, you should work with aggregation in the creation profile to consolidate lines with the same release date.

2.4.3 Maintaining Vendor Master Data

As we discussed in the previous sections, there are multiple data objects that you can maintain for your business partners: the general view, company code view, and purchasing organization data and its variations. You can create, change, and display master data records for all of the partner functions. There are several ways to do this, depending on your company's security policy. You should be able to create the complete vendor master record or partial records, restricted to general and purchasing data sections.

You can access the business partner maintenance using transaction codes that follow the SAP rule of 3sm, where the numbers in the transaction in example xx01 stands for create, xx02 for change, and xx03 for display functions. Or, you can navigate to the transactions using the SAP Easy Access menu paths.

Navigation options

To maintain the general data for your vendor, all you need is the account number. To maintain the company code and related accounting data, you'll also need the company code number. And finally, to maintain purchasing data, you have to specify the purchasing organization. Table 2.3 lists the transactions available to maintain the vendor master.

Maintain vendor master

Transaction	Menu Path
XK01: Create Vendor Centrally	LOGISTICS • MATERIALS MANAGEMENT • PURCHASING • MASTER DATA • VENDOR • CENTRAL • CREATE
XK02: Change Vendor Centrally	LOGISTICS • MATERIALS MANAGEMENT • PURCHASING • MASTER DATA • VENDOR • CENTRAL • CHANGE
XK03: Display Vendor Centrally	LOGISTICS • MATERIALS MANAGEMENT • PURCHASING • MASTER DATA • VENDOR • CENTRAL • DISPLAY
MK01: Create Vendor Purchasing	LOGISTICS • MATERIALS MANAGEMENT • PURCHASING • MASTER DATA • VENDOR • PURCHASING • CREATE

Table 2.3 Vendor Master Transaction Codes

Transaction	Menu Path
MK02: Change Vendor Purchasing	LOGISTICS • MATERIALS MANAGEMENT • PURCHASING • MASTER DATA • VENDOR • PURCHASING • CHANGE (CURRENT)
MK03: Display Vendor Purchasing	LOGISTICS • MATERIALS MANAGEMENT • PURCHASING • MASTER DATA • VENDOR • PURCHASING • DISPLAY (CURRENT)

Table 2.3 Vendor Master Transaction Codes (Cont.)

Maintenance Whenever you create a vendor master record, your company will discontinue, block, or archive another master record. Vendor hierarchies are maintained the same way, requiring you to update validity and add/remove nodes or partners (more on that in the upcoming sections of this chapter). Usually, a master data group within your business or IT organization is tasked with monitoring and maintaining your business partner records. Additional transactions are available to perform these tasks; the commonly used transaction codes are listed in Table 2.4.

Transaction	Menu Path
XK04: Vendor Changes (Centrally)	LOGISTICS • MATERIALS MANAGEMENT • PURCHASING • MASTER DATA • VENDOR • CENTRAL • CHANGES
XK05: Block Vendor (Centrally)	LOGISTICS • MATERIALS MANAGEMENT • PURCHASING • MASTER DATA • VENDOR • CENTRAL • BLOCK
XK06: Mark Vendor for Deletion (Centrally)	LOGISTICS • MATERIALS MANAGEMENT • PURCHASING • MASTER DATA • VENDOR • CENTRAL • FLAG FOR DELETION
XK07: Change Vendor Account Group	LOGISTICS • MATERIALS MANAGEMENT • PURCHASING • MASTER DATA • VENDOR • CENTRAL • ACCOUNT GROUP CHANGE
XK99: Mass Maintenance, Vendor Master	LOGISTICS • MATERIALS MANAGEMENT • PURCHASING • MASTER DATA • VENDOR • MASS MAINTENANCE

Table 2.4 Additional Vendor Master Maintenance Transactions

Transaction	Menu Path
MK04: Change Vendor (Purchasing)	LOGISTICS • MATERIALS MANAGEMENT • PURCHASING • MASTER DATA • VENDOR • PURCHASING • CHANGES
MK05: Block Vendor (Purchasing)	LOGISTICS • MATERIALS MANAGEMENT • PURCHASING • MASTER DATA • VENDOR • PURCHASING • BLOCK
MK06: Mark Vendor for Deletion (Purchasing)	LOGISTICS • MATERIALS MANAGEMENT • PURCHASING • MASTER DATA • VENDOR • PURCHASING • FLAG FOR DELETION

Table 2.4 Additional Vendor Master Maintenance Transactions (Cont.)

2.5 Vendor Hierarchies

Vendor hierarchies allow you to create flexible objects to reflect the organizational structure of your supplier. For example, if your vendor has a very complex sales department, multiple distribution centers, or retail stores, you can build hierarchies to reflect these structures.

You can use vendor hierarchies in purchasing documents to determine pricing, including rebates. For each hierarchy node marked as relevant for pricing, you can create a pricing condition record. If one or more nodes in a hierarchy contain pricing data, it's automatically used during purchase order processing. If you add a new vendor to any existing hierarchy, the vendor automatically inherits all pricing agreements that apply to that node.

Using hierarchies

A vendor hierarchy uses an account called a node (in a standard SAP system, you use account group 0012 to define a node) when the vendor master record is created. The node represents the freely definable level of your supplier organization, could represent your vendors' geographical/regional sales office structure, or number of distribution centers that supply your specific ordering plants. You assign a vendor account (standard account group 0001) to the lowest level node in your vendor hierarchy. You can then link the lower level node—called the dependent node—to the higher level node in the hierarchy. See Figure 2.12 for an example of a multilevel vendor hierarchy.

Nodes

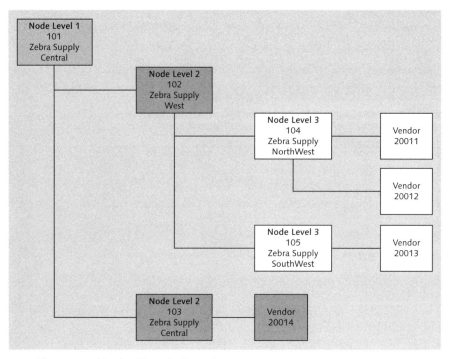

Figure 2.12 Vendor Hierarchy Example

Maintenance The structure of the vendor hierarchies is very flexible and easy to maintain. It allows you to move or change nodes within a hierarchy by moving all related vendor assignments with it, reducing maintenance time. In Table 2.5, you'll find some useful vendor hierarchy maintenance transactions for reference.

Transaction	Menu Path
MKH1: Maintain Vendor Hierarchy	LOGISTICS • MATERIALS MANAGEMENT • PURCHASING • MASTER DATA • VENDOR • HIERARCHY • CHANGE
MKH2: Display Vendor Hierarchy	LOGISTICS • MATERIALS MANAGEMENT • PURCHASING • MASTER DATA • VENDOR • HIERARCHY • DISPLAY

Table 2.5 Vendor Hierarchy Maintenance Transactions

2.6   Source Lists

When your procurement requirements are generated, you want them fulfilled as quickly as possible, and SAP gives you multiple ways to optimize
this task. Existing sources are suggested by the system in the predefined
sequence:

1. The system looks for a quota arrangement (covered in Section 2.7). If
   you maintained quotas, and the system found a valid entry, the vendor
   is selected based on the criteria maintained for the quotas.

2. If no quota arrangements are found, the system looks for source list entries,
   and the appropriate vendor and contract data, if maintained, are used.

3. If the source list records aren't found, the system looks for valid contracts or scheduling agreements (discussed in Chapter 4).

4. Purchasing info records are considered last after all previous checks
   fail to find a defined and active source of supply. (You'll read more
   about purchasing info records later in this chapter.)

A source list is one of the features used in optimizing Purchasing, as
mentioned earlier. It allows you to define possible sources for products
within a set of validity dates. You can maintain multiple allowed sources—
vendors—and reference multiple agreements.

Source lists can contain allowed, blocked, and fixed records. Fixed sources
take priority within defined a validity period. Blocked source list records
are ignored during processing of purchasing documents, and buyers can't
use blocked sources manually either. Source list functionality also gives
you the ability to set the MRP indicator to active to allow SAP to use
the source data in materials planning. A source list can be specific to an
individual material or can be set globally for all materials in the plant.
See Figure 2.13 for an example of a multivendor list showing some of
the data combinations described earlier.

Source lists are used in purchase requisition processing during the manual
or automated source determination procedures. They are also used during purchase order creation, where the source list is checked again if the
PO vendor is allowed. This helps you limit the number of suppliers to
a manageable number and also allows you to do business only with the
reliable and high-quality vendors.

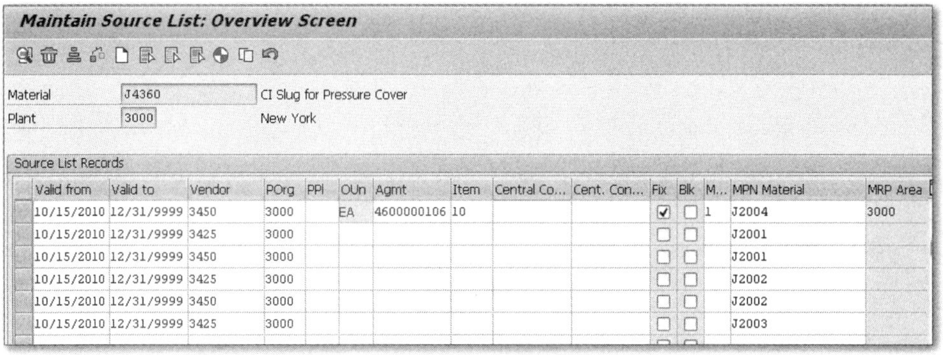

Maintain Source List: Overview Screen

Material J4360 CI Slug for Pressure Cover
Plant 3000 New York

Source List Records

Valid from	Valid to	Vendor	POrg	PPl	OUn	Agmt	Item	Central Co...	Cent. Con...	Fix	Blk	M...	MPN Material	MRP Area
10/15/2010	12/31/9999	3450	3000		EA	4600000106	10			☑	☐	1	J2004	3000
10/15/2010	12/31/9999	3425	3000							☐	☐		J2001	
10/15/2010	12/31/9999	3450	3000							☐	☐		J2001	
10/15/2010	12/31/9999	3425	3000							☐	☐		J2002	
10/15/2010	12/31/9999	3450	3000							☐	☐		J2002	
10/15/2010	12/31/9999	3425	3000							☐	☐		J2003	

Figure 2.13 Maintain Source List Overview Screen

There are multiple ways source lists can be generated:

- Manually using Transaction ME01
- From within the purchasing info record using Transaction ME11 or Transaction ME12
- From an outline agreement/contract using Transaction MK31N or Transaction MK32; using the mass-maintain transaction via the automatic generation transaction

Figure 2.14 shows the maintenance screen details.

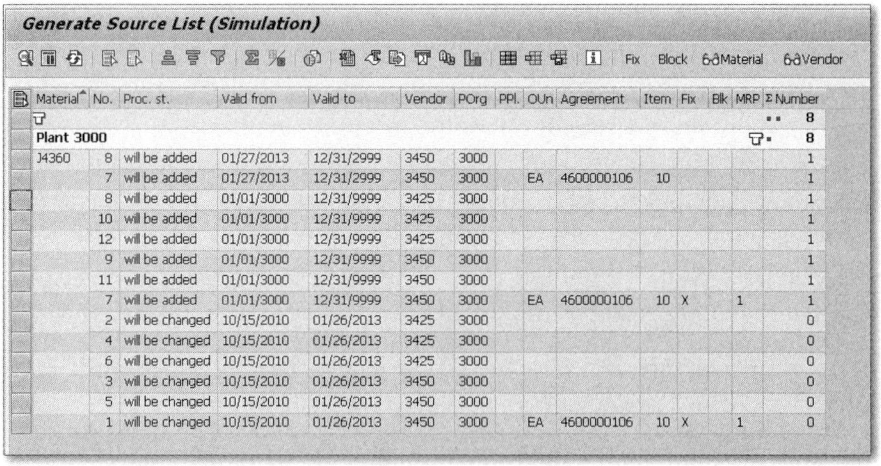

Generate Source List (Simulation)

Fix Block Material Vendor

Material	No.	Proc. st.	Valid from	Valid to	Vendor	POrg	PPl.	OUn	Agreement	Item	Fix	Blk	MRP	Σ Number
														8
Plant 3000														8
J4360	8	will be added	01/27/2013	12/31/2999	3450	3000								1
	7	will be added	01/27/2013	12/31/2999	3450	3000		EA	4600000106	10				1
	8	will be added	01/01/3000	12/31/9999	3425	3000								1
	10	will be added	01/01/3000	12/31/9999	3425	3000								1
	12	will be added	01/01/3000	12/31/9999	3425	3000								1
	9	will be added	01/01/3000	12/31/9999	3450	3000								1
	11	will be added	01/01/3000	12/31/9999	3450	3000								1
	7	will be added	01/01/3000	12/31/9999	3450	3000		EA	4600000106	10	X		1	1
	2	will be changed	10/15/2010	01/26/2013	3425	3000								0
	4	will be changed	10/15/2010	01/26/2013	3425	3000								0
	6	will be changed	10/15/2010	01/26/2013	3425	3000								0
	3	will be changed	10/15/2010	01/26/2013	3450	3000								0
	5	will be changed	10/15/2010	01/26/2013	3450	3000								0
	1	will be changed	10/15/2010	01/26/2013	3450	3000		EA	4600000106	10	X		1	0

Figure 2.14 Generate Source List: Maintenance View

Also, using the contract create or change transactions, you can create source list entries for additional variations tied to the J4 category:

▶ M: Material unknown

▶ W: Material group

Let's walk through an example on source list maintenance using Transaction ME01 (Maintain):   Maintenance

1. On the initial screen, specify the material and plant the records will be maintained for, and press ⎡Enter⎤ to continue.

2. On the next screen, maintain the validity periods for the allowed sources of supply, and enter the vendor and PURCHASING ORG.

3. Save your source list.

If you have a purchase requisition for an item without a material master but with the material group specified, the system will try to source it using source list defined records that reference a contract or info record without the same material group. You can fine-tune this type of source list by maintaining the materials exclusions indicator.

Refer to Table 2.6 for source list transactions and menu paths.

Transaction	Menu Path
ME01: Maintain	LOGISTICS • MATERIALS MANAGEMENT • PURCHASING • MASTER DATA • SOURCE LIST • MAINTAIN
ME03: Display	LOGISTICS • MATERIALS MANAGEMENT • PURCHASING • MASTER DATA • SOURCE LIST • DISPLAY
ME04: Changes	LOGISTICS • MATERIALS MANAGEMENT • PURCHASING • MASTER DATA • SOURCE LIST • CHANGES
ME0M: By Material	LOGISTICS • MATERIALS MANAGEMENT • PURCHASING • MASTER DATA • SOURCE LIST • LIST DISPLAYS • BY MATERIAL
ME05: Generate	LOGISTICS • MATERIALS MANAGEMENT • PURCHASING • MASTER DATA • SOURCE LIST • FOLLOW-ON FUNCTIONS • GENERATE

Table 2.6 Source List Maintenance Transactions

Transaction	Menu Path
ME06: Analyze	LOGISTICS • MATERIALS MANAGEMENT • PURCHASING • MASTER DATA • SOURCE LIST • FOLLOW-ON FUNCTIONS • ANALYZE
ME07: Delete	LOGISTICS • MATERIALS MANAGEMENT • PURCHASING • MASTER DATA • SOURCE LIST • FOLLOW-ON FUNCTIONS • DELETE

Table 2.6 Source List Maintenance Transactions (Cont.)

2.7 Quota Arrangement

Supply source Quota arrangement allows you to provide a mechanism to determine the source of supply if a requested material needs to be procured from different sources—internal or external—and have set quota values. For example, you need to control a certain material purchases to be split between two vendors A and B, where one will supply 80% and the other 20% of your material requests for a defined total quantity of 1,000 pieces. Using this functionality and the defined quota, the system automatically suggests requisitions to fulfill the quota numbers. The total quantity ordered from vendor A is 800 pcs, and the total quantity ordered from vendor B is 200 pcs. These quotas specify percentages of a total requirement to be procured from the defined sources.

Quota arrangements are common practice when you need to protect the inbound flow of goods and address issues such as uncontrollable price hikes, embargos, geopolitical situations, currency fluctuations, and other disadvantages of using a single source of supply.

Activate To activate the quota arrangement functionality, follow these steps:

1. Maintain quota arrangement usage in Customizing where you define the quota usage code.

2. Specify which of the purchasing documents are applicable for quota allocation calculations—from purchase orders, scheduling agreements, planned orders, purchase requisitions, MRP and production orders, and all the way to invoicing.

3. Assign the code defined in customization to the material master of an item you're planning to manage using quota arrangements (see Figure 2.15 for example).

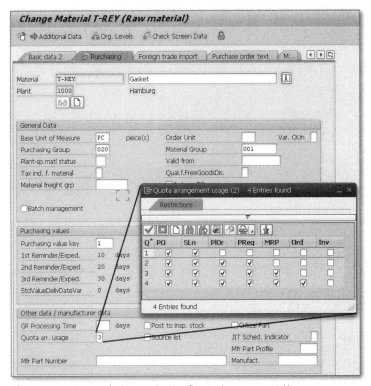

Figure 2.15 Material Master: Assign Quota Arrangement Usage

To maintain the quota, run Transaction MEQ1 (Maintain), and follow these steps:

Maintain

1. On the initial screen, enter the material number and plant the quota is maintained for, and press ⌈Enter⌉ to continue.

2. On the next screen, populate the header data. Header level data includes a validity period; the system stops taking part in sourcing when your requirements date is outside of the defined bracket. You can also define the minimum quantity of your requirement for quota arrangement to be applied during MRP.

3. To maintain line item details, select the line, and then click on the ITEM OVERVIEW button or press [F7] on your keyboard.

Quota fields

On the detailed view of the quota arrangement item, you can maintain the following fields (see Figure 2.16 for an example of the item overview screen and fields):

▶ P
Procurement type can be internal or external procurement.

▶ S
Special procurement type allows you to define usage of consignment, subcontracting, and other flavors of procurement types.

▶ VENDOR
This suppliers account number works together with the external procurement set for the procurement type.

▶ PPL
Procurement plant used to procure goods that works together with the internal procurement set for the procurement type.

▶ PVER
Production version to be used when procuring from the defined source. You need to use a different BOM or lot sizing in repetitive manufacturing.

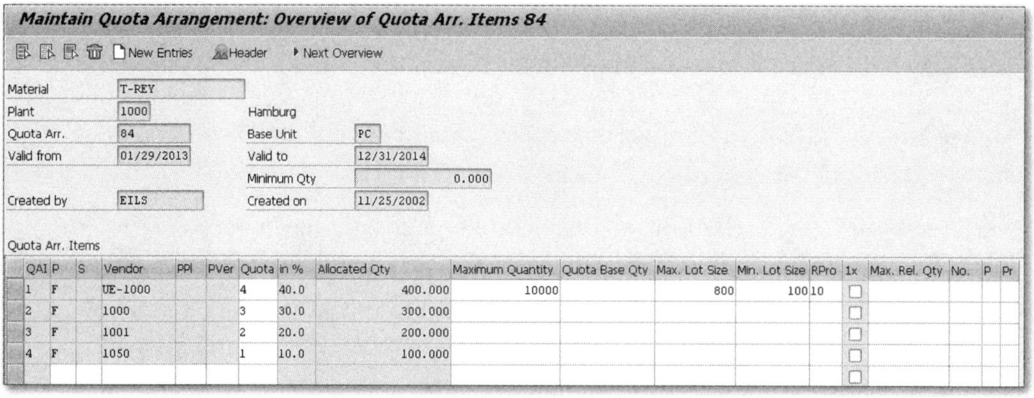

Maintain Quota Arrangement: Overview of Quota Arr. Items 84

New Entries   Header   ▶ Next Overview

Material	T-REY
Plant	1000	Hamburg
Quota Arr.	84	Base Unit	PC
Valid from	01/29/2013	Valid to	12/31/2014
		Minimum Qty	0.000
Created by	EILS	Created on	11/25/2002

Quota Arr. Items

QAI	P	S	Vendor	PPl	PVer	Quota	in %	Allocated Qty	Maximum Quantity	Quota Base Qty	Max. Lot Size	Min. Lot Size	RPro	1x	Max. Rel. Qty	No.	P	Pr
1	F		UE-1000			4	40.0	400.000	10000		800	100	10	☐				
2	F		1000			3	30.0	300.000						☐				
3	F		1001			2	20.0	200.000						☐				
4	F		1050			1	10.0	100.000						☐				
														☐				

Figure 2.16 Maintain Quota Arrangement Overview Screen

► QUOTA

Quota number that represents a portion of requirements to be supplied from the sources you're maintaining.

► IN %

Quota in percent shows the QUOTA column number converted to the percent distribution between sources of supply.

► ALLOCATED QTY

Represents the allocated quantity from the totals of all requisitions, purchase orders, contract release orders, scheduling agreement delivery schedules, and planned orders that are assigned to a source of supply (provided that these documents are to be taken into account according to the QUOTA ARR. USAGE indicator). The quota-allocated quantity is updated automatically for each order proposal to which a quota arrangement is applied.

► MAXIMUM QUANTITY

The source will no longer be considered after the allocation reaches this value.

► QUOTA BASE QTY

Treated as an additional quota-allocated quantity. You can use the quota base quantity when you add a new vendor to the mix and don't want all requirements to be assigned to this new source of supply until its quota allocated quantity exceeds the quantity of the existing sources.

► MAX. LOT SIZE

Controls the maximum order quantity you can allocate to a source of supply during the order proposal. If a requirement exceeds the maximum lot size defined here, several order proposals are suggested equal to the maximum lot size, until the total required quantity is covered.

► MIN. LOT SIZE

Defines a minimum quantity for an order proposal. If a minimum lot size has been entered, and the quantity required is less than the minimum order quantity, the order proposal is generated with a quantity equal to the minimum lot size.

> **Note**
>
> Minimum and maximum lot sizes are considered for auto generated proposals created during an MRP run, where maximum quantity is also checked during manual purchase requisition and PO creation. If maintained, minimum and/or maximum lot sizes from quota arrangement take precedence over the material master lot size settings.

▶ RPro

Rounding profile modifies the order proposal to purchasing units of delivery, such as rounding to a full pallet quantity, for example.

▶ 1X

The once-only indicator controls how the source is being considered. If checked, this source will be considered only once for matching the amount of the maximum lot size. If the total requirement is larger than the maximum lot size, the remaining quantity will be split among other sources defined in the arrangement.

Other fine-tuning options within quota arrangements allow you to manipulate controls related to period-related releases and sequencing of splits when proposals are generated. The preceding list covers the most frequently used features and controls quota arrangements offer.

Finally, save your quota arrangement when you complete the data maintenance.

Table 2.7 provides common quota arrangement transactions and menu paths.

Transaction	Menu Path
MEQ1: Maintain	LOGISTICS • MATERIALS MANAGEMENT • PURCHASING • MASTER DATA • QUOTA ARRANGEMENT • MAINTAIN
MEQ3: Display	LOGISTICS • MATERIALS MANAGEMENT • PURCHASING • MASTER DATA • QUOTA ARRANGEMENT • DISPLAY
MEQ4: Changes	LOGISTICS • MATERIALS MANAGEMENT • PURCHASING • MASTER DATA • QUOTA ARRANGEMENT • CHANGES

Table 2.7 Quota Arrangements Maintenance Transactions

Transaction	Menu Path
MEQM: Changes	LOGISTICS • MATERIALS MANAGEMENT • PURCHASING • MASTER DATA • QUOTA ARRANGEMENT • LIST DISPLAYS • BY MATERIAL
MEQ6: Analyze	LOGISTICS • MATERIALS MANAGEMENT • PURCHASING • MASTER DATA • QUOTA ARRANGEMENT • FOLLOW-ON FUNCTIONS • ANALYZE
MEQ7: Delete	LOGISTICS • MATERIALS MANAGEMENT • PURCHASING • MASTER DATA • QUOTA ARRANGEMENT • FOLLOW-ON FUNCTIONS • DELETE
MEQ8: Monitor	LOGISTICS • MATERIALS MANAGEMENT • PURCHASING • MASTER DATA • QUOTA ARRANGEMENT • FOLLOW-ON FUNCTIONS • MONITOR

Table 2.7 Quota Arrangements Maintenance Transactions (Cont.)

2.8   Purchasing Info Records

When you process your purchase requisitions into purchase orders, a certain amount of information is repeated over and over again, such as purchase price, delivery tolerances, planned delivery time, standard order quantity, or confirmation controls. To optimize this process and save a lot of time for users, you can use a reference document such as a contract or a purchasing info record. This is the most popular data source object in optimized purchasing.

Purchasing info records allow you to store information such as material, vendor, destination plant that is to receive the goods, price with validity dates, and planned delivery time. Info records can be plant-specific, so each of your facilities using the same vendor and materials can use different data such as price or planned delivery time. Data from the info records is copied into the purchase order, proposing these predefined values as defaults into the line items.

Using purchasing info records

> **Note**
>
> Info records can be used not only for materials or services with master records, but also in situations where master records aren't maintained using material group and info record short text describing the item you're purchasing.

Info records have data views that are common for the entire enterprise, and views that are specific to the purchasing organization. Let's go over each of the sections in detail because this is the most commonly used method in procurement process optimization.

2.8.1   General Data

The top section of the screen houses the common set of data applicable to the entire organization, and you can define details related to your supplier (see Figure 2.17).

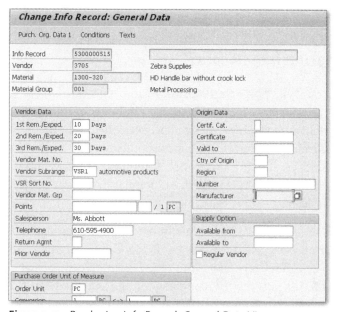

Figure 2.17   Purchasing Info Record: General Data View

Vendor data   In the VENDOR DATA section, you can maintain reminders (or expediters) in which positive values specify days after requested delivery days, and negative values specify that reminders will be sent x days prior to the requested delivery date. Messages will be issued and sent to your supplier. You can also maintain vendor material number and material group. VENDOR SUBRANGE, mentioned earlier in Section 2.4, can be assigned here to provide a link between the material or material group and the subrange defined in the vendor master. You can also maintain your supplier sales contact information here, which might be different from the information on the vendor master.

The PURCHASE ORDER UNIT OF MEASURE section allows you to store the default order unit of measure and conversion rate, and activate the variable purchase order unit.

PO UoM

The ORIGIN DATA section gives you details for foreign trade data such as certificate of origin, country and region of origin, and manufacturer information.

In the SUPPLY OPTION section, you can maintain the validity period for this source or vendor, and you can also mark this record as REGULAR VENDOR, which serves the same purpose as a fixed vendor on source lists we've mentioned earlier in this chapter.

2.8.2 Purchasing Organization Data 1

This is a purchasing organization-specific portion of the info record. Here you can maintain information either for the entire purchasing organization and/or make it plant-specific if needed. There are two main sections as shown in Figure 2.18, which we'll discuss in the following subsections.

Control Section

The data in this section is applied during purchase order creation and includes planned delivery time, purchasing group, standard order quantity, minimum order quantity, and maximum quantity. If you maintain rounding profiles with the RNDG PROF. field, your requested quantities will be converted according the rounding profile rules. For example, a less than pallet requirement is rounded up to a full pallet size order. By selecting the NO MTEXT checkbox, you'll choose the purchasing info record's PO text over the material master's purchasing texts during PO creation. If you require your suppliers to send you the acknowledgement of your purchase order receipt. You need to check the box for the ACKN.

RQD field. The CONF. CTRL checkbox allows you to define a default confirmation control for purchase order material. You can preset the required subsequent documents and procedures by choosing, for example, an inbound delivery shipping notification, simple confirmation, or rough goods receipt (rough GR).

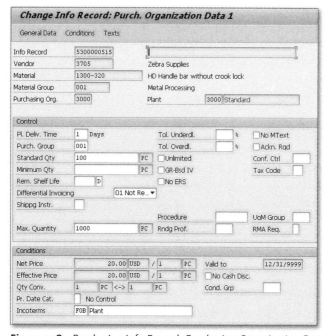

Figure 2.18 Purchasing Info Record: Purchasing Organization Data 1

You can also assign a tax relevancy in the TAX CODE field, which defaults to your PO line. If you manage your inventory using batch management, you can specify minimum remaining shelf life, which is checked at goods receipt posting. During goods receipt, the system also checks data for overdelivery and underdelivery tolerance that can be preset here in percentage or order quantity. If you use blanked POs and want to have open lines for unspecified amounts of overdeliveries over a certain period of time, select the UNLIMITED overdelivery checkbox. If you choose to do so, the overdelivery tolerance setting will be cleared.

You can also require material to follow the three-way match procedure by selecting the GR-BSD IV (goods receipt Invoice Verification) checkbox.

Some of the vendors you partner with allow for immediate payment upon receipt of goods using Evaluated Receipt Settlement (ERS). If you want certain materials to be excluded from this process and if you require an invoice document to be presented for payment every time you purchase a material, you need to check the No ERS flag.

Other invoicing features are set here as well, such as DIFFERENTIAL INVOIC-ING (BAdI-activated enhancement), which makes your material relevant for differential invoicing so you can enter incoming invoices as provisional, differential, or final. Shipping instructions allow you to capture vendor compliance with your shipping instructions at the time of goods receipt and allows you to track and calculate compliance scores in vendor evaluation. If your GR inspection discovers any quality issues with the supplied materials, your supplier may require you to obtain return material authorization before you ship the goods back. You can set the RMA REQ. field to match your needs.

Differential invoicing

Conditions

In the CONDITIONS section, you maintain basic pricing information and quantity conversion. If you need to maintain scales and multiple validity periods, you can do this in the detailed pricing CONDITIONS table (covered further in Section 2.8.3). Selecting the No CASH DISC. indicator lets the system know that during purchase order creation, no cash discount is granted for the item. You can also define how the pricing date is established by setting PR. DATE CAT. field to one of the six predefined options ranging from No CONTROL to GR DATE. INCOTERMS can also be maintained here.

Pricing and quantity

2.8.3   Purchasing Organization Data 2

In this simple data section of the purchasing info record, you can maintain the reference document numbers and relevant validity dates for these documents (see Figure 2.19). The two types of reference documents shown include your supplier quotation document number and last purchase order document number created using the purchasing info record reference and the PO date.

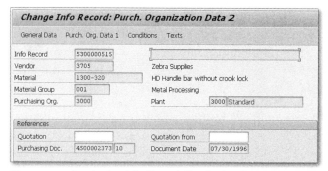

Figure 2.19 Purchasing Info Record: Purchasing Organization Data 2

The pricing CONDITIONS button provides access to detailed maintenance of PO-relevant conditions, including the basic gross price condition PB00. You can use all standard pricing maintenance functions, including validity dates and scales. See Figure 2.20 for a maintenance screen example.

The TEXTS button takes you to the purchasing texts maintenance part of the purchasing info record transaction. If you remember from the earlier sections, the MTEXTS field activates the use of purchasing info record texts over material master texts during purchase order creation.

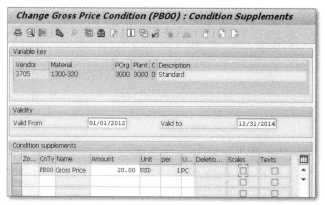

Figure 2.20 Purchasing Info Record: Pricing Condition Maintenance

2.8.4 Transactions

Manual generation Purchasing info records can be generated manually using direct transactions and automatically during maintenance of quotations, contracts, or purchase orders. Purchasing info records can also be updated every time a new goods receipt is posted against the PO. See Table 2.8 for a list of common purchasing info record maintenance transactions and menu paths.

Transaction	Menu Path
ME11: Create Info Record	LOGISTICS • MATERIALS MANAGEMENT • PURCHASING • MASTER DATA • INFO RECORD • CREATE
ME12: Change	LOGISTICS • MATERIALS MANAGEMENT • PURCHASING • MASTER DATA • INFO RECORD • CHANGE
ME13: Display	LOGISTICS • MATERIALS MANAGEMENT • PURCHASING • MASTER DATA • INFO RECORD • DISPLAY
ME14: Changes	LOGISTICS • MATERIALS MANAGEMENT • PURCHASING • MASTER DATA • INFO RECORD • CHANGES
ME15: Flag for Deletion	LOGISTICS • MATERIALS MANAGEMENT • PURCHASING • MASTER DATA • INFO RECORD • FLAG FOR DELETION
MEMASSIN: Mass Maintenance	LOGISTICS • MATERIALS MANAGEMENT • PURCHASING • MASTER DATA • INFO RECORD • MASS MAINTENANCE

Table 2.8 Purchasing Info Records Maintenance Transaction Codes

2.9   Pricing

Pricing is one of the most important activities in purchasing; you have to make sure that the price entered in a purchase order is correct because the purchase document represents a legal bond between your company and your vendors. You also have to make sure that all of the costs involved in purchasing a material and bringing it through the dock doors of your company are considered. That includes not only the price of the material you're buying, but also all of the shipping, handling, and customs costs. Furthermore, you have to be able to include all of the taxes to which the material is subject.

Vendors have list prices, special discounts, volume discounts, and also surcharges that may affect the final price of a material. To calculate all discounts and surcharges, SAP ERP uses conditions that are determined based on rules set in Customizing.

Schema The set of conditions that are valid for pricing are called *pricing schemas* (as shown in Figure 2.21), and they are determined depending on data assigned to the purchasing organization and the vendor: the schema group for vendor and the schema group for purchasing organization. The schema group for vendor is assigned in the PURCHASING DATA screen of the vendor master in Transaction MK01 or MK02 (LOGISTICS • MATERIALS MANAGEMENT • PURCHASING • MASTER DATA • INFO RECORD • CREATE), and the schema group for purchasing organization is assigned in the system configuration in the IMG path MATERIALS MANAGEMENT • PURCHASING • CONDITIONS • DEFINE PRICE DETERMINATION PROCESS • DETERMINE CALCULATION SCHEMA FOR STANDARD PURCHASE ORDERS.

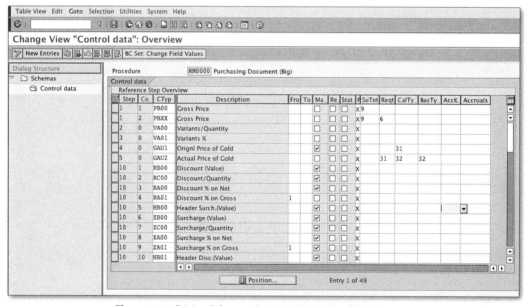

Figure 2.21 Pricing Schemas Contain Pricing Condition Types

If you're a functional analyst, then you need to configure different pricing schemas that contain different conditions depending on your pricing needs. You also need to configure schema groups for vendors and schema groups for purchase organization, and then configure the schema determination according to the combination of their values (see Figure 2.22).

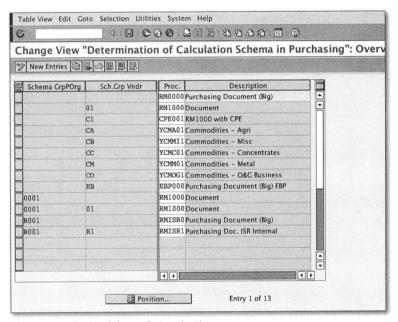

Figure 2.22 Pricing Schema Determination

2.9.1 Using Conditions in Purchasing Documents

After the pricing schemas and their determination are configured, you can start using those conditions in purchasing documents. Each pricing schema contains header and item conditions, referring to where these conditions can be used. Some conditions can even be set as available for use on both the header and the item levels.

The conditions you enter in the purchasing info record are valid only for one material when it's purchased from a specific vendor. To enter conditions that apply for all the items you buy from a vendor, all the items in a material group, or all the items included in a contract, you can use condition records.

Purchasing info record conditions

To enter conditions in a purchasing info record, follow these steps:

1. In the PURCHASING ORGANIZATION view of Transaction ME11 or Transaction ME12, enter a price and a price unit.

2. Click on the CONDITIONS button.

3. If you're changing an info record you'll see a list of validity dates for conditions; select the one that applies to your prices.

4. On the CHANGE GROSS PRICE CONDITION screen (see Figure 2.23), enter new conditions as required. For example, for condition FRB1 for freight value, enter the value in your document's currency and press the Enter key.

5. Save your info record.

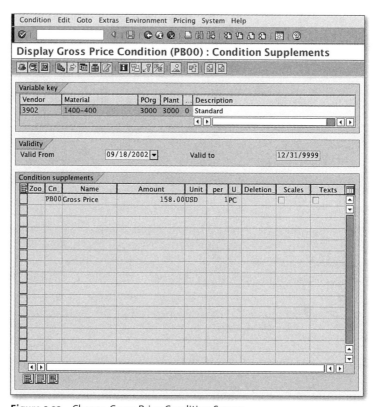

Figure 2.23 Change Gross Price Condition Screen

2.9.2 Condition Records

You create condition records to make prices appear in purchasing documents. Condition records are master data entries that create a combination of elements called a *condition*. The elements in the condition are set in Customizing, and each of these condition settings is called a *condition type*. In the example shown in Figure 2.24, the condition record will give the company a 13% discount when they buy using purchasing organization 3000, for everything it buys from vendor 3902 SCT, Inc; the condition record uses condition type RL01.

Display pricing

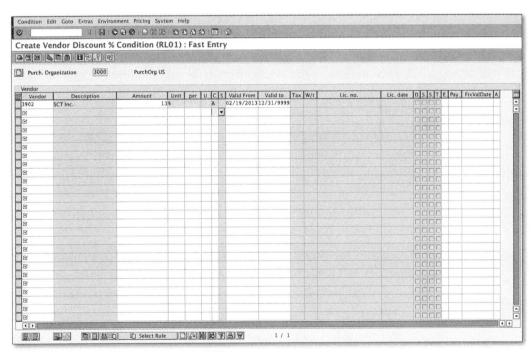

Figure 2.24 Create Vendor Discount Condition

Condition records are created in Transaction MEK1 (LOGISTICS • MATERIALS MANAGEMENT • PURCHASING • MASTER DATA • CONDITIONS • OTHER • CREATE). To create a new condition record, follow these steps:

Condition fulfillment

1. Choose a condition type; for example, LP00 for an incomplete pallet surcharge.

2. Select a key combination by clicking on the KEY COMBINATION button. These key combinations refer to the combination of field values that will make this condition relevant in a purchasing document. For the example of condition type LP00, select VENDOR.

3. Enter the values for all of the fields or elements. The values in these fields are compared to the values in a specific purchasing document or in the purchasing info record. When the values match the ones entered in the condition record, the system considers the condition fulfilled, and then it includes that condition type in that document. In the LP00 surcharge for a vendor example, enter the vendor number, the amount of the surcharge in the vendor's currency, and the price unit. Also enter the validity period for this condition record and save.

Entering Price Conditions

Two types of conditions are used in a purchasing document: header conditions and item conditions. The item conditions have the individual pricing elements for each line in the purchasing document, and the header conditions include pricing elements that apply to the whole document. The header conditions also include the sum of all the individual item conditions; ultimately, it calculates the total document (order) value.

To enter price conditions on a purchase order in Transaction ME21N or Transaction ME22N (LOGISTICS • MATERIALS MANAGEMENT • PURCHASING • PURCHASE ORDER • CREATE • VENDOR KNOWN), as shown in Figure 2.25, follow these steps:

1. Enter the material number, the quantity, and the price in the ITEM OVERVIEW section of the PO.

2. In the ITEM detail section, select the CONDITIONS tab.

3. At the bottom, enter new conditions as required. For example, condition FRB1 for freight value, enter the value in your document's currency, and press the ⌷Enter⌷ key.

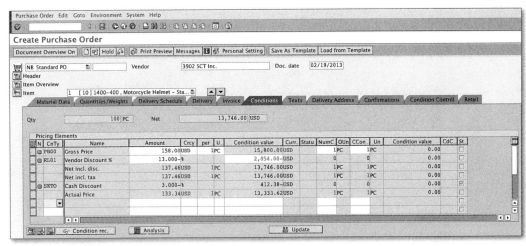

Figure 2.25 Fulfilled Conditions in the Purchasing Document

2.10 Taxes

In the Purchasing subcomponent, you have the option to determine taxes in the purchasing documents (purchase orders, purchasing contracts, or scheduling agreements) or not, and then let the follow-up process of Invoice Verification do the calculation. You can also use the same condition determination just described for pricing to determine taxes in purchasing documents.

In either case, there is data to be maintained to make your purchases tax relevant. One is a configuration setting for the plant, in which your system analyst needs to make sure that the right tax indicator is set for the plant or plants for which you're executing the purchases. This is done in Customizing in the path MATERIALS MANAGEMENT • PURCHASING • TAXES • ASSIGN TAX INDICATORS FOR PLANTS, as shown in Figure 2.26.

Tax master data

To configure taxes, follow the IMG path MATERIALS MANAGEMENT • PURCHASING • TAXES • SET TAX INDICATOR FOR PLANT to set that a plant is relevant for tax determination. Then, set the tax relevance for each vendor and for each material. This is done because not all vendors fall in the same tax category; import vendors may not charge a sales tax, for example. In the same way, some materials may fall into categories that make them tax exempt.

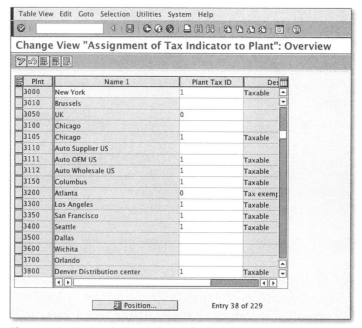

Figure 2.26 Setting the Tax Indicator for Each Plant

2.10.1 Adding Tax Relevance

The tax relevance is determined in the purchasing documents for each of its line items. When you define that all three elements—plant, vendor, and material—are relevant for some kind of sales tax, then it's adopted by the document.

Tax relevance for materials   The tax relevance for each material is set in the material master in the PURCHASING view. You need to maintain the TAX IND. F MATERIAL field. This field requires that you previously set the different options in Customizing.

To add tax relevance to a material as shown in Figure 2.27, follow these steps:

1. In Transaction MM02 (LOGISTICS • MATERIALS MANAGEMENT • MATE-RIAL MASTER • CHANGE • IMMEDIATELY), select the PURCHASING view.

2. Enter the plant and purchasing organization for which you're making the change.

3. In the TAX IND. F. MATERIAL field, enter the appropriate value.

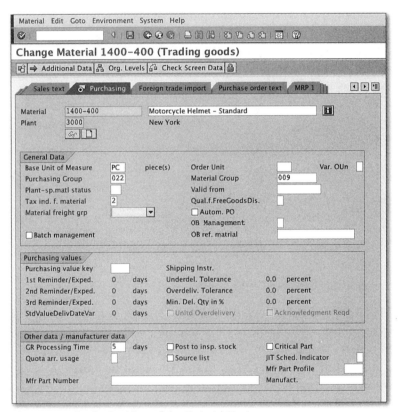

Figure 2.27 Purchasing View of the Material Master

Similarly, tax relevance for vendors is set in the vendor master in the CONTROL view in the SALES/PUR.TAX field (see Figure 2.28). Selecting this checkbox indicates that this vendor will add a sales tax in its sales invoice.

Tax relevance for vendors

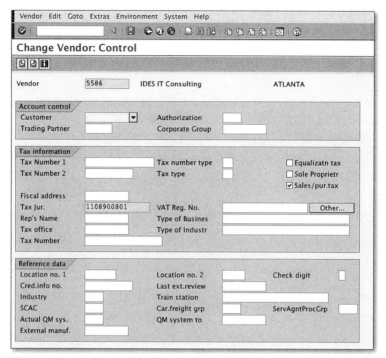

Figure 2.28 Setting the Sales/Purchasing Tax Flag in the Vendor Master

2.10.2 Adding the Tax Code

Additionally, you need to enter the appropriate tax code in the purchasing info record. This defaults the correct tax code in the INVOICE tab of the ITEM detail section of a purchase order, for example (see Figure 2.30). Keep in mind that purchasing info records have to be created for each material/vendor/purchasing organization combination.

For vendors To add tax relevance to a vendor as shown in Figure 2.29, follow these steps:

1. In Transaction MK02 (LOGISTICS • MATERIALS MANAGEMENT • PURCHASING • MASTER DATA • VENDOR • PURCHASING • CHANGE), select the vendor number and the purchasing organization.

2. Select the CONTROL data view and press Enter.

3. In the TAX INFORMATION section, enter all of the tax-relevant information for the vendor, and click SAVE.

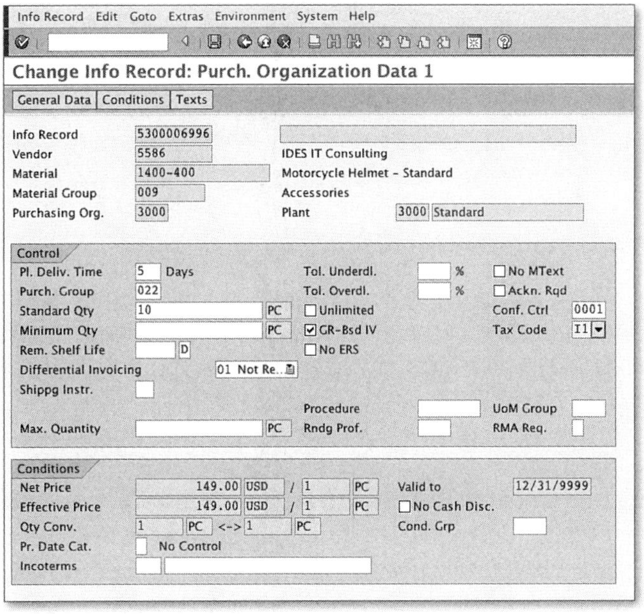

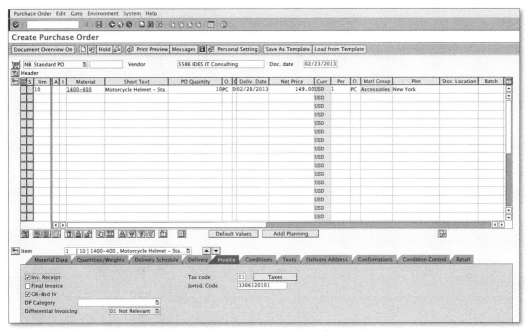

Figure 2.29 Setting the Tax Indicator in the Purchasing Info Record

Figure 2.30 Purchasing Documents with the Tax Code from the Info Record

> **Note**
>
> The tax code is set in Customizing by the finance areas, and each tax code can be assigned a different tax percentage, so make sure to consult with your finance department for details about the right code to use.

2.10.3 Creating Condition Records

So far, by the use of this basic master data, the purchasing documents can determine whether items are relevant for taxes, and specific tax codes can be copied from purchasing info records. If you need the purchasing documents to explicitly show the amount for taxes, then you need to create condition records for them.

Rules for plants and tax codes

As we explained in Section 2.9, condition records are the set of rules that help determine if an entry in the purchasing document is relevant or complies with that condition. So you can create condition records for imports, condition records for domestic purchases, for different plants, and for different tax codes. Please see Figure 2.31.

The standard SAP ERP system condition for taxes is called NAVS, you have the option of creating entries based on different combination of the following key fields: Tax indicator for Material, Tax indicator for Plant, Country of origin and destination, and Account Assignment. A tax percentage and a tax code have to also be entered.

Condition records for taxes are created in Transaction MEK1 (LOGISTICS • MATERIALS MANAGEMENT • PURCHASING • MASTER DATA • TAXES • CREATE).

Create

To create a new condition record, follow these steps:

1. First you have to choose the condition type NAVS for Non-Deductible Tax.

2. Select a key combination by clicking on the KEY COMBINATION button. There are a few options available, depending on how your purchases are taxed. Choose the one that applies to your business.

3. Enter the values for all the fields or elements. The values in these fields will be compared to the values from a specific purchasing document, specifically the material's and plant's tax indicators, along with the check for an import or domestic purchase.

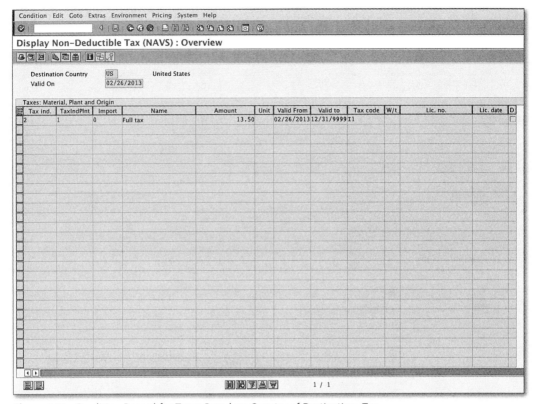

Figure 2.31 Condition Record for Taxes Based on Country of Destination, Tax Indicator for Material, and Tax Indicator for Plant

4. When the values match the ones entered in the condition record, the system considers the condition fulfilled, and then it includes that condition type in that document. At this point, the value you enter for the tax percentage you entered is brought to the pricing schema of the purchasing document.

5. When the combination of the values of these fields fulfills the condition record, the percentage and tax code are adopted by the purchasing documents and they are added to the total value of the order, as shown in Figure 2.32.

Creating and maintaining pricing conditions

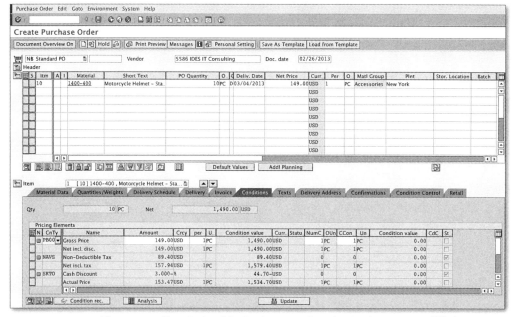

Figure 2.32 Non-Deductible Tax Appears when the Conditions are Fulfilled

Table 2.9 lists the transactions and menu paths that will help you create and maintain condition records.

Transaction	Menu Path
MEK1: Create Conditions	LOGISTICS • MATERIALS MANAGEMENT • PURCHASING • MASTER DATA • CONDITIONS • OTHER • CREATE
MEK2: Change	LOGISTICS • MATERIALS MANAGEMENT • PURCHASING • MASTER DATA • CONDITIONS • OTHER • CHANGE
MEK3: Display	LOGISTICS • MATERIALS MANAGEMENT • PURCHASING • MASTER DATA • CONDITIONS • OTHER • DISPLAY
MEKE: By Vendor	LOGISTICS • MATERIALS MANAGEMENT • PURCHASING • MASTER DATA • CONDITIONS • DISCOUNTS/SURCHARGES • BY VENDOR
MEKF: By Material Type	LOGISTICS • MATERIALS MANAGEMENT • PURCHASING • MASTER DATA • TAXES • MATERIAL TYPE

Table 2.9 Condition Records for Pricing

2.11 Other Master Data

Of the many other complete sets of master data in the SAP ERP system, some interact directly with the Purchasing subcomponent and some don't. We chose to introduce routes and batches because they play an important role in some purchasing business scenarios.

2.11.1 Routes

Routes are used in purchasing primarily in stock transport orders. These types of orders include a SHIPPING tab in the ITEM details section, which takes shipping and sales data from the material, the plant, the storage location, and the ship-to address. This information is used to determine a shipping point and a route that are used to create an outbound delivery in the shipping plant.

Stock transport orders

Other purchasing processes that use a similar determination and thus routes include returns to vendors with delivery, and subcontracting with delivery. These processes also require that your material, plant, and vendor include sales information to determine all of the shipping data, including the route.

Routes are part of the SAP Transportation Management master data objects, and they include a point of origin, a point of destination, sometimes way points in between, and, most importantly, a travel time. These travel times directly affect the purchasing lead times and are included in purchasing documents if an inbound delivery is being used. Longer lead times are also translated into earlier planning of materials, which means that MRP will generate the material requirements while taking into account this information.

Routes are created by the Logistics Execution (LE) or Sales and Distribution (SD) teams, and you need to make sure that these teams know about your requirements for shipping between plants and returns or shipping to vendors so that they can also create the routes your process needs.

2.11.2 Batches

Some industries, such as pharmaceutical or food, rely completely on batch management to know when their raw materials, semifinished products, and finished products were manufactured, when they expire, and where they've been used in the manufacturing process. Batches also help them know which customers the final products were sold and shipped to.

Batch information is used and kept throughout the entire logistics process. You can buy specific batches when you order raw materials from your vendors, or they can be captured upon receipt in the warehouse. You can determine exactly how much stock you have of any given batch in storage and when the expiration date is. You can also determine if a material can be received into stock based on the manufacturing date and the remaining shelf life.

Batch definition To use batches, you need to first configure how batches are defined in the system. You can set the system as the following:

- BATCH UNIQUE AT PLANT LEVEL
  With this setting, the system allows the same batch number for the same material in different plants.

- BATCH UNIQUE AT MATERIAL LEVEL
  With this setting, the system has a unique batch number for a material across plants.

- BATCH UNIQUE AT CLIENT LEVEL FOR A MATERIAL
  With this setting, no two batch numbers will be the same, independent of material and plant.

This is done in Customizing in the IMG path LOGISTICS GENERAL • BATCH MANAGEMENT • SPECIFY BATCH LEVEL AND ACTIVATE STATUS MANAGEMENT.

Then for every material in Transaction MM02 (LOGISTICS • MATERIALS MANAGEMENT • MATERIAL MASTER • MATERIAL • CHANGE • IMMEDIATELY), you'll have to set the BATCH MANAGEMENT flag in any of the plant level views of the material master: SALES/PLANT DATA, PURCHASING, or PLANT DATA/STORAGE.

2.12   Summary

In this chapter, we covered a range of master data objects that you can use in procurement functions. We identified influencing master data objects such as material master, service master, business partners, source lists, quota arrangements, purchasing info records, pricing, taxes, routes, and more. Depending on your procurement processes, you may need to use all or just a few of them, and reading this chapter should help you identify, maintain, and describe the relationship of those data objects to your procurement process with ease.

Based on the information we've covered, you can now tell that there is a lot of master data to maintain, which is why it's very important to keep it clean all the time.

Now, together with the information from Chapter 1 that introduced you to the procurement enterprise structure of your company and armed with the wealth of information about master data, we're ready to move on to Chapter 3, where we'll begin dissecting the procurement processes starting with planning and forecasting.

All procurement activities start with recognizing the demand, which is monitored by company planners. They are the ultimate players in performing the balancing act among needs, wants, and must-haves using planning and forecasting functionalities.

3 Planning and Forecasting

In Chapter 2, we covered the majority of master data objects that influence the procurement procedures along the way. This chapter introduces you to the first system steps that initiate procurement activities. We cover the planning procedures, including material requirements planning (MRP) and consumption-based planning, and talk in detail about planning methods that play a key role in monitoring demand, on-hand stock, incoming receipts, and order proposals. We demonstrate how MRP differs from consumption-based planning and flexible planning, as well as how material master data influences the planning run. You'll learn how consumption-based planning can use your materials' past consumption history to determine future requirements. We also touch briefly on flexible planning, which is part of Production Planning's Sales and Operations Planning (SOP), and its role in procurement.

> **Note**
>
> Planning and forecasting is a vast subject that covers both internal and external procurement aspects. It's impossible to cover all flavors and to be true to the scope of this book, so we address only the planning procedures that impact external procurement processes.

Planning procedures

The planning procedures (MRP procedures) are responsible for generating order proposals (planned orders, purchase requisitions, and delivery schedules), which are then directed to either purchasing or production, depending on master data and configuration settings. Figure 3.1 shows the different types of flavors and methods for planning procedures. All planning procedures use a common execution component—MRP—which brings material master data and all of these different flavors together at the planning run.

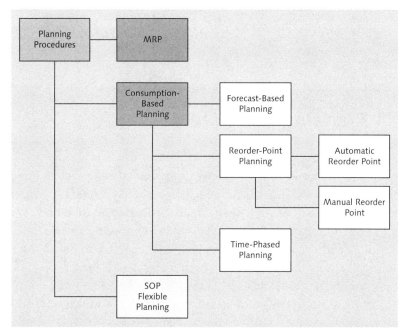

Figure 3.1 Planning Procedures: Overview

We'll start with the overview of MRP, introduce you to the basic principles influencing master data objects (from Chapter 2), and step through some of the most frequently used transactions used in executing the MRP process.

3.1 Material Requirements Planning Procedures

Supply versus demand

The purpose of MRP is to look at overall material demand and make sure that the quantities of this material are available on the date it's requested. On-hand balances are checked during the process, and procurement proposals—for internal or external procurement—are generated as a result in the form of planned orders later converted to either production or purchase orders. Planners (MRP controllers) can manage the process in a variety of flavors (planning procedures) as mentioned before. These procedures require master data settings, bills of material (BOMs), routings, and work centers, among the core objects. The following MRP procedures are covered in the upcoming sections:

- Material requirements planning
- Consumption-based planning
  - Reorder point planning
  - Forecast-based planning
  - Time-phased planning

3.1.1 Material Requirements Planning

MRP uses current and future sales numbers for the net requirements calculation. These relevant requirements include not only the customer sales orders, but also material reservations, all dependent requirements coming from BOMs used in production, and Planned Independent Requirements (PIRs) representing forecast values. These calculations can be very precise and translate to exact daily requirements, allowing you to work with relatively low levels of safety stock. Applying this procedure across multiple MRP areas (covered in the next sections of this chapter), groups of materials, or people responsible for managing product lines makes the planning process easy to manage and execute. MRP also helps maintain the balance between the optimal service level and the cost of carrying inventory.

Current/future information

The MRP process cascades through the following steps (see the flowchart in Figure 3.2 for details):

Process

- **Calculate net requirement**
  All of your requirements quantities are compared to available stock. The system may consider your on-hand warehouse stock, confirmed receipts, and consumption requirements (incoming sales orders, PIRs, and material reservations). If the available stock, including receipts from purchasing and production, is smaller than the required quantity, the system creates procurement proposals, such as planned orders or purchase requisitions.

▶ **Check lot-sizing procedure**
Identified material requirement quantities are resized according to the lot-size procedure specified in the material master record. Lot-sizing is discussed in more details later in this chapter.

▶ **Scheduling**
Procurement proposal dates are determined. Delivery dates are calculated for materials procured externally; production dates are calculated for materials produced in-house.

▶ **Process-dependent requirements**
During a BOM explosion, dependent requirements of components are processed through the same checklist we're walking through now.

▶ **Other requirements**
Material forecasts are checked for unplanned consumption; that is, consumption above planned issues of components during the production process.

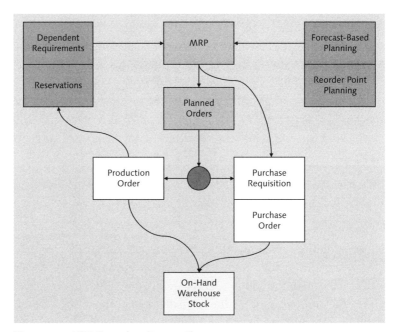

Figure 3.2 MRP Procedure Process Flow

3.1.2 Consumption-Based Planning

Consumption-based planning uses forecast information based on the past material consumption, as well as other statistical methods, to determine the future requirements. Translating this to procurement speak, MRP triggers a procurement request if your forecast recognized a past consumption record and reacted to it, or your on-hand and available stock levels fall below the reorder point. This method is very simple to implement and easy to maintain, with light material master data maintenance. One of the major prerequisites, however, is up-to-date inventory management. The other requirement is that your material consumption numbers are relatively consistent.

Requirements based on statistics

Consumption-based planning supports three different MRP procedures, which we'll discuss in the following subsections.

Reorder Point Planning

In this MRP procedure, the system checks whether the planned available stock (on-hand balance plus firmed incoming receipts) will fall below the reorder point (calculated level of stock needed to cover average consumption requirements during the replenishment lead time) specified on the material master record. If so, a procurement proposal will be created. See Figure 3.3 for an overview of the reorder point planning principles.

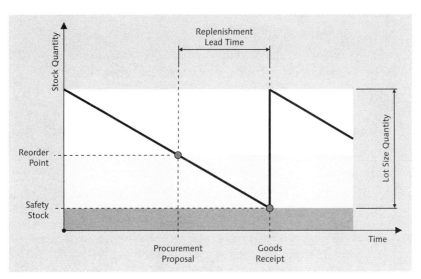

Figure 3.3 Reorder Point Planning: Overview

Because your future requirements have already been considered within the set reorder point level, material reservations, sales, and dependent requirements aren't considered in the net requirements calculation. One of the key values that is important for defining the reorder point data is safety stock, which takes the following into consideration:

Safety stock

▸ Historical consumption data or future requirements

▸ Supplier or production delivery time

▸ Desired service level

▸ Deviations from the forecasted requirements

▸ Average material consumption

▸ Replenishment lead time

Planning types

You can choose between two commonly used reorder point planning types:

▸ **Manual reorder point planning**
Levels are set and adjusted manually by the MRP controller or master data governance body within your organization.

▸ **Automatic reorder point planning**
The system determines the reorder point using the forecast data.

Process steps

When you settle on the type of planning, the system will follow these steps:

▸ **Monitor stock levels**
All relevant consumption and receiving transactions make your stock balances fluctuate. The system looks for the dips below the reorder point before the alarm is set for procurement proposals.

▸ **Calculate net requirement**
The system compares plant available stock and firmed receipts with the reorder point, and if the total available stock is less than the reorder point quantity, the need for replenishment is identified.

▸ **Check lot-sizing procedure**
Identified shortages of materials are resized according to the lot-size procedure specified in the material master record.

▸ **Scheduling**
Procurement proposal dates are finally determined. Delivery dates for a purchase order is calculated for materials procured externally, and production dates are calculated for materials procured internally.

Forecast-Based Planning

This procedure uses the historical consumption data collecting information from all movement types defined for consumption updates to determine future requirements. We'll walk through the forecast process in detail in Section 3.3.

Forecasting calculates these future requirements using defined time intervals (daily, weekly, etc.), continuously reacting and updating the forecasted data based on the latest consumption numbers. Forecast requirements are reduced by posted consumption, and if the true consumption is higher in the current period, future forecast requirements are reduced as well. Current forecast requirements aren't reduced. Average reduction of the forecast requirements is based on average daily consumption, and actual consumption postings are ignored.

Future requirements

The average daily requirements are calculated using the following formula:

Average daily requirements = forecast requirements ÷ number of workdays in the forecast period

The forecast requirements are reduced by using the following formula:

FR = number of workdays worked × average daily requirements

So when you decide on this type of planning, the system follows these steps to execute the procedure:

Forecast steps

▶ **Calculate net requirement**
The system copies the forecast requirements and performs a check for every forecast period if the forecast requirements are covered by plant available stock and/or firmed receipts. If the total available stock is inadequate, the system generates procurement proposals.

▶ **Check lot-sizing procedure**
Identified shortages of materials are resized according to the lot-size procedure specified in the material master record.

▶ **Scheduling**
Procurement proposal dates are finally determined for purchase orders or production orders.

Time-Phased Planning

If you have suppliers delivering goods to your warehouses on a particular day of the week according to defined intervals (such as weekly deliveries on Monday), you can apply this method to plan your materials in the matching cycle. You can use the planning calendar to maintain holidays and shift the requirements to be processed either before or after the nonworkday if needed (planning calendar maintenance is discussed in Section 3.2.4). If you use SAP Retail, you can use the planning cycle from the vendor master (covered in Chapter 2) using vendor subranges to fine-tune these types of planning scenarios.

This method can be used by both MRP and consumption-based planning. If you're planning on using MRP combined with time-phased planning, all relevant requirements are included in the net requirements calculation. If you want to use it in consumption-based planning mode, your requirements have to come from the forecast, and only forecast requirements are included in the net requirements calculation. In time-phased planning, the system follows these steps to execute the procedure:

- ▶ **Calculate net requirement**
  Requirements are calculated within a determined time interval, including planning cycle, purchasing processing time, planned delivery time, goods receipt processing time, and safety stock from the MRP run to the next MRP planning run. The system reduces the calculated requirements by on-hand stock and firmed incoming receipts. The remaining shortage quantity is used for the procurement proposal.

- ▶ **Lot-sizing procedure**
  The lot-for-lot procedure is the most frequently used sizing procedure, and this simply copies your calculated shortages planning proposal. You can, however, use other sizing methods, and shortages of materials are resized according to the lot-size procedure specified in the material master record.

- ▶ **Scheduling**
  Procurement proposal dates are determined using your planning cycle.

3.2 Master Data in Planning

You need master data to run MRP, which includes the material master, BOMs, quota arrangements, MRP profiles that help in master data default settings, and other configurable data objects such as planning calendars, MRP types, MRP areas, MRP controllers, or lot-sizing procedures. In this section, we'll cover the important foundation pieces of master data—some that are set in IMG Customizing and some that aren't. We'll talk about MRP types, MRP areas, MRP groups, and planning calendars as some of the key configurable mater data objects. Let's start with the MRP type, which ties directly into what we've covered so far.

3.2.1 MRP Type

An MRP type is a key that identifies and controls which planning procedure is used in a planning run for your materials. This assignment is done on the material master record together with other planning parameters. We'll cover them in detail shortly when we talk about MRP views in the material master.

MRP types are set in Customizing and offer several predelivered options that we've already covered when talking about the planning procedures in Section 3.1. Figure 3.4 shows the IMG configuration table for MRP Types.

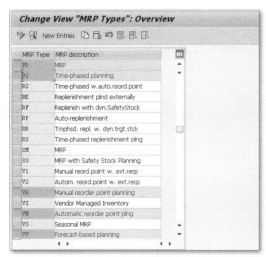

Figure 3.4 MRP Types: Pre-Delivered Options Configuration View

Configure types To configure the MRP types, you have to access the IMG configuration Transaction SPRO and use the following menu path: MATERIALS MANAGEMENT • CONSUMPTION-BASED PLANNING • MASTER DATA • CHECK MRP TYPES.

The MRP type controls include the MRP PROCEDURE field, which is the main indicator that specifies the procedure used for material planning (see Figure 3.5 for an example of MRP TYPE PD).

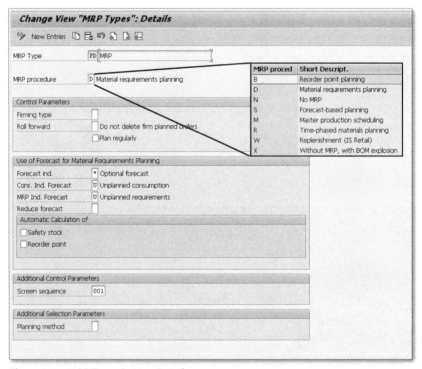

Figure 3.5 MRP Type: Setting Details

Moving down the screen, in the CONTROL PARAMETERS section, you can maintain the following:

▶ FIRMING TYPE
This setting controls firming of the planning results and how procurement proposals are firmed and scheduled. You can choose one of the following settings:

- ▶ 0: Planning results not firmed
- ▶ 1: Automatic firming and order proposals rescheduled out
- ▶ 2: Automatic firming without order proposal
- ▶ 3: Manual firming and order proposals rescheduled out
- ▶ 4: Manual firming without order proposal

> **Note**
>
> You can specify the firming date manually at the execution of the planning run, and the planning time fence is automatically extended to the date you've entered.

- ▶ ROLL FORWARD
  The master production scheduling process—not covered in this book—uses this option to control how MPS is updated in a specific planning period.

- ▶ PLAN REGULARLY
  Indicates that materials with this MRP type need to be planned in regular intervals—basically your system includes the planning cycle in the MRP process—used in retail systems.

In the USE OF FORECAST FOR MATERIAL REQUIREMENTS PLANNING section, you can define how your planning procedure interacts with forecasts using the following parameters:

MRP forecast

- ▶ FORECAST IND.
  Defines whether forecast data will be applied in planning.

- ▶ CONS. IND. FORECAST
  Controls whether total consumption or unplanned consumption values are used for the forecast.

- ▶ MRP IND. FORECAST
  Defines whether forecast values are applicable in the net requirements calculation. If you choose to use it, you have a choice to apply them as the following:

  - ▶ G: TOTAL REQUIREMENTS

  - ▶ U: UNPLANNED REQUIREMENTS

▶ Reduce forecast

Controls how forecast requirements are reduced. You have a choice of the following:

  ▶ "BLANK": Reduce forecast value by consumption

  ▶ 1: Reduce forecast value in first period by consumption—reduces forecast requirements exclusively in the current month

  ▶ 2: Reduce forecast value in first period by average value—reduces forecast requirements in current month by average value

In the Automatic Calculation of section, you can define the behavior of the following:

▶ Safety stock
  If set, the system calculates the safety stock automatically.

▶ Reorder point
  If set, the system calculates the reorder point automatically.

3.2.2 MRP Areas

Independent MRP and forecasting

An MRP area is an organizational unit defined to perform MRP and forecasting independently from other logical planning areas. In a majority of the simple installations, you won't require those multiple areas to deal with the granular view of your planning requirements, so you won't activate this functionality. In the following subsections, we'll discuss how to plan with and without MRP areas.

Planning without MRP Areas

All material requirements (dependent requirements, PIRs, and sales requirements) for all storage locations within a plant are planned together at plant level. Your material master MRP settings are applicable at the plant level, and finally based on your procurement type, either in-house production or external procurement is triggered. No MRP area activation is required.

Planning at storage location

SAP also provides the functionality to run planning at the storage location level, so you can exclude certain storage locations form the plant MRP or plan them separately altogether. Depending on your requirements, which can include a physical location of the facilities or type of use (service-only facility), you can set options in Customizing to suit your needs.

To plan your storage locations separately, you need to maintain the material master MRP 4 view, where you set the MRP indicator to 2 STORAGE LOCATION STOCK PLANNED SEPARATELY—as shown in Figure 3.6—and define a reorder point and replenishment quantities.

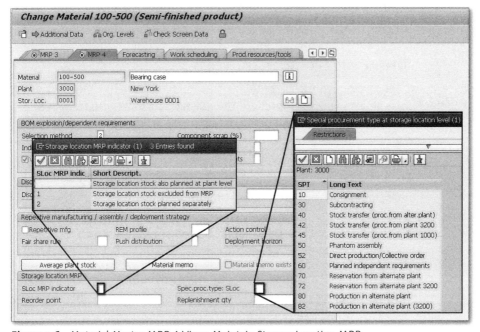

Figure 3.6 Material Master MRP 4 View: Maintain Storage Location MRP

You can apply the following procurement scenarios without the use of MRP areas:

Procurement scenarios

▶ **Stock transfer within plant**
In this scenario, the SPEC.PROC.TYPE: SLOC key must be blank. The storage location stock is procured from another storage location of the same plant. When you execute the planning run, the reorder point is checked against the available on-hand balances, and if the stock falls below the reorder point level, a reservation for a stock transfer is created.

▶ **External procurement**
To trigger this scenario, the SPEC.PROC.TYPE: SLOC key must be set to one of the special procurement types allowing for purchasing from an external vendor, such as 30-SUBCONTRACTING.

▶ **Stock transfer from another plant**
The SPEC.PROC.TYPE: SLOC key will drive the process, where in shortage situations, the planning run creates a stock transport requisition for the receiving plant. Finally, the stock transport requisition is converted to a stock transport purchase order.

Planning with MRP Areas

Different MRP master data

If you need even more granular planning functionality, and each of the areas needs to have a subset of MRP master data that is different between them, you can activate MRP area planning. If you're live on SAP ERP, and you're turning this functionality on, you also need to plan a conversion of your material master—adding MRP area segments to MRP views and forecasting views. Conversions of planning files also need to be performed; you can access this using the IMG configuration transaction and following the menu path PRODUCTION • MATERIAL REQUIREMENTS PLANNING • PLANNING FILE ENTRIES • CONVERT PLANNING FILE ENTRIES FOR MRP AREAS.

You can define the MRP areas within an individual plant; however, you can't set them up to create an MRP area that spans multiple plants. See Figure 3.7 for a view of the configuration maintenance screen.

MRP area types

You can use one of the three types of MRP areas:

▶ **01: plant**
A unique, single plant MRP area assignment that can include the plant with all storage locations and subcontractor stock.

▶ **02: storage location**
One or more storage locations of a single plant assigned to an MRP area. Remember that a plant storage location can be assigned to only one MRP area.

▶ **03: vendor**

A unique, single plant subcontracting vendor per MRP area. Again, subcontracting vendors can be assigned to only one MRP area.

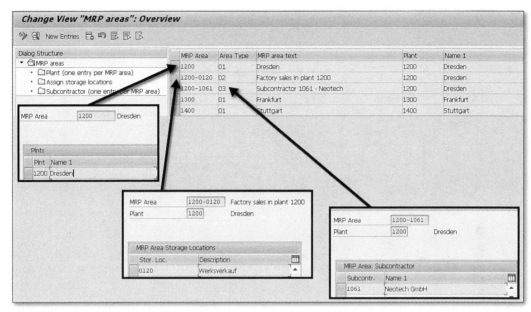

Figure 3.7 MRP Area: Overview Screen

To set up the MRP areas, you have to access the IMG configuration transaction to first activate the MRP areas and then maintain them:

▶ **Activate**
MATERIALS MANAGEMENT • CONSUMPTION-BASED PLANNING • MASTER DATA • MRP AREA • ACTIVATE MRP FOR MRP AREAS

▶ **Maintain**
MATERIALS MANAGEMENT • CONSUMPTION-BASED PLANNING • MASTER DATA • MRP AREA • DEFINE MRP AREAS

After your MRP areas are defined, you'll notice that everything from material master data, forecasting and consumption, to planning and evaluation require using the MRP area field. Every planning procedure is carried out for defined MRP areas. So each MRP area has its own set of planning data, including the MRP procedures, lot-sizing procedures, and independent forecasting based on independently collected consumption data—per MRP area assignment. Figure 3.8 shows the material master maintenance view of MRP area examples. Also, the evaluation of planning results—if done using individual display—require you to specify the MRP area.

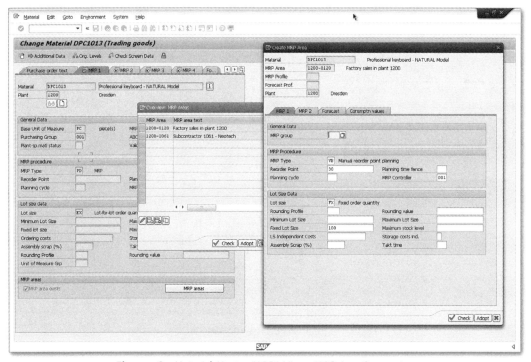

Figure 3.8 Material Master MRP1 View: MRP Area Segment

> **Note**
>
> Individual display is limited to a single MRP area. Collective display, however, shows you planning results across multiple MRP areas.

Delete data segments

You can also delete MRP area master data segments if they are no longer needed. To do this, run the material master Transaction MM02 (Data Change) and then select the MRP 1 view to open the OVERVIEW: MRP AREAS dialog box. Choose the MRP area for deletion, and click the DELETE LINE icon ⊟. All planning data of this MRP area are automatically transferred to the plant MRP area.

3.2.3　MRP Groups

To execute your planning, you need certain parameters defined for the plant that you can maintain in customizing to control things such as number ranges, MRP controllers, allowed special procurement keys, float dates, conversion rules for planned orders, and various planning run parameters. If plant controls aren't detailed enough, and you want to apply different controls to a group of materials, you need to use MRP groups.

Plant controls

The *MRP group* allows you to apply common planning parameters and controls to a group of materials that have the same planning and procurement requirements. This includes external procurement controls where you define document types, horizon controls for planning and rescheduling, and planning run details. Here you can also set a maximum MRP interval, and use of safety stock. If your MRP group settings are common across specific material types, you can also create a default entry in configuration that is proposed when a new material master record is created. To set up the MRP groups, you need to run the IMG customization in the sequence shown and with following the menu paths:

Apply common parameters/ controls

▸ Materials Management • Consumption-Based Planning • MRP Groups • MRP Groups • Carry Out Overall Maintenance of MRP Groups

▸ Materials Management • Consumption-Based Planning • MRP Groups • MRP Groups • Define MRP Group for Each Material Type

MRP group assignment to the material master can be maintained using material master Transaction MM01 (Create) or Transaction MM02 (Change) on the MRP 1 view (see Figure 3.9).

> **Note**
>
> When planning is executed, the system checks that the MRP group is assigned to a material. If the field isn't maintained, it's planned using common plant parameters.

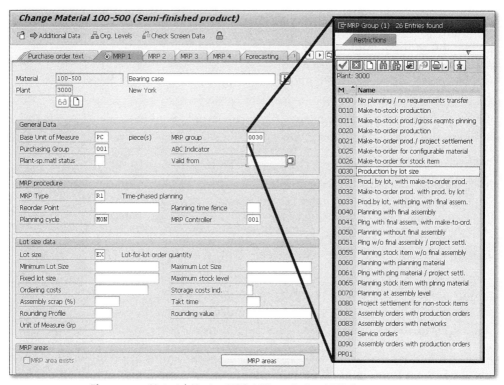

Figure 3.9   Material Master MRP 1 View: Assign MRP Group

3.2.4   Planning Calendar

As you recall from Chapter 2, Section 2.4.2, we talked about alternative purchasing data on the vendor master using planning cycles, delivery cycles, and both using planning calendars. Also in this chapter, we already covered time-phased planning, which uses the planning calendar.

In the following subsections, we'll discuss the planning calendar in more details, and explain how to assign and maintain one.

Assigning Planning Calendars

Flexible time periods Planning calendars define flexible time periods for MRP for a plant and groups together the procurement proposals to creating a lot that falls within the periods defined in the planning calendar. To control which materials will use this method, assign the planning calendar to the material master record in MRP VIEW 1 and MRP VIEW 2 using Transaction MM01 or Transaction MM02. Remember, when you're setting up your materials, the following two important facts will impact your results:

▶ If your material master MRP VIEW 1 has the MRP TYPE set to PD - MRP and the LOT SIZE field set to PK - PERIOD LOT SIZE ACC. TO PLNG CALENDAR, the planning calendar entered on the MRP VIEW 2 is used during planning.

▶ If your material MRP VIEW 1 has the MRP TYPE set to R1 - TIME-PHASED PLANNING, the planning cycle is used for planning your requirements, and the planning calendar entered on the MRP VIEW 2 is used for the delivery cycle; that is, days on which suppliers deliver the goods.

Maintaining Planning Calendars

To maintain planning calendars, you have two options. You can access the planning calendar via IMG Customizing or by using the SAP Easy Access menu. Either way, you initiate the maintenance process, and a transport request is required to move your changes between your SAP environments. Table 3.1 lists the transactions available to maintain the planning calendar.

Transaction	Menu Path
MD25: Create Periods	LOGISTICS • MATERIALS MANAGEMENT • MATERIAL REQUIREMENTS PLANNING (MRP) • MRP • MASTER DATA • PLANNING CALENDAR • CREATE PERIODS
MD26: Change Periods	LOGISTICS • MATERIALS MANAGEMENT • MATERIAL REQUIREMENTS PLANNING (MRP) • MRP • MASTER DATA • PLANNING CALENDAR • CHANGE
MD27: Display Periods	LOGISTICS • MATERIALS MANAGEMENT • MATERIAL REQUIREMENTS PLANNING (MRP) • MRP • MASTER DATA • PLANNING CALENDAR • DISPLAY

Table 3.1 Planning Calendar Maintenance Transactions

To maintain your planning calendars via IMG Customizing, use the menu path MATERIALS MANAGEMENT • CONSUMPTION-BASED PLANNING • MASTER DATA • MAINTAIN PLANNING CALENDAR.

3.3   Forecasting

In this section, we'll talk about how to apply materials forecasting in the various consumption-based planning procedures we discussed and the different ways you can create forecasts in the SAP ERP system. We'll show you different forecasting models and how to use them appropriately. Finally, we'll put all of these pieces together and show you how to run your forecasts.

How to use forecasting

When forecasting, you need to do a combination of things covered earlier in this chapter:

1. Define the MRP type to determine the use of the forecast.

2. Assign the MRP type to the material master record on MRP VIEW 1.

3. Maintain the material master forecast view with valid forecasting parameters.

Forecasts usually have a defined period in which materials consumption is measured and analyzed, such as daily, weekly, and monthly intervals. Because materials forecasting is based on historical consumption values, they also must be available—whether updated automatically (using consumption movement types postings) or manually. If you're introducing a new material, which obviously won't have any historical data available, you can still run a forecast by using a reference material and a reference plant's consumption values up until a defined date that the new material consumption data will start recording. Figure 3.10 shows the material master record forecasting view maintenance screen.

Regardless of where the data comes from and how it's being analyzed (manual or automatic model selection, covered in Section 3.3.2), you need to understand the behavior. Understanding how the data moves is key to properly assigning the forecasting models and getting the expected results. In most examples from collective consulting experiences, we notice that a wrong model selection can be disastrous for the business, causing a variety of issues from inadequate inventory levels and increased carrying costs to missed deliveries and loss of customers. We suggest that you always plan for corrections.

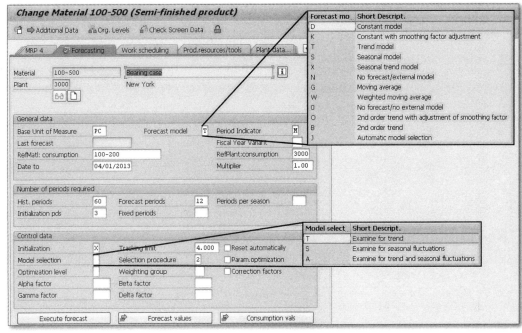

Figure 3.10 Material Master Forecasting View

Now that you have a general idea of what forecasting is, we'll discuss the different forecasting models and how to choose the right one for you, as well as control data, profile, and execution steps.

3.3.1 Forecast Models

Planning for the future can be difficult as you start identifying the data and confirming accuracy. Crunching through the consumption numbers, trying to understand them, and attempting to detect patterns is usually the first step in deciding between appropriate forecast models. SAP provides the following models out of the box:

▶ **Constant model**

SAP models

This is the simplest of forecast models with time series basically stationary and completely random (see Figure 3.11). "The values of this time series appear to have been independently drawn from a common probability distribution, suggesting that future observations will be drawn from the same distribution." (*people.duke.edu/~rnau/411mean. htm*).

▶ **Trend model**
This trend model is commonly seen in the business world where consumption values constantly rise or fall over a long period of time (see Figure 3.11).

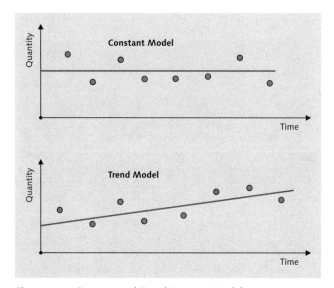

Figure 3.11 Constant and Trend Forecast Models

▶ **Seasonal model**
Use this model when your data has clearly identifiable and periodically recurring peaks and valleys, changing from season to season, differing from the stable mean value (see Figure 3.12).

▶ **Seasonal trend model**
This consumption model shows continuous increase or decrease of the mean value (see Figure 3.12). The seasonal model and the seasonal trend model both predict the seasonal cycles, but the trend projection for the seasonal model assumes that the future trend will be the same as in the previous series of periods, whereas the seasonal trend model will show a clear upward or downward direction.

▶ **Other forecast models**

If you can't detect any repeatable patterns and behavior that would make use of any of the preceding models, and if your past consumption values shows irregular consumption flow, you can still execute forecasts using *moving average* or *weighted moving average* models.

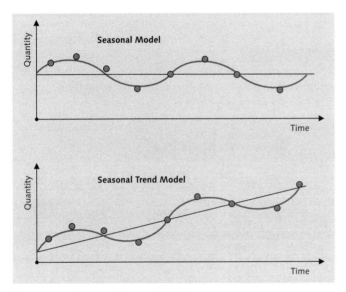

Figure 3.12 Seasonal Forecast Models

In the next section, we explain how to set the controls to start the SAP-delivered forecasts.

3.3.2 Forecast Control Data

For the forecast to be carried out, you have to set all relevant control parameters in the FORECASTING view's CONTROL DATA section (refer to Figure 3.10). In the following subsections, we'll discuss these controls in detail.

Selecting a Model

We briefly covered the different types of forecast models you can choose between using the combination of two field dropdowns: FORECAST MODEL and MODEL SELECTION. You can choose to set up one of three available solutions:

▸ **Manual model selection**
Set the MODEL SELECTION field to blank. You must analyze past consumption data, choose the appropriate forecast model, and set the FORECAST MODEL field to the determined setting. Don't set this field to J-AUTOMATIC MODEL SELECTION.

▸ **Automatic model selection**
If you want to rely on the system to pick the model for you automatically, the system can analyze your historical data according to your selection in the MODEL SELECTION field:

   ▸ T: EXAMINE FOR TREND

   ▸ S: EXAMINE FOR SEASONAL FLUCTUATIONS

   ▸ A: EXAMINE FOR TREND AND SEASONAL FLUCTUATIONS

> **Note**
>
> If the system can't determine the appropriate models during automatic model selection, CONSTANT MODEL will be applied as a default.

▸ **Manual model selection with additional checks**
Use this option if you want to set a specific forecast model manually in the FORECAST MODEL field. Also choose one of the choices from the MODEL SELECTION field to additionally analyze historical consumption data for a seasonal or trend behavior.

Initializing a Model

After you select the forecast models for your materials, you need to set the INITIALIZATION indicator (refer to Figure 3.10). The initialization procedure calculates the model parameters, such as basic value, trend value, and seasonal indices. The initialization procedure takes place the first time you execute your forecast, each time the planning series are forecasted, and when changes are made to time series settings.

Set historical values

The forecast models are initialized automatically. To execute initialization, you need a set number of historical values available, which depends on the forecast model used in the procedure. Table 3.2 shows the default system requirements.

Forecast Model	Number of Historical Periods
▶ Constant ▶ Moving Average ▶ Weighted Moving Average	1
▶ Trend ▶ Second Order Trend with Smoothing Factor	3
▶ Seasonal	1 season
▶ Seasonal Trend	1 season + 3

Table 3.2 Forecast Model Initialization Data Requirements

Choosing Optional Forecast Parameters

Some of the additional parameters available on the FORECASTING view of the material master (refer to Figure 3.10) may be used as optional or required depending on the forecast model you've planned to use. These parameters include the following:

▶ WEIGHTING GROUP
Used with the weighted moving average model and specifies how many historical period values should be included in the forecast and how they are weighted in the calculations.

▶ PERIODS PER SEASON
Used with seasonal models and specifies the number of periods per season.

The following factors are used by the system, depending on the model, for exponential smoothing. Thus, for example, only the alpha and the delta factors are required for the constant model, whereas all of the smoothing factors are required for the seasonal trend model.

Exponential smoothing

▶ ALPHA FACTOR
Used for exponential smoothing of the basic value (required for the constant and seasonal trend models).

▶ BETA FACTOR
Used to smooth the trend value (required for the seasonal trend model).

▶ GAMMA FACTOR
Used to smooth the seasonal index (required for the seasonal trend model).

▶ DELTA FACTOR
Used in every forecast model to smooth the mean absolute deviation.

3.3.3 Material Forecast Profile

Template The forecast profile in the material master applies to individual material master records, and it's assigned to each applicable MRP area. A forecast profile is like a template that allows you to use forecast parameter settings without maintaining individual MRP area settings. Fields that you normally see on the FORECASTING screen can be set to default values, and, if needed, you can write-protect them to avoid potentially unwanted master data changes from being made. Figure 3.13 shows the FORECAST PROFILE maintenance screen.

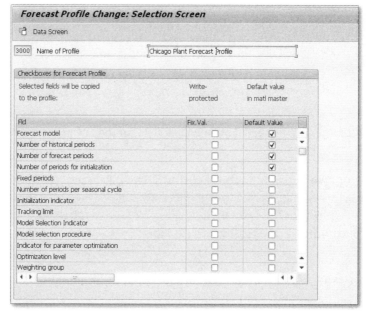

Figure 3.13 Forecast Profile Definition

To assign the forecast profile, run Transaction MM02 (Material Master Change). When you get to the MRP VIEW 1 maintenance screen, click on the MRP AREAS button to access the MRP AREA SELECTION popup window. The FORECAST PROF. column stores the value of the profile that will be applied to the selected MRP area (see Figure 3.14). You run the forecast based on a forecast profile, either online or in the background. We'll talk about forecast execution next, in Section 3.3.4.

Assign forecast profile

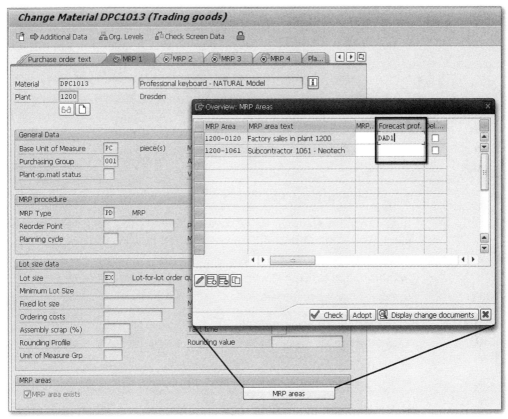

Figure 3.14 MRP Area Assignment of a Forecast Profile

To maintain the forecast profiles, you can use transactions listed in Table 3.3.

Transaction	Menu Path
MP80: Create Forecast Profile	LOGISTICS • MATERIALS MANAGEMENT • MATERIAL REQUIREMENTS PLANNING (MRP) • MATERIALS FORECAST • PROFILES • CREATE
MP81: Change	LOGISTICS • MATERIALS MANAGEMENT • MATERIAL REQUIREMENTS PLANNING (MRP) • MATERIALS FORECAST • PROFILES • CHANGE
MP82: Delete	LOGISTICS • MATERIALS MANAGEMENT • MATERIAL REQUIREMENTS PLANNING (MRP) • MATERIALS FORECAST • PROFILES • DELETE
MP83: Display	LOGISTICS • MATERIALS MANAGEMENT • MATERIAL REQUIREMENTS PLANNING (MRP) • MATERIALS FORECAST • PROFILES • DISPLAY

Table 3.3 Forecast Profile Maintenance Transactions

3.3.4 Executing a Forecast

In the previous sections, we've covered how to choose the right forecast parameters, and which of them are required to get correct results when you execute your forecast run. Now we're ready to put all that knowledge in motion and execute the forecast. There are a few ways to execute the forecast for your materials:

▶ **Individual forecast**
The forecast is executed for a single material in a single plant.

▶ **Total forecast**
The forecast run covers multiple materials for one or more plants.

▶ **Material master**
The forecast is executed from the material master FORECASTING view.

Table 3.4 lists some of the commonly used forecasting transactions and menu paths for your reference.

Transaction	Menu Path
MP30: Execute Individual Forecast	LOGISTICS • MATERIALS MANAGEMENT • MATERIAL REQUIREMENTS PLANNING (MRP) • MATERIALS FORECAST • FORECAST • INDIVIDUAL FORECAST • EXECUTE
MP31: Change	LOGISTICS • MATERIALS MANAGEMENT • MATERIAL REQUIREMENTS PLANNING (MRP) • MATERIALS FORECAST • FORECAST • INDIVIDUAL FORECAST • CHANGE
MP32: Display	LOGISTICS • MATERIALS MANAGEMENT • MATERIAL REQUIREMENTS PLANNING (MRP) • MATERIALS FORECAST • FORECAST • INDIVIDUAL FORECAST • DISPLAY
MP38: Execute Total Forecast	LOGISTICS • MATERIALS MANAGEMENT • MATERIAL REQUIREMENTS PLANNING (MRP) • MATERIALS FORECAST • FORECAST • TOTAL FORECAST • EXECUTE
MP33: Reprocess	LOGISTICS • MATERIALS MANAGEMENT • MATERIAL REQUIREMENTS PLANNING (MRP) • MATERIALS FORECAST • FORECAST • TOTAL FORECAST • REPROCESS
MP39: Print	LOGISTICS • MATERIALS MANAGEMENT • MATERIAL REQUIREMENTS PLANNING (MRP) • MATERIALS FORECAST • FORECAST • TOTAL FORECAST • PRINT
MPBT: Execute (Background)	LOGISTICS • MATERIALS MANAGEMENT • MATERIAL REQUIREMENTS PLANNING (MRP) • MATERIALS FORECAST • FORECAST • TOTAL FORECAST • EXECUTE (BACKGROUND)
MPDR: Print (Background)	LOGISTICS • MATERIALS MANAGEMENT • MATERIAL REQUIREMENTS PLANNING (MRP) • MATERIALS FORECAST • FORECAST • TOTAL FORECAST • PRINT (BACKGROUND)
MM02: Change Immediately	LOGISTICS • MATERIALS MANAGEMENT • MATERIAL MASTER • MATERIAL • CHANGE • IMMEDIATELY

Table 3.4 Forecasting Transaction Codes

Let's walk through an example of forecast execution using Transaction MP38 (Total Forecast Execute). Because this transaction is designed to run your forecast en masse, your selection screen gives you the options to run it using a variety of different options (see Figure 3.15).

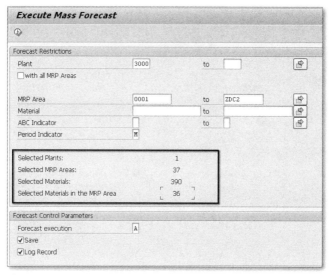

Figure 3.15 Execute Mass Forecast: Selection Screen

In our example, we'll execute the forecast for a single plant, specifying MRP areas to narrow down the number of materials for processing.

1. Enter the PLANT, and enter the MRP AREA or select WITH ALL MRP AREAS (which basically selects all materials within a plant specified).

2. Then enter the range of MATERIAL, ABC INDICATOR, and PERIOD INDICATOR; that is whether materials selected use monthly (M), weekly (W), or daily (D) forecast periods.

3. After you're done specifying your selection criteria, press Enter to execute the initial selection and update the summary section, as shown in Figure 3.15. The summary list shows the following:

   ▶ Number of plants selected

   ▶ Number of MRP areas selected

▶ Selected material count

▶ Selected material count per MRP area

4. You can also choose to run your forecast for a current or future period and save and log the records. You set these parameters in the FORECAST CONTROL PARAMETERS section at the bottom of the screen. In our example, we've selected A for current period.

5. When ready, simply use the EXECUTE icon or press F8 to execute.

> **Note**
>
> You can also execute this job in the background by clicking on PROGRAM • EXECUTE IN BACKGROUND, or using the F9 function key.

Execute in background

During the execution, your forecast procedure uses the historical consumption data and calculates the future requirements using a defined time interval selected (daily, weekly, etc.). When the transaction completes, the list of processed materials is displayed together with the historical consumption values used and forecasted requirements, as shown in Figure 3.16.

> **Note**
>
> Transaction MP30 and Transaction MP38 don't allow changes to historical values of consumption data before the forecast run.

If you're planning on making individual material changes to your historical consumption values (both planned and unplanned), run Transaction MM02 (Material Master Change), or use the menu path LOGISTICS • MATERIALS MANAGEMENT • MATERIAL MASTER • MATERIAL • CHANGE • IMMEDIATELY. Now follow these steps:

Make individual material changes

1. Select the FORECASTING view, and click on the CONSUMPTION VALUES button. The new screen appears allowing you to maintain the values. To toggle between planned and unplanned consumption values, click on the button at the bottom of the screen.

```
┌─────────────────────────────────────────────────────────────────────────┐
│  Total Forecast: List of Results                                          │
├─────────────────────────────────────────────────────────────────────────┤
│                                                                           │
├─────────────────────────────────────────────────────────────────────────┤
│  Execute Mass Forecast                                                    │
│                                                                           │
│  Material no.   M-10             Flatscreen MS 1775P                       │
│  MRP area                                                                 │
│  Plnt        3000                New York                                  │
│  Client                                                                   │
├─────────────────────────────────────────────────────────────────────────┤
│  Basic data                                                               │
│  Forecast date       04/01/2013      Unit               PC                │
│  Forecast model                      Service level      0.0               │
│  Period indicator    M               Paramtr profile                      │
├─────────────────────────────────────────────────────────────────────────┤
│  Control data                                                             │
│  Initialization      X               Tracking limit     4.000             │
│  Model selection     A               Procedure selection 2                │
│  Parameter optimizatioX              Optimization level  F                │
│  Alpha factor        0,23            Beta factor         0,00             │
│  Gamma factor        0,00            Delta factor        0,30             │
│  Basic value            33.717       Trend value                 0.000    │
│  MAD                    18.576       Error total               124.859    │
│  Safety stock           50.000       Reorder pnt.                8.000    │
├─────────────────────────────────────────────────────────────────────────┤
│  No. of values                                                            │
│  Consumption         60              Forecast periods    12               │
│  Initial. periods    0               Fixed periods       0                │
│  Periods per season  12                                                   │
├─────────────────────────────────────────────────────────────────────────┤
│  Historical data                                                          │
│  Period              Original    Corrected value                          │
│  03/2013             0.000            34.000                               │
│  02/2013             0.000            78.000                               │
│  01/2013             0.000            20.000                               │
│  12/2012             0.000            10.000                               │
│  11/2012             0.000            30.000                               │
│  10/2012             0.000             3.000                               │
│  09/2012             0.000            20.000                               │
│  08/2012             0.000            78.000                               │
│  07/2012             0.000             5.000                               │
│  06/2012             0.000            78.000                               │
│  05/2012             0.000             0.000                               │
│  04/2012             0.000             0.000                               │
│  03/2012             0.000             0.000                               │
│  02/2012             0.000             0.000                               │
│  01/2012             0.000             0.000                               │
├─────────────────────────────────────────────────────────────────────────┤
│  Forecast results                                                         │
│  Period              Original    Corrected value                          │
│  04/2013             34.000           34.000                              │
│  05/2013             34.000           34.000                              │
│  06/2013             34.000           34.000                              │
│  07/2013             34.000           34.000                              │
│  08/2013             34.000           34.000                              │
│  09/2013             34.000           34.000                              │
│  10/2013             34.000           34.000                              │
│  11/2013             34.000           34.000                              │
│  12/2013             34.000           34.000                              │
│  01/2014             34.000           34.000                              │
│  02/2014             34.000           34.000                              │
│  03/2014             34.000           34.000                              │
└─────────────────────────────────────────────────────────────────────────┘
```

Figure 3.16 Total Forecast Results: Summary

2. Maintain the corrected values, and click SAVE to apply your changes. Figure 3.17 shows the FORECASTING view. Locate the buttons on the bottom of the screen that allow you to execute the follow-on actions, such as executing the forecast, maintaining the forecast, and using consumption values.

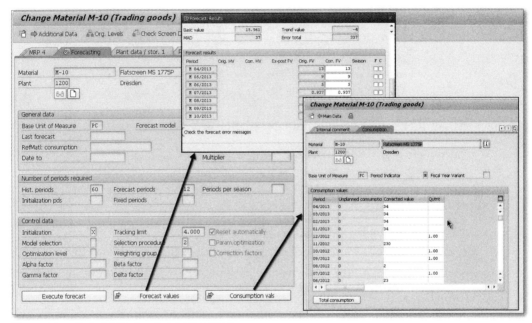

Figure 3.17 Material Master: Forecasting View

3.4   Sales and Operations Planning and Flexible Planning

Another way to create demand in SAP is by using the Sales and Operations Planning (SOP) functionality, which is best suited for mid- and long-term planning scenarios. SOP provides the ability to forecast future sales, plan production, and perform feasibility estimates with simulative modes. SOP provides you with two ways to run your planning: standard SOP and flexible planning. *Standard* SOP planning is based on predefined sets of infostructures and comes pretty much ready for use out of the box. *Flexible*

Mid- and long-term planning

planning, on the other hand, can use any custom infostructures defined to meet your requirements and those of available standard structures.

> **Note**
>
> SOP is best suited for finished materials, not for the materials components, unless you use characteristics planning. We won't describe the entire SOP functionality in detail here because that would require a dive into ABAP programming and technical steps beyond the scope of this book. Instead, we'll simply cover the basics of the standard and flexible planning forecasting component and how it influences the procurement process. For more information on SOP, refer to *Demand and Supply Planning with SAP APO* by Sandeep Pradhan (SAP PRESS 2013).

Planning methods

There are three planning methods for you to choose from:

▶ **Consistent planning**
Data is maintained at the lowest level of the planning hierarchy, but you can access it from any level. Changes made at one level immediately affects other levels consistently.

▶ **Level-by-level planning**
Data is stored at all levels, and each of the levels can be planned separately, allowing you to plan top-down or bottom-up because of the hierarchical structure of the planning tables.

▶ **Delta planning**
Data maintained at one level aggregates to higher levels in the hierarchy automatically. Changes at one level, however, aren't automatically disaggregated, which creates a difference between lower and higher planning levels. You also don't need the planning hierarchy to use this method.

All of the planning data produced by these methods is version controlled, and you should transfer it to the active version only when you're ready. A00 is the default SAP standard active version, which is used by the demand management. You'll see it now in the form of PIRs, which MRP now uses to act upon and create procurement proposals for.

Just like with every other functionality in SAP ERP, you also have some required building blocks that need to be maintained to fit your needs.

In the next sections, we'll talk about a few of the most important master data types needed for SOP, other than a basic material master as a base.

3.4.1 Defining an Infostructure

You can define your own planning structures, which you can then use for flexible planning. These structures basically define the planning levels or characteristics representing your company organizational units down to the material at the lowest level. Each of the levels can be picked from the characteristics field catalog menu and copied into your infostructures. This function is usually performed by ABAP technical team members, so we'll only mention that such an option is available for you.

> **Note**
>
> You can't change base SOP structures within the reserved range of S001 to S499. You can use them, however, as a base for your own, and then you can maintain them as needed using the available field catalog.

You can maintain the info structures using one of the transactions listed in Table 3.5.

Transaction	Menu Path
MC21: Create	TOOLS • ABAP WORKBENCH • DEVELOPMENT • SAP BUSINESS WORKFLOW • REPORTING • WORKFLOW INFORMATION SYSTEM (WIS) • ENVIRONMENT • INFO STRUCTURES • CREATE
MC22: Change	TOOLS • ABAP WORKBENCH • DEVELOPMENT • SAP BUSINESS WORKFLOW • REPORTING • WORKFLOW INFORMATION SYSTEM (WIS) • ENVIRONMENT • INFO STRUCTURES • CHANGE
MC23: Delete	TOOLS • ABAP WORKBENCH • DEVELOPMENT • SAP BUSINESS WORKFLOW • REPORTING • WORKFLOW INFORMATION SYSTEM (WIS) • ENVIRONMENT • INFO STRUCTURES • DISPLAY

Table 3.5 Info Structure Maintenance Transaction Codes

3.4.2 Maintaining a Planning Hierarchy

Infostructure
organizational level

A planning hierarchy uses the organizational levels defined in the info-structures you want to use for planning. This master data object allows you to assign the key data for your materials to a planning level defined in your infostructure. You can copy characteristic values, move them between planning levels, and set proportional factors. The proportional factors determine how a key figure at one level is distributed to another using defined units of measure. See Table 3.6 for some of the transactions used for planning hierarchy maintenance.

Transaction	Menu Path
MC61: Create	LOGISTICS • SALES AND DISTRIBUTION • SALES INFORMATION SYSTEM • PLANNING • FLEXIBLE PLANNING • MASTER DATA • PLANNING HIERARCHY • CREATE
MC62: Change	LOGISTICS • SALES AND DISTRIBUTION • SALES INFORMATION SYSTEM • PLANNING • FLEXIBLE PLANNING • MASTER DATA • PLANNING HIERARCHY • CHANGE
MC63: Display	LOGISTICS • SALES AND DISTRIBUTION • SALES INFORMATION SYSTEM • PLANNING • FLEXIBLE PLANNING • MASTER DATA • PLANNING HIERARCHY • DISPLAY
MC59: Postprocess	LOGISTICS • SALES AND DISTRIBUTION • SALES INFORMATION SYSTEM • PLANNING • FLEXIBLE PLANNING • MASTER DATA • PLANNING HIERARCHY • POSTPROCESS

Table 3.6 Planning Hierarchy Maintenance Transaction Codes

3.4.3 Product Group

Combine/classify
materials

In SOP, you can use product groups to combine materials with similar planning requirements and classify them as single or multilevel. Multi-level product groups contain other product groups, and the lowest level contains materials. Single-level groups contain materials only. Figure 3.18 shows a graphical display of a product group using Transaction MC91 (Product Group).

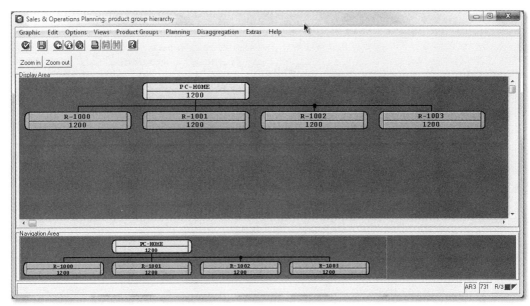

Figure 3.18 Product Group Hierarchy Display Using Transaction MC91

Product groups also require a proportion factor to be applied, which is used when your plan is disaggregated to a lower level where the sum of proportion factors usually rounds up to 100%. Some of the most commonly used product group maintenance transactions are listed in Table 3.7.

Transaction	Menu Path
MC84: Create	LOGISTICS • SALES AND DISTRIBUTION • SALES INFORMATION SYSTEM • PLANNING • FLEXIBLE PLANNING • MASTER DATA • PRODUCT GROUP • CREATE
MC86: Change	LOGISTICS • SALES AND DISTRIBUTION • SALES INFORMATION SYSTEM • PLANNING • FLEXIBLE PLANNING • MASTER DATA • PRODUCT GROUP • CHANGE
MC85: Display	LOGISTICS • SALES AND DISTRIBUTION • SALES INFORMATION SYSTEM • PLANNING • FLEXIBLE PLANNING • MASTER DATA • PRODUCT GROUP • DISPLAY

Table 3.7 Product Group Maintenance Transactions

Transaction	Menu Path
MC91: Product Group	LOGISTICS • SALES AND DISTRIBUTION • SALES INFORMATION SYSTEM • PLANNING • FLEXIBLE PLANNING • MASTER DATA • PRODUCT GROUP • GRAPHIC • PRODUCT GROUP
MC92: Overview	LOGISTICS • SALES AND DISTRIBUTION • SALES INFORMATION SYSTEM • PLANNING • FLEXIBLE PLANNING • MASTER DATA • PRODUCT GROUP • GRAPHIC • OVERVIEW

Table 3.7 Product Group Maintenance Transactions (Cont.)

3.4.4 Setting Up a Forecast Profile

The forecast profile stores the forecast period definition, controls, and smoothing parameters data. This set of configurable parameters can then be transported across your environments and applied during SOP.

To set up your profiles, use Transaction MC91, and then on the initial screen choose to add a new entry, copy an existing profile, or maintain an existing profile (see Figure 3.19 for the overview screen). For our example, access change mode for profile 3000: FLEX PLAN FORECAST MODEL. Double-click the profile to get to the profile details. Figure 3.20 shows the configuration details of the forecast profile.

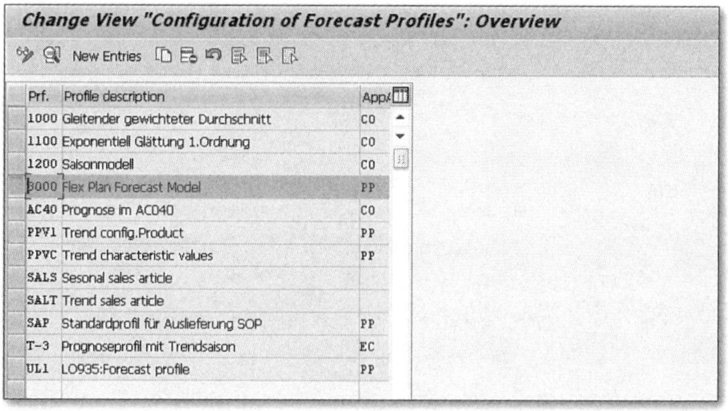

Figure 3.19 Maintain Forecast Profile Overview

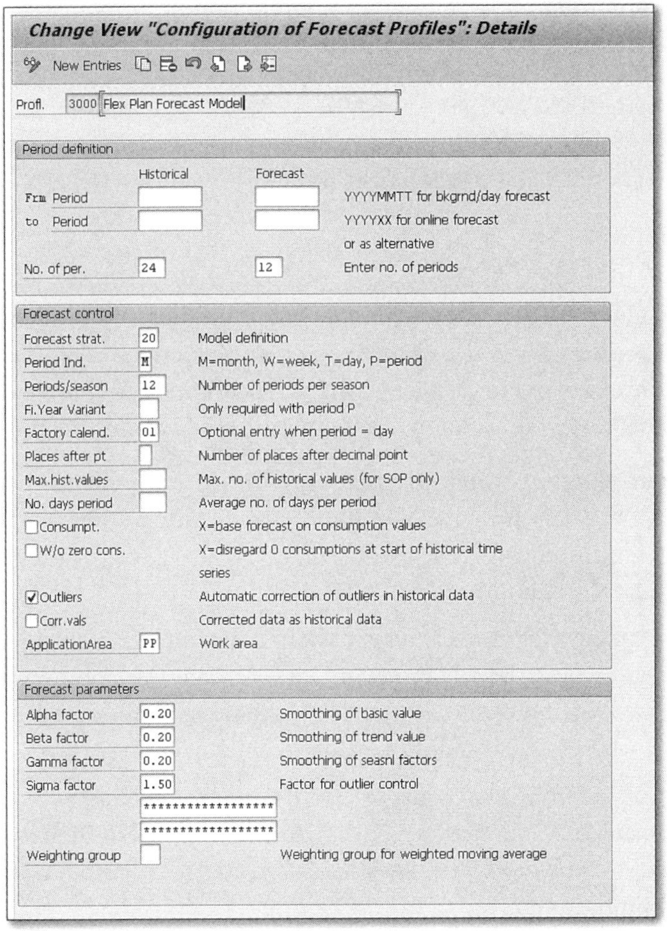

Figure 3.20 Configuration of the Forecast Profile: Details

The forecast profiles in SOP are different from those in the material master (refer to Section 3.3.3). In SOP, you can use this defined forecast profile to forecast a group of materials, whereas in the material master forecasting, each material has to have its own profile. Table 3.8 lists the maintenance transaction for forecasts profiles. Bear in mind that this is considered configuration, and the maintenance action will create a transport request.

Forecast group
of materials

Transaction	Menu Path
MC96: Forecast Profile	LOGISTICS • SALES AND DISTRIBUTION • SALES INFORMATION SYSTEM • SETTINGS • FORECAST PROFILE

Table 3.8 SOP Forecast Profile Configuration Transaction

3.4.5 SOP Process Steps

When you decide to use the SOP functionality for your planning process, you need to execute a few steps to make the planning entries available for your MRP process and to create the actual procurement proposals at the end. This process is also shown in Figure 3.21. Follow these steps:

1. Execute your planning using Transaction MC93 (Create) where you create the preliminary plan and save it with the version number (version 001 is proposed by default). You can overwrite it and give it its own value and description.

2. After you evaluate the results and approve of what you see, you need to activate your plan. Use Transaction MC8V (Copy) to copy your approved plan version to an SAP-required default version A00.

3. Delete the active version if needed using Transacton MC8W (Delete). This action makes your plan ready for the transfer to demand, which you do by executing Transaction MC90 (Transfer Material to Demand Management). You'll notice the new PIRs are created to represent your active plan numbers created in the initial step.

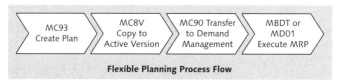

Figure 3.21 SOP Process Steps: Planning to MRP

In Table 3.9, you'll find the process steps transactions again with the menu paths for your reference.

Transaction	Menu Path
MC93: Create	LOGISTICS • SALES AND DISTRIBUTION • SALES INFORMATION SYSTEM • PLANNING • CREATE
MC94: Change	LOGISTICS • SALES AND DISTRIBUTION • SALES INFORMATION SYSTEM • PLANNING • CHANGE
MC95: Display	LOGISTICS • SALES AND DISTRIBUTION • SALES INFORMATION SYSTEM • PLANNING • DISPLAY
MC8V: Copy	LOGISTICS • SALES AND DISTRIBUTION • SALES INFORMATION SYSTEM • PLANNING • FLEXIBLE PLANNING • PLANNING • COPY
MC8W: Delete	LOGISTICS • SALES AND DISTRIBUTION • SALES INFORMATION SYSTEM • PLANNING • FLEXIBLE PLANNING • PLANNING • DELETE
MC90: Transfer Material to Demand Management	LOGISTICS • SALES AND DISTRIBUTION • SALES INFORMATION SYSTEM • PLANNING • FLEXIBLE PLANNING • ENVIRONMENT • TRANSFER MATERIAL TO DEMAND MANAGEMENT

Table 3.9 SOP Process Step Transactions

Now with all planning and forecasting steps finally completed, we can talk about the execution of the MRP run and analysis of the planning results.

3.5 Planning Execution

Finally we arrive at the time where all of the pieces we've talked about in this chapter so far fall together—during the execution of planning. In all of the previous sections, you've learned about influencing factors driving planning behavior from configuration to master data, from consumption-based planning and forecasting through SOP standard and flexible planning. Now you'll be able to see it all in action by scheduling the planning run. You have a couple of options for execution: total planning or single-item planning.

However, before the planning run can be executed, all of the required master data objects must be in place, and materials in scope must have planning file entries maintained. Table 3.10 lists the related planning run transactions. Also, MRP must be active for the plant you want to run

Prerequisites for execution

planning for, and MRP views must exist for materials at that plant. After all of these prerequisites are fulfilled, you can execute planning material requirements for materials with changed requirements or stock levels.

Transaction	Menu Path
MD20: Create	LOGISTICS • MATERIALS MANAGEMENT • MATERIAL REQUIREMENTS PLANNING (MRP) • MRP • PLANNING • PLANNING FILE ENTRY • CREATE
MD21: Display	LOGISTICS • MATERIALS MANAGEMENT • MATERIAL REQUIREMENTS PLANNING (MRP) • MRP • PLANNING • PLANNING FILE ENTRY • DISPLAY

Table 3.10 Planning Table Entry Maintenance Transactions

3.5.1 Total Planning

Mass processing

SAP provides you with an efficient method of executing planning for all materials within a planning plant, which is called *regenerative planning*. You can also choose to plan for materials with changes that occurred since the last planning run and are relevant and considered in the new planning run. This is called *net change planning*. You can also control the scope of the planning run by setting your selection parameters and execute your run for the following:

▶ One or more plants

▶ Single MRP area

▶ Multiple MRP areas

▶ Combinations of plant and MRP areas

> **Note**
>
> Total planning is usually executed as a background job due to its massive scope and hunger for system resources. Use parallel processing option whenever possible to speed up the execution time by spreading the workload to several sessions or servers.

You can influence materials selection for the total planning run by activating the user exit in enhancement M61X0001, which allows you to pull in materials based on additional criteria, such as MRP controller.

Table 3.11 lists two of the transaction codes relevant to this process and the corresponding menu paths.

Transaction	Menu Path
MD01: Online	LOGISTICS • MATERIALS MANAGEMENT • MATERIAL REQUIREMENTS PLANNING (MRP) • MRP • PLANNING • TOTAL PLANNING • ONLINE
MDBT: As Background Job	LOGISTICS • MATERIALS MANAGEMENT • MATERIAL REQUIREMENTS PLANNING (MRP) • MRP • PLANNING • TOTAL PLANNING • AS BACKGROUND JOB

Table 3.11 MRP Total Planning Transactions

3.5.2 Single-Item Planning

In the previous section, we covered a mass-processing scenario. In this method, on the other hand, the single-item planning scope covers just one material. You have a couple of options to execute single-item planning:

▶ **Single-item, with multilevel planning**
All levels of the BOM are in scope of the planning run.

▶ **Single-item, at single-level planning**
One material is planned, and only if a planned order is created, its BOM is exploded, creating dependent requirements for the next level.

Let's walk through an example of executing planning using Transaction MD02 (Single-Item, Multilevel Planning). See Figure 3.22 for an example of the selection options:

1. Enter the MATERIAL, PLANT, and MRP AREA if you're using this type of planning. The PRODUCT GROUP checkbox in the SCOPE OF PLANNING section is usually left blank unless you use product groups.

2. Specify the following MRP CONTROL PARAMETERS section fields to control how MRP data is used and modified:

   ▶ PROCESSING KEY
   In our example, "NETCH" is entered, which calculates net changes for the total horizon.

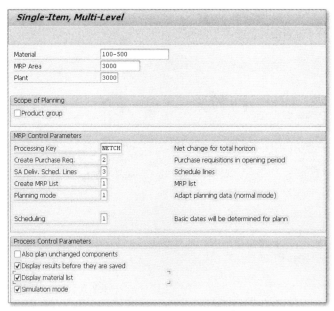

Figure 3.22 Transaction MD02: Process Control Parameters

- ▶ CREATE PURCHASE REQ.
  Controls whether purchase requisitions or planned orders are created.

- ▶ SA DELIV. SCHED. LINES
  Controls whether and how the schedule lines are created for scheduling agreements.

- ▶ CREATE MRP LIST
  Controls whether the list for MRP results is generated.

- ▶ PLANNING MODE
  Controls how you look at already existing planning data in the new MRP run.

- ▶ SCHEDULING
  Controls how date calculations are performed for planned orders.

3. Set the PROCESS CONTROL PARAMETERS that control the subsequent processing mode:

   - ▶ Without an interactive check of the planning result, the DISPLAY RESULTS BEFORE THEY ARE SAVED option isn't selected.

▶ With an interactive check of the planning result per material, you can display results before save. The DISPLAY RESULTS BEFORE THEY ARE SAVED option has to be checked to enable it, and you can also review planning in simulation mode. All materials are planned in memory, without saving to the database. This allows you to test the planning run and apply corrections immediately before a final run and save.

Table 3.12 lists the transactions for execution of individual materials—single item—in multilevel or single-level mode.

Transaction	Menu Path
MD02: Multilevel Single-Item Planning	LOGISTICS • PRODUCTION • MRP • PLANNING • MULTILEVEL SINGLE-ITEM PLANNING
MD03: Single-Level Single-Item Planning	LOGISTICS • PRODUCTION • MRP • PLANNING • SINGLE-LEVEL SINGLE-ITEM PLANNING

Table 3.12 Single-Level Planning Transaction Codes

3.6 Evaluation and Analysis

The planning run will apply all of the components we've covered in the previous sections to determine how much product is needed to satisfy the demand. The difference between the demand and the supply—the short-age—is identified, and a planning proposal is created either by planned orders or purchase requisition. You can review these results, you can check for planned orders and purchase requisitions, and apply changes where needed by using the MRP list and stock/requirement reports. You can also access planned orders and purchase requisitions directly and adjust proposed quantities to suit your needs.

In the following sections, we'll discuss the different options you have to review the system information.

3.6.1 MRP List

The MRP list displays the results of the last MRP planning run for a material, and it's not updated until you perform an MRP run again. The

Planning run results

structure and information stored is similar to that of the stock requirements list, but it's static in nature, and real-time information isn't captured.
When you execute planning, MRP results are stored in the planning tables.
You can access them and review the data later, looking for exception
messages alarming the planner to abnormal situations requiring immediate attention. Figure 3.23 shows an example of the collective list for an
MRP controller.

> **Note**
>
> The MRP list is created only if you select Create MRP List in the MRP Control
> Parameters at the time of the MRP run.

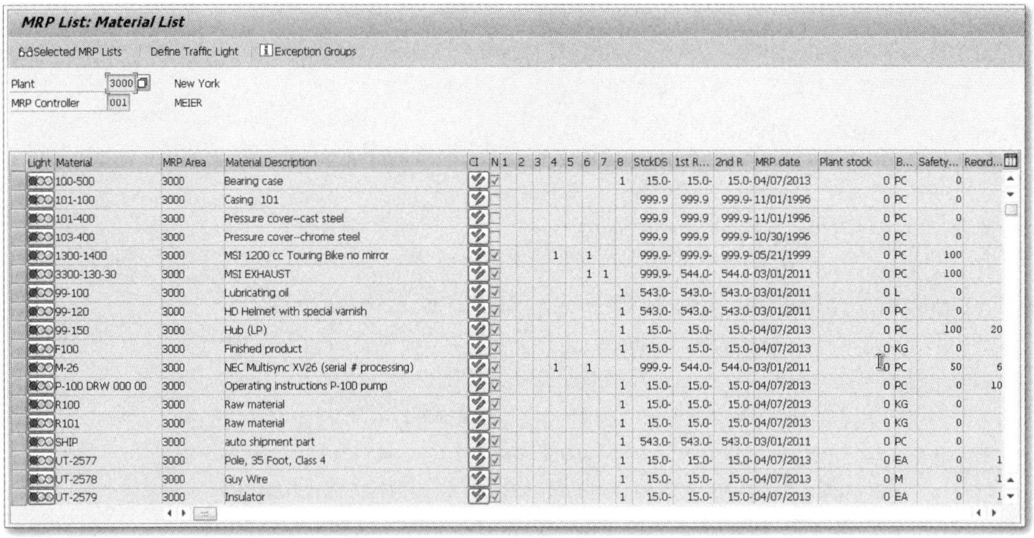

Figure 3.23 Transaction MD05: MRP List Collective Access

Table 3.13 lists MRP List transaction codes and menu paths for your
reference.

Transaction	Menu Path
MD05: MRP List – Material	Logistics • Materials Management • Material Requirements Planning (MRP) • MRP • Evaluations • MRP List–Material

Table 3.13 MRP List Transaction Codes

Transaction	Menu Path
MD06: MRP List – Collective Display	LOGISTICS • MATERIALS MANAGEMENT • MATERIAL REQUIREMENTS PLANNING (MRP) • MRP • EVALUATIONS • MRP LIST – COLL. DISPL.
MDLD: Print of MRP List	LOGISTICS • MATERIALS MANAGEMENT • MATERIAL REQUIREMENTS PLANNING (MRP) • MRP • EVALUATIONS • PRINT OF MRP LIST

Table 3.13 MRP List Transaction Codes (Cont.)

3.6.2 Stock Requirements List

Dynamic results

The stock/requirements list allows you to display the last MRP run results updated dynamically with the latest real-time information about stock balances, receipt, and goods issues—individually or collectively for multiple materials. Just like the MRP list we've talked about before, the stock requirements share the same common features and reporting elements (refer to Figure 3.23 and Figure 3.24 for reference).

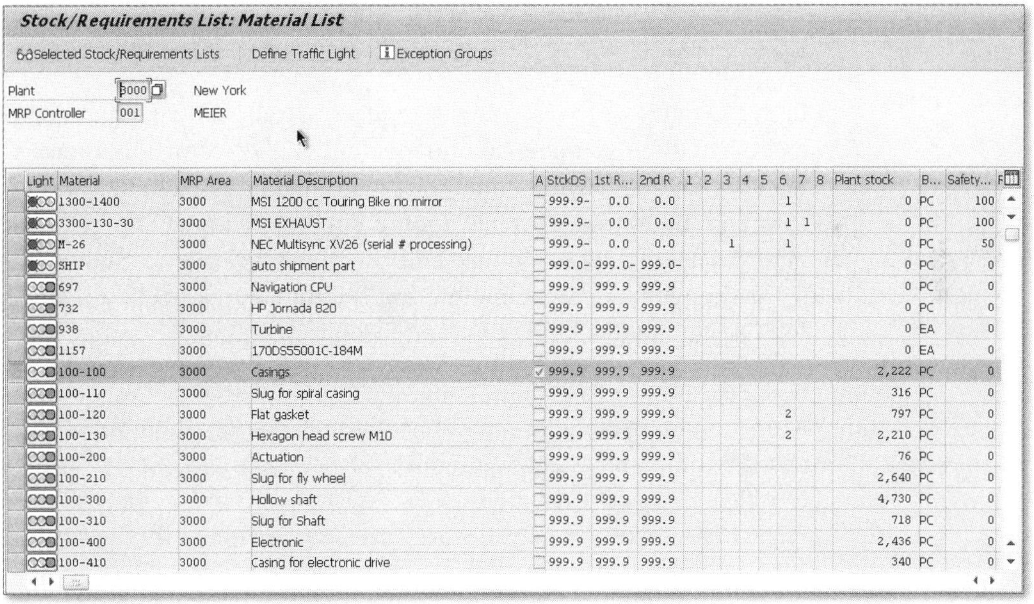

Light	Material	MRP Area	Material Description	A	StckDS	1st R...	2nd R	1	2	3	4	5	6	7	8	Plant stock	B...	Safety...
	1300-1400	3000	MSI 1200 cc Touring Bike no mirror		999.9-	0.0	0.0						1			0	PC	100
	3300-130-30	3000	MSI EXHAUST		999.9-	0.0	0.0						1	1		0	PC	100
	M-26	3000	NEC Multisync XV26 (serial # processing)		999.9-	0.0	0.0			1			1			0	PC	50
	SHIP	3000	auto shipment part		999.0-	999.0-	999.0-									0	PC	0
	697	3000	Navigation CPU		999.9	999.9	999.9									0	PC	0
	732	3000	HP Jornada 820		999.9	999.9	999.9									0	PC	0
	938	3000	Turbine		999.9	999.9	999.9									0	EA	0
	1157	3000	170DS55001C-184M		999.9	999.9	999.9									0	EA	0
	100-100	3000	Casings	✓	999.9	999.9	999.9									2,222	PC	0
	100-110	3000	Slug for spiral casing		999.9	999.9	999.9									316	PC	0
	100-120	3000	Flat gasket		999.9	999.9	999.9						2			797	PC	0
	100-130	3000	Hexagon head screw M10		999.9	999.9	999.9						2			2,210	PC	0
	100-200	3000	Actuation		999.9	999.9	999.9									76	PC	0
	100-210	3000	Slug for fly wheel		999.9	999.9	999.9									2,640	PC	0
	100-300	3000	Hollow shaft		999.9	999.9	999.9									4,730	PC	0
	100-310	3000	Slug for Shaft		999.9	999.9	999.9									718	PC	0
	100-400	3000	Electronic		999.9	999.9	999.9									2,436	PC	0
	100-410	3000	Casing for electronic drive		999.9	999.9	999.9									340	PC	0

Figure 3.24 Transaction MD04: Collective Access – Stock/Requirements List

> **Note**
>
> You can customize the look and feel of the report both for MRP lists and stock/requirements lists. And if this isn't enough, you can activate a customer exit to include additional data columns.

Table 3.14 lists the stock/requirements list transactions and their menu paths for your reference.

Transaction	Menu Path
MD04: Stock/Requirements List	LOGISTICS • MATERIALS MANAGEMENT • MATERIAL REQUIREMENTS PLANNING (MRP) • MRP • EVALUATIONS • STOCK/REQMTS LIST
MD07: Stock/Requirements: Collective Display	LOGISTICS • MATERIALS MANAGEMENT • MATERIAL REQUIREMENTS PLANNING (MRP) • MRP • EVALUATIONS • STOCK/REQUIREMENTS: COLLECTIVE DISPLAY

Table 3.14 Stock/Requirements List Transaction Codes

3.7 Summary

In this chapter, we covered the prerequisites to any subsequent procurement activities—planning and forecasting. You've learned that most of your requirements will be recognized through procedures that include MRP and consumption-based planning. You've also learned about related master data objects that drive the MRP process. We also considered the forecasting process; discussed forecast models, control data, and material forecast profiles; and finally walked through execution of the forecast.

In our discussion of SOP and flexible planning, you learned about another method of forecasting for mid- to long-term planning where we covered infostructures, planning hierarchies, forecast profiles, and an overall flexible planning process flow on a transaction-by-transaction basis. And finally, we walked through the execution and planning run evaluation processes.

Now, armed with all this knowledge, you'll be able to perform all of these processes and understand their contribution to the core procurement activities that we'll cover next in Chapter 4.

All of the items used in a company in its productive or operating processes are acquired through the action of purchasing. This action happens in different ways, depending on what is being purchased.

4 Purchasing

Purchasing is the process through which a company buys materials that are essential to its business processes. A manufacturing company buys raw materials that will be transformed or assembled to produce a finished product that will later be sold. A trading company buys finished products in large quantities from different manufacturers and later sells them in smaller lots to its clients.

Today, these materials are being bought all around the world from companies in different countries. Buyers need tools to make sure they are buying the right material at the right price and that will show up in the warehouse dock at the right time. In this chapter, we'll describe how the SAP ERP system, and specifically the Materials Management (MM) component, supports the whole purchasing cycle as shown in Figure 4.1. We'll explain each of the tools the system has and take a practical approach to show you how to use each of them.

The Purchasing submodule is part of Materials Management in SAP ERP and supports every step of the purchasing process. You can use Purchasing to do the following:

► Invite vendors to submit quotes.

► Create contracts to guarantee the conditions of the purchase.

► Create scheduling agreements to guarantee on-time delivery upon requirements.

Purchasing activities

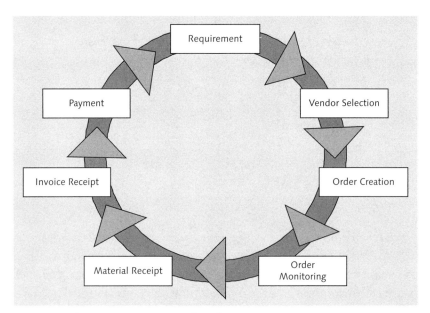

Figure 4.1 The Continuous Process of Purchasing

▶ Create purchase requisitions either manually or based on material requirements, and optionally submit them to an approval process.

▶ Create purchase orders (POs) either manually or based on purchase requisitions, and also submit them to an approval process.

▶ Evaluate a vendor's performance based on its timely deliveries and accuracy to deliver orders.

In this chapter, we'll discuss each of these activities in turn. We'll start with the first activity: working with quotations from vendors.

4.1   Requests for Quotation (RFQ)

Requests for quotations (RFQs) are created in the SAP ERP system to invite vendors to submit quotes for materials the company needs to buy. These requests can be sent to either existing vendors or to vendors that haven't yet been created in the system through the use of the one-time vendor functionality. In this section, we'll explain how to create and maintain an RFQ, as well as how to process the RFQ when the vendor returns it with prices and conditions.

4.1.1   Creating an RFQ

When you create an RFQ, you're creating a document that will be sent to different vendors with a list of materials you need them to quote (see Figure 4.2 and Figure 4.3). This list contains the estimated quantity you'll be buying from them, a date when the material is required to be delivered to your company, and a deadline for the vendor to submit a response. The vendors in return will send price and conditions for each of the materials included in the document. With this information, you'll update the same RFQ document, and then those prices and conditions can be compared with the ones sent by other vendors using a price comparison list. The best bid can be saved to an info record, and you can send rejection letters to the rest of the vendors.

Bid invitation to vendors

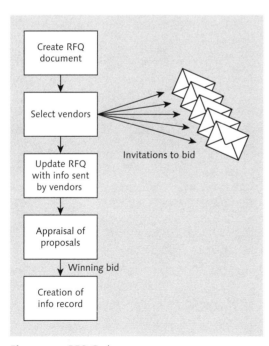

Figure 4.2 RFQ Cycle

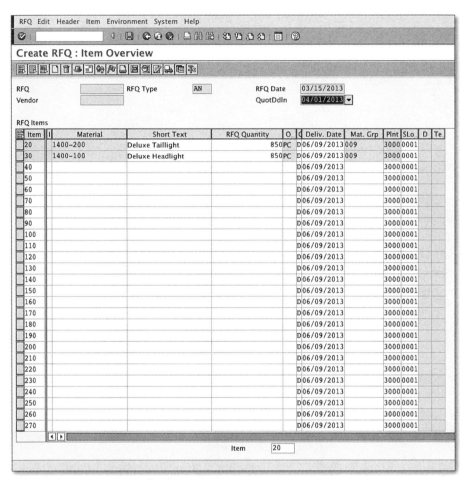

Figure 4.3 Required Delivery Date in RFQ

RFQ references RFQs can be created with reference to other RFQs, which is useful if you bid the same items periodically, and also to send the same request to several different vendors. You can also create RFQs with reference to an existing purchase requisition or with reference to an existing purchasing agreement. This way, you can quote items that are requested by members of the organization or get a new quote at the end of the validity of a contract.

When the vendors send back their proposals, you have to maintain quotations in the SAP ERP system. In a quotation, you can enter all of the conditions that make up the total price such as the unit price, and any discounts or surcharges that may apply. You can also capture the delivery lead time and the country of origin. All of this data will be used to create the purchasing info records when the winning bid is selected.

When you create an RFQ, you need to create a different document number for each vendor (see Figure 4.4). To create an RFQ, follow these steps:

Create RFQ

1. Use Transaction ME41, and in the ITEM section, enter the material number, quantity, and delivery date. Repeat this step as many times as materials are needed.

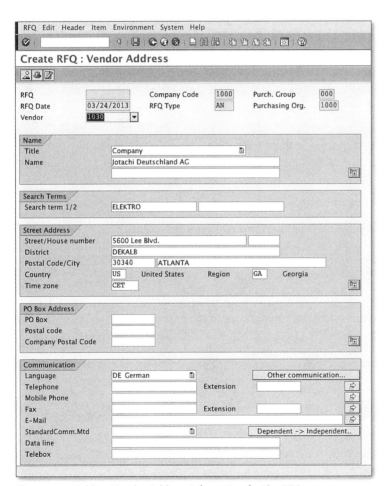

Figure 4.4 Adding Vendor Address Information for the RFQ

2. Go to the Vendor Address screen by choosing Header • Vendor Address, by clicking the little envelope icon on the button bar, or by pressing F7.

3. Enter a vendor number, and make sure the address and contact information is correct.

4. Save the document. Repeat this step for as many vendors as you want to invite.

4.1.2 Processing the Quotation

When the vendors send you back their quotes, you can enter their pricing conditions and delivery times by maintaining the quotation. This is done in Transaction ME47 or by following the path Logistics • Materials Management • Purchasing • RFQ/Quotation • Quotation • Maintain. In the initial screen, you enter the price and delivery date. You can also set comments chosen from a previously configured list, and even set a rejection indicator if needed, triggering the printout of a rejection letter to the vendor (see Figure 4.5).

Saving the Quote to an Info Record

One very important step is the selection of a value in the InfoUpdate field. With the right value, an info record is created automatically for that material and that vendor upon saving the quotation.

InfoUpdate options

There are four options to select for this field:

▸ Blank: No updating.

▸ A: Update with or without plant.

▸ B: Update with plant (if no plant ban).

▸ C: Update without plant (if no plant requirement).

When you select the winning bid, you have to maintain the quote and update the value of this field using any of those three values. All of the conditions from the quotation are written to an info record. The quotation number and item are also written to the info record.

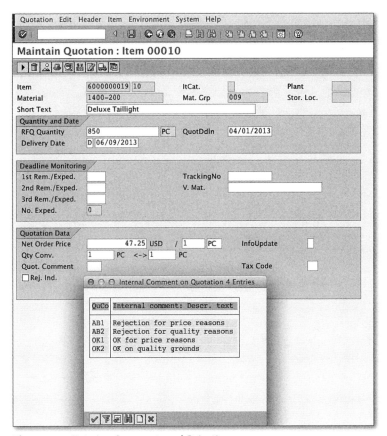

Figure 4.5 Entering Comments and Rejections

When you change a quotation, the conditions are also changed in the info record.

Comparing the Quotes

After you've captured all of the offers, you can compare them using the price comparison report to look at how individual prices compare to each other. To reach this report, go to Transaction ME49, or follow the path Logistics • Materials Management • Purchasing • RFQ/Quotation • Quotation • Price Comparison. The price comparison report gives you a visual comparison of the total value of the order for each item, ranking the price of each vendor for each item, and a percentage of how far off the average is for each of the items (see Figure 4.6).

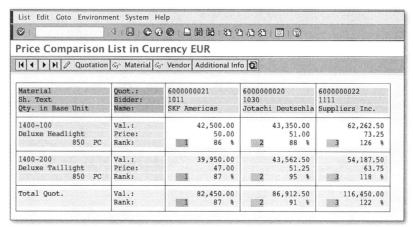

Figure 4.6 Price Comparison Report Showing Ranking and Comparison to the Average Price of Each Item

Ranked comparison

This report should help you make a decision on which vendor to select. To do this, the report shows you a ranked comparison of the prices of each vendor based on the quantity entered in the RFQ document. It shows you the unit price and total value for the whole lot. It also shows you the variance from the mean price among the different vendors. In Figure 4.6, you can see that the vendor with the best quote for material 1400-100, quoted 24% (86% of the mean price) below the mean price, while the worst quoted 26% above it.

If you selected to create an info record when you created the PO, all of the conditions contained in it are automatically copied. If you selected not to create an info record when you updated the quotation, you can still create the PO based on the quotation, and all of the conditions will be copied at that point.

Table 4.1 provides a list of transactions for RFQ and quotation maintenance.

Transaction	Menu Path
ME41: Create (RFQ)	LOGISTICS • MATERIALS MANAGEMENT • PURCHASING • RFQ/QUOTATION • REQUEST FOR QUOTATION • CREATE

Table 4.1 RFQ and Quotation Maintenance Transaction Codes

Transaction	Menu Path
ME42: Change (RFQ)	LOGISTICS • MATERIALS MANAGEMENT • PURCHASING • RFQ/QUOTATION • REQUEST FOR QUOTATION • CHANGE
ME43: Display (RFQ)	LOGISTICS • MATERIALS MANAGEMENT • PURCHASING • RFQ/QUOTATION • REQUEST FOR QUOTATION • CHANGE
ME4S: By Collective Number (Display)	LOGISTICS • MATERIALS MANAGEMENT • PURCHASING • RFQ/QUOTATION • REQUEST FOR QUOTATION • LIST DISPLAYS • BY COLLECTIVE NUMBER
ME47: Maintain (Quotation)	LOGISTICS • MATERIALS MANAGEMENT • PURCHASING • RFQ/QUOTATION • QUOTATION • MAINTAIN
ME48: Display (Quotation)	LOGISTICS • MATERIALS MANAGEMENT • PURCHASING • RFQ/QUOTATION • QUOTATION • DISPLAY
ME49: Price Comparison	LOGISTICS • MATERIALS MANAGEMENT • PURCHASING • RFQ/QUOTATION • QUOTATION • PRICE COMPARISON

Table 4.1 RFQ and Quotation Maintenance Transaction Codes (Cont.)

4.2 Outline Agreements

In the SAP ERP system, contracts or other binding agreements between two companies to supply goods or services on a long-term basis are represented by *outline agreements*. After a company realizes that it's going to enter one of these relationships, the company can set up an outline agreement in the SAP ERP system to control and monitor its execution. Different types of agreements can be set up depending on their reach inside the system, on how they will be measured, or on the triggering mechanism for releasing partial quantities.

Contracts/binding

In the SAP ERP system, outline agreements are divided into two basic types: contracts and scheduling agreements. On both of them, you have to set a target value or a target quantity that you've negotiated with your vendor and based upon which that vendor is giving you specific benefits. We'll discuss each type in greater detail in the following sections.

4.2.1 Contracts

Several types of contracts exist in the SAP ERP system, as detailed in Table 4.2.

Document Type	Contract Type	Description
CCTR	Central contract	Valid for several different plants
DC	Distributed contracts	Available across different SAP instances
MK	Quantity contracts	Belong to a specific plant and have a target quantity
WK	Value Contracts	Belong to a specific plant and have a target currency value

Table 4.2 Document Types

The two most used types of contracts are value contracts and quantity contracts (we'll discuss how to create them later in the "Creating a Contract" section). You can create a contract within your purchasing organization or create a central contract for a reference purchasing organization that is valid for all associated purchasing organizations. By using plant-based pricing conditions, each plant can determine individual pricing, which allows for different transportation costs to different places. Also, vendor partner roles can be determined at the plant level so that the right member of the vendor organization can deliver the materials.

A central contract is useful when a central purchasing organization is buying for the entire corporate group, and it's necessary that all of the associated purchasing organizations are set up in the same SAP ERP system.

Distributed contracts

Similarly, there is another type of contract that helps you buy for an entire corporate group, but the contract is distributed among independent distributed SAP ERP systems. The prerequisite to use this type of contract is that all of the purchase organizations and purchasing groups exist in all of the systems.

There are other communications prerequisites that have to be met before the contracts can be distributed by Application Link Enabling (ALE).

Creating a Contract

In this section, we focus on how to create a contract for stock material; however, contracts can also be created for account assigned items or for services.

To create a contract, follow the path LOGISTICS • MATERIALS MANAGEMENT • PURCHASING • OUTLINE AGREEMENT • CONTRACT • CREATE, or go directly to Transaction ME31K.

You can create a contract either manually by typing all of the required data or by referencing other purchasing documents such as purchase requisitions, or RFQ/quotations. If you want to use a reference document, either click the REFERENCE TO PREQ button for a purchase requisition, or click the REFERENCE TO RFQ button for an RFQ (see Figure 4.7). Reference document

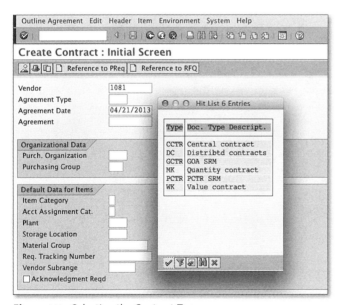

Figure 4.7 Selecting the Contract Type

If you create the contract manually, you need to follow these steps: Manual creation

1. In the first screen of Transaction ME31K, select a vendor number, agreement type, purchase organization, and purchasing group at a minimum (see Figure 4.7). Press Enter to proceed to the header screen.

2. In the next screen, enter the header data, such as the contract's validity end date and the maximum contract value, if applicable. The header copies information from the vendor about the terms of payment and cash discounts, which you can edit if they don't apply for the contract (see Figure 4.8). Press Enter to continue to the ITEM OVERVIEW screen.

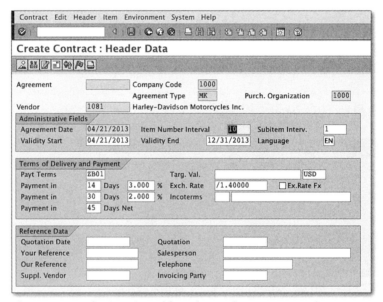

Figure 4.8 Header Data Copied from the Vendor Master Record

3. In the ITEM OVERVIEW screen, enter the materials and quantities that will be committed for purchase from the vendor (see Figure 4.9). At this point, you can still choose to copy from a reference document or proceed to enter the materials manually.

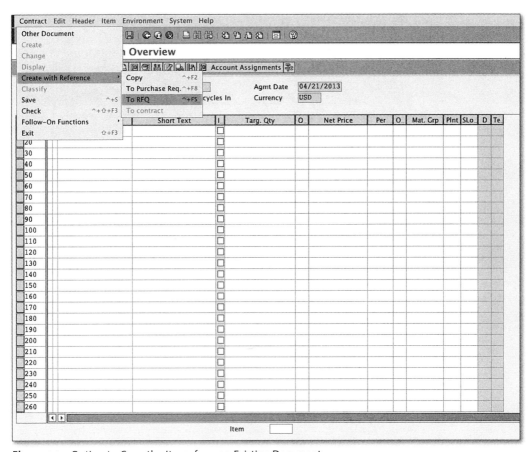

Figure 4.9 Option to Copy the Items from an Existing Document

If you copy the items from a reference document by selecting CON-
TRACT • CREATE WITH REFERENCE • TO PURCHASE REQ or TO RFQ, then
all of the pricing conditions are copied along with the materials and
quantities; if you're entering the contract manually, you have to enter
the pricing conditions at both the header and item level.

Referencing
method

4. By selecting the menu entry ITEM • CONDITIONS, you can enter all of
the conditions you've negotiated with the vendor, including all of the
discounts and all of the surcharges (see Figure 4.10).

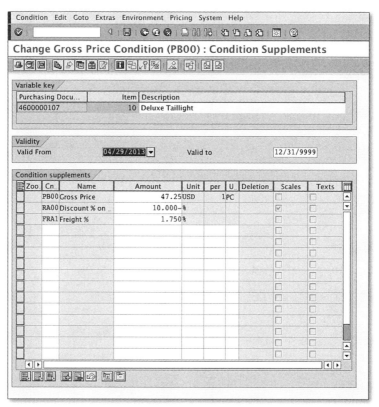

Figure 4.10 Item Conditions Copied from a Reference Document or Entered Manually

Value contracts

As we discussed previously, you can either create a contract based on value or based on quantity. Value contracts (agreement type WK) are based on a fixed target monetary value on purchases of a set of materials that you enter in the contract. You enter a target contract value in the document's header (refer back to Figure 4.8) as you start creating the document. After completing the header's data, you can proceed to entering the materials that will be part of the contract. When the materials are entered in the contract, you can enter a quantity for each one, but it's not required; remember these contracts depend on a global value and not on individual quantities (see Figure 4.11).

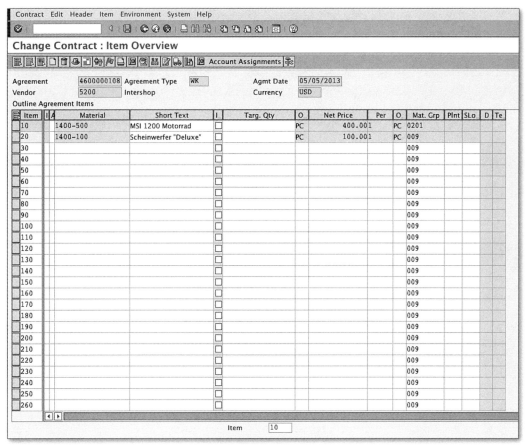

Figure 4.11 Materials Entered in a Value Contract: No Individual Quantity Needed

Quantity contracts (agreement type MK), on the other hand, don't require you to enter a target value in the header, but they do require that you enter a target quantity for each of them in the item details.

Quantity contracts

Both types of contracts, value (WK) and quantity (MK) allow you to create an item without entering a plant. You can then use these same documents in several different plants, as long as they belong to the same purchasing organization.

Referencing and Updating the Contract

Contracts are reference documents that need to be updated constantly with either the quantities or the values of the POs created for the materials they contain. Fortunately, you don't have to worry about updating them manually.

Source lists After you create the contract document, it's a good practice to create or update the source list (see Figure 4.12) for that material with the contract number, so that when you create a PO, it's automatically referenced, and all of the conditions are copied into it. Otherwise, you have to reference it manually every time you create a PO. Source lists are discussed in detail in Chapter 2.

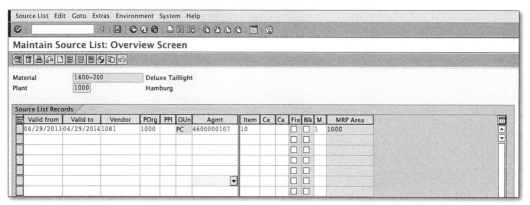

Figure 4.12 Source List

Contract release order — Each PO that is created with reference to the contract, known as a *contract release order*, is registered in the contract's history, and the item quantities and values entered in the PO are discounted from the contract's target value or quantity. To reach the statistics for the contract (see Figure 4.13), select the menu option HEADER • STATISTICS • GENERAL. After you get to the target quantity or value of the contract, you'll see a warning message or an error, depending on the configuration of your system, telling you that the maximum quantity or the maximum amount of the agreement has been reached.

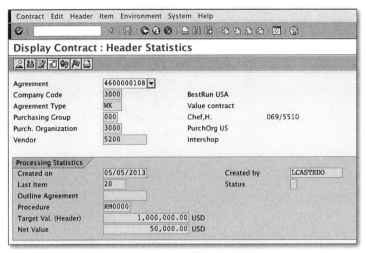

Figure 4.13 Contract Header Statistics Showing the Net Value and Total Target Value

Value contracts have the statistic of how much of the target value has been released at the header level, and the quantity contracts can be reviewed at the item level. The documentation can be displayed in the release documentation in the item statistics (see Figure 4.14) by choosing ITEM • STATISTICS.

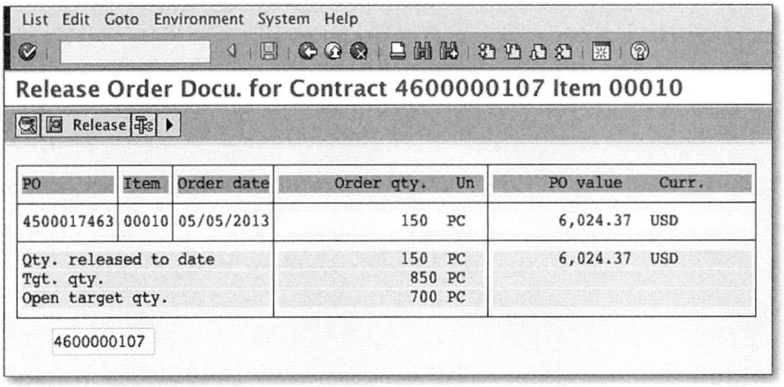

Figure 4.14 Item Statistics for Released Documentation

Table 4.3 lists some useful transactions for working with contracts.

Transaction	Path
ME31K: Create	LOGISTICS • MATERIALS MANAGEMENT • PURCHASING • OUTLINE AGREEMENT • CREATE
ME32K: Change	LOGISTICS • MATERIALS MANAGEMENT • PURCHASING • OUTLINE AGREEMENT • CHANGE
ME33K: Display	LOGISTICS • MATERIALS MANAGEMENT • PURCHASING • OUTLINE AGREEMENT • DISPLAY

Table 4.3 Contracts Transactions

4.2.2 Scheduling Agreements

Scheduling agreements are another type of outline agreement, and they are a very powerful purchasing tool that can be used to plan the delivery and create a very integrated relationship with your vendor. The scheduling agreement can take forecasting information for a given material and send it over to the vendor to provide full visibility of your material requirements so that the vendor can take that information and also plan purchases from its vendors, production, and transportation schedules.

Visible planning and horizon

Scheduling agreements cover the entire planning horizon and mark a date range as firm, or go ahead for build and ship; transition, representing the next firm zone where changes to requirements are still acceptable; and forecast, where changes may occur more freely.

When working with scheduling agreements, you send releases or transmissions to your vendor with information that covers the whole planning horizon. As shown in Figure 4.15, you can send 52 weeks of requirements every week in a rolling schedule format so your vendor knows exactly what to ship, how much to commit with its own vendors, and how much to plan ahead.

The information that is sent in each release to the vendor can use different periods, or time buckets, for each of the zones. For example, if the vendor can deliver to you daily, you can send daily requirements in the firm zone, weekly requirements in the trade-off zone, and monthly requirements in the forecast zone. This is set in from the item detail screen; follow the menu ITEM • MORE FUNCTIONS • ADDITIONAL DATA.

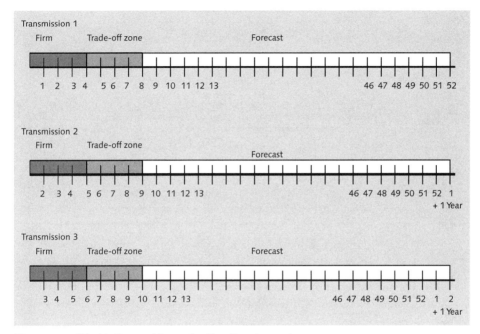

Figure 4.15 Weekly Demand Becoming Firm Requirements

Note

Be very mindful about the timing for sending releases to your vendors. When working with daily buckets, there is a risk of duplicating order quantities or leaving "orphan" requirements that won't be covered. If the release is sent before the specified day, the vendor may duplicate orders for the first days included in the trade-off zone, and if it's sent after the specified day, the number of days you skip will also be skipped by the vendor during order creation.

Weekly buckets, as shown in Figure 4.16, won't present the same problem; if the release is late, the impact is shown in the current week, where the quantity is reduced by the requirements of the skipped days. Any open quantities from previous days are still shown and still marked as FIRM.

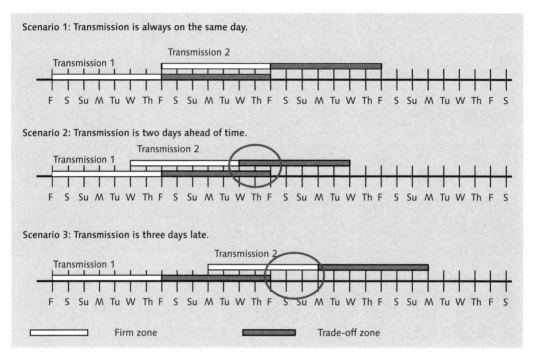

Figure 4.16 Weekly Buckets for Late or Early Releases

Combination of daily/weekly buckets

Working with weeks along the overall scheduling agreement horizon creates one problem for purchasing: the delivery date is always on the Monday of the specified week. To solve this problem, use a combination of daily and weekly buckets so that as time goes by, a requirement that was marked for a specific calendar week becomes a shipping instruction for a specific day (see Figure 4.17).

Creating a Scheduling Agreement

Now let's discuss how to create a scheduling agreement. These documents are always created for stock materials because their intention is take the material requirements planning (MRP) requirements and send them to the vendor.

Follow the path LOGISTICS • MATERIALS MANAGEMENT • PURCHASING • OUTLINE AGREEMENT • SCHEDULING AGREEMENT • CREATE • VENDOR KNOWN, or use Transaction ME31L.

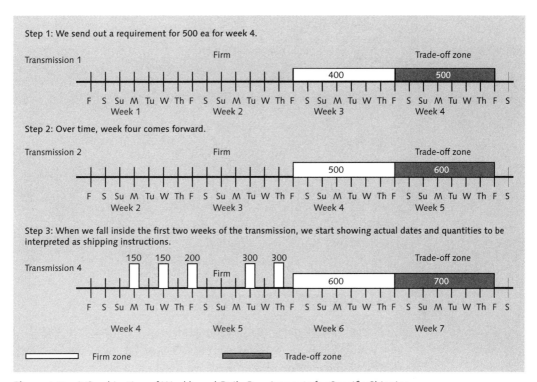

Step 1: We send out a requirement for 500 ea for week 4.

Step 2: Over time, week four comes forward.

Step 3: When we fall inside the first two weeks of the transmission, we start showing actual dates and quantities to be interpreted as shipping instructions.

Figure 4.17 A Combination of Weekly and Daily Requirements for Specific Shipping Instructions

You can create a scheduling agreement either manually by typing all of the required data, or by referencing other purchasing documents such as purchase requisitions, RFQ/quotations, or a contract. If you want to use a reference document, click REFERENCE TO PREQ for a purchase requisition, click REFERENCE TO RFQ for an RFQ, or click REFERENCE TO CONTRACT for a contract.

If you create the contract manually, you need to follow these steps:

Create contract manually

1. In the first screen of Transaction ME31L, select a VENDOR number, the AGREEMENT TYPE LP, PURCH. ORGANIZATION, and PURCHASING GROUP at a minimum (see Figure 4.18). Press ⌷Enter⌷ to proceed to the header screen.

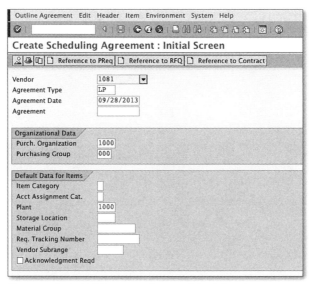

Figure 4.18 Initial Screen to Create a Scheduling Agreement

2. Enter the header data, such as the contract's VALIDITY END date and the maximum contract value, if applicable. The header copies information from the vendor about the terms of payment and cash discounts, which you can edit if they don't apply for the contract (see Figure 4.19).

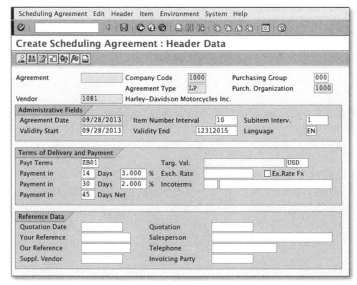

Figure 4.19 Entering the Validity Date for the Contract Target Value

3. Press [Enter] to continue to the ITEM OVERVIEW screen.

4. Enter the materials and quantities that will be committed for purchase from the vendor (see Figure 4.20). At this point, you can still choose to copy from a reference document or proceed to enter the materials manually.

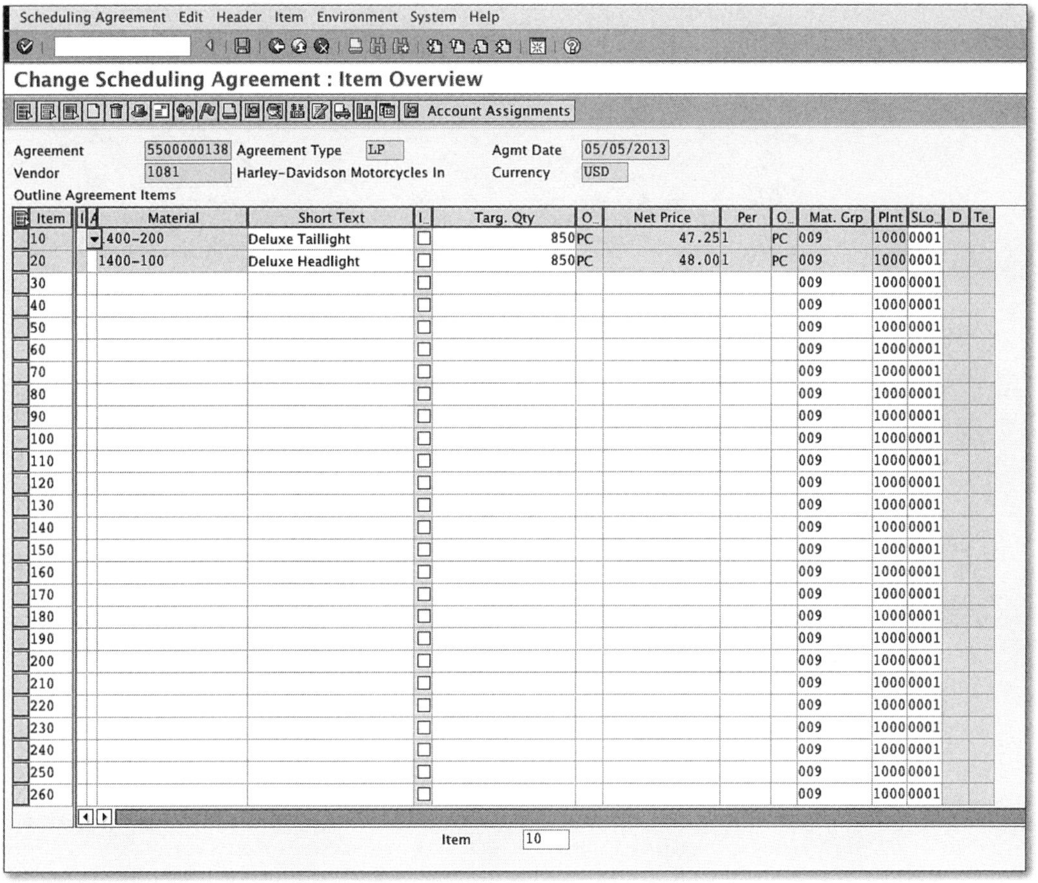

	Scheduling Agreement	Edit	Header	Item	Environment	System	Help

Change Scheduling Agreement : Item Overview

Account Assignments

Agreement	5500000138	Agreement Type	LP	Agmt Date	05/05/2013
Vendor	1081	Harley–Davidson Motorcycles In		Currency	USD

Outline Agreement Items

Item	I A	Material	Short Text	I	Targ. Qty	O	Net Price	Per	O	Mat. Grp	Plnt	SLo	D	Te
10		400–200	Deluxe Taillight		850	PC	47.25	1	PC	009	1000	0001		
20		1400–100	Deluxe Headlight		850	PC	48.00	1	PC	009	1000	0001		
30										009	1000	0001		
40										009	1000	0001		
50										009	1000	0001		
60										009	1000	0001		
70										009	1000	0001		
80										009	1000	0001		
90										009	1000	0001		
100										009	1000	0001		
110										009	1000	0001		
120										009	1000	0001		
130										009	1000	0001		
140										009	1000	0001		
150										009	1000	0001		
160										009	1000	0001		
170										009	1000	0001		
180										009	1000	0001		
190										009	1000	0001		
200										009	1000	0001		
210										009	1000	0001		
220										009	1000	0001		
230										009	1000	0001		
240										009	1000	0001		
250										009	1000	0001		
260										009	1000	0001		

Item   10

Figure 4.20 Overview Screen: Materials and Estimated Target Quantity

If you copy the items from a reference document by selecting the menu entry SCHEDULING AGREEMENT • CREATE WITH REFERENCE • PURCHASE REQ or RFQ, then all of the pricing conditions are copied along with the

Copy from reference

materials and quantities. If you're entering the contract manually, you have to enter the pricing conditions at both the header level and item level.

1. By selecting the menu entry ITEM • CONDITIONS, you can enter all of the conditions you've negotiated with the vendor, including all of the discounts and surcharges (see Figure 4.21).

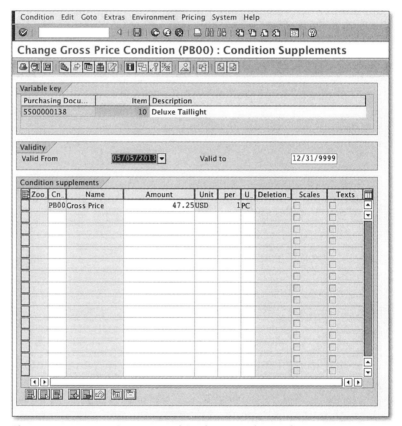

Figure 4.21 Entering Discounts and Surcharges in the Conditions Screen

2. Select the menu option ITEM • MORE FUNCTIONS • ADDITIONAL DATA, and enter the duration for the FIRM ZONE and the TRADE-OFF ZONE. Everything after the trade-off zone is considered the forecast zone (see Figure 4.22).

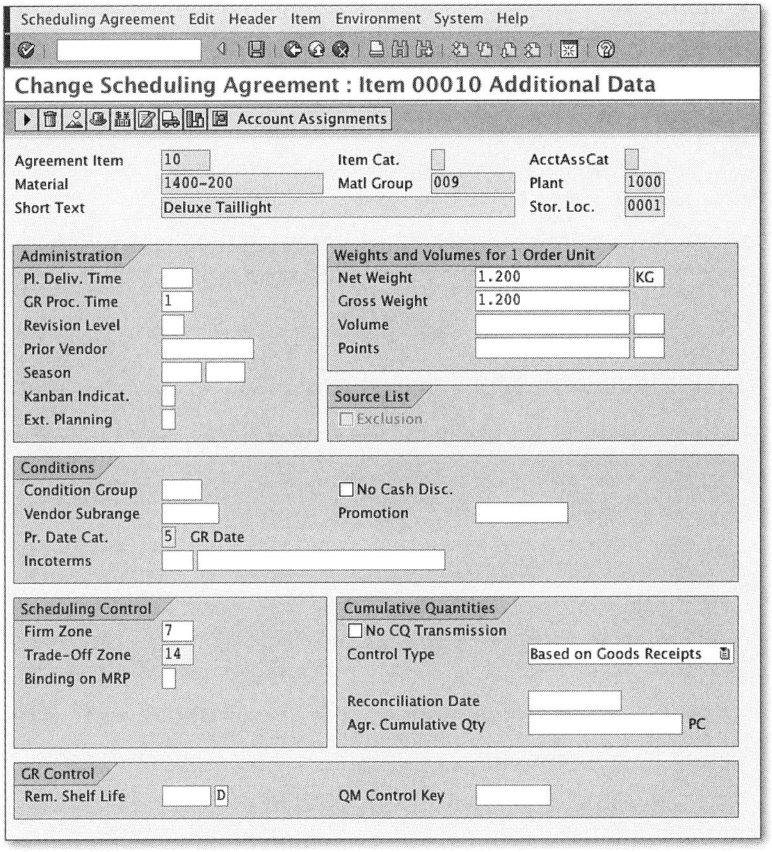

Figure 4.22 Entering the Duration for the Firm Zone and Trade-Off Zone

Generating Schedule Lines

To have the MRP system generate the schedule lines in the scheduling agreement, you need to make sure that every material that is included in a scheduling agreement has a source list that is relevant for MRP and that automatically generates schedule lines. These schedule lines are included in the scheduling agreement for the complete planning horizon. To generate the schedule lines automatically, make sure the SOURCE LIST USAGE IN MRP is set to 2 (see Figure 4.23). Source lists are described in detail in Chapter 2.

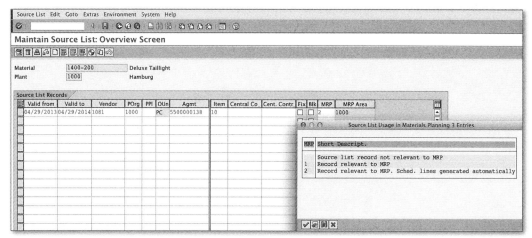

Figure 4.23 Generating Schedule Lines Automatically

Generating Output

After MRP runs, the schedule lines are generated and passed to the scheduling agreement. From there, you can generate an output to send them to your partner. Of course, when you have to send out releases for hundreds or maybe even thousands of parts, manual isn't the way to go. The best way to guarantee that the releases are sent in a timely manner, especially in a high-volume environment, is to use electronic communications in which the releases are sent automatically every time they are produced by the MRP system.

Electronic communication

Electronic communications out of the SAP ERP system vary from emails to direct interfaces with your vendors, but the most widely adopted form of communications is through Electronic Data Interchange (EDI). EDI has been the international standard for many years, and it's based on international standards set by ANSI and EDIFACT.

EDI

To get an output from the scheduling agreement, use Transaction NACR to create a condition record for output type LPH1 for the scheduling agreement. This output type generates a DELFOR01 IDoc, which can be sent to your vendor according to its EDI setup.

In return, the vendor sends back a shipping notification DESADV01, which is recorded in the scheduling agreement.

The outbound DELFOR01 IDoc contains the header and item information for the scheduling agreement, including the forecast information for each of the items for the whole planning horizon.

The IDoc indicates the firm and trade-off zones with an end date for each of them according to the settings of the scheduling control data in the scheduling agreement's item additional data. For firm, it sends the end date as "End of material go-ahead," and for trade-off, it sends an end date as "End of production go-ahead." This way, the vendor is always kept informed of all of the document details. The rest of the schedule lines are considered forecast information (see Figure 4.24).

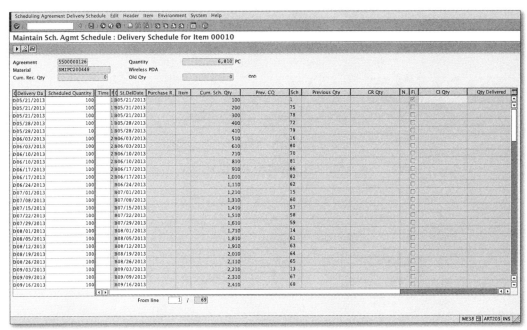

Figure 4.24 Schedule Lines Produced by MRP and Passed to the Scheduling Agreement

Note

Starting EDI communications with vendors isn't an easy undertaking and is a big project by itself; normally a team formed of buyers, functional analysts, and basis analysts take on this challenge.

Table 4.4 lists some useful transactions for working with scheduling agreements.

Transaction	Menu Path
ME31L: Create from Known Vendor	LOGISTICS • MATERIALS MANAGEMENT • PURCHASING • SCHEDULING AGREEMENT • CREATE • VENDOR KNOWN
ME32L: Change	LOGISTICS • MATERIALS MANAGEMENT • PURCHASING • SCHEDULING AGREEMENT • CHANGE
ME33L: Display	LOGISTICS • MATERIALS MANAGEMENT • PURCHASING • SCHEDULING AGREEMENT • DISPLAY
ME38: Maintain	LOGISTICS • MATERIALS MANAGEMENT • PURCHASING • SCHEDULING AGREEMENT • DELIVERY SCHEDULE • MAINTAIN
ME9E: Print/Transmit	LOGISTICS • MATERIALS MANAGEMENT • PURCHASING • SCHEDULING AGREEMENT • DELIVERY SCHEDULE • PRINT/TRANSMIT

Table 4.4 Scheduling Agreements Transactions

4.3   Purchase Requisition

Purchase requisitions are the internal documents through which people request the purchase of a specific item or service. These documents include information about the material to be purchased, the quantity, the person responsible for the purchase, the preferred vendor, and the date the material or service is required at the company. It also includes internal financial information.

The MRP system can also create purchase requisitions for materials needed either for production or sales, which are normally not subject to an approval because the company has already gone through the process of production and sales planning.

Purchase types   Purchase requisitions can be created for different types of purchases:

- **Standard**
  Purchases of stock materials.

▶ **Subcontracting**

Purchases of services that a third party will execute to transform materials that belong to your company and will come back, most of the time with a different material number.

▶ **Consignment**

Purchases of materials that are kept in stock but belong to the vendor until they are actually used.

▶ **Stock transfer**

Requirements to move or purchase materials between plants or companies of the same enterprise group.

▶ **External service**

Purchases of services, one-time services, or services included in the service master.

Like other SAP documents, purchase requisitions have a header and the items details. Unlike other SAP documents, the header is dedicated only to add text notes that apply to all of the items in the requisition. SAP designed the requisition document with the final user in mind, who only cares about entering the items that need to be purchased. You can choose between conventional text processing and a continuous text editor, which allows automatic line breaks and searching and replacing texts.

Structure

The requisition items contain all of the necessary information for buying the required materials or services, all in a single screen.

4.3.1 Creating a Purchase Requisition Manually

To create a purchase requisition manually, follow the menu path MATERIALS MANAGEMENT • PURCHASING • PURCHASE REQUISITION • CREATE, or use Transaction ME51N. The screen presents you with three sections: HEADER, ITEM OVERVIEW, and ITEM details. Follow these steps:

1. Enter SHORT TEXTS in the header section if you need to do so.

2. In the ITEM OVERVIEW section, enter the basic information:

   ▶ ACCOUNT ASSIGNMENT

   ▶ ITEM CATEGORY

   ▶ MATERIAL NUMBER

▶ QUANTITY

▶ UNIT OF MEASURE

▶ PLANT

With this information, the system can fetch most of the rest of the information; for example, the material description, delivery address, material group, planned delivery time, valuation price, company code, purchasing group, and MRP controller (see Figure 4.25).

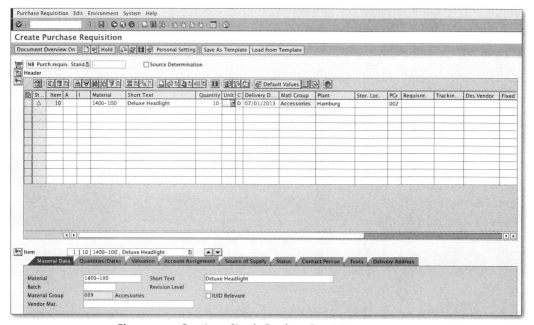

Figure 4.25 Creating a Simple Purchase Requisition

If necessary, the user can change the delivery address, which, by default, is the PLANT or STOR. LOC. address.

4.3.2 Assigning Source of Supply

Purchase requisitions need to be assigned a source of supply, which can be determined automatically if the material has only one info record or several info records and a source list. The vendor can also be entered manually.

To assign a source of supply, follow these steps:

1. Expand the ITEM DETAIL section of the purchase requisition.

2. Select the SOURCE OF SUPPLY tab.

3. If you know the vendor you want to assign, enter it in the VENDOR field. Otherwise, click on the ASSIGN SOURCE OF SUPPLY button and select a vendor from the list that is presented.

4. If necessary, run a price simulation by selecting a vendor and clicking on the PRICE SIMULATION button. You can also run a price simulation for all vendors by clicking on the PRICE SIMULATION ALL button.

Purchase requisitions can be subject to a release strategy, which will cause other people to review it and approve it. We'll describe this in detail in Section 4.5.

Table 4.5 lists some useful transactions for working with purchase requisitions.

Transaction	Menu Path
ME51N: Create	LOGISTICS • MATERIALS MANAGEMENT • PURCHASING • PURCHASE REQUISITION • CREATE
ME52N: Change	LOGISTICS • MATERIALS MANAGEMENT • PURCHASING • PURCHASE REQUISITION • CHANGE
ME53N: Display	LOGISTICS • MATERIALS MANAGEMENT • PURCHASING • PURCHASE REQUISITION • DISPLAY
ME54N: Individual Release	LOGISTICS • MATERIALS MANAGEMENT • PURCHASING • PURCHASE REQUISITION • RELEASE • INDIVIDUAL RELEASE
ME55: Collective Release	LOGISTICS • MATERIALS MANAGEMENT • PURCHASING • PURCHASE REQUISITION • RELEASE • COLLECTIVE RELEASE
ME5A: General List Display	LOGISTICS • MATERIALS MANAGEMENT • PURCHASING • PURCHASE REQUISITION • LIST DISPLAYS • GENERAL
ME56: Assign	LOGISTICS • MATERIALS MANAGEMENT • PURCHASING • PURCHASE REQUISITION • FOLLOW-ON FUNCTIONS • ASSIGN

Table 4.5 Purchase Requisition Transaction Codes

Transaction	Menu Path
ME57: Assign and Process	LOGISTICS • MATERIALS MANAGEMENT • PURCHASING • PURCHASE REQUISITION • FOLLOW-ON FUNCTIONS • ASSIGN AND PROCESS

Table 4.5 Purchase Requisition Transaction Codes (Cont.)

4.4 Purchase Orders

Authorization documents Purchase orders (POs) are legal written documents that authorize a vendor to deliver goods or services binding your company to pay for those goods or services at a later time. POs in the SAP ERP system are considered external documents and as such can be printed, sent by email, or sent by EDI to the vendor.

Procurement types There are different methods of purchasing goods, and in SAP ERP, these different ways are defined as *procurement types*. The procurement types detailed in Table 4.6 exist in the SAP ERP system.

Procurement Type	Definition or Use
Standard	Purchase of standard items that normally go into stock
Subcontracting	Purchase of some assembly or transformation service performed by the vendor to materials owned by the buyer
Consignment	Items that are ordered but remain the property of the vendor until used by the buyer
Stock transfer	Items that have to be internally transferred between plants
External service	Services provided by vendors

Table 4.6 Procurement Types in SAP ERP

PO header Like other documents in the SAP ERP system, the POs have a header section that contains information common to all of the items in the order, and an ITEM section that contains the detail for each of the items to be ordered (see Table 4.7 for a list of the fields in the PO header).

Field	Short Description
DOCUMENT TYPE	Distinguishes between a standard PO, a stock transfer order (STO), blanket order, or other custom order types.
DOCUMENT NUMBER	Number assigned uniquely to each PO.
VENDOR	The number of the partner supplying the goods or services.
PURCHASING ORGANIZATION	The organizational structure responsible for this purchase.
PURCHASING GROUP	Normally the person responsible for executing this purchase.
COMPANY CODE	The organizational structure for the legal entity under which this purchase is being executed.
RELEASE STRATEGY	If it applies, the steps to be followed to approve this purchase.
HEADER TEXTS	Any free-form texts that need to be communicated to the vendor for this purchase.
HEADER CONDITIONS	Pricing conditions that apply to the whole order, including discounts or surcharges. You can enter some of these manually, but they are usually the sum of all of the item pricing conditions.

Table 4.7   Some of the Fields Contained in the PO Header

The ITEM section contains the specific information of the items that are being ordered to the vendor (see Table 4.8 for the list of fields in the item overview section of the PO).

PO items

Field	Short Description
ITEM CATEGORY	Indicates the procurement type: standard items, subcontracting, consignment, or services
ACCOUNT ASSIGNMENT	Indicates if the purchase is going to be put into stock, or expensed to a cost center, asset, internal order, or other
MATERIAL NUMBER	The number that uniquely identifies an item within the SAP ERP system and the company

Table 4.8   Some of the Fields Contained in the PO Items

Field	Short Description
MATERIAL DESCRIPTION	The text that describes the item
ORDERED QUANTITY	The quantity of the material to be supplied by the vendor
UNIT OF MEASURE	The unit of measure that qualifies the quantity ordered to the vendor
UNIT PRICE	The unitary price of the item
CURRENCY	The currency being used for this purchase, in most cases, depends on the country for the vendor's address
PLANT	Organizational structure under which the items will be stocked and accounted for
STORAGE LOCATION	The specific stock holding unit that will account for the material and its stock value
DELIVERY DATE	The date required for the delivery at the location indicated in the Incoterms
DELIVERY ADDRESS	The physical address where the goods are to be delivered
ITEM TEXTS	Free-form texts that have to be communicated to the vendor
ITEM CONDITIONS	Pricing conditions for the item, including gross price, discounts, surcharges, taxes, and net price
ORDER CONFIRMATIONS	Any communication received from the vendor to confirm and accept the PO and the conditions, or to communicate delivery dates

Table 4.8 Some of the Fields Contained in the PO Items (Cont.)

Creation methods

Different Ways to Create a Purchase Order

The following details the different methods you can use to create a PO:

▶ *Automatically* through mass conversion of MRP generated purchase requisitions into POs. This requires that both the vendor and the material are set up to allow automatic PO creation in the vendor master and the material master, and all of the data for the PO comes from the master data: info record, source list, and material master. This normally happens in the background by scheduling a job that runs the automatic creation of POs from requisitions program from Transaction ME59N.

- *Semi-automatically* by reviewing and converting requirements for a given vendor. This is done using the ordering Transaction ME58 for assigned purchase requisitions in the path Logistics • Materials Management • Purchasing • Purchase Order • Create • via Requisition Assignment List. Some data can be typed manually. This enables you to correct any quantities that you consider inaccurate or maybe adjust the delivery dates.

- *Manually* by copying data from a purchase requisition. This is done within the PO create transaction by selecting one or several requisition items and copying them into the PO. Here you also can type and complete some information manually. This is done in Transaction ME21N, or by following the path Logistics • Materials Management • Purchasing • Purchase Order • Create • Vendor/Supplying Plant Known.

- *Manually* by typing the complete information for the header and all of the different items in the same Transaction ME21N.

4.4.1 Creating Purchase Orders Automatically

When you create a PO manually, you need to know the values to be entered in the previously mentioned fields. Some fields are automatically filled with values coming from the master data. The description, for example, comes from the material master, the price and pricing conditions usually come from the info record or can be entered manually, and the delivery address is usually copied from either the plant's address or the storage location address, or can be entered manually if the delivery needs to happen at a different location.

In previous sections, we discussed the RFQ process to bid purchases of new materials from vendors, but a material may also be directly quoted from a specific vendor without creating an RFQ in the SAP ERP system. When the material is then bought for the first time, the PO can create an info record based on the conditions entered in the PO. In this case, you need to create the source lists manually.

Purchase bid without RFQ

As we mentioned, both the materials and the vendors need to have been set up in master data to apply for this method. Once this is done, follow these steps:

1. Go to Transaction ME59N or follow the menu path Logistics • Materials Management • Purchasing • Purchase Requisition • Follow

ON FUNCTIONS • CREATE PURCHASE ORDER • AUTOMATICALLY VIA PUR-
CHASE REQUISITIONS.

2. Enter the selection values in the selection screen. At the minimum, required fields are PLANT and PURCHASING ORGANIZATION.

3. Push the EXECUTE button. You will see the result of the run in the resulting screen.

4.4.2 Converting Purchase Requisitions to POs

To convert groups of purchase requisitions to purchase orders, go to Transaction ME58 or follow the path LOGISTICS • MATERIALS MANAGE-
MENT • PURCHASING • PURCHASE REQUISITION • FOLLOW ON FUNCTIONS •
CREATE PURCHASE ORDER • VIA ASSIGNMENT LIST.

1. From the selection screen enter the purchasing group, purchase organization, the plant, the vendor, and any other selection criteria you want to enter.

2. In the OVERVIEW OF ASSIGNMENTS screen, click on the purchasing organization number under the vendor. This line contains the general purchasing data for the requisitions assigned to that vendor and also the number of requisitions to be processed.

3. Push the PROCESS ASSIGNMENT button. A pop-up window will ask you to enter/confirm the basic data for the purchase order: document type, PO date, purchasing group, and purchasing organization. Complete and press Enter .

4. On the CREATE PURCHASE ORDER screen, drag the requisitions from the left side (DOCUMENT OVERVIEW) column into the shopping cart at the top left of the main screen. Repeat this step for each requisition.

5. Make any adjustments to the quantities or dates if necessary.

6. Save the purchase order.

4.4.3 Creating a Purchase Order Manually

To create a PO manually, execute Transaction ME21N or follow the path LOGISTICS • MATERIALS MANAGEMENT • PURCHASING • PURCHASE ORDER •
CREATE • VENDOR/SUPPLYING PLANT KNOWN. This transaction, as others

we've described in this chapter, separates on one single screen the header information, the item information, and the item detail information. Follow these steps:

1. Select the document type (for standard POs, select NB, and for STOs, select UB).

2. Select a vendor to buy from.

3. The header data, on the top, is divided into several tabs (see Figure 4.26). In the ORG.DATA tab, enter the purchasing organization, purchasing group, and company code that apply for your order. (See Table 4.6 earlier in this chapter for other header fields you may enter.)

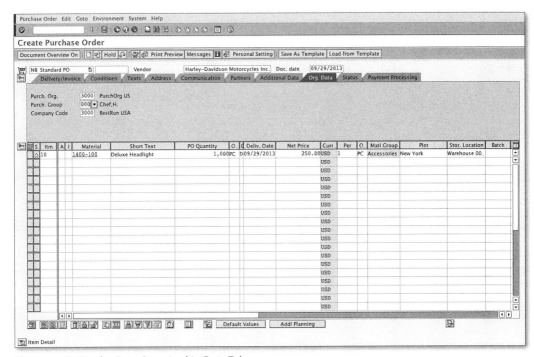

Figure 4.26 Header Data Organized in Data Tabs

4. In the middle section, you find the line item overview section, where you enter all of the relevant information for the item you're buying. (See Table 4.8 for the detailed description of each field in this section.)

5. After you've completed the line items entry and press the ⎡Enter⎤ key, you'll see the bottom section item detail section. Here you'll find detailed information about the material, quantities, delivery schedule, pricing conditions, delivery, and invoice requirements. Most of this information comes from a collection of master data, including the material master, vendor master, and purchasing info records. Review this information and make sure it's complete (see Figure 4.27).

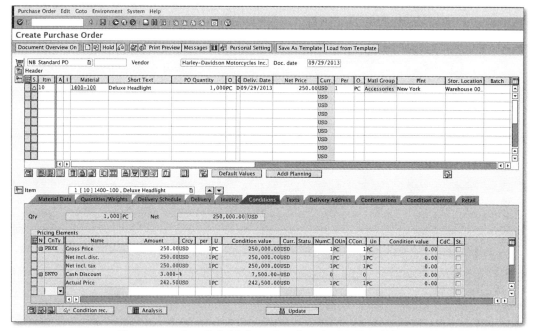

Figure 4.27 Item Detail Information Organized in Data Tabs

6. Save your PO. The system gives you a PO number as a result.

Creating a purchase order output

After a PO is created, it's natural to think that you need to communicate your purchasing need to the vendor. As external documents, you can do many things with a PO. The standard output types allow you to print, email, or send the document via EDI.

The standard output types and forms for POs is NEU, and, depending on the medium you choose for the output, you can send it in different ways as listed in Table 4.9.

Medium	Description	Form Name	Use
1	Print output	MEDRUCK	Prints a PO
2	Fax output	MEDRUCK	Sends a fax to the vendor
5	External send	MEDRUCK	Sends a PDF version by email to the vendor
6	EDI	ORDERS/ ORDCHG	Generates an IDoc to be sent as an EDI message

Table 4.9 Standard Output Types and Forms for Purchase Orders

4.4.4 Printing or Emailing a Purchase Order

The PO forms that will be printed or sent by email were created during the implementation process of your SAP ERP system. The next step is to generate an output condition record so that when a new PO is created, it also generates one of these forms. This is done in Transaction NACE (Conditions for Output Control). This transaction allows you to create output conditions for most of the documents or processes in the SAP ERP system (see Figure 4.28).

Within Transaction NACE, follow these steps to create the message:

1. Select application EF.

2. Click the CONDITION RECORDS button.

3. Select the output type for which you want to create a condition record. The standard PO output is NEU.

4. Select the key combination. You can choose from the following purchasing output determinations:

   ▶ PURCHASING ORG/VENDOR FOR EDI

   ▶ DOCUMENT TYPE/PURCH. ORG./VENDOR

   ▶ DOCUMENT TYPE

   ▶ PURCHASING ORGANIZATION

5. Enter the data for the key combination that you chose, and execute.

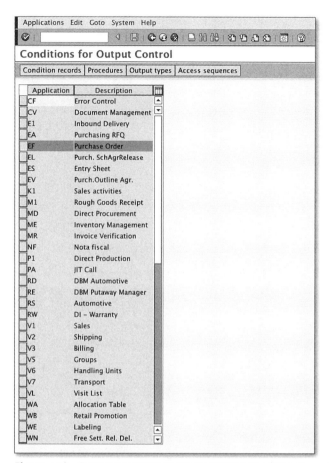

Figure 4.28 Transaction NACE to Create Output Condition Records

6. In the following screen, complete the data, and make sure you enter a partner function, which is usually "VN" for vendor (see Figure 4.29). Also in the MEDIA column, make sure you select the right option: PRINT, EMAIL, EDI, and so on.

7. In the DATE/TIME column, you can tell the system to generate the output as soon as you save the PO, or at a later time by the use of another transaction, you can also select to produce the output with a batch job or with a time specification.

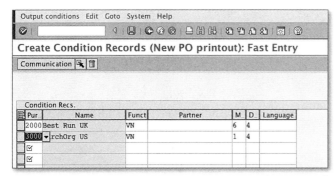

Figure 4.29 Transaction NACE: Creating Output Condition Records

8. If you're printing, click on the COMMUNICATION button. There you can specify the printer to use and specify whether the printout has to come out immediately or if only a new spool will be generated.

If you set up the output message to be printed later and not at the time you save the PO, then you need to follow these steps to print/send your PO form:

Print later

1. Go to Transaction ME9F or follow the path LOGISTICS • MATERIALS MANAGEMENT • PURCHASING • PURCHASE ORDER • MESSAGES • PRINT/ TRANSMIT.

2. Enter the search parameters that allow you to print all the POs you need, or directly enter the PO number in the DOCUMENT NUMBER field.

3. From the list of resulting purchase orders, select the ones you want to output by clicking the little selection box at the far left.

4. Click on the OUPTUT MESSAGE button.

The successfully output messages will have a green check mark on the left and the ones with errors will have a red X.

Table 4.10 lists some useful transactions for working with POs.

Transaction	Menu Path
ME21N: Create	LOGISTICS • MATERIALS MANAGEMENT • PURCHASING • PURCHASE ORDER • CREATE VENDOR/SUPPLYING PLANT KNOWN
ME22N: Change	LOGISTICS • MATERIALS MANAGEMENT • PURCHASING • PURCHASE ORDER • CHANGE
ME23N: Display	LOGISTICS • MATERIALS MANAGEMENT • PURCHASING • PURCHASE ORDER • DISPLAY
ME29N: Individual Release	LOGISTICS • MATERIALS MANAGEMENT • PURCHASING • PURCHASE ORDER • RELEASE • INDIVIDUAL RELEASE
ME28: Collective Release	LOGISTICS • MATERIALS MANAGEMENT • PURCHASING • PURCHASE ORDER • RELEASE • COLLECTIVE RELEASE
ME58: Create Via Assignment List	LOGISTICS • MATERIALS MANAGEMENT • PURCHASING • PURCHASE REQUISITION • CREATE PURCHASE ODER • VIA ASSIGNMENT LIST
ME59N: Create Automatically via Purchase Requisitions	LOGISTICS • MATERIALS MANAGEMENT • PURCHASING • PURCHASE REQUISITION • CREATE PURCHASE ODER • AUTOMATICALLY VIA PURCHASE REQUISITIONS
ME2L: List Displays By Vendor	LOGISTICS • MATERIALS MANAGEMENT • PURCHASING • PURCHASE ORDER • LIST DISPLAYS • BY VENDOR
ME2M: List Displays By Material	LOGISTICS • MATERIALS MANAGEMENT • PURCHASING • PURCHASE ORDER • LIST DISPLAYS • BY MATERIAL
ME2C: List Displays By Material Group	LOGISTICS • MATERIALS MANAGEMENT • PURCHASING • PURCHASE ORDER • LIST DISPLAYS • BY MATERIAL GROUP
ME2N: List Displays By PO Number	LOGISTICS • MATERIALS MANAGEMENT • PURCHASING • PURCHASE ORDER • LIST DISPLAYS • BY PO NUMBER
ME2W: List Displays By Supplying Plant	LOGISTICS • MATERIALS MANAGEMENT • PURCHASING • PURCHASE ORDER • LIST DISPLAYS • BY SUPPLYING PLANT

Table 4.10 Purchase Order Transactions

Transaction	Menu Path
NACE: Conditions for Output Control	There is no menu path for this transaction.
ME9F: Print/Transmit	LOGISTICS • MATERIALS MANAGEMENT • PURCHASING • PURCHASE ORDER • MESSAGES • PRINT/TRANSMIT

Table 4.10 Purchase Order Transactions (Cont.)

4.5   Release Strategies

In Purchasing, users create documents that represent commitments to other companies. For that reason, it's possible to prevent the printing, transmitting, or in the case of purchase requisitions, turning into POs without the document going through an approval process.

Approval

In the SAP ERP system, approvals for purchasing documents are given through the use of a release strategy, and purchasing documents need to be relevant to an overall release strategy. This is done in configuration during the definition of document types. A release strategy is the set of rules, set in configuration, that determines which materials or amounts must be approved and by whom. You can configure release strategies for the following:

▶ RFQs

▶ Purchase requisitions

▶ POs

▶ Outline agreements

When you set up a release strategy, you assign it to a document type; for example, NB for a standard purchase requisition. When you create a new document, the system automatically checks if the parameters of your release strategy apply to that document. If it does, the document gets that release strategy assigned, and a release indicator shows the status.

In a release strategy, you set steps for release, and as you progress through those steps the release indicator changes, letting you know which follow-up steps can be executed on the document.

Types There are two types of release strategies. Release strategies without classification are *only* for purchase requisitions, and release strategies with classification are for all purchasing documents, including purchase requisitions. We'll explain how to set up each in the following sections.

4.5.1 Release Strategy without Classification

Value amount The release strategy without classification is very straightforward. You set up a value amount over which the document needs to be released and assign a release strategy to it (see Figure 4.30).

You can further refine the determination of the release strategy by using a plant (mandatory field), a material group, and an account assignment category.

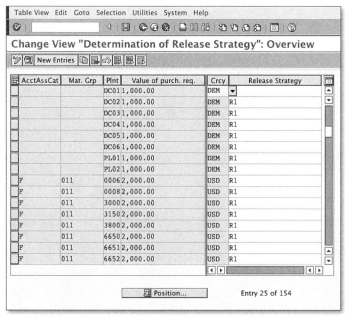

Figure 4.30 Release Strategy without Classification

Setup steps To set up and activate a strategy, in the IMG configuration, first choose Materials Management • Purchasing • Purchase Requisition • Set

Up Procedure Without Classification. Then, double-click on each of the activities indicated in the menu to complete the following steps:

1. **Create release codes**
   These represent the people who should release the document: manager, director, controller, and so on. The code is added to the security profile of the user who will go into the system and release the document.

2. **Create a release indicator or use one of the SAP delivered ones**
   These indicators represent the allowed follow-up operations that can be performed as the document is released by the different approvers.

3. **Set the release points**
   The release points indicate which release code has to approve before which other release point. You can also indicate whether any of the release points is a mandatory prerequisite for the next point.

4. **Assign release indicators**
   In this activity, you assign the release indicators that are valid for each release point. Here it's very important to have a release step in which the document is completely blocked. This step should be the first one so that it's assigned upon creation of the document. This way, you prevent any follow-on steps on that newly created purchasing document.

5. **Determine the release strategy**
   Here you tell the system which release strategy has to be used by setting combinations of the following fields:

   ▸ Account Assignment Category

   ▸ Material Group

   ▸ Plant

   ▸ Value of Purchase Requisition (with currency)

> **Note**
>
> One thing to keep in mind when working with this type of release strategy is that even if the overall value of the purchase document determines whether the document is subject to a release strategy or not, the release is based on an item-by-item basis.

4.5.2   Release Strategy with Classification

With the release strategy with classification, you have more flexibility to determine which documents are subject for release and which aren't. There are two main differences that may make you decide you want to use this scheme and not the one discussed in the previous section. One is the flexibility you get by using the SAP Classification System.

Characteristics You can create characteristics and assign them to a class that will be used for the release strategy determination. Although you have more flexibility by creating these characteristics, you're still restricted to the fields that are available during the strategy determination. These fields reside in a structure called CEBAN for purchase requisitions and CEKKO for the rest of the purchasing documents, which are the communication structures for release strategy determination that provide access to the purchasing document's field values. You can include any of these fields in your class and use them as the filter or selection criteria for strategy determination.

Workflow The second big difference is the possibility of using *workflow* to communicate to people that they need to approve a purchasing document. SAP delivers a standard workflow for this, and it's automatically used every time a purchasing document needs an approval.

What you do in the system is assign a release code to a user in the system who is defined as an agent in the workflow. That way, each time that agent needs to review and approve a purchasing document, a message will be sent to that person's SAP inbox with a link to review that document.

To set up a release strategy using classification, follow the IMG path MATERIALS MANAGEMENT • PURCHASING • PURCHASE REQUISITION • PROCEDURE WITH CLASSIFICATION, and then complete the following steps:

1. **Edit the characteristics**
   In the SAP Classification System, you have to define characteristics, which are like fields in a structure called a class. As discussed earlier, these fields need to correspond to the fields included in the communication structures for release strategy determination. So, for example, if you need to check on the document type, create characteristic FRG_EKKO_BSART, go directly to the ADDL DATA tab, and enter a reference to table CEKKO and field name BSART. Press the ⌷Enter⌷ key, and the

characteristic copies all of the descriptions and field values from that reference field. Save your characteristic, and do the same for other fields you need to check in your strategy.

2. **Edit the classes**

   After you've defined your characteristics, you have to assign them to a class. Create a class with class type 032, for Release Strategy, and assign your characteristics there (see Figure 4.31).

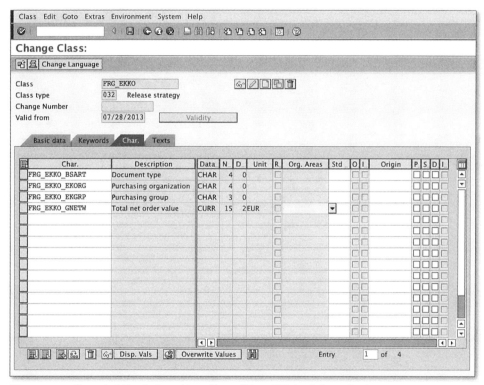

Figure 4.31 Characteristics Assigned to a Class of Type 032 for Release Strategy

3. **Create release groups**

   Here you define if the approval is for the overall document or for each item. You have to create a release group for each document type, which is similar to what you did in the procedure without classification, but here you also have to assign a class to each of these groups. The class corresponds to the class you created in the previous step.

4. **Create release codes**

   These represent the people who should release the document: manager, director, controller, and so on. The code is added to the security profile of the user who will go into the system and release the document. You need to assign each code to a release group from the previous step.

5. **Create a release indicator or use one of the SAP-delivered ones**

   These indicators represent the allowed follow-up operations that can be performed as the document is released by the different approvers.

6. **Set release strategies**

   Here you create a strategy and assign it to a release group. For each strategy, you'll define the following:

   ▸ The release codes that are going to be used.

   ▸ The release prerequisites for those release codes (see Figure 4.32).

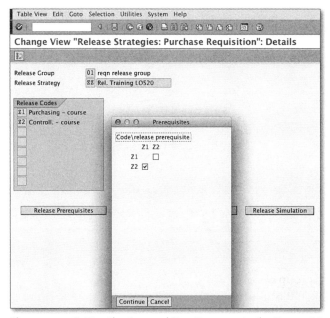

Figure 4.32 Setting the Approval Step Sequence in the Prerequisites Table

   ▸ The release statuses. Don't forget to have a status in which the document is completely blocked (see Figure 4.33).

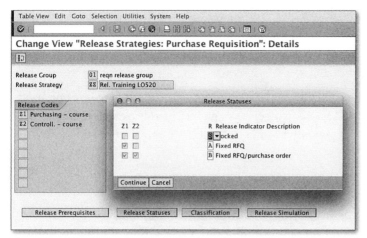

Figure 4.33 Assigning the Statuses in the Release Status Table

▶ The values for each characteristic in the class. Here is where you enter your selection criteria (see Figure 4.34).

Figure 4.34 Entering the Values to Check for Each Characteristic

7. **Assign workflow roles to release codes**

In this step, you link your release strategy to the different workflow agents. You'll enter an SAP ERP internal user that will be responsible to release a step in your strategy.

Create PO for assignment

After you have set up your strategy, your next step is to create a purchasing document and see how it gets assigned to the release strategy depending on the values you entered in classification (see Figure 4.35).

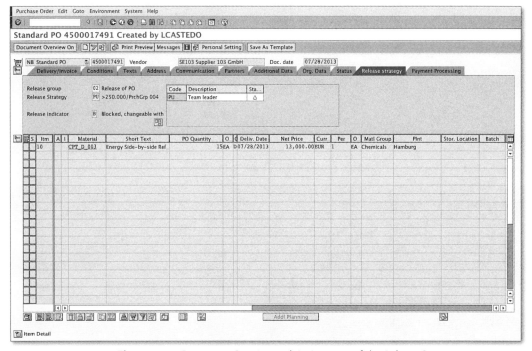

Figure 4.35 Document Creation and Assignment of the Release Strategy

Table 4.11 details the transactions and configurations steps you'll use when creating and maintaining a release strategy.

Transaction/ Configuration Steps	Menu Path
Define release strategy for purchase requisition without classification	IMG • MATERIALS MANAGEMENT • PURCHASING • PURCHASE REQUISITION • RELEASE PROCEDURE • SET UP PROCEDURE WITHOUT CLASSIFICATION
Define release strategy for purchase requisition with classification	IMG • MATERIALS MANAGEMENT • PURCHASING • PURCHASE REQUISITION • RELEASE PROCEDURE • PROCEDURE WITH CLASSIFICATION
Define release strategy for contracts with classification	IMG • MATERIALS MANAGEMENT • PURCHASING • CONTRACT • RELEASE PROCEDURE FOR CONTRACTS
Define release strategy for scheduling agreements with classification	IMG • MATERIALS MANAGEMENT • PURCHASING • SCHEDULING AGREEMENTS • RELEASE PROCEDURE FOR SCHEDULING AGREEMENTS
ME29N: Individual Release (Purchase Order)	LOGISTICS • MATERIALS MANAGEMENT • PURCHASING • PURCHASE ORDER • RELEASE • INDIVIDUAL RELEASE
ME28: Collective Release (Purchase Order)	LOGISTICS • MATERIALS MANAGEMENT • PURCHASING • PURCHASE ORDER • RELEASE • COLLECTIVE RELEASE
ME54N: Individual Release (Purchase Requisition)	LOGISTICS • MATERIALS MANAGEMENT • PURCHASING • PURCHASE REQUISITION • RELEASE • INDIVIDUAL RELEASE
ME54N: Collective Release (Purchase Requisition)	LOGISTICS • MATERIALS MANAGEMENT • PURCHASING • PURCHASE REQUISITION • RELEASE • COLLECTIVE RELEASE
ME35K: Release (Contract)	LOGISTICS • MATERIALS MANAGEMENT • PURCHASING • OUTLINE AGREEMENTS • CONTRACT • RELEASE
ME35L: Release (Scheduling Agreement)	LOGISTICS • MATERIALS MANAGEMENT • PURCHASING • OUTLINE AGREEMENTS • SCHEDULING AGREEMENT • RELEASE

Table 4.11 Release Strategy Transactions and Configuration Steps

4.6 Return Materials to Vendor

Sometimes, things don't go as well as you would like them to go and you run into the problem of receiving materials out of spec, damaged, or something completely different to what you ordered. The normal business process is to return the goods to the vendor.

In the SAP ERP system, you have two different ways of returning materials to vendors. One is purely an Inventory Management activity (which we'll discuss briefly), and the other is initiated by Purchasing (which we'll discuss in detail).

4.6.1 Returns in Inventory Management

In Inventory Management, the return is done by posting a return to vendor in Transaction MIGO (follow menu path LOGISTICS • MATERIALS MANAGEMENT • INVENTORY MOVEMENT • GOODS MOVEMENTS • MIGO) (see Figure 4.36), and follow these steps:

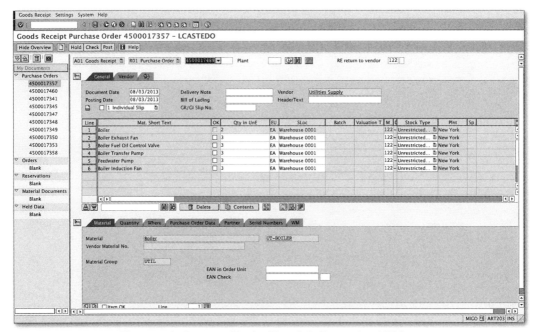

Figure 4.36 Return to Vendor Directly in Transaction MIGO

1. Post a goods receipt for a PO, but replace the default movement type 101 with 122.

2. As you enter your PO number, the items that have already been received will be listed. Select the item and the correct quantity, and post the material document.

This scenario may apply to simple returns in which the vendor comes and picks up the merchandise or when the items are being destroyed.

4.6.2 Returns to Vendor in Purchasing

From Purchasing, after you have a return authorization from the vendor, the buyer needs to create a new line in the PO for each item that will be returned. The simplest way to do this is to change the original PO and create a new item by copying the item to be returned. This is done with these steps:

1. Select an item and click on the Copy button under the Item Overview section.

2. After the new item is created, scroll to the right and click the Returns Items field (see Figure 4.37).

3. When you select the Return flag and press ⌨Enter, the system checks several things:

   ▸ That the material has sales views

   ▸ That the vendor has the indicator set for Return Vendor

   ▸ That the return vendor exists as a customer (normally a ship-to account group is used to create these customers)

   ▸ That the material's sales data and the vendor exist in the same sales organization, distribution channel, and division

   ▸ That a shipping point can be determined for the combination of shipping conditions of the return vendor (vendor master), plant (from the PO), and storage location (from the PO)

If all of these conditions are met, then the PO item gets a new tab created for Shipping (see Figure 4.37). When you see this new Shipping tab appear, check that all of the data is complete, including the route. Save the document.

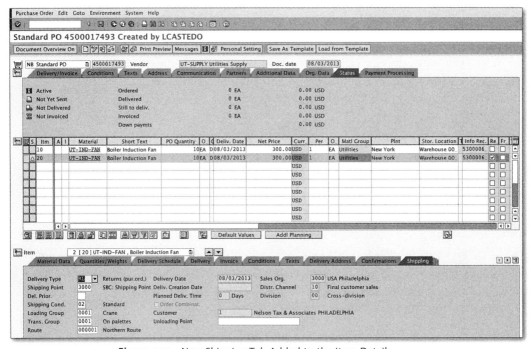

Figure 4.37 New Shipping Tab Added to the Item Details

Create an outbound delivery

After the PO is saved, you can create an outbound delivery using Transaction VL10G (menu path LOGISTICS • LOGISTICS EXECUTION • OUTBOUND PROCESS • GOODS ISSUE FOR OUTBOUND DELIVERY • OUTBOUND DELIVERY • CREATE • COLLECTIVE PROCESSING OF DOCUMENTS DUE FOR DELIVERY • PURCHASE ORDERS).

1. Enter the shipping point from the SHIPPING tab information, and enter the PO number.

2. Make sure that the date range covers the delivery date of your return item, and click EXECUTE.

3. In the next screen, select your PO number at the leftmost of the screen, and click on the BACKGROUND button.

4. If everything goes right, you'll again see your PO number with a green light on the left. Click on the SHOW/HIDE DELIVERY button, and the delivery number is shown on the rightmost column.

The delivery acts as the instruction for the warehouse to pick the product and ship it out to the vendor (see Figure 4.38). If the storage location is managed with SAP Warehouse Management, then an STO can be created as a follow-on function for the delivery. After the STO is confirmed, then the delivery can be goods issued, and the credit memo can be processed by AP.

Normally, the delivery type is RL, and this is set in configuration under the IMG path PURCHASE ORDER • RETURNS ORDER • RETURNS TO VENDOR.

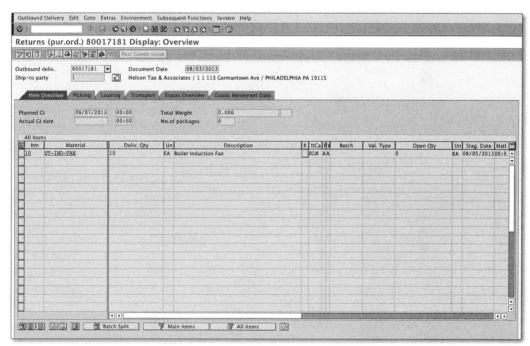

Figure 4.38 Return Delivery Informing the Warehouse What to Pick, Pack, and Ship to the Vendor

In Table 4.12 we provide you with a list of useful transactions that apply to the return to vendor scenarios.

Transaction	Menu Path
ME22N: Change Purchase Order	LOGISTICS • MATERIALS MANAGEMENT • PURCHASING • PURCHASE ORDER • CHANGE
MIGO: Goods Movement (MIGO)	LOGISTICS • MATERIALS MANAGEMENT • INVENTORY MANAGEMENT • GOODS MOVEMENT• GOODS MOVEMENT (MIGO)
VL10G: Create Delivery for Sales and Purchase Orders	LOGISTICS • LOGISTICS EXECUTION • OUTBOUND PROCESS• GOODS ISSUE FOR OUTBOUND DELIVERY • OUTBOUND DELIVERY • CREATE • COLLECTIVE PROCESSING OF DOCUMENTS DUE FOR DELIVERY • SALES ORDERS AND PURCHASE ORDERS

Table 4.12 Returns to Vendor Transactions

4.7 Vendor Evaluation

In the standard SAP ERP system, you can rate and evaluate vendors based on a scoring range from 1 to 100 points, which is used to measure the performance of your vendors on the basis of four main criteria. You can then determine and compare the performance of your vendors by reference to their overall scores. The vendor evaluation system ensures that evaluation of vendors is objective because all vendors are assessed according to uniform criteria, and the scores are computed automatically.

In the SAP ERP system, vendor evaluation is completely integrated with Purchasing within MM. This means that information such as delivery dates, prices, and quantities can be taken from POs.

Vendor evaluation also uses data from the Quality Management (QM) component, such as the results of incoming inspections or quality audits — all with the purpose of letting you know how timely, how accurate, and with how much quality your purchases are being delivered to you by your vendors.

4.7.1 Performance Criteria

The following are the main criteria available in the standard system for procurement of materials:

- ▶ Price
- ▶ Quality
- ▶ Delivery
- ▶ General service/support

In addition to these four criteria, the system provides the external service provision criterion, which serves as a basis for evaluating those vendors you employ as external service providers.

External service provision

You can also define your own criteria, as required. You can assign different weights to the individual criteria, and, at the end, the vendor's overall score is computed by taking into account the weighted scores awarded for each of the main criteria.

To create a more detailed evaluation, each main criterion can be divided into several subcriteria. Subcriteria are the smallest units for which scores are awarded in vendor evaluation, and the system calculates a score for the relevant higher-level main criterion based on the scores a vendor receives for the various subcriteria.

Subcriteria

The standard delivered system provides you with certain subcriteria that help you form a basis for evaluation. You can also define your own additional subcriteria if you need to. If you need to create your own subcriteria, you first have to select the main criterion for which you want to add more subcriteria and then add it by double-clicking on SUBCRITERIA and then by clicking on the NEW ENTRIES button. Enter a sequence number, a description, and a scoring method. This scoring method determines the origin of the score (see Figure 4.39).

Vendor evaluation can compute the scores of these subcriteria in three different ways, and you can select which method to use:

Compute subcriteria methods

- ▶ **Automatically**
  Scores are calculated by the system based on the available data.
- ▶ **Semi-automatically**
  You manually enter scores for selected items, and then the system calculates the higher-level scores based on your input.
- ▶ **Manually**
  You enter your scores for a subcriterion for each vendor.

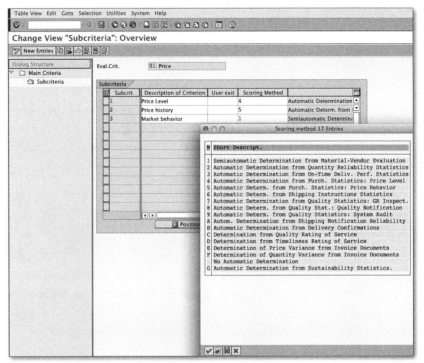

Figure 4.39 Choosing the Scoring Method

Vendor evaluation can only be maintained for manual criteria, and this is done in Transaction ME61 (LOGISTICS • MATERIALS MANAGEMENT • MASTER DATA • VENDOR EVALUATION • MAINTAIN). The scores for all of the automatic criteria are collected automatically in the background every time you post goods receipts or use Invoice Verification for POs (see Figure 4.40).

Automatic subcriteria

The system calculates the scores for automatic subcriteria on the basis of data from other areas of the enterprise outside the vendor evaluation system (e.g., goods receiving or QM). This is set up in configuration in the IMG path MATERIALS MANAGEMENT • PURCHASING • VENDOR EVALUATION • DEFINE CRITERIA.

The automatic subcriteria provided in the standard system should be enough for the evaluation of a vendor from whom you procure materials, and you don't necessarily have to maintain scores for manual or semiautomatic subcriteria to perform evaluations.

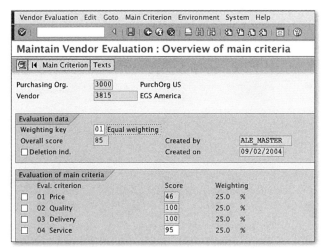

Figure 4.40 Setting the Weighting Key to Distribute the Scores for Manual Criteria

The system allows for a maximum of 20 subcriteria for each main criterion. Table 4.13 shows the number of subcriteria provided in the standard system and the available number for you to configure in your system.

Main Criterion	SAP-Delivered Subcriteria	Growth Availability for Additional Subcriteria
Price	2	18
Quality	3	17
Delivery	4	16
Invoices	2	18

Table 4.13 Subcriteria Provided in the Standard System

There are no automatic subcriteria for the general service/support and external service provision main criteria. However, three semi-automatic subcriteria are included in the standard SAP system for the former and two for the latter. This means that you can define up to 17 and 18 additional manual or semi-automatic subcriteria, respectively, for these two main criteria.

It's a good rule of thumb to keep the number of manual subcriteria to a minimum to have a better overview and to minimize the maintenance effort.

4.7.2 Scoring

The following is a brief description of what is evaluated in the standard SAP ERP delivered main criteria and subcriteria.

Price

This main criterion evaluates the variations in price for every delivery a vendor makes and includes the following subcriteria:

- **Price level**
  Compares the relationship of a vendor's price to the market price. If the vendor's price is lower than the market price, the vendor receives a good score; if it's higher than the market price, the vendor is assigned a poor score.

- **Price history**
  Compares the development of the vendor's price with the market price. With this subcriterion, you can determine whether the vendor's price has increased or decreased over a certain period in comparison with changes in the market price over the same period.

Quality

This main criterion gathers the results of the quality inspections performed on the vendor's materials and includes the following subcriteria:

- **Goods receipt**
  Evaluates the quality of the material that the vendor delivers. Quality inspection takes place at the time of goods receipt.

- **Quality audit**
  Evaluates the quality assurance system used by a company in manufacturing products.

- **Complaints/rejection level**
  Evaluates whether the materials delivered by the vendor are regularly found to be faulty subsequent to incoming inspection.

Delivery

This main criterion gathers the data about the way materials are delivered according to time, quantity, and the vendor's own confirmation dates. It includes the following subcriteria:

▶ **On-time delivery performance**
Determines how precisely a vendor has adhered to the specified delivery dates.

▶ **Quantity reliability**
Determines whether a vendor has delivered the quantity specified in the PO.

▶ **Compliance with shipping instructions**
Determines how precisely a vendor complies with your instructions for shipping and packing of a material.

▶ **Confirmation date**
Determines whether a vendor adheres to a previously confirmed delivery date.

Invoices

This main criterion evaluates the pricing and quantity variances between POs and invoices and includes the following subcriteria:

▶ **Price variance**
Compares the invoice price to the PO price and checks for any variances.

▶ **Quantity variance**
Determines quantity variations against the received quantity during goods receipt.

4.7.3 Understanding How the Evaluation is Calculated

The results of vendor evaluation are displayed in the form of analyses that are part of the Purchasing Information System. In these results, you can generate ranking lists of the best vendors according to their overall scores or ranking lists for specific materials (see Figure 4.41).

Changes to evaluations are recorded in logs, and you have the option of printing out evaluation sheets.

How is the evaluation calculated?

Vendor evaluation is performed automatically in the background. When you start looking at the evaluation of your vendors, you have to do it in several levels. First, there is the overall score, which is the result of the combination of the scores for that vendor in the main criteria. At this top level, you can see a total of points out of 100 that each individual vendor obtained—much like a professor looks at the grades of his class at the end of a period.

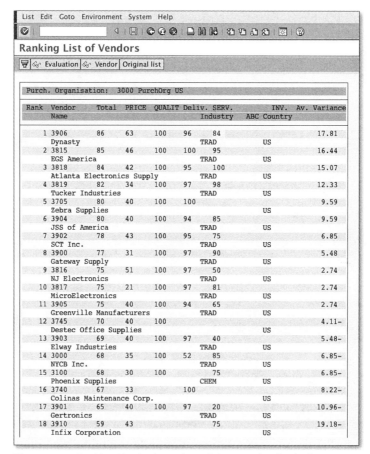

Figure 4.41 Ranking List Analysis: Overall Score and Individual Scores per Main Criteria

The OVERALL score is the sum of all of the main criteria selected as relevant for a vendor (see Figure 4.42). You can evaluate vendors according to several main criteria that you consider important. The scores for the main criteria are a more accurate representation of the performance of a vendor than the overall score.

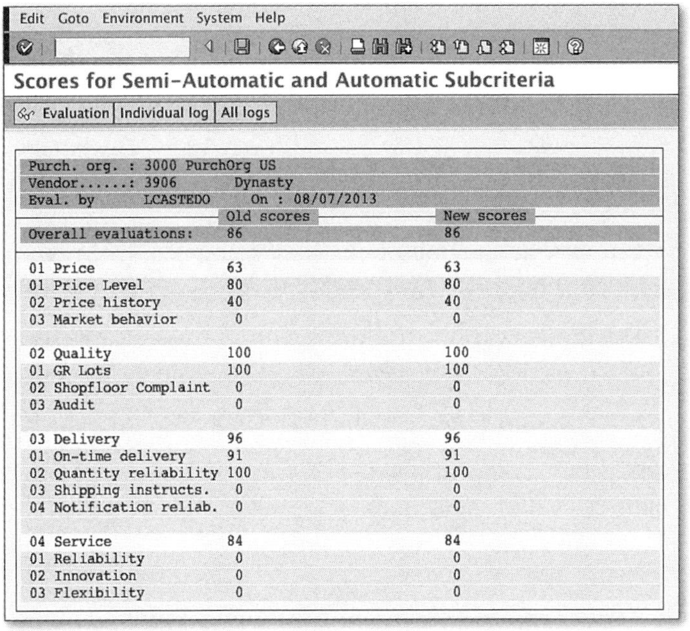

Figure 4.42 Each Criterion's Score Including the Subcriteria

You can determine the type and number of main criteria yourself to a maximum of 99. You can specify the number of main criteria for each purchasing organization and decide which main criteria are to be covered by the overall score.

4.7.4 Performing Vendor Evaluation

As we have discussed in previous paragraphs, there are different types of criteria for vendor evaluation: automatic, semi-automatic, and manual.

Automatic vendor evaluation is gathered and evaluated automatically in the background as receipts, quality inspections, invoice verification, and other transactions are posted in the system.

To generate the automatic and semi-automatic scores, follow these steps:

1. Go to Transaction ME63 or follow the path LOGISTICS • MATERIALS MANAGEMENT • PURCHASING • MASTER DATA • VENDOR EVALUATION • AUTOMATIC NEW EVALUATION.

2. From the selection screen, enter the vendor number and the purchase organization.

3. Push the EXECUTE button. In the resulting screen you can see the values for all the automatic and semi-automatic criteria (see Figure 4.42).

4. Press SAVE.

Manual To enter the values for manual criteria, follow these steps:

1. Go to Transaction ME61 or follow the path LOGISTICS • MATERIALS MANAGEMENT • PURCHASING • MASTER DATA • VENDOR EVALUATION • MAINTAIN.

2. Enter the purchasing organization number and the vendor number.

3. Push the EXECUTE button.

4. The manual criterions will appear as opened for input; enter the values for the vendor evaluation (see Figure 4.43 in the next section).

5. Save.

4.7.5 Comparing Performance

Scoring range To compare the performance of one vendor with another, it's necessary to establish a range (or scale) of possible scores. You can define your own scoring range from the worst-possible to the best-possible achievable score; for example, a range of 1 to 100 points. This scale provides you with a good overview and also permits quite a finely differentiated rating of individual vendors. This is set up in configuration when you maintain the purchasing organization data for vendor evaluation in the IMG path MATERIALS MANAGEMENT • PURCHASING • VENDOR EVALUATION • MAINTAIN PURCHASING ORGANIZATION DATA.

Of course, not all vendors are created equal, and you may have valid reasons to consider some criteria as more important for some vendors and less important for others. Fortunately, the scores a vendor is awarded for the main criteria can be weighted differently to reflect differences in the significance of the criteria.

In the SAP ERP system, you can use weighting factors to increase or reduce the importance of certain criteria when a score is calculated at the next highest level. These weighing factors are grouped under weighting keys. If you know that you'll want to carry out an evaluation repeatedly with certain main criteria and certain weighting factors, you can save this combination under a weighting key. Weighting keys are maintained in configuration in the IMG path MATERIALS MANAGEMENT • PURCHASING • VENDOR EVALUATION • DEFINE WEIGHTING KEYS. As described previously, when you maintain the vendor evaluation in Transaction ME61, you can assign a weighting key.

Weighing factors and keys

When you carry out the next vendor evaluation, just enter the relevant weighting key instead of entering a weighting factor for each individual criterion. The system then automatically sets all of the weighting factors. These weighting keys are set up in configuration and then used during the vendor evaluation maintenance (see Figure 4.43).

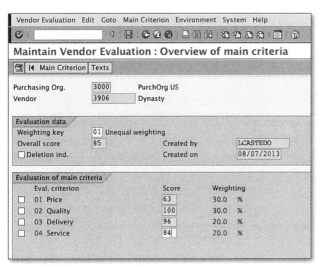

Figure 4.43 Displaying the Cumulative Scores for the Automatic Criteria and Entering the Score for the Manual Criteria

In Table 4.14, we list the most useful transactions that let you enter and display vendor evaluation.

Transaction	Menu Path
ME61: Maintain Vendor Evaluation	LOGISTICS • MATERIALS MANAGEMENT • PURCHASING • MASTER DATA • VENDOR EVALUATION • MAINTAIN
ME62: Display	LOGISTICS • MATERIALS MANAGEMENT • PURCHASING • MASTER DATA • VENDOR EVALUATION • DISPLAY
ME63: Automatic New Evaluation	LOGISTICS • MATERIALS MANAGEMENT • PURCHASING • MASTER DATA • VENDOR EVALUATION • AUTOMATIC NEW EVALUATION
ME64: Compare Evaluations	LOGISTICS • MATERIALS MANAGEMENT • PURCHASING • MASTER DATA • VENDOR EVALUATION • COMPARE EVALUATIONS
ME6A: Changes	LOGISTICS • MATERIALS MANAGEMENT • PURCHASING • MASTER DATA • VENDOR EVALUATION • CHANGES
ME65: Ranking Lists	LOGISTICS • MATERIALS MANAGEMENT • PURCHASING • MASTER DATA • VENDOR EVALUATION • LIST DISPLAYS • RANKING LISTS
ME6B: Evaluations per Material/Material Group	LOGISTICS • MATERIALS MANAGEMENT • PURCHASING • MASTER DATA • VENDOR EVALUATION • LIST DISPLAYS • EVALUATIONS PER MATERIAL/MATERIAL GROUP
ME6C: Vendors Without Evaluation	LOGISTICS • MATERIALS MANAGEMENT • PURCHASING • MASTER DATA • VENDOR EVALUATION • LIST DISPLAYS • VENDORS WITHOUT EVALUATION
ME6D: Vendors Not Evaluated Since	LOGISTICS • MATERIALS MANAGEMENT • PURCHASING • MASTER DATA • VENDOR EVALUATION • LIST DISPLAYS • VENDORS NOT EVALUATED SINCE

Table 4.14 Vendor Evaluation Transactions

4.8 Reporting

Standard SAP functionality allows you to obtain several reports based on the transactional data produced in the MM component. Because SAP

ERP is a real-time system, these reports vary their results and become obsolete almost immediately.

> **Note**
>
> As SAP consultants, we always mention to our customers that SAP's reports should be displayed on screen, maybe downloaded to your computer for further analysis in a spreadsheet program or some other kind of tool, and that for the same reason, they shouldn't be printed.

In this section, we provide a quick view of the most common reports that give a good view of your operation. We also discuss a couple of tools that can help you get more information out of the system.

The purchasing information that is available in the form of reports in the SAP ERP system is vast and gives you access to information about the following:

Purchasing information

- POs issued to vendors in a time period
- Goods delivered for POs
- Delays in deliveries
- Value of orders issued in the purchasing organization or by an individual purchasing group
- How accurately invoices match the POs

There are two types of reports in the SAP ERP system and specifically within the Purchasing submodule:

- **List displays**
  Lists of live transactional data that give you access to real-time information.
- **Analyses**
  Statistical reports of information gathered based on transactional data, which can give you valuable insight into your purchasing activities.

We'll discuss each of these reports in more detail in the following sections.

4.8.1 List Displays

Master records
information You can use the list display reports to look at the information in the master records database and also to look at transactional data as it happens in the system. Each has a plethora of selection fields so that you can accurately find results based on your search criteria. The information in these reports can be very extensive, and we suggest that you enter as many search parameters as you can to minimize the number of results.

These reports allow drilldown capability, so from the report list, you can double-click on an item, and the system will take you to the display transaction for that item.

Info Records

In Table 4.15 we list the most commonly used report transactions for info records. All of them give you more or less the same information, but the ways to find and view the info record information are different. See Figure 4.44 for a view to the result of running this report.

Transaction	Menu Path
ME1L: Display Info Record By Vendor	LOGISTICS • MATERIALS MANAGEMENT • PURCHASING • MASTER DATA • INFO RECORD • LIST DISPLAYS • BY VENDOR
ME1M: By Material	LOGISTICS • MATERIALS MANAGEMENT • PURCHASING • MASTER DATA • INFO RECORD • LIST DISPLAYS • BY MATERIAL
ME1W: By Material Group	LOGISTICS • MATERIALS MANAGEMENT • PURCHASING • MASTER DATA • INFO RECORD • LIST DISPLAYS • BY MATERIAL GROUP
ME1P: Order Price History	LOGISTICS • MATERIALS MANAGEMENT • PURCHASING • MASTER DATA • INFO RECORD • LIST DISPLAYS • ME1P – ORDER PRICE HISTORY
ME1E: Quotation Price History	LOGISTICS • MATERIALS MANAGEMENT • PURCHASING • MASTER DATA • INFO RECORD • LIST DISPLAYS • QUOTATION PRICE HISTORY
ME1L: By Vendor	LOGISTICS • MATERIALS MANAGEMENT • PURCHASING • MASTER DATA • INFO RECORD • LIST DISPLAYS • BY VENDOR

Table 4.15 Main Info Record Reports

Figure 4.44 List Display for Info Records by Vendor Listing all Materials Supplied by Each Vendor

Purchasing Master Data

Following up with list display reports, in Table 4.16, we list the transactions you can use to display more purchasing master data: source lists, quota arrangements, and vendors.

Master Data	Transaction	Menu Path
Source lists	MEOM: By Material	LOGISTICS • MATERIALS MANAGEMENT • PURCHASING • MASTER DATA • SOURCE LIST • LIST DISPLAYS • BY MATERIAL

Table 4.16 Master Data Reports

Master Data	Transaction	Menu Path
Quota arrangements	MEQM: By Material	LOGISTICS • MATERIALS MANAGEMENT • PURCHASING • MASTER DATA • QUOTA ARRANGEMENT • LIST DISPLAYS • BY MATERIAL
Vendor	MKVZ: Purchasing List	LOGISTICS • MATERIALS MANAGEMENT • PURCHASING • MASTER DATA • VENDOR • LIST DISPLAYS • PURCHASING LIST

Table 4.16 Master Data Reports (Cont.)

As shown in Figure 4.45, you can view vendors within a purchasing organization that display specific pricing changes.

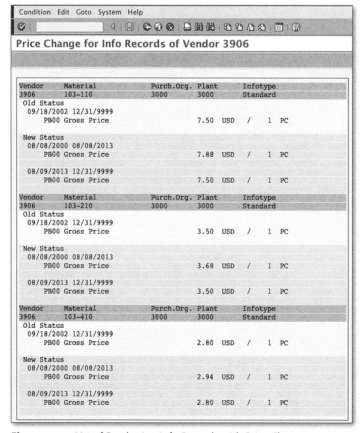

Figure 4.45 List of Purchasing Info Records with Price Changes

Vendor Evaluation

Table 4.17 provides useful transaction codes you can use to work with evaluating and reporting on your vendor evaluation.

Transaction	Menu Path
ME65: Ranking Lists	LOGISTICS • MATERIALS MANAGEMENT • PURCHASING • MASTER DATA • VENDOR EVALUATION • LIST DISPLAYS • RANKING LISTS
ME6B: Evaluations per Material/Material Group	LOGISTICS • MATERIALS MANAGEMENT • PURCHASING • MASTER DATA • VENDOR EVALUATION • LIST DISPLAYS • EVALUATIONS PER MATERIAL/ MATERIAL GROUP
ME6C: Vendors Without Evaluation	LOGISTICS • MATERIALS MANAGEMENT • PURCHASING • MASTER DATA • VENDOR EVALUATION • LIST DISPLAYS • VENDORS WITHOUT EVALUATION
ME6D: Vendors Not Evaluated Since	LOGISTICS • MATERIALS MANAGEMENT • PURCHASING • MASTER DATA • VENDOR EVALUATION • LIST DISPLAYS • VENDORS NOT EVALUATED SINCE

Table 4.17 Vendor Evaluation Reports Transactions

Conditions/Prices

With these reports, you'll see a list of time-dependent conditions for the pricing condition records. The conditions come from purchasing info records, outline agreements, POs, and other master data. Table 4.18 lists the most useful transactions for reviewing conditions and prices.

Transaction	Menu Path
MEKA: General Overview	LOGISTICS • MATERIALS MANAGEMENT • PURCHASING • MASTER DATA • CONDITIONS • PRICES • LIST DISPLAYS • GENERAL OVERVIEW
MEKB: By Contract	LOGISTICS • MATERIALS MANAGEMENT • PURCHASING • MASTER DATA • CONDITIONS • PRICES • LIST DISPLAYS • BY CONTRACT
MEKC: By Info Record	LOGISTICS • MATERIALS MANAGEMENT • PURCHASING • MASTER DATA • CONDITIONS • PRICES • LIST DISPLAYS • BY INFO RECORD
MEKD: By Material Group	LOGISTICS • MATERIALS MANAGEMENT • PURCHASING • MASTER DATA • CONDITIONS • PRICES • LIST DISPLAYS • BY MATERIAL GROUP
MEK32: Condition Index	LOGISTICS • MATERIALS MANAGEMENT • PURCHASING • MASTER DATA • CONDITIONS • PRICES • LIST DISPLAYS • CONDITION INDEX

Table 4.18 Reports for Conditions/Prices

Conditions/Surcharges

With these reports, you'll see a list of time-dependent conditions for the condition records for discounts and surcharges. The conditions come from purchase info records, outline agreements, POs, and other master data. Table 4.19 lists the most frequently used reports for listing and reviewing surcharges. For a sample of the resulting report, please look at Figure 4.46.

Transaction	Menu Path
MEKA: General Overview	LOGISTICS • MATERIALS MANAGEMENT • PURCHASING • MASTER DATA • CONDITIONS • SURCHARGES • LIST DISPLAYS • GENERAL OVERVIEW
MEKE: By Vendor	LOGISTICS • MATERIALS MANAGEMENT • PURCHASING • MASTER DATA • CONDITIONS • SURCHARGES • LIST DISPLAYS • BY VENDOR
MEKK: By Vendor Sub-Range	LOGISTICS • MATERIALS MANAGEMENT • PURCHASING • MASTER DATA • CONDITIONS • SURCHARGES • LIST DISPLAYS • BY VENDOR SUB-RANGE
MEKG: By Condition Group	LOGISTICS • MATERIALS MANAGEMENT • PURCHASING • MASTER DATA • CONDITIONS • SURCHARGES • LIST DISPLAYS • BY CONDITION GROUP
MEKF: By Material Type	LOGISTICS • MATERIALS MANAGEMENT • PURCHASING • MASTER DATA • CONDITIONS • SURCHARGES • LIST DISPLAYS • MEKF – BY MATERIAL TYPE
MEKI: By Incoterms	LOGISTICS • MATERIALS MANAGEMENT • PURCHASING • MASTER DATA • CONDITIONS • SURCHARGES • LIST DISPLAYS • BY INCOTERMS
MEKJ: By Invoicing Party	LOGISTICS • MATERIALS MANAGEMENT • PURCHASING • MASTER DATA • CONDITIONS • SURCHARGES • LIST DISPLAYS • BY INVOICING PARTY
MEKP: Involving Info Records	LOGISTICS • MATERIALS MANAGEMENT • PURCHASING • MASTER DATA • CONDITIONS • VENDOR PRICE CHANGES • LIST DISPLAYS • INVOLVING INFO RECORDS
MEKR: Involving Contracts	LOGISTICS • MATERIALS MANAGEMENT • PURCHASING • MASTER DATA • CONDITIONS • VENDOR PRICE CHANGES • LIST DISPLAYS • INVOLVING CONTRACTS
MEKL: Involving Scheduling Agreements	LOGISTICS • MATERIALS MANAGEMENT • PURCHASING • MASTER DATA • CONDITIONS • VENDOR PRICE CHANGES • LIST DISPLAYS • INVOLVING SCHEDULING AGREEMENTS

Table 4.19 Conditions/Surcharges Reports

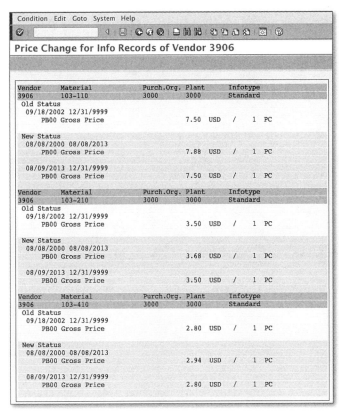

Figure 4.46 Vendor Price Changes Report Showing Price Histories

Purchase Requisitions

With these reports, you can display a list of requisitions according to your search criteria and drill down all of the way to the MRP requirement. Table 4.20 lists the most frequently used reports for listing and reviewing purchase requisitions. For an example of these lists, please look at Figure 4.47.

Transaction	Menu Path
ME5A: General	LOGISTICS • MATERIALS MANAGEMENT • PURCHASING • PURCHASE REQUISITION • LIST DISPLAYS • GENERAL
MSRV2: By Service	LOGISTICS • MATERIALS MANAGEMENT • PURCHASING • PURCHASE REQUISITION • LIST DISPLAYS • BY SERVICE

Table 4.20 Reports for Purchase Requisitions

Transaction	Menu Path
MELB: Transactions per Tracking Number	LOGISTICS • MATERIALS MANAGEMENT • PURCHASING • PURCHASE REQUISITION • LIST DISPLAYS • MELB – TRANSACTIONS PER TRACKING NUMBER
ME5W: Resubmission	LOGISTICS • MATERIALS MANAGEMENT • PURCHASING • PURCHASE REQUISITION • LIST DISPLAYS • RESUBMISSION
ME5J: By Project	LOGISTICS • MATERIALS MANAGEMENT • PURCHASING • PURCHASE REQUISITION • LIST DISPLAYS • BY ACCOUNT ASSIGNMENT • BY PROJECT

Table 4.20 Reports for Purchase Requisitions (Cont.)

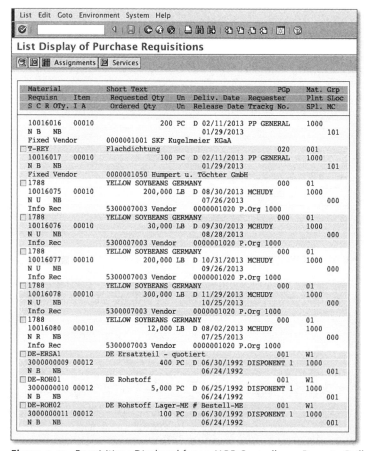

Figure 4.47 Requisitions Displayed for an MRP Controller or Buyer to Drill Down to the MRP Requirement

Purchase Orders

With these reports, you can display a list of requisitions according to your search criteria and drill down all of the way to the MRP requirement. Table 4.21 lists the most frequently used reports for listing and reviewing purchase orders.

Transaction	Menu Path
ME2L: List Displays By Vendor	LOGISTICS • MATERIALS MANAGEMENT • PURCHASING • PURCHASE ORDER • LIST DISPLAYS • BY VENDOR
ME2M: By Material	LOGISTICS • MATERIALS MANAGEMENT • PURCHASING • PURCHASE ORDER • LIST DISPLAYS • BY MATERIAL
ME2C: By Material Group	LOGISTICS • MATERIALS MANAGEMENT • PURCHASING • PURCHASE ORDER • LIST DISPLAYS • BY MATERIAL GROUP
ME2N: By PO Number	LOGISTICS • MATERIALS MANAGEMENT • PURCHASING • PURCHASE ORDER • LIST DISPLAYS • BY PO NUMBER
ME2W: By Supplying Plant	LOGISTICS • MATERIALS MANAGEMENT • PURCHASING • PURCHASE ORDER • LIST DISPLAYS • BY SUPPLYING PLANT
ME2J: By Project	LOGISTICS • MATERIALS MANAGEMENT • PURCHASING • PURCHASE ORDER • LIST DISPLAYS • BY ACCOUNT ASSIGNMENT • BY PROJECT

Table 4.21 Purchase Order Reports

Outline Agreements

With these reports, you can display a list of outline agreements, and from here, you can drill down and look at each document. Table 4.22 lists the most frequently used reports for listing and reviewing outline agreements.

Transaction	Menu Path
ME3L: List Outline Agreements By Vendor	LOGISTICS • MATERIALS MANAGEMENT • PURCHASING • OUTLINE AGREEMENT • LIST DISPLAYS • BY VENDOR

Table 4.22 Reports for Outline Agreements

Transaction	Menu Path
ME3M: By Material	LOGISTICS • MATERIALS MANAGEMENT • PURCHASING • OUTLINE AGREEMENT • LIST DISPLAYS • BY MATERIAL
ME3C: By Material Group	LOGISTICS • MATERIALS MANAGEMENT • PURCHASING • OUTLINE AGREEMENT • LIST DISPLAYS • BY MATERIAL GROUP
ME3B: By Tracking Number	LOGISTICS • MATERIALS MANAGEMENT • PURCHASING • OUTLINE AGREEMENT • LIST DISPLAYS • BY TRACKING NUMBER
ME3N: By Agreement Number	LOGISTICS • MATERIALS MANAGEMENT • PURCHASING • OUTLINE AGREEMENT • LIST DISPLAYS • BY AGREEMENT NUMBER
MELB: Transactions per Tracking Number	LOGISTICS • MATERIALS MANAGEMENT • PURCHASING • OUTLINE AGREEMENT • LIST DISPLAYS • TRANSACTIONS PER TRACKING NUMBER

Table 4.22 Reports for Outline Agreements (Cont.)

4.8.2 Analyses

Info system

The SAP ERP system can collect statistical information in what is called the info system. The *info system* consists of a collection of databases called infostructures; these structures collect data every time a transaction is posted. Information about inventory movements such as material receipts, material issues, purchases, and so on is collected.

This data is collected without links to the original document that created it. So you know how many receipts for a certain material you had in the warehouse in a period of time, but you don't know who posted it, which vendor it came from, the PO that originated that receipt, or any other document-related information.

Purchasing info system

The purchasing info system, or PURCHIS, focuses its attention on purchasing data, so you know how much you've bought from each vendor, how many orders, and for which materials. You can list the top vendors you buy from or the top materials that you buy.

To display the information from the infostructures, there is a set of standard analyses that provide you with a very extensive variety of views of the data. In addition, there is the possibility of running what is called *flexible evaluations*, where you select an infostructure and create your own report from that data.

Table 4.23 includes a list of the most helpful purchasing info system analyses. Use LOGISTICS • LOGISTICS CONTROLLING • PURCHASING INFORMATION SYSTEM • STANDARD ANALYSES to reach them.

Transaction	Description
MCE1: Purchasing Group	This analysis gives you a view of the purchases that each of the purchasing groups have done during the past periods. You can select to show all of the data for one or many purchasing groups over a date range, or you can filter by purchase organization and/or vendor.
MCE3: Vendor	This analysis shows you all of the purchases from a vendor or group of vendors. You have several fields to put together your search criteria and select the data over a period of time. This report shows you data such as PO value, invoice amount, order quantity, and more.
MCE5: Material Group	In this analysis, you can very quickly identify who your vendors are for each of the material groups. You can detect vendors that go across multiple material groups or maybe find that a vendor that you thought sold products from a certain material group really doesn't.
MCE7: Material	Similar to the material group analysis, you can enter individual material numbers and look at who sells them to your company, how much you've bought in a specific period, and who in your organization has done the purchasing.
MCE8: Service	This analysis allows you to look at individual services, letting you know how much you've bought and who has bought it.
ME6H: Vendor Evaluation	This report shows you the overall score for a vendor or group of vendors and the scores per individual main criterion or subcriterion. By changing the drilldown level, you can see the individual scores by plant, purchasing organization, or month.

Table 4.23 Purchasing Info System Reports

Drilldown levels All of these listed analyses can be viewed from different drilldown levels, which allow you to view the totals at different levels:

- ▸ Purchasing organization
- ▸ Plant
- ▸ Purchasing group
- ▸ Vendor
- ▸ Month
- ▸ Material
- ▸ Service

Each report has a different set of drilldown levels depending on the info-structure or structures where the data is being retrieved. You can display the drilldown levels of each analysis by clicking the DISPLAY STANDARD DRILLDOWN button (see Figure 4.48).

Most of these analysis will also allow you to change the display currency.

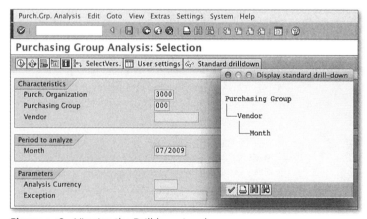

Figure 4.48 Viewing the Drilldown Levels

Key figures Each report also has a set of key figures, which are the fields that are available in each analysis. These key figures can be shown on the screen or can be brought up in a pop-up window by double clicking on any value figure on the screen (see Figure 4.49).

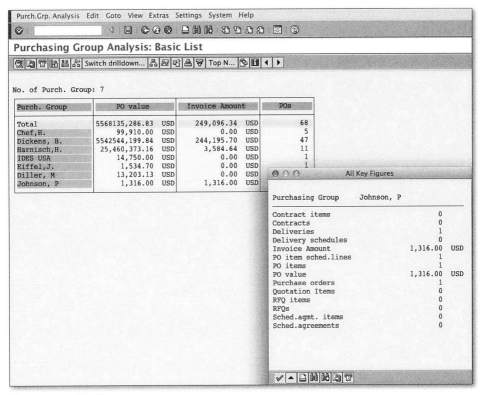

Figure 4.49 Key Figures

4.9 Summary

In this chapter, we discussed the different tools and documents provided by Purchasing in MM of the SAP ERP system to help you execute the different steps of the purchasing cycle.

We covered how to create an RFQ and send it to several vendors, and how to manually create a purchase requisition or how this is created automatically by the MRP system. We also discussed how these requisitions are converted to POs and how you can send them to the vendors by paper, email, or EDI.

Also in this chapter, we covered the different types of outline agreements and their possible uses. As part of creating these documents, we also discussed how they can be subject to approval levels and how this happens in the SAP system with the use of release strategies.

Another process covered in this chapter was the possibility of initiating in the system a return of goods to the vendor, and how to evaluate the vendors using criteria such as price, accuracy, punctuality, and quality of products.

And last, we gave you a look at how to obtain reports for all of these processes; including transactional reports or display lists, and also the analyses included in the PURCHIS purchasing info system.

Unfortunately, procurement processes aren't as simple as creating the purchase order for a supplier and then receiving and paying for the goods. That's why SAP makes special functions available to help you.

5 Special Procurement Functions

In Chapter 4, we covered common purchasing documents and procedures from contracts to scheduling agreements to purchase orders (POs) for standard items. You've learned how to order products using the material master and how to procure things without using the material master. Your business requirements, however, will usually go way outside this common path and into business procedures such as subcontracting, third-party ordering, cross-company transactions that move goods between sister companies and affiliates, and stock transfers between your own facilities. You can also trigger procurement transactions using Kanban—where procurement requirements are generated by the change in the status—commonly used in manufacturing environments. If you're on a retail system, you also trigger procurement using load builder, which is a feature that allows you to build truckloads of goods from a supplier based on configured order size definitions.

This chapter supplements the information you learned in Chapter 4, and finishes the complete view of core procurement activities, both standard and special. With that, let's start with the overview of the SAP subcontracting functionality.

5.1 Subcontracting

In this section, we walk through the first of the frequently used special procurement scenarios—subcontracting. There are many reasons to use subcontractors, but in general it's due to inability of the company to produce or to procure enough material in peak periods of demand at the cost lower than that proposed by a contract manufacturer. The classic SAP subcontracting scenario assumes that you're providing your contractor with the PO and all of the needed components using an outbound delivery, where components are defined in the bill of materials (BOM) for the finished good and listed on the PO. The subcontractor then provides the facilities and labor and assembles the final product and sends it back to you—all for a set price.

You then post goods receipt for the finished goods, consume components provided to the vendor, and at the end, you process the invoice from your supplier for the subcontracting service provided. We'll discuss this process in more detail in Section 5.1.2.

5.1.1 Master Data

The minimum master data needed to execute a subcontracting scenario requires some configuration to function correctly end to end; that is, from requirements to invoice payment.

Item category The process is driven by the item category of the PO—SUBCONTRACT-ING—which is predefined by SAP and can't be changed. This item category is also reflected in the purchasing info record definition as infotype subcontracting. The same item category flows through the purchasing documents from RFQ to receipt. Subcontracting orders must also have a BOM that lists all of the components you need to provide to the vendor making the product assembly for you. SAP provides a number of tools to allow provision of these components and monitoring.

In the following subsection, we'll start with a short overview of the underlying master data objects that drive this process.

Material Master

The material master drives the majority of the planning activities, and you now know that material requirements planning (MRP) views are behind most of the influencing factors. For the subcontracting scenario to work, your material master has to be defined to drive requirements directly to create subcontracting purchase requisitions. You can control that by using SAP predelivered special procurement key 30: SUBCONTRACTING, which you apply in the MRP 2 view and/or individual MRP AREA of material master transactions if this is how your planning strategies are defined. See Figure 5.1 for an example showing Transaction MM02.

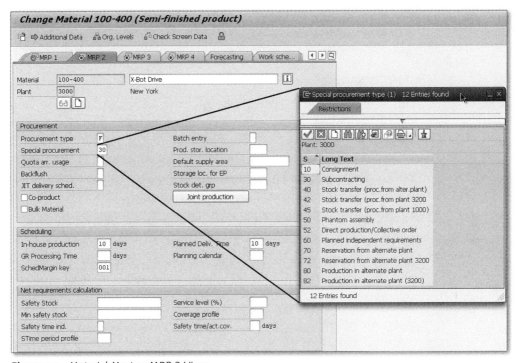

Figure 5.1 Material Master: MRP 2 View

The special procurement key is also very important if you manage the subcontractor as an MRP area, especially if you run other vendor deliveries to that subcontractor (we'll cover this in the example scenario further in this section). This information copies into the procurement proposal of the MRP run results either into a planned order or into a purchase requisition, depending on your planning configuration settings. To automatically convert the requirements to a purchase requisition, you need to set your procurement type on the material master by following these steps:

Convert requirements

1. Run Transaction MM02 (Material Master Change) if you're performing maintenance of an existing record or Transaction MM01 (Create) if you're creating a new entry.

2. In the procurement section of the same material master view, set the PROCUREMENT TYPE to F (EXTERNAL PROCUREMENT).

> **Note**
>
> Refer to Chapter 2 for detailed information on material master and transaction code references.

Bill of Materials

All finished goods subject for subcontracting need a list of components defined in a BOM, which is then used as a reference when components need to be provided to your subcontracting vendor. The BOM is defined the same way you define the assemblies to be produced internally in Production Planning (PP). The components are copied into your subcontract order during the BOM explosion. You can manipulate the BOM that is copied into your PO by adding or deleting items as needed.

Rules to automate selection

If you have only one set of BOMs, it's very easy to define master data for this process, but if you have many versions and alternatives to choose from, you can apply specific BOM selection methods to help automate the process:

▶ **Quantity**
Derived based on the lot size interval maintained on the BOM header. The MRP 4 view SELECTION METHOD field has to be blank. Figure 5.2 shows the material master MRP 4 example set to allow this procedure.

▶ **Validity date**
Validity date of the alternative BOMs is considered during BOM selection. The material master MRP 4 view selection method needs to be set to 1.

▶ **Production version**
Applicable if you have different versions for each of your suppliers. Maintain the production version on the MRP 4 view again, and also maintain the correct production version when creating purchasing documents.

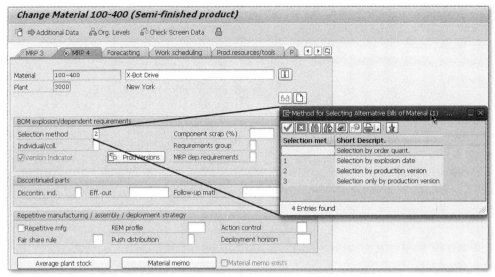

Figure 5.2 MRP 4 View: Selection Method Assignment

To maintain the components of the assembly, follow these steps:

Maintain assembly components

1. Run Transaction CS02 (Change BOM).

2. On the initial screen, enter the main assembly material number and plant, and specify the BOM usage type as 1 (PRODUCTION).

3. On the next screen, you'll find the list of components needed to build the assembly with item category (ICT) of L (material). Here you specify the quantities needed to build a base quantity of the assembly (1, for this example). See Figure 5.3 for the BOM example.

Change material BOM: General Item Overview

Material	100-400	X-Bot Drive
Plant	3000	New York
Alternative BOM	1	

Material / Document / General

Item	ICt	Component	Component description	Quantity	Un	A...	SIs	Valid From	Valid to
0010	L	100-420	Circuit board	1	PC	☐	☐	11/14/1994	12/31/9999
0020	L	101-100	Gearbox	1	PC	☑	☐	05/30/2013	12/31/9999
0030	L					☐	☐		

Figure 5.3 BOM: General Item Overview

BOM maintenance

In Table 5.1 you'll find some of the BOM maintenance transactions for your reference.

Transaction	Menu Path
CS01: Create	LOGISTICS • PRODUCTION • MASTER DATA • BILLS OF MATERIAL • BILL OF MATERIAL • MATERIAL BOM • CREATE
CS02: Change	LOGISTICS • PRODUCTION • MASTER DATA • BILLS OF MATERIAL • BILL OF MATERIAL • MATERIAL BOM • CHANGE
CS03: Display	LOGISTICS • PRODUCTION • MASTER DATA • BILLS OF MATERIAL • BILL OF MATERIAL • MATERIAL BOM • DISPLAY

Table 5.1 BOM Maintenance Transaction Codes

Subcontracting Info Record

Source determination

The second important component in the subcontracting process is the purchasing info record, which drives the source determination used in creation of purchase requisitions and POs. We covered the purchasing info records in detail in Chapter 2, so you can go back to refresh your memory on the basics and general usage of purchasing info records, if necessary.

The subcontracting scenario needs a special version of the purchasing info record that is defined as a subcontracting category type, indicated during the purchasing info record creation. Usually, the price maintained in the info record reflects the price for the service applied to build the assembly and not a price for the finished product that reflects what you paid for the part itself—strictly because you're supplying the components.

Maintain existing

To maintain the existing subcontracting info record, follow these steps:

1. Run Transaction ME12 (Info Record Change), and specify the info record category as SUBCONTRACTING together with the other information such as vendor, material number, purchasing organization, plant, or info record number.

2. On the detail screens, you'll see the info category confirming that it is in fact a subcontracting info record. You can maintain pricing and other relevant information here as well (see Figure 5.4).

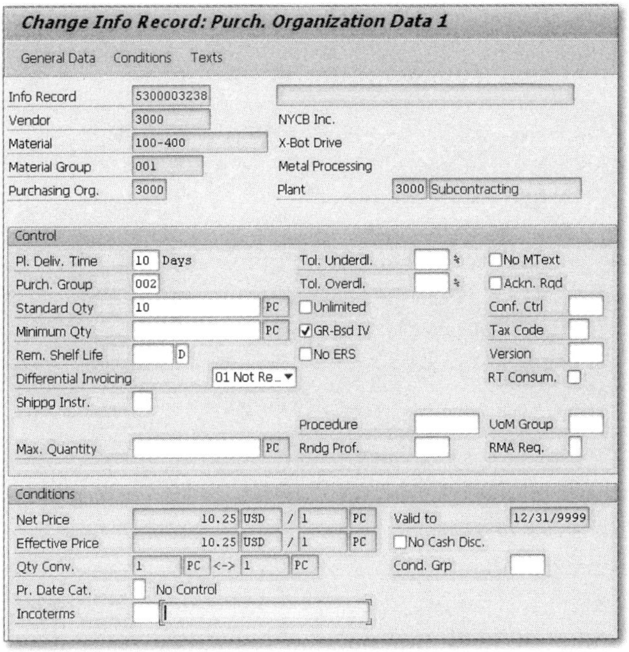

Figure 5.4 Subcontracting Purchasing Info Record: Purchasing Org Data

5.1.2 Subcontracting Process Flow Overview

You now have all required master data and configuration ready to support your subcontracting process. Let's now walk through a hypothetical subcontracting scenario as shown in Figure 5.5.

Imagine you're running plant 3000, and you have a main assembly material 100-400 (X-Bot Drive) that will be put together by a subcontracting vendor 3000 (NYCB Inc.). This material will have a BOM with some components provided by your company—plant 3000—and one of the components will be a subassembly—101-100 (Gearbox)—that will be built by another subcontractor, 5595 (Big Things Etc.), which you'll send to 3000 (NYCB Inc.), once received in your warehouse. You also plan, forecast, and manage inventory provided to vendor 5595 in your SAP system, as the MRP area. This will drive one of the components 100-120 (Flat Gasket) to be provided directly to them instead of your own warehouses (see the BOM hierarchy chart in Figure 5.6).

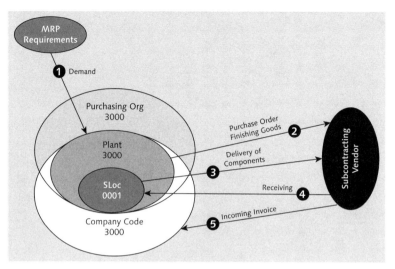

Figure 5.5 Subcontracting Process Flow

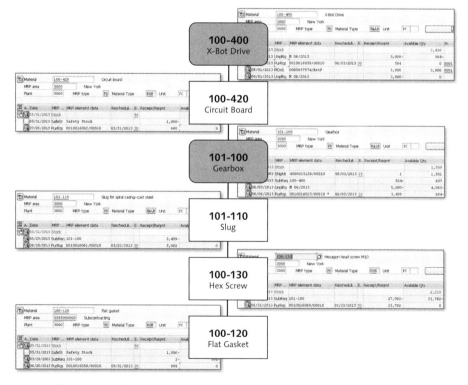

Figure 5.6 BOM Hierarchy Chart

Purchase requisitions and POs will be processed, and components will be provided to subcontractors. Finally, you'll receive the finished electronic assembly into your inventory and pay the incoming invoices for all parts and services performed.

Master data will drive all of the subsequent activities, and we'll walk you through this hypothetical scenario from demand to payment. Let's start with demand and planning.

Step 1: Process Demand

Demand for the X-Bot Drive sample material will come either from forecasts or the sales side of the world, and it will follow your standard planning procedures during the MRP run. If your planning configuration and settings allow for immediate purchase requisition creation, they will be created immediately; otherwise, planned orders will be created. You can analyze the results and consider next steps (refer to Chapter 3 for details on planning and forecasting steps).

In our scenario, the forecast drives the requirements for the X-Bot Drive, and all subsequent component demand creates dependent requirements calling for procurement proposals as well. You'll see the results of your planning run at the end of the MRP execution in Transaction MD02 (Stock/Requirements List) if you choose to display the MRP list. See the MRP results created for each of your example materials showing screen captures of Transaction MD04 (Stock Requirements List views) in Figure 5.7 and Figure 5.8.

Forecast

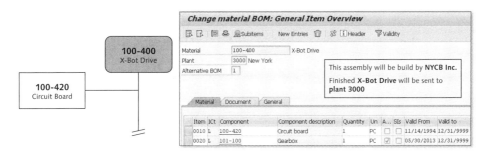

Figure 5.7 Transaction MD04: Stock/Requirements List Summary (Part 1)

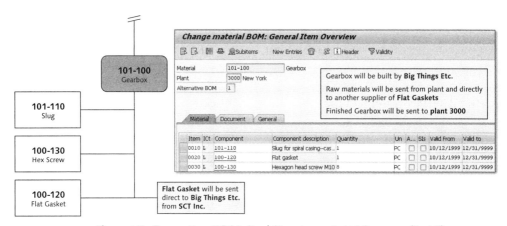

Figure 5.8 Transaction MD04: Stock/Requirements List Summary (Part 2)

See Table 5.2 for related transactions discussed in the subcontracting section (for a complete list of planning transactions, refer to Chapter 3).

Transaction	Menu Path
MD02: Multilevel Single-Item Planning	LOGISTICS • PRODUCTION • MRP • PLANNING • MULTILEVEL SINGLE-ITEM PLANNING
MD04: Stock/Reqmts List	LOGISTICS • MATERIALS MANAGEMENT • MATERIAL REQUIREMENTS PLANNING (MRP) • MRP • EVALUATIONS • STOCK/REQMTS LIST

Table 5.2 Reference Planning Transaction Codes

Step 2: Purchase Order

In the previous step, we talked about planning and processing requirements and dependent requirements of all items in the scenario. A couple of the purchase requisitions—for material 100-400 (X-Bot Drive) and for subassembly material 101-100 (Gearbox)—are referencing the components and showing the exploded view of the applicable BOM discussed in previous sections. You can access the component list by getting to the purchase requisition change Transaction ME52N. Figure 5.9 shows the MATERIALS tab with components displayed.

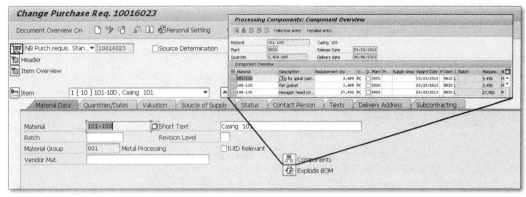

Figure 5.9 Purchase Requisition: Components List

Now you should review the list of created purchase requisitions by using Transaction ME5A, which lists the requisitions. You can perform sourcing if you want to only assign a source of supply using Transaction ME56. If you want to assign the source and process the requisition into POs, use Transaction ME57 (see an example of the sourcing transaction in Figure 5.10). For more details on conversions, refer to Chapter 4.

Review list of purchase requisitions

```
Assign Source of Supply to Requisitions

🔍 📭  Assign Automatically  📖 Assignments  📑 Assignment  Assign Manually


Material        Short Text                        PGp   Mat. Grp
Requisn   Item   Requested Qty  Un Deliv. Date Requester  Plnt SLoc
S C R QTy. I A   Ordered Qty    Un Release Date Trackg No.  SP1. MC


☐ 101-100        Casing 101                  001   001
  10016023  00010        3,499 PC  D 06/06/2013 MCHUDY   3000 0001
  N U   NB   L                        05/23/2013              001
  Info Rec      5300004251 Vendor  0000005595 P.Org 3000
☐ 100-120        Flat gasket                 001   001
  10016057  00010        7,644 PC  D 07/12/2013 MCHUDY   3000
  N U   NB                          07/01/2013              001
  Info Rec      5300003741 Vendor  0000003902 P.Org 3000
```

Figure 5.10 Assign Source of Supply

If you have a release procedure in place, approvals have to be applied before any further processing can take place. You can perform the conversion of purchase requisitions to POs using different transactions such as Transaction ME58 or Transaction ME59N. Using either one of these transactions produces a number of POs, including a couple of subcontract orders. In the scenario you're following, two of your purchase requisitions will be converted to subcontracting POs and require you to provide

Release procedure

components to vendors to complete the assemblies needed. Figure 5.11 shows material 100-400 and material 101-100.

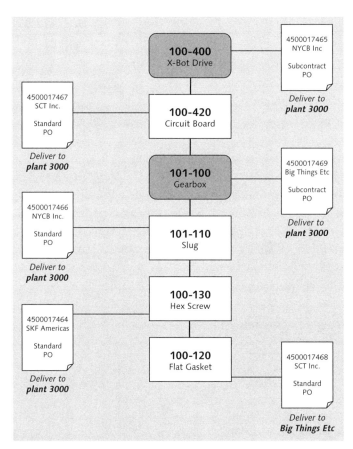

Figure 5.11 Purchase Orders: Scenario Overview

Your sample materials 100-400 (X-Bot Drive) and 101-100 (Gearbox) are both subcontracted items. This means that the POs created will have item category L (subcontracting) on the corresponding PO lines, and the components listed include items copied from purchase requisitions. You can re-explode the BOMs if you suspect changes took place between the time the requisition was generated and PO creation.

Most components will be delivered to plant 3000 and supplied to the subcontractors using the outbound delivery process from your facilities. This will be true for materials 100-420 (Circuit Board), 101-110 (Slug), and 100-130 (Hex Screw) as shown in Figure 5.10. The only exception to this rule is material 100-120 (Flat Gasket), which needs to be provided directly from the supplier 3902 (SCT Inc.) to the subcontractor 5959 (Big Things Etc.), making material 101-100 (Gearbox). This means that this PO will have a different delivery address assignment, so you need to enter the subcontracting vendor's number and check the subcontractor flag (SC VEND) (see Figure 5.12).

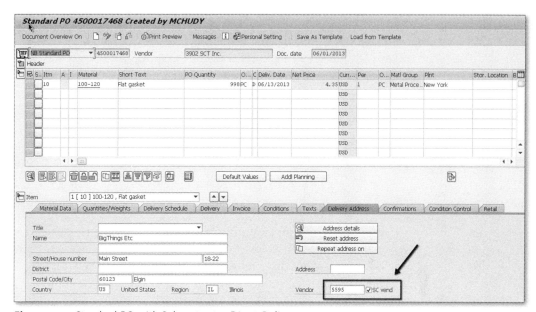

Figure 5.12 Standard PO with Subcontractor Direct Delivery

You now have all the POs placed for all assemblies and necessary components. Standard receiving procedures apply to receive all of these materials into your own inventory, and after they show up as on hand and available, you can provide the materials as needed to the corresponding subcontractors. You can find commonly used transactions in the purchasing step of the subcontracting process in Table 5.3.

Transaction	Menu Path
ME5A: General List of Purchase Requisitions	LOGISTICS • MATERIALS MANAGEMENT • PURCHASING • PURCHASE REQUISITION • LIST DISPLAYS • GENERAL
ME56: Assign Source of Supply	LOGISTICS • MATERIALS MANAGEMENT • PURCHASING • PURCHASE REQUISITION • FOLLOW-ON FUNCTIONS • ASSIGN
ME57: Assign Source of Supply and Process	LOGISTICS • MATERIALS MANAGEMENT • PURCHASING • PURCHASE REQUISITION • FOLLOW-ON FUNCTIONS • ASSIGN AND PROCESS
ME58: Create PO Via Requisition Assignment List	LOGISTICS • MATERIALS MANAGEMENT • PURCHASING • PURCHASE ORDER • CREATE • VIA ASSIGNMENT LIST
ME59N: Create PO Automatically via Purchase Requisitions	LOGISTICS • MATERIALS MANAGEMENT • PURCHASING • PURCHASE ORDER • CREATE • AUTOMATICALLY VIA PURCHASE REQUISITIONS
ME21N: Create Purchase Order	LOGISTICS • MATERIALS MANAGEMENT • PURCHASING • PURCHASE ORDER • CREATE • VENDOR/SUPPLYING PLANT KNOWN
ME22N: Change	LOGISTICS • MATERIALS MANAGEMENT • PURCHASING • PURCHASE ORDER • CHANGE

Table 5.3 Reference Purchasing Transaction Codes

Step 3: Delivery of Components

The POs placed with your supplier list the exploded BOM components for materials you need to provide to the subcontractor to complete the manufacturing process. These components can be managed as a separate bucket designed just for this process.

Monitor stock provided to vendor

Components provided to your subcontractors are managed in a separate stock category called *stock provided to vendor*. This is shown on the books of the company as your own inventory. Stock provided to vendor also has special characteristics and use restrictions:

▸ Managed at the plant level, with the vendor code designation and available for MRP.

- Maintained and transferable between two stock types:

  - Unrestricted stock in which consumption can be posted only from unrestricted stock

  - Quality inspection stock

- Stock of material provided to vendor allowed for physical inventory.

Just as with regular materials, you can monitor your stock provided to vendor with these steps:

1. Access Transaction MMBE (Stock Overview) or Transaction ME2O (SC Stock at Vendor).

2. When using Transaction MMBE, check the SPECIAL STOCKS indicator on the initial selection screen.

3. After your material information is displayed, double-click on the STOCK PROVIDED TO VENDOR line to access the information showing per vendor quantity breakdown (see Figure 5.13).

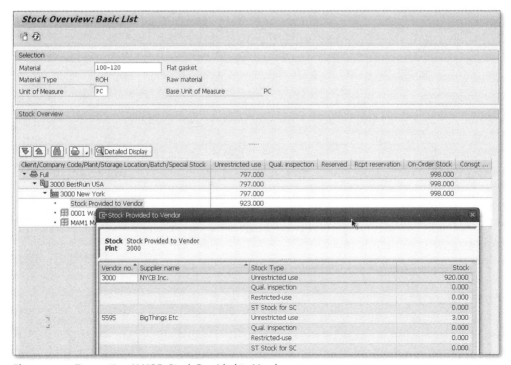

Figure 5.13 Transaction MMBE: Stock Provided to Vendor

When accessing this data using Transaction ME2O (Stock at Subcontractor), you can provide the subcontractor vendor account and plant, and use components or assembly as a selection criteria. The report shows you what has been already provided to the subcontractor, including the material number and also the requirements generated from unprocessed subcontract purchase requisitions, POs, delivery documents, or external deliveries from other vendors supplying the subcontractor directly (see Figure 5.14).

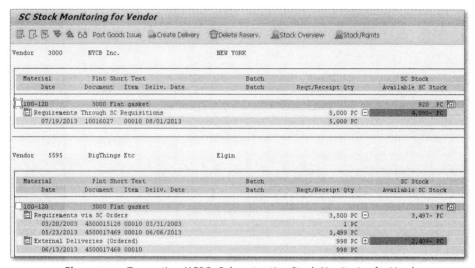

Figure 5.14 Transaction ME2O: Subcontracting Stock Monitoring for Vendor

Supply materials to subcontractors Now that you know how to monitor stock provided to a vendor, we'll walk through the different ways of supplying materials to your subcontracting partners. As we mentioned earlier, you can supply them from your own plant using either a logistics outbound delivery process or inventory management transfers, or directly via a PO from another vendor with the subcontract vendor as the delivery address. Transaction ME2O (Stock at Subcontractor) enables you to execute all of these delivery flavors from one spot.

You can provide the materials to your subcontractor by following these steps:

1. Click the Post Goods Issue button on the transaction button ribbon or use function key F7 to perform an immediate transfer posting using movement type 541 from your on-hand inventory directly to stock provided to the vendor (see Figure 5.15). This initiates immediate transfer of material 100-420 from plant 3000 and storage location 0002.

2. In the pop-up window, you can specify the quantity to be delivered or press Enter to continue. Transaction ME2O (Transfer Posting) completes, and the confirmation message appears.

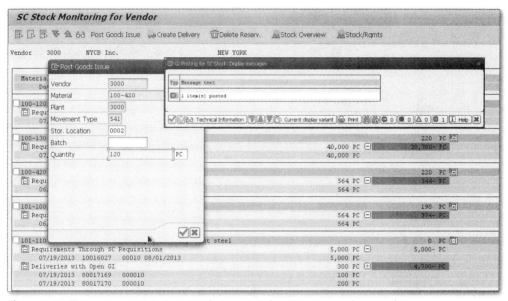

Figure 5.15 Transaction ME2O: Post Goods Issue to Subcontracting Stock at Vendor

The second method is to use the outbound delivery in the process. You can access the same Transaction ME2O and click on the Create Delivery button on the ribbon or press Ctrl + F5.

Outbound delivery

1. In the pop-up window, overwrite the proposed delivery quantity, and press Enter to continue. The delivery document is created, and the confirmation message appears with the delivery number issued (see Figure 5.16). You're providing material 101-110 from plant 3000 and storage location 0002.

2. If your Logistics business processes require it, execute the subsequent pick/pack steps, and finally the post goods issue will remove the quantities of materials from your on-hand inventory location and transfer it to the stock provided to vendor category, thereby increasing the stock balance numbers.

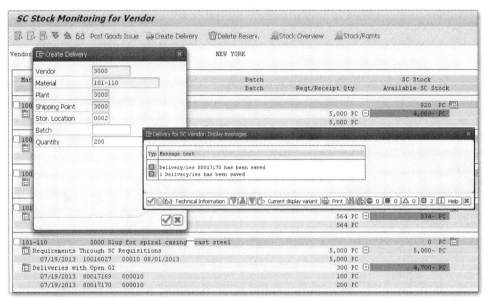

Figure 5.16 Transaction ME2O: Create Delivery to Subcontracting Stock at Vendor

Transfer posting The third method of providing your subcontractor with components from your own plant is by initiating the transfer posting using inventory transactions such as Transaction MIGO or the older Transaction MB1B using movement type 541.

Components from different vendor The fourth method we've partially covered is providing components from another vendor and delivering them directly to the subcontract partner. You can order them at the regular vendor, and then simply enter the subcontractor's delivery address in the PO DELIVERY tab, and select the indicator SC VEND (refer to Figure 5.12 for examples). The components are posted directly to the material provided to the vendor at the time of the goods receipt.

After all of the required components are provided to the subcontractor, check the material status by running Transaction ME2O (SC Stock Monitoring). All of the materials now have the status AVAILABLE—showing green—and all requirements are no longer displayed, as shown in Figure 5.17.

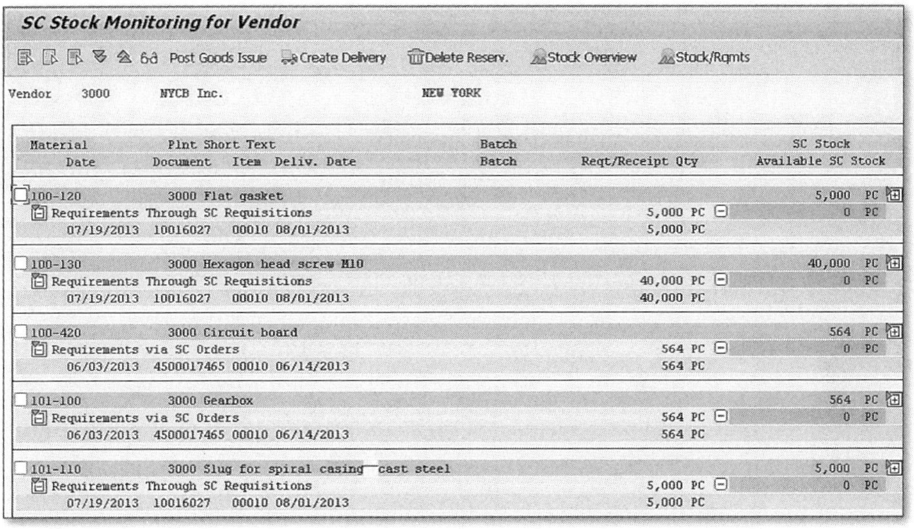

Check material status

Figure 5.17 Subcontracting Stock Monitoring: Components Provided to Vendor

You can also run Transaction MBLB (Stocks at Subcontractor) to report on materials, on-hand balances, and valuation of all materials at the subcontractor. It's important to have all required components because during receipt of the finished assemblies, the components are consumed from inventory at the same time. So if you have any shortages, the receipt transaction won't complete.

All of the transactions used to monitor and provide components to your subcontractor are listed for your reference in Table 5.4.

Transaction	Menu Path
MMBE: Stock Overview	INFORMATION SYSTEMS • GENERAL REPORT SELECTION • MATERIALS MANAGEMENT • INVENTORY MANAGEMENT • STOCK OVERVIEW

Table 5.4 Reference Subcontracting Monitoring and Provision Transaction Codes

Transaction	Menu Path
MBLB: Stock with Subcontractor	LOGISTICS • MATERIALS MANAGEMENT • PURCHASING • PURCHASE ORDER • REPORTING • SC STOCK PER VENDOR
ME2O: SC Stock per Vendor	LOGISTICS • MATERIALS MANAGEMENT • PURCHASING • PURCHASE ORDER • REPORTING • SC STOCK PER VENDOR
MIGO: Goods Movement	LOGISTICS • MATERIALS MANAGEMENT • INVENTORY MANAGEMENT • GOODS MOVEMENT • GOODS MOVEMENT (MIGO)
MB1B: Transfer Posting	LOGISTICS • MATERIALS MANAGEMENT • INVENTORY MANAGEMENT • GOODS MOVEMENT • TRANSFER POSTING

Table 5.4 Reference Subcontracting Monitoring and Provision Transaction Codes (Cont.)

Step 4: Receiving

In the example scenario, you post goods receipts for all component materials, receiving them into plant 3000, before sending them out to the subcontractors as described in Step 3. Now we'll talk about the actual receipt of finished goods.

When the subcontracting vendor is ready to send the final products back to you, use your standard inbound delivery processing. Upon arrival, goods receipt posting automatically places materials into your on-hand inventory at the plant storage location and consumes components from stock provided to the vendor at the same time.

Post goods receipt   Follow these steps to post a goods receipt:

1. Access Transaction MIGO or Transaction MIGO_GR.

2. Specify the type of transaction you're posting by selecting GOODS RECEIPT in the ACTION dropdown field, and then selecting a type of receipt in the next ACTION field where you pick PURCHASE ORDER.

3. Specify the subcontracting PURCHASE ORDER number, and press ⌷Enter⌷ to continue.

4. Purchase order details are displayed, and you can explode the main PO line to show the list of components that will be consumed when the receipt is posted. You have to check the OK checkbox, verify the receiving quantity, and when ready click the POST button or use `Shift` + `F11` (see Figure 5.18).

We'll talk in detail about different flavors of inbound processing (such as receiving using inbound deliveries) in the upcoming chapters.

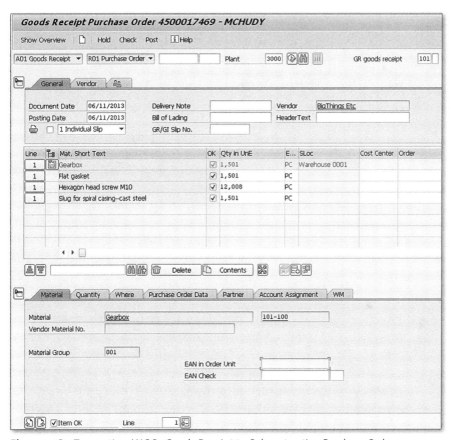

Figure 5.18 Transaction MIGO: Goods Receipt to Subcontracting Purchase Order

Your subassembly 101-100 Gearbox was received into plant 3000 from vendor 5959 (Big Things Etc.), and then was sent as a component to 3000

(NYCB Inc.) for final assembly of 100-400 (X-Bot Drive). So both receipts consumed components provided to the subcontractor using movement type 543 (in column M...), and posted finished assemblies to on-hand inventory using movement type 101 (in column M...) (see Figure 5.19). This figure shows material and material document for the receipt of the product in LINE 1 of each screen shown, and consumption of provided components right below it.

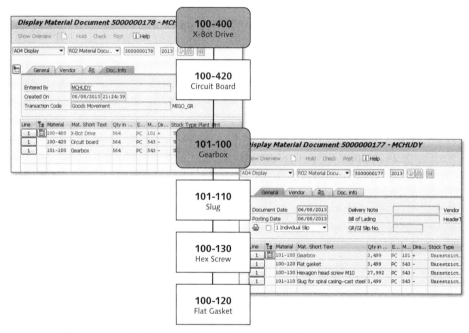

Figure 5.19 Goods Receipt for Subcontracting Orders

Verify stock positions In this scenario, the stock positions at the vendors have changed to reflect the consumption of components provided. You can verify this by running Transaction ME2O (SC Stock per Vendor) to monitor the report after the receipt takes place. It now shows no open unprocessed requirements and confirms the goods movement has completed the process. We captured some of the transaction codes used in the receiving process for your reference in Table 5.5.

Transaction	Menu Path
MIGO: Goods Movement (MIGO)	LOGISTICS • MATERIALS MANAGEMENT • INVENTORY MANAGEMENT • GOODS MOVEMENT • GOODS MOVEMENT (MIGO)
MIGO_GR: GR for Purchase Order (MIGO)	LOGISTICS • MATERIALS MANAGEMENT • INVENTORY MANAGEMENT • GOODS MOVEMENT • FOR PURCHASE ORDER • GR FOR PURCHASE ORDER (MIGO)

Table 5.5 Goods Receipt Transaction Codes

Step 5: Incoming Invoice

You're now ready to process incoming invoice receipts and pay for the subcontracting services provided. In the example scenario, we've created two subcontract POs for the following:

▸ Subassembly 101-120: Gearbox with vendor 5959, Big Things Etc.

▸ Assembly 100-400: X-Bot Drive with vendor 3000, NYCB Inc.

The next step is to enter the incoming vendor invoices into the system. This function is usually performed by the finance department. We'll talk a bit more about the invoicing in detail in the next chapters, so we only give a brief overview of Transaction MIRO (Enter Incoming Invoice) here. When you start the transaction for the first time and you have multiple company codes in your organizational structure, you'll be asked to specify the company code before you access the detailed data screen (see Figure 5.20). You can now fill in all the required information to process your vendor's invoice:

1. Specify the INVOICE DATE in the BASIC DATA tab.

2. On the bottom portion of the transaction screen, select the PO REFERENCE tab where you enter the PURCHASE ORDER NUMBER.

3. Specify the invoice amount in the BASIC DATA tab of the transaction, and then you can either simulate posting to check for errors or click the SAVE button to create the invoice document for your PO.

Pay for services

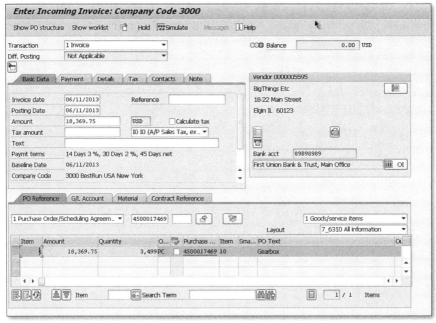

Figure 5.20 Transaction MIRO: Enter Incoming Invoice

With the invoice processing and outgoing payment to the vendor, you've completed the subcontracting process steps. See Table 5.6 for transaction code and menu path information.

Transaction	Menu Path
MIRO: Goods Movement (MIGO)	LOGISTICS • MATERIALS MANAGEMENT • LOGISTICS INVOICE VERIFICATION • DOCUMENT ENTRY • ENTER INVOICE

Table 5.6 Enter Invoice Transaction Code

5.2 Third-Party Order

Third-party sales orders are a pretty common scenario in the business world. In this scenario, you're basically arranging to ship goods directly from your supplier to the customer on your behalf. In SAP ERP, your order will have a third-party item category defined to immediately create a purchase requisition, and via your standard procurement processes, you'll end up creating a PO and sending it to your vendor. The PO presented to your vendor will have the shipping address of your customer instead of your own facilities.

Upon delivery, your vendor will notify you that the goods left their facilities. This triggers your receiving process, which then ends up with invoice and payables to your supplier. You finish up with a billing document to your customer. We'll cover the process steps shown in Figure 5.21 in detail in Section 5.2.3.

Process steps

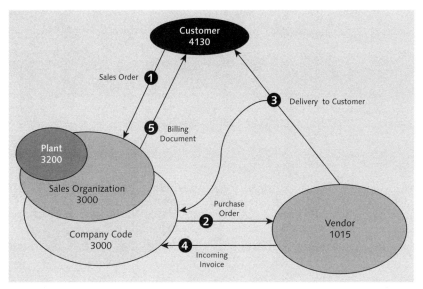

Figure 5.21 Third-Party Process Flow Overview

5.2.1 Configuration Prerequisites

Just like the previous subcontracting scenario, you also must have certain configuration settings and master data in place before you can execute this model.

The first configuration piece is on the MM side of the SAP world. In the MM component, there need to be the correct account assignment controls and combinations that are required to collect accounting postings into the correct buckets. The standard SAP system has this setup ready for you to use in the configuration table shown in Figure 5.22−1 (THIRD-PARTY)−defining the account assignment category for third-party process with detailed posting controls and fields where you can define whether certain fields are required, optional, or not needed at all. To do this, run Transaction SPRO by following the menu path MATERIALS MANAGEMENT • PURCHASING • ACCOUNT ASSIGNMENT • MAINTAIN ACCOUNT ASSIGNMENT CATEGORIES.

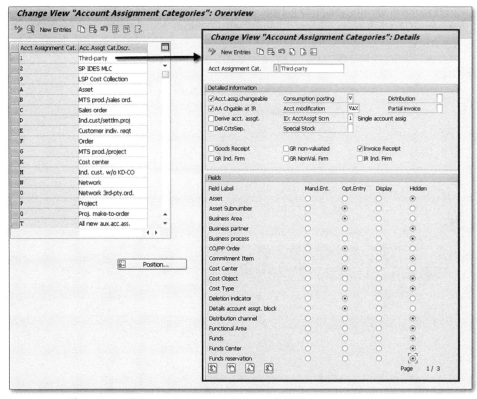

Figure 5.22 Account Assignment Category Overview

Assign purchasing item/account assigned category

The second piece of the puzzle is in the assigning the allowed purchasing item category and account assigned category that we just talked about. Access the following configuration node: MATERIALS MANAGEMENT • PURCHASING • ACCOUNT ASSIGNMENT • DEFINE COMBINATION OF ITEM CATEGORIES/ACCOUNT ASSIGNMENT CATEGORIES. In this configuration screen, you link the item category (ITCAT.) with the account assignment category (ACC.ASSGT CAT.DSCR.) to create allowed combinations. Figure 5.23 shows the standard configuration for this scenario.

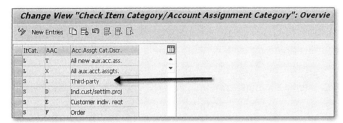

Figure 5.23 Item Category/Account Assignment Category Overview

And finally, the third required configuration piece is related to the sales document type, item category, and schedule line category definition, assignment, and determination. You can access the maintenance view using customizing Transaction VOV6 (Maintain Schedule Line Categories) or the SAP IMG menu. This configuration applies a component of the sales order in which the order type can be specific to the third party if you need to isolate this activity at the document level, or if you're using standard document type OR (standard order), verify usage of item category TAS (third party item). The schedule line category CS (leg) is a final piece that ties back to the MM configuration portion we covered earlier, which is assigning the defined PURCHASING item category (5 - THIRD PARTY), and the account assignment category (1 - THIRD PARTY) to complete the process (see Figure 5.24 for configuration details). This assignment provides the transfer mechanism of the requirements between sales order and subsequent purchasing documents.

Transfer between sales order and purchasing documents

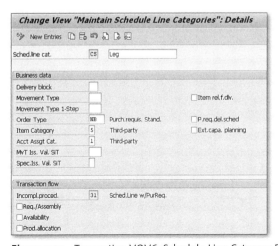

Figure 5.24 Transaction VOV6: Schedule Line Category Definition

Schedule line The schedule line makes a connection to the purchasing side of this scenario to define the behavior of to-be-generated purchase requisitions. This schedule line configuration setting allows you to transition your sales order to a purchase requisition and finally to a purchase order. Table 5.7 shows how data is passed between these documents, and what item categories and account assignment are applied on the purchasing side of this scenario.

Sales Order	Purchase Requisition	Purchase Order
Material	Material	Material
Quantity	Quantity	Quantity
Item Category: TAS Schedule Line: CS	Item Category: S Account Assignment: 1	Item Category: S Account Assignment: 1
Delivery Date	Delivery Date	Delivery Date

Table 5.7 Data Transfers from Sales Order to Purchase Order

In Table 5.8, you can find the transaction codes and IMG configuration path to maintain entries we've just discussed.

Transaction	Menu Path
SPRO: Customizing – Edit Project	MATERIALS MANAGEMENT • PURCHASING • ACCOUNT ASSIGNMENT • MAINTAIN ACCOUNT ASSIGNMENT CATEGORIES
SPRO: Customizing – Edit Project	MATERIALS MANAGEMENT • PURCHASING • ACCOUNT ASSIGNMENT • DEFINE COMBINATION OF ITEM CATEGORIES/ACCOUNT ASSIGNMENT CATEGORIES

Table 5.8 Account Assignment/Item Category Definition Transaction Codes

5.2.2 Master Data

Default item category This leads us to the next step needed to complete this process—editing the material master data. Access this screen using Transaction MM02 (Material Master Change). If required by your business needs, you can permanently default the item category of your material to TAS (THIRD-PARTY ITEM) by using standard configuration values in the material master SALES ORG 2 view and setting the item category group field to BANS (THIRD-PARTY

ITEM). Figure 5.25 shows the material master view for the SALES ORG 2 tab. This setting causes your item category determination to always select item category TAS for orders with materials to be exclusively procured from an external supplier and shipped directly to your customers.

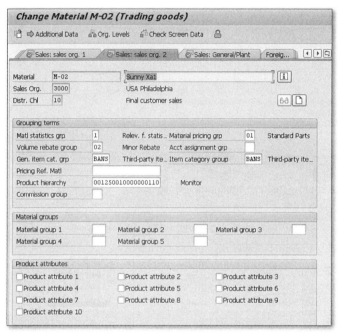

Figure 5.25 Material Master: Sales Org 2 View Maintenance

However, if you need flexibility in processing your orders in a variety of different ways and only sometimes have your supplier send the goods to your customers, leave the settings alone, and treat this item as your standard setting (e.g., NORM). Make sure, however, that in your item category determination, you allow for a manual selection of item category TAS—this is normally done by a system analyst in Customizing. You can also refer back to Section 5.2.1 detailing the item categories and schedule lines.

5.2.3 Third-Party Process Flow Overview

Let's get back to our scenario. You're a marketing company (company code 3000, BestRun USA) that doesn't have any manufacturing or inventory capability. You're leveraging your relationship with a supplier to fulfill your requirements and ship direct to the customer on your behalf. Your customer (4130, CompuTech) places an order with your sales organization 3000. The sales order item category is determined to be TAS, and when saved, a subsequent purchase requisition and finally a PO is issued to your supplier—vendor 1015, Wollner AG. Figure 5.26 shows the TAS item category in the sales order overview.

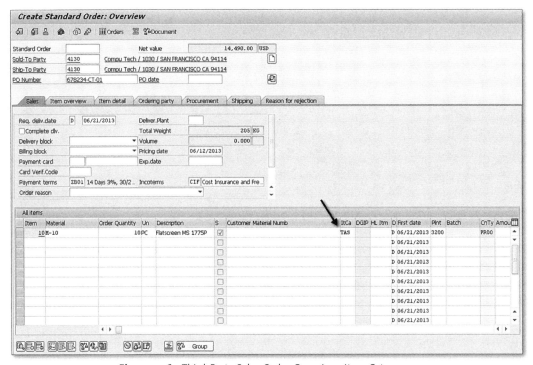

Figure 5.26 Third-Party Sales Order Overview: Item Category

Your vendor ships the goods from its warehouse directly to your customer and notifies you about the completed delivery (this might be a manual step requiring a phone call, fax, email, etc.). The vendor then presents you (company code 3000, BestRun USA) with the invoice, which is received by your accounts payables department. You can complete your scenario now by issuing the standard billing document to your customer and collect the receivables.

Next let's walk through execution of all of the required steps in detail. You may want to refer to the process overview steps shown in Figure 5.5 earlier in this chapter.

Step 1: Creating a Third-Party Sales Order

We'll start the process by creating the third-party sales order using Trans-action VA01 (Create Order).

Transaction VA01

1. On the CREATE SALES ORDER INITIAL SCREEN, enter the sales order document type, such as "OR" (standard order), and enter the SALES ORGANIZATION as "3000", DISTRIBUTION CHANNEL as "10", and DIVISION as "00", for this example. Press Enter.

2. Enter the number for the CUSTOMER SOLD-TO—for this example, use "4130 - CompuTech"—and press Enter to determine other partners.

3. On the line item, enter the MATERIAL. For this example, enter "M-10" as defined earlier for the third-party process on the material master SALES ORG 2 view.

4. Enter the requested quantity in the PO QUANTITY column. Enter the price in NET PRICE column if pricing conditions aren't maintained, and the TAS item category will be determined for you as shown in Figure 5.27.

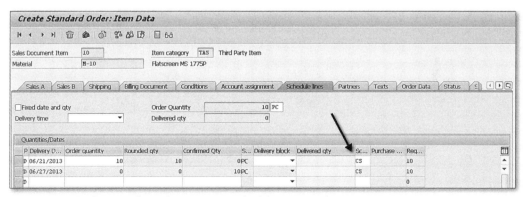

Figure 5.27 Third-Party Sales Order Item Data: Schedule Line Details

Review details Now you can review the details of the schedule lines created. Note that the CS-Leg schedule line category has been determined. See Figure 5.27 for details.

1. To get to this screen, select your item on the Overview screen, and then click on the Schedule Lines For Item icon on the bottom of the screen or select Go To • Item • Schedule Lines from the pulldown menus, and click on the Purch Requisition icon on the bottom portion of the screen.

2. On the detail overview of the purchase requisition, you'll see all of the data proposed for the PO to be created upon conversion of the purchase requisition (see Figure 5.28 for more details).

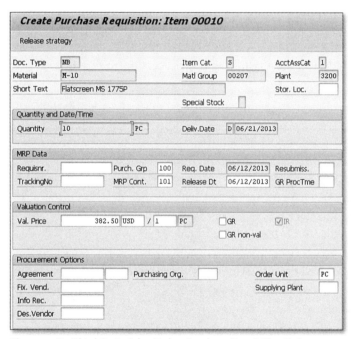

Figure 5.28 Third-Party Sales Order: Purchase Requisition Data

3. After you're done reviewing all your entries, save your order. Not only is your sales order created and saved, but the corresponding purchase requisition is created and saved as well.

4. Verify the order by going back to the schedule line details, and now you'll see the actual document number in the PURCHASE REQUISITION column.

In Table 5.9, you can find some of the sales order transactions that we've used or can be used in this process.

Transaction	Menu Path
VA01: Create	LOGISTICS • SALES AND DISTRIBUTION • SALES • ORDER • CREATE
VA02: Change	LOGISTICS • SALES AND DISTRIBUTION • SALES • ORDER • CHANGE
VA03: Display	LOGISTICS • SALES AND DISTRIBUTION • SALES • ORDER • DISPLAY

Table 5.9   Create Sales Order Transaction Codes

Step 2: Create Purchase Order

In this step, you create a PO from an already created purchase requisition. This procedure is identical to the steps in the subcontracting process covered in the previous sections.

Create PO from purchase requisition

Again, conversion can be done manually using Transaction ME21N (Create Purchase Order), or it can be done using conversion Transaction ME59N (Automatically via Purchase Requisitions).

At the end, you'll have a PO issued to your vendor (in this scenario, it's Vendor 1015) where the delivery address belongs to your customer. Figure 5.29 shows the DELIVERY ADDRESS tab of the PO you just created.

Note
Note that the PO item column A (ACCOUNT ASSIGNMENT) with the value 1 (THIRD-PARTY) and column I (ITEM CATEGORY) with value S (THIRD-PARTY) are the results of the configuration settings described earlier in Section 5.2.1.

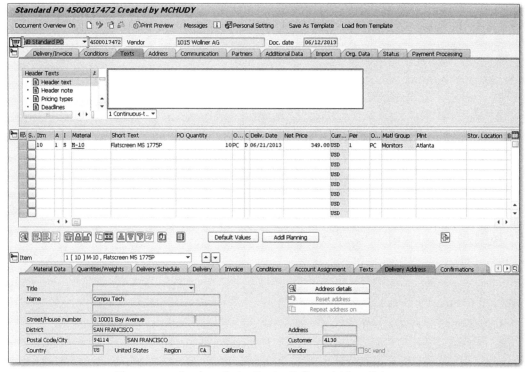

Figure 5.29 Purchase Order Create: Delivery Address Tab

Step 3: Delivery to Customer: Receiving

Goods receipt for PO

The vendor sends the goods to your customer and notifies you that the delivery has been completed. This is a trigger to execute the goods receipt transaction for your PO. This is procedurally almost exactly the same as what we've covered in the subcontracting scenario. Perform the steps as follows:

1. Start the goods receipt process using Transaction MIGO (Goods Receipt for PO) and selecting goods receipt for the PO.

2. Specify the PO number created in the previous steps.

3. Verify that all of the data is correct, mark the item OK checkbox on the bottom of the Transaction MIGO screen, and click the POST button.

The material document is created and captures your receipt information.

Step 4: Enter Incoming Invoice

The next step is to enter the incoming invoice into the system. This is also similar to what we've discussed in the subcontracting scenario before, so we'll only give you a brief refresher on performing these steps.

1. To record the incoming invoice from your vendor use Transaction MIRO (Enter Incoming Invoice).

2. On the entry screen, specify the invoice date.

3. On the bottom portion of the transaction screen, select the PO REFERENCE tab—and there you enter your purchase order number from the previous steps.

4. Specify the invoice amount in the BASIC DATA tab of the transaction, and you can either simulate posting to check for errors or click the SAVE button to create the invoice document for your PO.

Step 5: Send Billing Document

We're now back to the Sales and Distribution (SD) side of the world to finish off the process and send the invoice to the customer. You can do this using Transaction VF01 (Create Billing Document).

Send invoice to customer

1. On the CREATE BILLING DOCUMENT initial screen, enter the sales order number from the previous steps in the DOCUMENT column, and press `Enter`.

2. Verify the pricing condition details: locate condition type VPRS – COST, which should equal the purchase price you've been invoiced for from your supplier. This value will be used for calculations of your profits that will ultimately post to Profitability Analysis (CO-PA). See Figure 5.30 for details.

3. Save your billing document to complete the process.

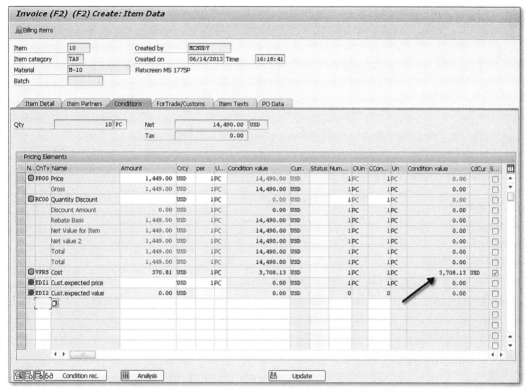

Figure 5.30 Create Invoice: Cost Condition on the Condition Tab

In Table 5.10, you can find some of the billing transactions that we've demonstrated or can be used instead to create/maintain invoices.

Transaction	Menu Path
VF01: Create	LOGISTICS • SALES AND DISTRIBUTION • BILLING • BILLING DOCUMENT • CREATE
VF02: Change	LOGISTICS • SALES AND DISTRIBUTION • BILLING • BILLING DOCUMENT • CHANGE
VF03: Display	LOGISTICS • SALES AND DISTRIBUTION • BILLING • BILLING DOCUMENT • DISPLAY

Table 5.10 Billing Document Transaction Codes

5.3 Stock Transport Orders

When you have a company with multiple plants or warehouses, stock movements between your own facilities are common in almost any type of industry, especially in the hub-spoke relationships, and SAP provides multiple methods to accommodate this need. In this section, we'll concentrate on stock transport orders (STOs), which use purchasing documents to initiate movement. The STO can be processed using Logistics Execution components (delivery, pick, pack, warehouse management transfer orders) or just simple Inventory Management movements.

Internal movement

An STO is a form of internal PO placed by the requesting plant as demand on another issuing plant within the same organizational structures — company code and sales organization. This transfer can be executed using a procedure that either involves creation of an outbound delivery or just a simple inventory posting of movement types to complete the transfer of goods. You can have the following types of STO procedures:

Definition and procedures

- **Without outbound delivery**
  You use a two-step procedure where the shipping plant places the inventory in in-transit, and receiving at the requesting plant places the inventory in the plant's own unrestricted stock (see Section 7.3.3 for details).

- **With outbound delivery**
  When delivering between plants or storage locations (see Section 7.3.4 and Section 7.3.5 for more details):

  - One-step procedure: Goods receipt at the receiving plant immediately post goods issue at the shipping plant.

  - Two-step procedure: Goods issue in the shipping plant is executed first, and goods are then placed in the receiving plant stock in transit. The second step posts a final transfer from in-transit to own stock at the plant.

You can use the STO process not only between plants, but also between storage locations, which gives you even more flexibility to move stock between lower level enterprise structures.

Using the STO process gives you the ability to treat these types of transfers with a high degree of flexibility, visibility, and traceability across all involved components:

▶ **Planning**
The plant-to-plant relationship can be formalized, and MRP can be applied easily to use the demand coming out of one plant and place it on another.

▶ **Procurement**
The requirements can be converted to purchase requisitions and then into STOs using the same functions as any other standard purchasing documents.

▶ **Logistics**
You can plan and schedule deliveries and shipments just like you do with any other type of outbound deliveries processed from your shipping/supplying plant perspective to manage transportation costs.

▶ **Inventory Management**
This gives you the ability to monitor the stock in transit and to treat the receiving of your intra-company shipments as you would any other incoming vendor delivery.

▶ **PO history and document flow**
All STO transactions and actions taken are recorded in the PO history, along with whether outbound deliveries are used in the document flow.

Other transfer methods
You can move inventory between plants using other methods such as the following:

▶ **Plant-to-plant transfer postings**
You can use this method to bypass the Logistics component and apply inventory movements instead (we'll talk in detail about the transfer postings in Chapter 8).

▶ **Cross-company code STO with delivery and billing document**
This is basically a cross-company PO process, which we'll cover in the next section of this chapter.

5.3.1 Configuration Prerequisites

The STO scenario requires document types specific to the intra-company movements and a set of movement types to accommodate the postings. The default purchasing document type for this process is a UB (STOCK TRANSPORT ORDER), and the corresponding item category is U (STOCK TRANSFER). If you're planning on using the STO with outbound delivery, the provided default delivery type for movements within the same company code is NL.

Document types

We won't go through all configuration nodes needed to set up the STO process; we'll just mention some of those that are relevant for processes using outbound deliveries. You can find all of the related configuration nodes in the IMG Customizing using Transaction SPRO and the following menu path: MATERIALS MANAGEMENT • PURCHASING • PURCHASE ORDER • SET UP STOCK TRANSPORT ORDER.

If you need to set up the STOs between storage locations, use the following menu path: MATERIALS MANAGEMENT • PURCHASING • PURCHASE ORDER • SET UP STOCK TRANSPORT ORDER • SET UP STOCK TRANSFER BETWEEN STORAGE LOCATIONS.

When dealing with STOs with outbound deliveries, one of the important configuration pieces is to link your plants to the customer master account representing the plant within the sales area responsible for the STO shipments. We'll discuss this more in the master data section, along with the purchasing document type, shipping plant, delivery type, and ATP checking rule.

Link plant to customer master account

Figure 5.31 shows the configuration of an outbound delivery scenario in node ASSIGN DELIVERY TYPE AND CHECKING RULE. This configuration setting plays an important part in outbound delivery processing; item category determination, which pulls in the links to schedule lines; and eventually movement types used in the STO with outbound delivery two-step process.

> **Note**
>
> If you're *not* planning on using the outbound deliveries in your STO processing, you don't have to maintain any of the Logistics settings because direct inventory movement will be applied instead.

Ty.	DT Dscr.	SPl	Name 1	DlTy.	Descript...	CRl	Descri...	S...	R...	Delivery type 1	Delivery type 2	DT...	A..	Req. ...	A
UB	Stock transpor...	3000	New York	NL	Replenish...	A	SD order						E		
UB	Stock transpor...	3050	UK												
UB	Stock transpor...	3100	Chicago	NL	Replenish...	B	SD deliv...								
UB	Stock transpor...	3105	Chicago												
UB	Stock transpor...	3110	Auto Suppl...												
UB	Stock transpor...	3111	Auto OEM ...												
UB	Stock transpor...	3112	Auto Whol...												
UB	Stock transpor...	3150	Columbus	NL	Replenish...	A	SD order								
UB	Stock transpor...	3200	Atlanta			B	SD deliv...			NL	NLCC				
UB	Stock transpor...	3300	Los Angeles												

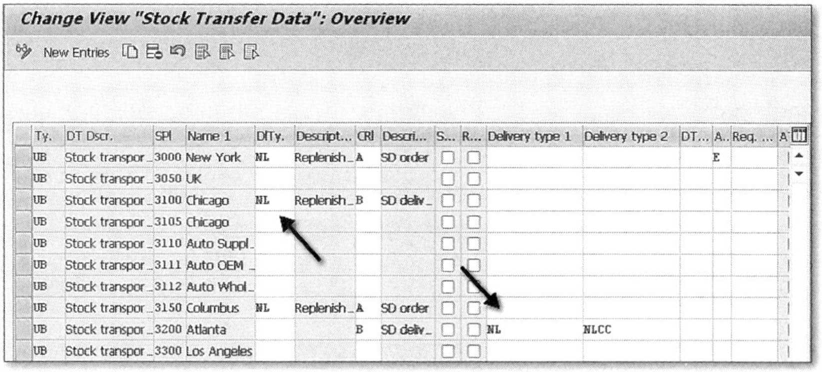

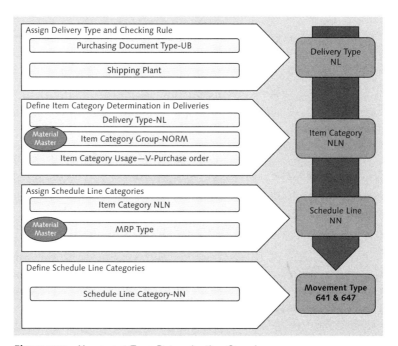

Figure 5.31 STO Type: Delivery Type Assignment

How does the system determine the actual movement type for the STO transaction? We mentioned the actual link between UB type purchasing and the outbound delivery type document earlier. When the logistics process is used—whether the one-step or two-step version—you have to perform the goods issue posting, which consumes the goods at the supplying plant, and determine which movement type to use when doing so.

Figure 5.32 Movement Type Determination Overview

Looking at the flowchart in Figure 5.32, you'll follow the corresponding steps:

1. Start with assignment of the delivery document type to the STO purchasing document, supplying plant, and assignment of the available to promise (ATP) checking rule. This is maintained in the STOCK TRANSPORT settings section in IMG node ASSIGN DELIVERY TYPE AND CHECKING RULE. In our example, you maintain the combination of order type UB, your shipping plant 3100, delivery type NL, and checking rule B.

   Delivery document type assignment

2. Maintain the item category determination for the replenishment delivery in IMG Logistics Execution, in the SHIPPING section, in the node DEFINE ITEM CATEGORY DETERMINATION IN DELIVERIES. The delivery type and the item category group of the material you're processing (stored on material master SD in the SALES ORG. 2 view) and the item category usage V will determine the item category NLN.

   The item category NLN—in standard delivered SAP systems—is linked to the schedule line category NN with assignment to the MRP TYPE, which is also maintained on the material master MRP 1 view. This is done in the sales document related IMG node—ASSIGN SCHEDULE LINE CATEGORIES.

3. In the IMG node DEFINE SCHEDULE LINE CATEGORIES, the schedule line category NN links MOVEMENT TYPE 641 to the two-step procedure, and it links MOVEMENT TYPE 647 to the one-step procedure (see Figure 5.33).

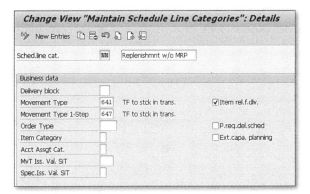

Figure 5.33 Schedule Line NN: Movement Type 641/647 Assignment

5.3.2 Master Data

With basic supporting configuration out of the way, you need to make sure that you have all master data in place to support the STO process. This includes a variety of information, but you'll need to maintain the data discussed in the following subsections at a minimum.

Customer Master

Outbound delivery — If you're planning on using outbound delivery in your process, your outbound delivery needs a customer master account. This customer account must be assigned to the individual plants involved in the process. Figure 5.34 displays the configuration assignment screen of the DEFINE SHIPPING DATA FOR PLANTS node.

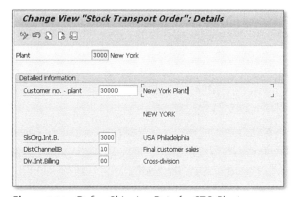

Figure 5.34 Define Shipping Data for STO Plants

To create the customer master, run Transaction XD01. So, in our example, PLANT 3000 has a customer master record 30000 (New York Plant) assigned in sales organization 3000. This data will be applied to the delivery header when an outbound delivery is created.

Shipping — Make sure you maintain the SHIPPING CONDITIONS in the SALES AREA DATASHIPPING tab, as shown in Figure 5.35. This is used in the shipping point determination for the deliveries you're creating together with the materials master sales organization view loading group. The plant, loading group, and shipping condition determine the shipping point that will be proposed by the system.

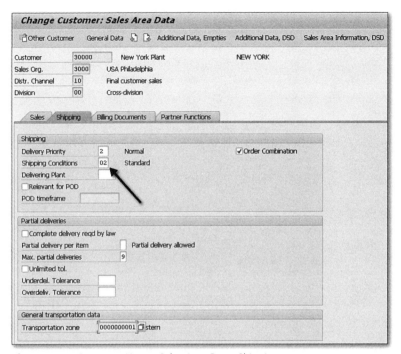

Figure 5.35 Customer Master Sales Area Data: Shipping

You need to maintain the same type of records for all plants or storage locations depending on the flavor you pick, and assign them per the steps described previously. Table 5.11 lists some of the customer master maintenance transactions for your reference.

Transaction	Menu Path
XD01: Create Customer	LOGISTICS • SALES AND DISTRIBUTION • MASTER DATA • BUSINESS PARTNER • CUSTOMER • CREATE • COMPLETE
VD01: Sales and Distribution Create	LOGISTICS • SALES AND DISTRIBUTION • MASTER DATA • BUSINESS PARTNER • CUSTOMER • CREATE • SALES AND DISTRIBUTION
XD02: Customer Master Change	LOGISTICS • SALES AND DISTRIBUTION • MASTER DATA • BUSINESS PARTNER • CUSTOMER • CHANGE • COMPLETE

Table 5.11 Customer Master Maintenance Transaction Codes

Transaction	Menu Path
VD02: Customer Master Sales and Distribution Change	LOGISTICS • SALES AND DISTRIBUTION • MASTER DATA • BUSINESS PARTNER • CUSTOMER • CHANGE • SALES AND DISTRIBUTION
XD03: Customer Master Display	LOGISTICS • SALES AND DISTRIBUTION • MASTER DATA • BUSINESS PARTNER • CUSTOMER • DISPLAY • COMPLETE
VD03: Customer Master Sales and Distribution Display	LOGISTICS • SALES AND DISTRIBUTION • MASTER DATA • BUSINESS PARTNER • CUSTOMER • DISPLAY • SALES AND DISTRIBUTION

Table 5.11 Customer Master Maintenance Transaction Codes (Cont.)

Material Master

Shipping point determination

As mentioned previously, some material master data is needed to help in shipping point determination (see Figure 5.36). In general, you need to follow these rules when you have to set the data for materials being moved between locations:

▶ Maintain LOADINGGRP on the SALES: GENERAL/PLANT view, and make sure you have accounting data for the material in the shipping PLANT field and the correct sales area (Sales Org/Distribution Chanel).

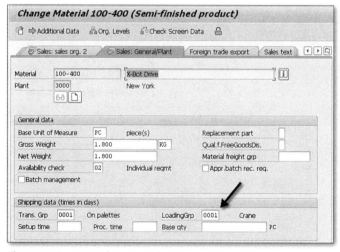

Figure 5.36 Material Master Sales General/Plant Data View

▶ Maintain the PURCHASING view, which is required to create the STO purchasing document, view, and accounting data for the receiving plant. If you always want the STOs to be used in the procurement proposal, you can set the SPECIAL PROCUREMENT key to 40 - STOCK TRANSFER (see Figure 5.37).

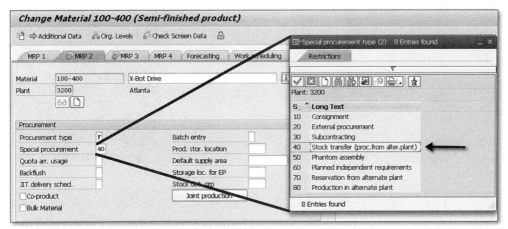

Figure 5.37 Material Master: MRP 2 Data View

There are several transactions related to material master maintenance, and we've covered most of them extensively in Chapter 2, if you need to refresh your memory.

Next we'll walk you through execution of different STO scenarios involving both delivery and nondelivery versions.

5.3.3 Two-Step Stock Transport Order without Outbound Delivery

The two-step STO without outbound delivery is a transfer that allows you to process goods movement and track its progress along the way but without detailed logistics steps—such as delivery picking, transfer order processing, and shipment processing. It's simply relying on Inventory Management movements executed at the time where stock movements occur.

Avoid detailed logistics steps

> **Note**
>
> STO without outbound delivery must use the two-step procedure; no other method is available.

Because no outbound delivery is involved, you're not using Logistics, only standard Purchasing and Inventory Management modules are engaged in this scenario. See Figure 5.38 for the process overview.

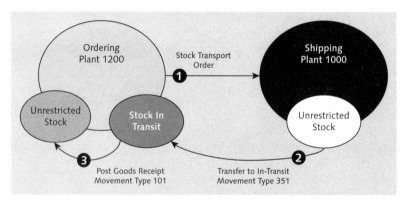

Figure 5.38 STO without Outbound Delivery: Two-Step Procedure

We'll transfer a sample material YY-270 between supplying plant 1000 (Hamburg) and ordering plant 1200 (Dresden). The STO without outbound delivery requires the following steps and transactions to execute. In the following subsections, we'll explain each step shown in the figure in more detail.

Step 1: Create Stock Transport Order

You first need to create the STO document type UB in the receiving plant 1000 where the supplying facility is plant 1200. Looking at the enterprise structure, you see that plant 1200 and plant 1000 belong to the same company code, and they are servicing the same sales area.

1. You're in plant 1200, and you enter the STO manually using Transaction ME21N and purchasing document order type UB.

2. Enter your materials, and you'll notice the item category U in the line item data (see Figure 5.39).

3. Alternatively, if you use purchase requisitions generated manually or by the planning run, the purchase requisitions can be automatically adopted into the PO document using Transaction ME59N. We used a similar procedure when discussing the subcontracting scenario earlier.

4. Notice that the PO doesn't have the SHIPPING data tab because we didn't make provisions for outbound delivery to be created.

Figure 5.39 Transaction ME21N: Stock Transport Create Transaction Screen

In Table 5.12, you'll find some of the transactions applied in the PO create process.

Transaction	Menu Path
ME59N: Automatically via Purchase Requisitions	LOGISTICS • MATERIALS MANAGEMENT • PURCHASING • PURCHASE ORDER • CREATE • AUTOMATICALLY VIA PURCHASE REQUISITIONS
ME21N: Display	LOGISTICS • MATERIALS MANAGEMENT • PURCHASING • PURCHASE ORDER • CREATE • VENDOR/SUPPLYING PLANT KNOWN

Table 5.12 Reference Purchasing Transaction Codes

Step 2: Post Goods Issue in the Issuing Plant

At the time of delivery, plant 1000 (Hamburg) has to issue the goods from its on-hand inventory to the STO you created in the previous step. You're the inventory clerk at plant 1000, and you enter the goods issue for the STO using Transaction MIGO. Now let's walk through the execution steps.

1. On the initial screen, specify the type of transaction you're posting by selecting GOODS ISSUE in the first action dropdown field, and then selecting PURCHASE ORDER in the next action field. MOVEMENT TYPE 351 - TF TO STCK IN TRANS is automatically proposed into the transaction.

2. Specify the STO PO number, and press Enter to continue.

3. All relevant STO data are pulled into the screen. Mark the item OK box, verify the issue quantity, and then click the POST button or press Shift + F11. See Figure 5.40 for an example. All stock reports reflect the inventory balance changes and show them in the report MMBE we've talked about before when using Transaction MB5T (Display Stock In-Transit).

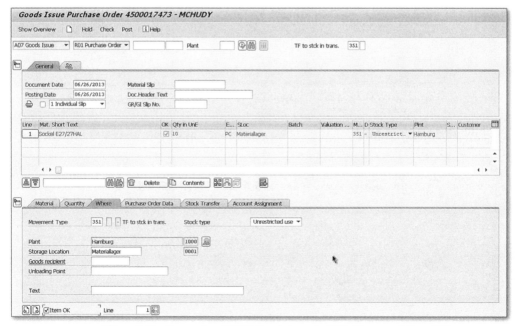

Figure 5.40 Transaction MIGO Goods Issue to STO: Movement Type 351

4. On the initial screen of Transaction MB5T, specify the selection criteria that will include the material you're monitoring (YY-270), shipping plant 1000, and destination plant 1200.

5. Press Enter to get a list of all relevant STO documents, materials, quantities being moved to in-transit, and value associated with it (see Figure 5.41).

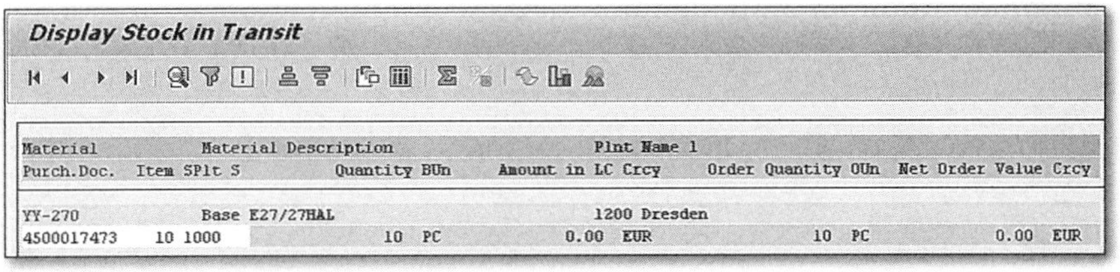

Figure 5.41 Display Stock In-Transit

Table 5.13 lists some of the reference transactions for this process step.

Transaction	Menu Path
MIGO: Goods Movement (MIGO)	LOGISTICS • MATERIALS MANAGEMENT • INVENTORY MANAGEMENT • GOODS MOVEMENT • GOODS MOVEMENT (MIGO)
MB5T: Stock in Transit CC	INFORMATION SYSTEMS • GENERAL REPORT SELECTION • MATERIALS MANAGEMENT • INVENTORY MANAGEMENT • STOCK IN TRANSIT CC
MMBE: Stock Overview	INFORMATION SYSTEMS • GENERAL REPORT SELECTION • MATERIALS MANAGEMENT • INVENTORY MANAGEMENT • STOCK OVERVIEW

Table 5.13 Goods Issue to In-Transit Reference Transaction Codes

Step 3: Post Goods Receipt in the Receiving Plant

When the goods arrive in the receiving plant, which in our example is plant 1200 (Dresden), the standard procedure is applied to receive and post the goods receipt using your STO created in Step 1 as a reference using Transaction MIGO or Transaction MIGO_GR (see Figure 5.42).

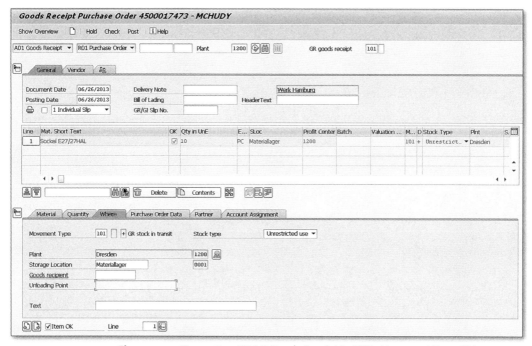

Figure 5.42 Transaction MIGO Goods Receipt to STO: Movement Type 101

1. On the initial screen, specify the type of transaction you're posting by selecting GOODS RECEIPT in the action dropdown field and then selecting PURCHASE ORDER in the next action field.

2. Specify the STO number, and press [Enter] to continue. You'll see all STO details next, and the default movement type is set to 101.

3. Mark the item OK checkbox either in the main line item level detail portion of the screen or at the bottom of the screen.

4. Verify the receiving quantity, and when you're ready, click the POST button. This creates the material document and moves the quantities from in-transit to the final on-hand inventory at plant 1200 (Dresden) storage location 0001.

5. You can then rerun Transaction MB5T (Stock in Transit) report just like in the post goods issue step before, or rerun Transaction MMBE (Stock Overview).

In the next section, we'll talk about the STO process using Logistics components.

5.3.4 One-Step Stock Transport Order with Outbound Delivery

In this scenario, we'll describe the one-step STO process using Logistics outbound delivery and a single goods movement posting. If your business requirements and reality on the ground don't call for a full blown two-step process, this is an ideal candidate. It allows you to use the outbound delivery for scheduling purposes and for creation of all delivery-related output, but instead of separate goods issue at the shipping plant and a separate goods receipt at the requesting plant, you post both movements at the same time during delivery post goods issue (PGI).

Simultaneous movements

> **Note**
>
> With this scenario, there is no stock in transit to monitor because the inventory changes ownership immediately on post.

The material document posts movement type 647 to move the inventory from on-hand to the in-transit bucket at the shipping plant, and movement type 101 at the ordering plant to move the goods from in transit to the on-hand inventory. You can control the timing of the goods movement and choose whether you want to physically execute the posting at the shipping plant or receiving plant. Let's walk through an example scenario between shipping plant 3100 (Chicago) and ordering plant 3300 (Los Angeles) using supplying material PROD302. The scenario process flow is available for your review in Figure 5.43, and we'll walk you through it step by step in the following subsections.

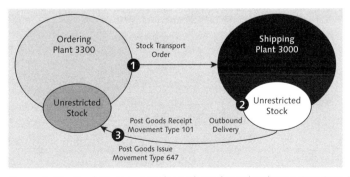

Figure 5.43 Stock Transport Order with Outbound Delivery: One-Step Procedure

Step 1: Create Stock Transport Order

First, just like in the previous scenario, you need to create the PO type, which is UB - STOCK TRANSPORT ORDER, using Transaction ME21N. Again, if you use purchase requisitions, they can be automatically adopted into the PO document using Transaction ME59N.

1. Enter your SUPPLYING PLANT "3100 Chicago" in the header details, and populate the organizational data, including PURCH. ORG. as "3000", PURCH. GROUP as "100", and COMPANY CODE as "3000" as shown in Figure 5.44.

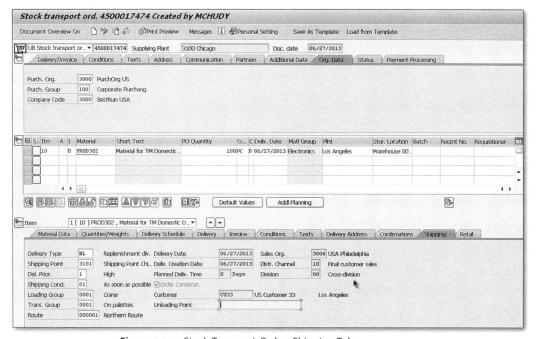

Figure 5.44 Stock Transport Order: Shipping Tab

2. Enter the line item information—"PROD302" for MATERIAL, the PO QUANTITY, and "Los Angeles" for the requesting plant (PLNT). Notice that the purchase order this time has the SHIPPING data tab, which includes all information required for Logistics subsequent steps for the outbound delivery to be created (see Figure 5.44). This tab includes the information about the ship-to account, which connects you to the customer master, and the shipping condition and the line item

material loading group stored on the material master—both used in shipping point determination. This information will be used in the next step during processing of the delivery due list.

Step 2: Create Outbound Delivery

The outbound delivery starts the Logistics process and is created when the requested material becomes available as the STO delivery deadline approaches. Using the delivery due list (in our example, we'll use Transaction VL10B), you can process all STO requirements for a shipping point, which is linked to the shipping plant. You can also create deliveries that are then used for execution of picking and transportation activities if you use Transportation Management components in your Logistics processes.

Start of Logistics process

To run this utility, follow these steps:

1. Execute Transaction VL10B, Transaction VL10D, Transaction VL10G, or Transaction VL10H, if you want to run your STOs together with any other sales orders you normally process. On the selection screen, specify the SHIPPING POINT; in our example, we'll use shipping point 3101 (Chicago), linked to plant 3100. Also, deliveries are very sensitive to dates, so the report will find all those STOs with delivery dates within the selection date range.

2. In our example, we'll ask to process the STO creates in the previous step only. Simply select the PURCHASE ORDERS tab, enter your STO number in the PURCHASING DOCUMENT field, and click the EXECUTE button (or use the [F8] function key) (see Figure 5.45).

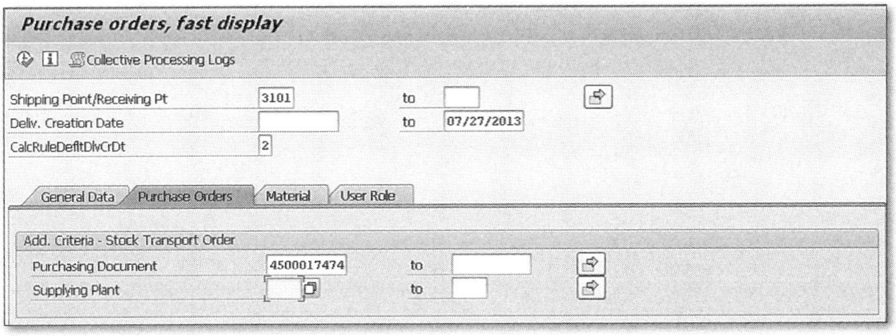

Figure 5.45 Delivery Due List: Initial Screen

Compliant
STO POs The report lists all of the STO POs that comply with the selection parameters (see Figure 5.46 for an example of the STO). Each line will have a traffic light indicating the delivery status. When it's possible to create a delivery, the status will be yellow; when the delivery can't be created, the status will be red. Normally, this is due to a lack of stock in the warehouse or the delivery date is far in the past. To create the deliveries, select the orders you want to process, and click on the BACKGROUND button or press ⌈Shift⌉ + ⌈F7⌉.

Figure 5.46 Create Delivery in the Background

When the system finishes processing, it highlights the STO orders that were successfully processed in green. In our case, the STO 4500017474 was successfully processed, creating outbound delivery 80017171, as shown in Figure 5.47. Click on the SHOW/HIDE DELIVERY icon or press ⌈Shift⌉ + ⌈F8⌉ to make the delivery numbers appear on the screen.

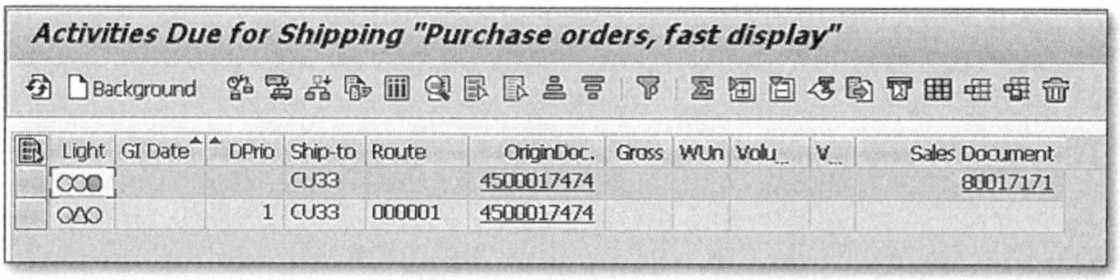

Light	GI Date	DPrio	Ship-to	Route	OriginDoc.	Gross	WUn	Volu_	V_	Sales Document
◯◯●			CU33		4500017474					80017171
◯▲◯		1	CU33	000001	4500017474					

Figure 5.47 Create Delivery: Processing Completed

In Table 5.14, you can find some of the outbound delivery transactions we've mentioned.

Transaction	Menu Path
VL10B: Purchase Orders	LOGISTICS • LOGISTICS EXECUTION • OUTBOUND PROCESS • GOODS ISSUE FOR OUTBOUND DELIVERY • OUTBOUND DELIVERY • CREATE • COLLECTIVE PROCESSING OF DOCUMENTS DUE FOR DELIVERY • PURCHASE ORDERS
VL10D: Purchase Order Items	LOGISTICS • LOGISTICS EXECUTION • OUTBOUND PROCESS • GOODS ISSUE FOR OUTBOUND DELIVERY • OUTBOUND DELIVERY • CREATE • COLLECTIVE PROCESSING OF DOCUMENTS DUE FOR DELIVERY • PURCHASE ORDERS ITEMS
VL10G: Sales Orders and Purchase Orders	LOGISTICS • LOGISTICS EXECUTION • OUTBOUND PROCESS • GOODS ISSUE FOR OUTBOUND DELIVERY • OUTBOUND DELIVERY • CREATE • COLLECTIVE PROCESSING OF DOCUMENTS DUE FOR DELIVERY • SALES ORDERS AND PURCHASE ORDERS
VL10H: Sales Orders and Purchase Orders (Items)	LOGISTICS • LOGISTICS EXECUTION • OUTBOUND PROCESS • GOODS ISSUE FOR OUTBOUND DELIVERY • OUTBOUND DELIVERY • CREATE • COLLECTIVE PROCESSING OF DOCUMENTS DUE FOR DELIVERY • SALES ORDERS AND PURCHASE ORDERS (ITEMS)

Table 5.14 Outbound Delivery Processing Transaction Codes

Step 3: Execute Picking and Post Goods Movement

To complete your delivery steps, picking activities will take place where you specify and confirm that what was requested has been supplied from the warehouse. If you use SAP Warehouse Management functionality, you have to execute transfer order creation and confirmation and, as required, issue the packing slip to list what has been picked and packed.

Finally, when you're ready to send the goods on the road, you need to issue required paperwork such as a bill of lading by running Transaction VL71 (Output from Deliveries). Finally, after the picking process is complete, you can post the goods movement transaction.

Paperwork

Remember that this is a one-step posting transaction, so you can either execute this at the time of shipping from the supplying plant or at the time of receipt at the ordering plant.

Usually, you want to post the goods movement at the time you ship the goods if you need to get all the paperwork to accompany your shipment on the road. You can post the goods movement individually using Transaction VL02N (Delivery Change) or en-masse using Transaction VL06G (Deliveries Due for PGI).

In our example, we're ready to post goods movement to our sample delivery created at the previous step.

1. Run Transaction VL02N, enter the delivery document number, and press Enter to continue.

2. On the subsequent screen, you can review the picking status by looking at the PICKING tab.

3. Click the POST GOODS ISSUE button or press Shift + F8 (see Figure 5.48). The goods are immediately transferred from the supplying plant 3100 (Chicago) to the receiving plant 3300 (Los Angeles) in a single posting. See the material document detail in Figure 5.49, which shows movement type 647 removing goods from inventory in plant 3100 and storage location 0001, and moving them to in transit. An immediate movement type 101 posts the goods to on-hand at plant 3300 and storage location 0001.

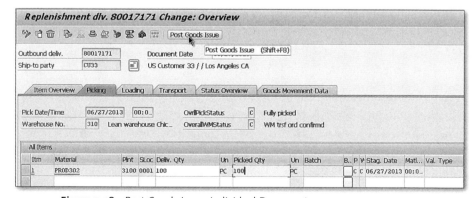

Figure 5.48 Post Goods Issue: Individual Document

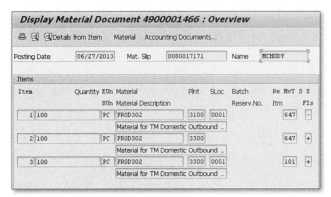

Figure 5.49 Material Document Showing One-Step Transfer Posting Details

You can find a list of transactions commonly used in the process step to post goods movements in Table 5.15.

Transaction	Menu Path
VL02N: Single Document	LOGISTICS • LOGISTICS EXECUTION • OUTBOUND PROCESS • GOODS ISSUE FOR OUTBOUND DELIVERY • OUTBOUND DELIVERY • CHANGE • SINGLE DOCUMENT
VL06G: Collective Processing via Outbound Delivery Monitor	LOGISTICS • LOGISTICS EXECUTION • OUTBOUND PROCESS • GOODS ISSUE FOR OUTBOUND DELIVERY • POST GOODS ISSUE • COLLECTIVE PROCESSING VIA OUTBOUND DELIVERY MONITOR

Table 5.15 Outbound Delivery Post Goods Movement Transaction Codes

5.3.5 Two-Step Stock Transport Order with Outbound Delivery

Finally, we'll cover the last intra-company STO flavor: using outbound delivery and a separate goods issue and good receipt steps. The two-step STO scenario is ideal when separate issue and receipt are required, and to show stock in transit during the transportation time, giving the visibility of movement in your stock reporting transactions. This is the most frequently used transaction out of all of the STO scenarios.

In this scenario, there are two separate material documents, one for goods issue at the shipping plant with movement type 641, and another at the

Movement visibility

receiving location with movement type 101. You'll see in the following subsections how the goods postings truly follow the physical movement of goods. Take a look at the two-step STO process flow in Figure 5.50. After the steps are listed, we'll walk through an example scenario between shipping plant 3000 (New York) and ordering plant 3800 (Denver) using material P-103 (Precision Pump 103).

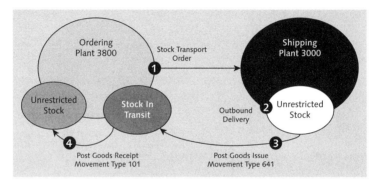

Figure 5.50 STO with Outbound Delivery: Two-Step Procedure

Step 1: Create Stock Transport Order

First, you need to create a new PO type—UB (Stock Transport Order)—using Transaction ME21N. Again, if you use purchase requisitions, they can be automatically adopted into the PO document using mass-convert Transaction ME59N. Follow these steps:

1. In the SUPPLYING PLANT field, enter "3000 New York" in the header data section and populate the organizational data as follows: purchasing organization as "3000", purchasing group as "100", and company code as "3000".

2. At the item level, enter MATERIAL as "P-103", specify the PO QUANTITY, and enter the destination plant (PLNT) as "Denver" (see Figure 5.51). The line item also gets the SHIPPING data tab that includes all information required for Logistics subsequent steps for the outbound delivery just as in the one-step scenario example discussed previously. If you need to find relevant transactions for this step, refer to Table 5.12.

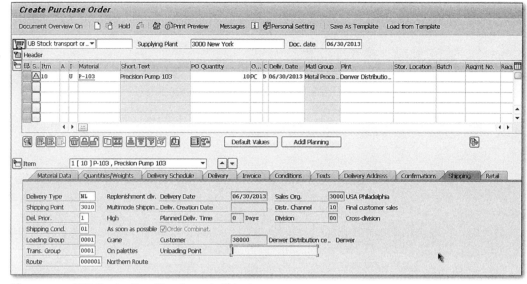

Figure 5.51 STO Create: Two-Step Scenario Shipping

Step 2: Create Outbound Delivery

The second step looks pretty much identical to the one-step scenario. Using the delivery due list—Transaction VL10B—you can process all STO requirements for a shipping point 3010 (New York), which is linked to the shipping plant 3000, and create deliveries that are then used for execution of picking and transportation activities just as demonstrated previously.

Upon successful execution, you'll find the delivery number for your STO showing with the green stop light indicator on the line (see Figure 5.52). We created delivery 80017179 for our STO 4500017475, which is now ready for picking at the warehouse. Figure 5.53 shows the delivery Pick-ing tab as an example of a document that's ready for processing.

Figure 5.52 Delivery Due List for Purchase Orders

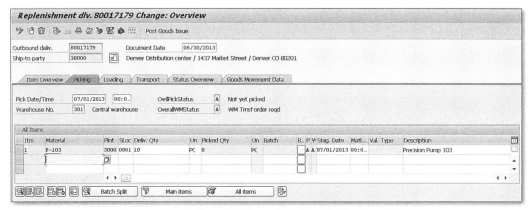

Figure 5.53 Outbound Delivery Overview: Picking Data Tab

Refer to Table 5.14 for delivery creation transaction codes and path information.

Step 3: Execute Picking and Post Goods Issue

Complete processing for shipping plant

To complete processing on the shipping plant side, you need to execute picking, whether it's done with or without warehouse functionality, confirming the quantities supplied to the STO delivery. Finally, you can post the goods issue transaction. This time the post goods issue movement is done explicitly at the time you ship the materials requested.

Again, just as in the one-step scenario, you can post the goods issue individually using Transaction VL02N (Delivery Change) or en-masse using Transaction VL10G (Deliveries Due for PGI). In our example, follow these steps:

1. Run Transaction VL10GN. On the initial screen, enter the SHIPPING POINT as "3010" and enter the planned goods movement date range (PLAND GDS MVMNT DATE) (see Figure 5.54).

2. You can use the DELIVERY document number if you choose the extended selection ALL SELECTION option button or use `Shift` + `F7`, and click the EXECUTE button or press `F8` to continue.

Figure 5.54 Transaction:VL10G: Outbound Deliveries for Goods Issue Initial Screen

3. On the subsequent screen shown in Figure 5.55, you'll get the list of all documents meeting your criteria. In our example, only one delivery is ready for post goods issue.

Figure 5.55 Transaction VL10G: Post Goods Issue

4. When ready, simply click the POST GOODS ISSUE button or use `Shift` + `F8` on your keyboard. You'll get a pop-up box asking for the posting date and time confirmation; the system proposes the current system date and time stamp.

5. Press `Enter` to confirm and continue. You'll get the confirmation message on the bottom of the screen stating the number of successful postings and the number of error transactions if any were to be reported. You can also access the error log to display details and research the failure to post reasons.

6. The goods are immediately transferred using movement type 641 from the supplying plant 3000 (New York), storage location (0001), to the receiving plant in-transit bucket of plant 3800 (Denver) (see the material document detail in Figure 5.56).

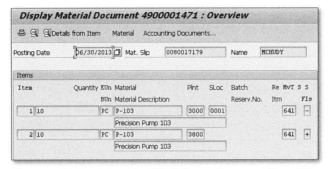

Figure 5.56 Goods Issue to STO Delivery: Movement Type 641

See inventory move The common stock reports reflect the inventory move between plants and show them in the Transaction MMBE (Stock Overview) report as well as in Transaction MB5T (Display Stock In-Transit). Just like in the two-step without outbound delivery scenario, given your initial selection matching the plants involved and material being transferred, you'll get a list of all relevant STO documents, materials, and quantities being moved to in-transit (see Figure 5.57). Refer to Table 5.13 for delivery movement posting transactions, and for monitoring of stock in transit transactions.

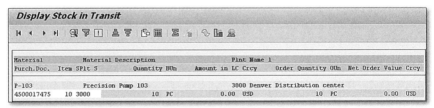

Figure 5.57 Display Stock In Transit

Step 4: Post Goods Receipt

When the goods arrive in the receiving plant—3800 (Denver), in our example—you can post the goods receipt using your STO created in Step 1 as a reference using Transaction MIGO or Transaction MIGO_GR.

1. Just like in the two-step scenario without delivery, on the initial screen for Transaction MIGO, you have to specify the type of transaction you're posting by selecting GOODS RECEIPT in the action dropdown

field and then selecting a type of receipt—PURCHASE ORDER—in the next action field.

2. Enter the STO number, and press `Enter` to continue. Data defaults from your STO, and the movement type is set to 101.

3. Check the item OK checkbox either in the main line item level detail portion of the screen or at the bottom of the screen, verify the receiving quantity, and when you're ready, click the POST button.

The material document is created for your goods receipt, quantities from in-transit are moved to the final on-hand inventory at plant 3800 (Denver) and storage location 0001, and if the destination was a warehouse location, the transfer order steps (creation and confirmation) complete the process. You can also rerun the Transaction MB5T (Stock in Transit) report just like in the post goods issue step, or rerun Transaction MMBE (Stock Overview) to verify that the in-transit bucket has been cleared.

For your reference, refer to the transaction codes and menu paths shown earlier in Table 5.13.

5.4 Cross-Company Code Stock Transport Order

We've talked about the STOs executed within a single company code extensively in the previous sections. Now we'll describe the process of procuring goods from a sister company and moving them across company codes.

A cross-company STO is a form of a PO that's placed by a requesting sister company plant as a demand on another company code issuing plant within the same sales organization. This transfer is executed using a procedure that involves the creation of an outbound delivery, intercompany billing document, or intercompany AP invoicing. Basically, this scenario can be executed either in the form of a one-step or a two-step procedure—just like the intra-company STOs. Because you're moving the goods between two different companies defined on the same instance of the SAP system, a form of internal settlement needs to be issued for the goods shipped, and a corresponding payables for goods received finalizes the process.

Definition

295

In the following sections, we'll go over configuration, master data, process flow, and all of the steps needed to perform the scenario from beginning to end (see Section 5.4.3).

5.4.1 Configuration Prerequisites

The cross-company code STO scenario requires document types specific to the cross-company movements and a set of movement types to accommodate the postings. The default purchasing document type for this process is a regular NB purchase order, and it's used with the default outbound delivery type NLCC.

Just like with the regular STO within the same company code boundaries, we won't go through all of the configuration nodes. You can find all of the related configuration nodes in the IMG Customizing using Transaction SPRO and the same menu path as we visited before: MATERIALS MANAGEMENT • PURCHASING • PURCHASE ORDER • SET UP STOCK TRANSPORT ORDER.

You also need to make sure that you link your customer master account representing the plant within the sales area responsible for cross-company PO shipments. You also need to maintain assignment of the purchasing document type, shipping plant, delivery type, and ATP checking rule. Figure 5.58 shows the configuration example.

Change View "Stock Transfer Data": Overview

Ty.	DT Dscr.	SPl	Name 1	DlTy.	Description	CRl	Description o...	S...	R...	De...	De...	DT...	A..	Req. ...	AT...
NB	Standard PO	3000	New York	NLCC	Replen.Cross-c_B		SD delivery	☐	☐						☐
NB	Standard PO	3050	UK					☐	☐						☐
NB	Standard PO	3100	Chicago	NLCC	Replen.Cross-c_B		SD delivery	☐	☐						☐
NB	Standard PO	3105	Chicago	NLCC	Replen.Cross-c_B		SD delivery	☐	☐						☐
NB	Standard PO	3110	Auto Supplier _	NLCC	Replen.Cross-c_B		SD delivery	☐	☐						☐
NB	Standard PO	3111	Auto OEM US	NLCC	Replen.Cross-c_B		SD delivery	☐	☐						☐
NB	Standard PO	3112	Auto Wholesal_	NLCC	Replen.Cross-c_B		SD delivery	☐	☐						☐
NB	Standard PO	3150	Columbus					☐	☐						☐
NB	Standard PO	3200	Atlanta					☐	☐						☐
NB	Standard PO	3800	Denver Distrib_					☐	☐						☐

Figure 5.58 Cross-Company Code PO: Delivery Type Assignment

Next, you need to set up the cross-company movement type determination for the outbound delivery goods issue transactions, which follows the same principles as the setup for the regular STOs.

Cross-company movement type determination

Looking at the flowchart in Figure 5.59, you start with the assignment of the delivery document type to the STO purchasing document, supplying plant, and assignment of the ATP (available to promise) checking rule. This is maintained in the STOCK TRANSPORT settings section in the IMG node ASSIGN DELIVERY TYPE AND CHECKING RULE that we've mentioned before. In our example, you maintain the combination of order type N, your shipping plant 3000, delivery type NLCC, and a checking rule B.

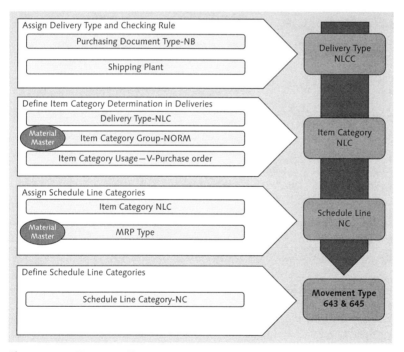

Figure 5.59 Movement Type Determination Overview

Next you need to maintain the item category determination for the delivery. This is done in IMG Logistics Execution, SHIPPING section, in the node DEFINE ITEM CATEGORY DETERMINATION IN DELIVERIES. The delivery type and the item category group of the material you're processing (stored on

Item category determination

the material master SD SALES ORG.2 view) and the item category usage V determine the item category NLC.

Item category link The item category NLC is linked to the schedule line category NC with assignment to the MRP type, which is also maintained on the material master MRP 1 view. This is done in the sales document-related IMG node—ASSIGN SCHEDULE LINE CATEGORIES. Finally, in the IMG node DEFINE SCHEDULE LINE CATEGORIES, the schedule line category NC links movement type 643 (see Figure 5.60).

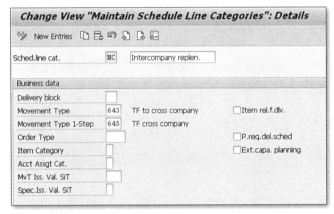

Figure 5.60 Schedule Line NC: Movement Type 643 Assignment

With this scenario, you have to create a billing document that requires a definition of the billing document type and copy controls between cross-company code delivery type NLCC and its item categories.

The delivery gets the values copied between the DL source document type (purchasing) and into the NLCC outbound delivery. Follow these steps:

1. Set up the copy control between purchasing and sales documents and delivery documents in Transaction VTLA. Figure 5.61 shows the configuration screen.

2. Set up the NLCC delivery type header and item data so they copy into the billing document type IV–INTERCOMPANY BILLING as shown in Figure 5.62. The configuration view of Transaction VTFL defines the copy control of delivery documents to billing documents.

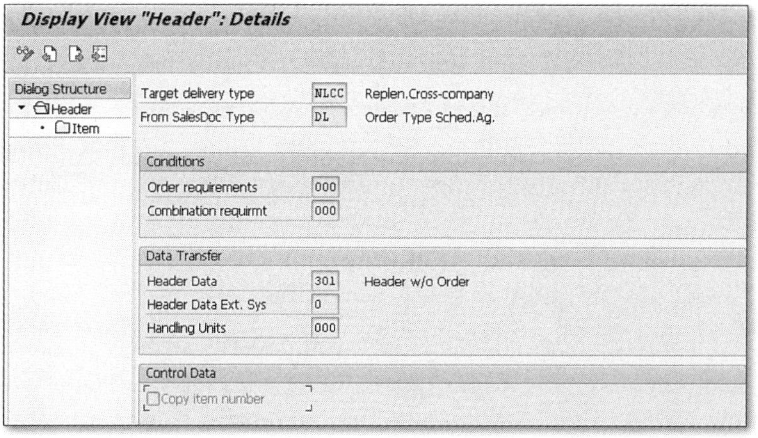

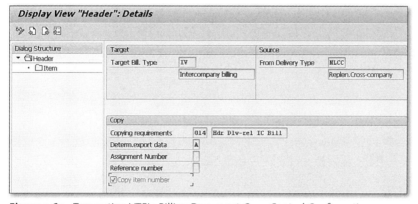

Figure 5.61 Transaction VTLA: Delivery Document Copy Control Configuration

Figure 5.62 Transaction VTFL: Billing Document Copy Control Configuration

5.4.2 Master Data

Just like with the standard STO within the same company code, you need to maintain the customer master and the material master; refer to Section 5.3.2 for a quick scan to refresh your memory. The only difference between this scenario and the previous one is in the customer master where this time, the payer as a partner function is required to complete the billing portion of this scenario. We also introduce the use of a vendor master for the supplying sister plant of a supplying company code. In this example scenario, you'll use customer plant 7000 representing the ordering plant 7000 of the company code 7000. You'll use both ship-to

Payer as a partner

and the bill-to for processing the delivery and the invoice, and the plant 7000 customer must be defined in the sales organization 3000.

On the supply side, plant 3000 will serve as the cross-company vendor defined in purchasing organization 7000 with account 3750 providing the goods (material 100-400 X-Bot Drive) to plant 7000. Vendor 3750 of company code 3000 will pay the incoming AP invoice.

Vendor Master

When you create a cross-company STO, you basically create a standard PO using purchasing document type NB. To complete this PO, as we mentioned, you have to enter a vendor account number. This vendor is defined as any other vendor; however, it also needs to be assigned to the supplying plant for the cross-company scenario to recognize that this is, in fact, your own sister company involved. This is done with the following steps:

1. Access the vendor master maintenance Transaction MK02 or Transaction XK02.

2. Enter the purchasing data on the initial screen, and after you're in the Transaction, select Extras and Add. Purchasing Data.

3. The pop-up window is displayed where you can maintain the Plant vendor assignment (see Figure 5.63).

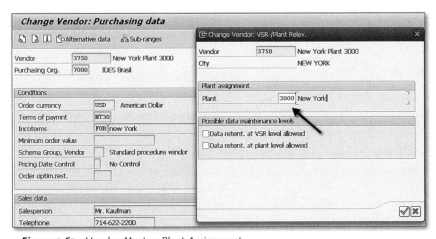

Figure 5.63 Vendor Master: Plant Assignment

In Table 5.16, you can find some of the customer master maintenance transactions for your reference.

Transaction	Menu Path
MK01: Create	LOGISTICS • MATERIALS MANAGEMENT • PURCHASING • MASTER DATA • VENDOR • PURCHASING • CREATE
MK02: Change (Current)	LOGISTICS • MATERIALS MANAGEMENT • PURCHASING • MASTER DATA • VENDOR • PURCHASING • CHANGE (CURRENT)
MK03: Display (Current)	LOGISTICS • MATERIALS MANAGEMENT • PURCHASING • MASTER DATA • VENDOR • PURCHASING • DISPLAY (CURRENT)
XK01: Create	LOGISTICS • MATERIALS MANAGEMENT • PURCHASING • MASTER DATA • VENDOR • CENTRAL • CREATE
XK02: Change	LOGISTICS • MATERIALS MANAGEMENT • PURCHASING • MASTER DATA • VENDOR • CENTRAL • CHANGE
XK03: Display	LOGISTICS • MATERIALS MANAGEMENT • PURCHASING • MASTER DATA • VENDOR • CENTRAL • DISPLAY

Table 5.16 Vendor Master Maintenance Transaction Codes

5.4.3 Cross-Company Code Purchase Order Process Flow Overview

Cross-company stock transport requires the Logistics components—the outbound delivery has to be used in the process—because it will be used as a base for the inter-company billing document. This scenario, however, can be executed using a one-step or a two-step version, just like STOs processed within the same company code described earlier. In the cross-company scenario, you'll also produce two separate material documents, one for goods issue at the shipping plant with movement type 643 or 645, and another at the receiving location with movement type 10. Take a look at the process flow in Figure 5.64.

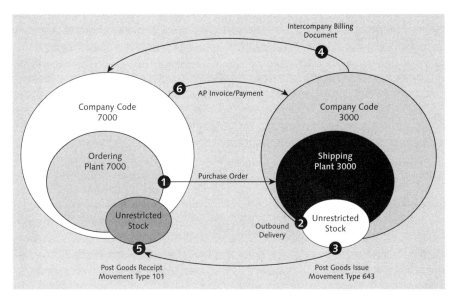

Figure 5.64 Cross-Company Stock Transport Order Process Flow

In the following subsections, we'll walk through an example of a cross-company PO between shipping plant 3000 (New York) of company code 3000 (BestRun USA), and ordering plant 7000 (São Paolo) of company code 7000 (BestRun Brazil), using material 100-400 X-Bot drive that we've used before in the subcontracting process.

Step 1: Create Stock Transport Order

You start the process in plant 7000 by creating the PO via conversion of the purchase requisition—such as using Transaction ME59N—or a direct PO creation using Transaction ME21N. This is pretty much the same procedure that we've talked about before when dealing with STOs with the difference being the document type. This time, you use the NB STANDARD PO to initiate the process, and you use the VENDOR account 3750 NEW YORK PLANT 3000 (see Figure 5.65).

You then follow these steps:

1. Enter "100-400" in the MATERIAL field, enter "X-Bot Drive" in the SHORT TEXT field, specify the PO QUANTITY needed, and enter the receiving plant (PLNT). The ordering plant 7000 shipping data configuration together with the material master data are used to determine

the data used on the Shipping tab, which is needed to execute the delivery creation in the next step.

2. Per the STO configuration, perform the availability check according to the rules assigned (refer to Figure 5.58).

3. The delivery date is calculated to give you the approximate dates for the delivery creation date needed for the shipping plant scheduling and a true delivery date representing the goods arrival date.

4. Save, and you'll see the example PO created number 4500017476.

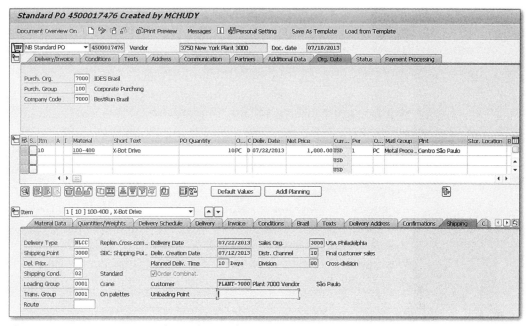

Figure 5.65 Cross-Company Code Purchase Order

Step 2: Create Outbound Delivery

This step looks pretty much identical to the intra-company scenario. Now you're in the shipping department of plant 3000. You're again using the delivery due list—Transaction VL10B—to create outbound deliveries for the cross-company POs. This time, the delivery type created will be of the NLCC document type per the configuration definition covered earlier in this section (refer to Figure 5.58, which shows the default document type NB STANDARD PO, linked to supplying plant 3000 - NEW YORK, and outbound delivery document type NLCC).

Upon successful execution, you'll find the delivery number for your PO showing with the green stop light indicator on the line (see Figure 5.66). See delivery 80017180 for cross-company PO 4500017476. Now you're ready to process the picking and shipping the goods to the requesting plant.

Figure 5.66 Delivery Due List for Purchase Order

Step 3: Execute Picking and Post Goods Issue

To complete processing on the shipping plant side, you again need to execute picking, and finally you can post the goods issue transaction. You can post the goods issue individually using Transaction VL02N (Delivery Change) or en-masse using Transaction VL10G (Deliveries Due for PGI). The goods are immediately consumed from the supplying plant 3000 – NEW YORK, storage location 0001, using movement type 643 (see the material document posted for goods issue transaction for our example delivery 80017180 in Figure 5.67). If you used a one-step version of the process, you consumed the goods issue in the shipping location using movement type 645 and immediately posted the goods receipt in the ordering location using movement type 101.

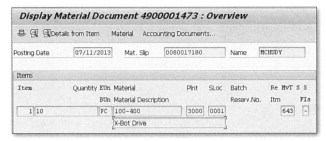

Figure 5.67 Goods Issue to Stock Transport Order Delivery: Movement Type 643

If you need to verify the stock situation after the posting, use Transaction MMBE (Stock Overview) report or Transaction MB5T (Display Stock In-Transit) using your initial selection matching the plants involved and material being transferred. The post goods issue updates the quantities between the UNRESTRICTED-USE STOCK and DELIVERY TO CUSTOMERS in the stock overview of the supplying plant, and the stock accounts and material expense accounts are updated. Refer to Table 5.15 for delivery posting transactions, and Table 5.13 for monitoring of stock in transit transactions.

Verification

Step 4: Create Intercompany Billing Document

The next step in our scenario is to create the intercompany invoice to pay for the goods supplied by the sister company. You can do this using Transaction VF01 (Create Billing Document). Follow these steps:

1. On the CREATE BILLING DOCUMENT initial screen, enter the same outbound delivery number from the previous step in the DOCUMENT column. You can also specify the billing document type IV-INTERCOMPANY BILLING, and press Enter.

2. On the INVOICE CREATE OVERVIEW OF BILLING ITEMS screen, verify that the material from the sample delivery showed up and that the pricing data is present as well (see Figure 5.68).

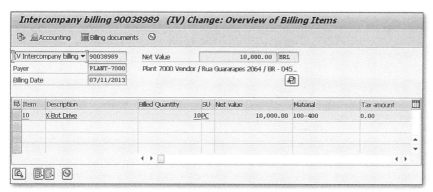

Figure 5.68 Intercompany Billing Document: Overview Screen

3. Upon review of all this data, you post the document by pressing the SAVE button. The financial document is released to accounting as well if you allow the automatic release.

Tips & Tricks

You can set up the invoicing process in such a way that whenever an intercompany invoice is created in the supplying company, the AP invoice receipt is triggered automatically in the issuing company code using EDI message category INVOIC.

Step 5: Post Goods Receipt

When the goods arrive in the receiving plant, you're ready to post goods receipt with reference to the cross-company PO number 4500017476 created in the first step of this scenario. Use Transaction MIGO or Transaction MIGO_GR. If you used the one-step procedure, no goods receipt posting has to be done as an extra step; it already posted when you executed the good issue to the outbound delivery in Step 3. Follow these steps:

1. On the initial screen, just like in the STO scenarios within the same company code, you have to specify the type of transaction you're posting by selecting GOODS RECEIPT in the action dropdown.

2. Select PURCHASE ORDER as the type of receipt in the next action field, and enter the PO number as "4500017476". Alternatively, you can choose OUTBOUND DELIVERY instead with a sample delivery as "80017180", and press Enter to continue. All information from the reference document is transferred, and the movement type is set to 101.

3. Check the item OK checkbox, verify the receiving quantity, and when ready click the POST button.

   As with all material movements, the material document is created showing relevant data such as received quantity, material number, receiving plant, storage location, and purchasing document. Figure 5.69 shows a view of Transaction MB03 (Material Document Display).

Figure 5.69 Transaction MIGO: Goods Receipt to STO with Movement Type 101

4. You can also rerun Transaction MB5T (Stock in Transit), or Transaction MMBE (Stock Overview) to verify that the transfer has been completed. Refer to Table 5.13 for transaction codes and menu paths.

Step 6: Post Invoice Receipt for Cross-Company Purchase Order

The next step is to enter the incoming invoice into the system. You can enter this invoice manually by creating it using Transaction MIRO. You can also automate this process by providing the output routine that creates an incoming EDI message that the ordering company code recognizes as an incoming invoice.

Enter invoice

1. To perform the manual entry, use Transaction MIRO (Enter Incoming Invoice).

Manual entry

2. On the entry screen, specify the invoice date.

3. On the bottom portion of the transaction screen, select the PO REFERENCE tab, and enter your PURCHASE ORDER number from the previous steps.

4. Specify the invoice amount in the BASIC data tab of the transaction.

5. Either simulate posting to check for errors or click the SAVE button to create the invoice document for your PO.

Refer to Table 5.6 for transaction codes and menu paths.

If you're planning on automating the creation of the invoice receipts, you need to know that this is done via output condition RD04 (Invoice Receipt MM) determined during intercompany billing document creation performed in Step 4 of this scenario. Automatic posting to a vendor account

Automatically create invoice receipts

is triggered when message type RD04 is processed into an EDI document (see Figure 5.70). This document uses a message category INVOIC for invoice and will use an internal processing variant FI that allows you to post the translated incoming invoice receipt directly in Financial Accounting (FI). With the last step of issuing the payment, the overview of the cross-company stock transport process is complete.

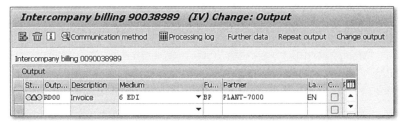

Figure 5.70 Intercompany Billing Document Output Condition RD04

5.5 Kanban

In this section, we'll spend a little bit of time talking about the lean production method called Kanban, which ties to most of the forms of the planning and procurement we've already discussed, including MRP, STOs, and straight purchasing.

Definition   Kanban (in Japanese, "signboard" or "billboard") was originally developed at Toyota to improve and maintain a high level of production efficiency. This method allows you to provide material to production lines on a regular basis in smaller manageable quantities, monitor inventory levels, track actual consumption, and place replenishment requests by using the card as a trigger to move existing inventory, send the requirements to produce more, or send a requisition to purchasing and out to the vendor to deliver goods when material is consumed. Kanban is an example of a "pull" approach according to the actual demand.

Automatic process   SAP allows you to use this procedure in the system and interact with procurement or the Inventory Management side automatically. Basically, the production process controls itself, reducing manual posting to a minimum, such as scanning a barcode or setting the status manually using a single transaction, instead of using the physical cards and boards. The SAP electronic version of the Kanban container represents the Kanban card.

The demand signal for material replenishment (internal or external) can be triggered by sending a card to the source of supply that will procure the needed material, specifying the requesting destination location or a production supply area, the material, and quantity needed. You can also trigger the goods receipt posting using a Kanban signal.

Trigger

See Figure 5.71 for the generic process overview.

Process overview

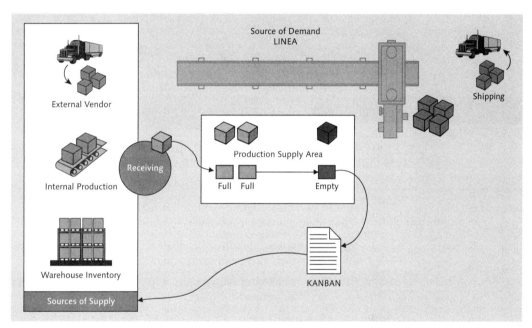

Figure 5.71 Kanban Process Flow Overview

When the bin on the factory floor becomes empty, the empty container and the Kanban card are returned to the inventory control person or set to EMPTY by the shop floor worker by executing one of the SAP Kanban signal or Kanban board transactions. Depending on the number of Kanbans in the cycle, the shop floor can replace the empty bin with another full bin already in the supply area. The inventory control can then trigger a request for materials that can come from a variety of sources, including your own production lines, via production orders, external vendor using a purchase requisition or a PO, and a reservation, stock transfer, or transfer posting from your on-hand inventory. Next, the full product bin is delivered, and the status of the Kanban is reset to FULL—completing the cycle.

> **Note**
>
> Design your Kanban in such a way that the process should never run out of needed material. Consumption of Kanban materials should be constant within intervals longer than the replenishment lead time. Maintaining the accurate number of bins/Kanbans that can serve as a buffer to compensate for the problems in case of availability issues in the supply chain.

In the following sections, we'll discuss different Kanban procedures, required master data, and how it all falls together using a Kanban board.

5.5.1 Kanban Procedures and Categories

SAP provides you with multiple ways to implement and use Kanban depending on your business requirements and industry needs. These procedures—also known as Kanban control cycle categories—are defined and applied in the control cycle. Let's review the available options in the following subsections.

Classic Kanban

Control cycle
In classic Kanban, the demand source, the supply source, and the procedure for the replenishment of the material, number of Kanbans, and quantity per each Kanban are defined in the control cycle. In this procedure, the Kanban signal triggers the replenishment only for the quantity defined in the control cycle. Also, to increase the number of Kanbans in the procedure, you have to redefine the control cycle.

One-Card Kanban

Container capacity
The one-card system requires two Kanbans, to guarantee the replenishment of the Kanban currently being used. This procedure is useful when you have a period when material isn't required continuously and when the replenishment is needed at about half of the container capacity. Before you can use this procedure, you must select one of the processes in the field and trigger replenishment when maintaining the control cycle (see the Section 5.5.2 for details).

Kanban with Quantity Signals

With the quantity signal, the replenishment signal isn't set by the manual Kanban status change. Instead, the posted actual consumption of the Kanban material sets the status to EMPTY when the preset quantity trigger is reached.

Actual
consumption

Event-Driven Kanban

In event-driven Kanban, material is provided based on actual consumption, and the actual Kanban is created only when required, that is, triggered by the defined event, for every requested material quantity. This Kanban eventually is deleted at the time the replenishment signal is issued.

5.5.2 Master Data

The Kanban procedure is based on the control cycle, which you define in SAP to replicate your process electronically, and it uses the material master and production supply and replenishment method areas, among other things specific to this process. For external procurement, you also need the vendor account number and a scheduling agreement number, if you want to reference and trigger just in time (JIT) calls, or a contract number to reference in creation of purchase requisitions or POs.

In the following subsections, we'll discuss the different parts of the master data you need to configure.

Production Supply Area

A production supply area represents the interim storage location on the shop floor that is used to provide parts to the production line. The production supply area requires some key fields to be maintained:

▶ PLANT
The supply area is plant specific.

▶ STOR. LOCATION
All goods movements related to the production supply area are performed using the assigned storage location.

▶ RESPONSIBLE

This is the user responsible for monitoring/processing activities at the supply area.

You need to maintain the supply area using Transaction PK05 (Maintain) (see Figure 5.72).

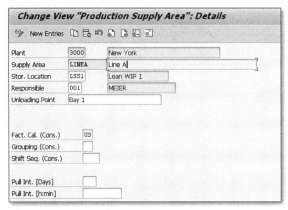

Figure 5.72 Production Supply Area: Details

Table 5.17 lists the menu paths and other related transactions for your reference.

Transaction	Menu Path
PK05: Maintain	LOGISTICS • PRODUCTION • KANBAN • PRODUCTION SUPPLY AREAS • MAINTAIN
PK06: Display	LOGISTICS • PRODUCTION • KANBAN • PRODUCTION SUPPLY AREAS • DISPLAY
PK05S: Fast Entry Production Supply Area	LOGISTICS • PRODUCTION • KANBAN • PRODUCTION SUPPLY AREAS • FAST ENTRY PRODUCTION SUPPLY AREA

Table 5.17 Production Supply Area Transaction Codes

Control Cycle

Define Kanban procedure

The control cycle is the key to the entire process. Here you define which Kanban procedure you're going to use (e.g., classic or event driven), the number of Kanbans in the cycle, and the replenishment strategy (choice between external procurement, in-house production, or stock transfer). Follow these steps:

1. Run Transaction PKMC (Control Cycle Maintenance). If you're creating a new record, first click the DISPLAY/CHANGE icon or press the [F7] key.

2. On the initial screen, enter the plant you're maintaining the control cycle for and the SUPPLY AREA in scope.

   On the right side of the main screen section, click the CREATE icon. The pop-up window appears where you can choose the first important data setting: CONTROL CYCLE CATEGORY (CLASSIC KANBAN or EVENT-DRIVEN KANBAN) (see Figure 5.73).

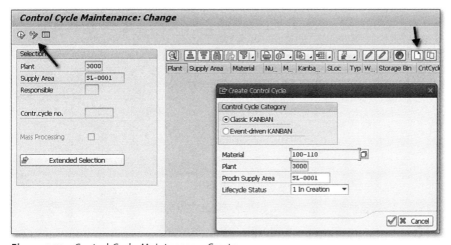

Figure 5.73 Control Cycle Maintenance: Create

3. You have to specify what MATERIAL the control cycle is created for, and you can also maintain the LIFECYCLE STATUS of the master record by choosing IN CREATION, CREATED, RELEASED, or LOCKED.

4. Press [Enter] to continue to the next screen.

Kanbans Section

Here you can maintain the details for your control cycle starting with the KANBANS section where you define the number of Kanbans (container) in the cycle and control quantities, for example. On the bottom of the screen, you'll find tabs with additional controls needed for the control cycle.

Replenishment Strategy Tab

The second major key data setting—REPLENISHMENT STRATEGY—allows you to define how the Kanban will be replenished. You can choose from IN-HOUSE PROD., EXT.PROCUREMENT, and STOCK TRANSFER. The individual procedures per strategy are predefined and may include production orders, POs, STOs, or simple transfer posting as well as reservations (which are processed by MRP). This is where you tie the Kanban to the procurement processes we've covered in detail already (see Figure 5.74).

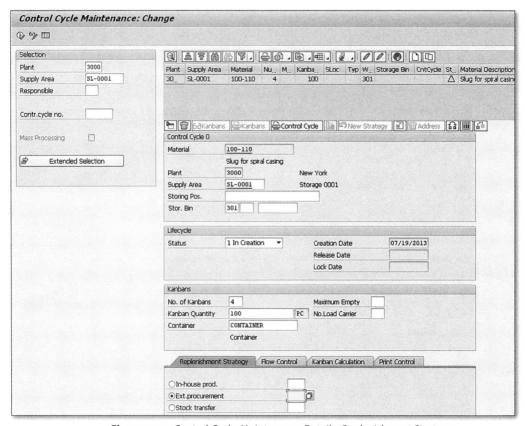

Figure 5.74 Control Cycle Maintenance Details: Replenishment Strategy

Flow Control Tab

In this section, you can define whether you need to post a separate transaction for goods receipt and the Kanban set to FULL—maintaining the SEPARATE GR field. If you don't set the flag, the status change automatically posts goods receipt, and if you post the goods receipt first, the Kanban status is automatically set to FULL.

If you set the INDEP. SOURCE flag, you'll hand over the replenishment control to the source of supply, which means that the consuming work center will set the status to EMPTY, but no replenishment is triggered, and the system automatically sets the status to WAIT.

The STATUS SEQUENCE field controls which Kanban status can be used during processing. You can define a specific status sequence if you have such a requirement. If no status sequence is defined, you have to use EMPTY and FULL. Other statuses are optional.

The TRIGGER REPLEN field controls what status is used to trigger the replenishment signal; if none is specified, the EMPTY status is used. If you want any other status to be used instead, you can select it from the dropdown: IN USE, WAIT, and TRIGGER QUANTITY are available.

The TRIGGER QUANTITY ties the KANBAN directly to the trigger replenishment option; it defines the quantity that will actually be used as a value for the replenishment signal.

Kanban Calculation Tab

This tab is used only if you decide to define your Kanban and employ the calculations to auto-calculate either the number of Kanbans needed or the quantity per container using standard SAP-provided formulas that include other parameters such as RTL (replenishment lead time), safety factors, and consumption per unit of time.

Print Control Tab

Here you define if the Kanban card should be printed. If you choose to print, you select whether it should be done at the time of goods receipt or at the time of replenishment signal. You can also define the printer you want the card to be printed on.

Table 5.18 contains the maintenance transactions for your reference.

Transaction	Menu Path
PKMC: Control Cycle Maintenance	LOGISTICS • PRODUCTION • KANBAN • CONTROL CYCLE • CONTROL CYCLE MAINTENANCE
PK17: Print Kanban	LOGISTICS • PRODUCTION • KANBAN • CONTROL CYCLE • PRINT KANBAN

Table 5.18 Kanban Control Cycle Transaction Codes

5.5.3 Kanban Board and Signals

Monitoring   There are a number of transactions that allow you to control all of your Kanban activities from a central perspective. SAP provides a nice interface to monitor and trigger signals either from the demand or supply point of view using Kanban board transactions. Let's walk through an example of the Kanban board using the demand source option and Transaction PK13N.

1. On the initial screen, enter the plant number, and press Enter.

2. On the next screen, you'll see the Kanban board with all active and inactive control cycles showing supply areas, materials, Kanban quantities, and individual Kanban color-coded statuses—showing FULL in green, EMPTY in red, WAIT in purple, and KANBAN ERROR postings in white with red outline (see Figure 5.75).

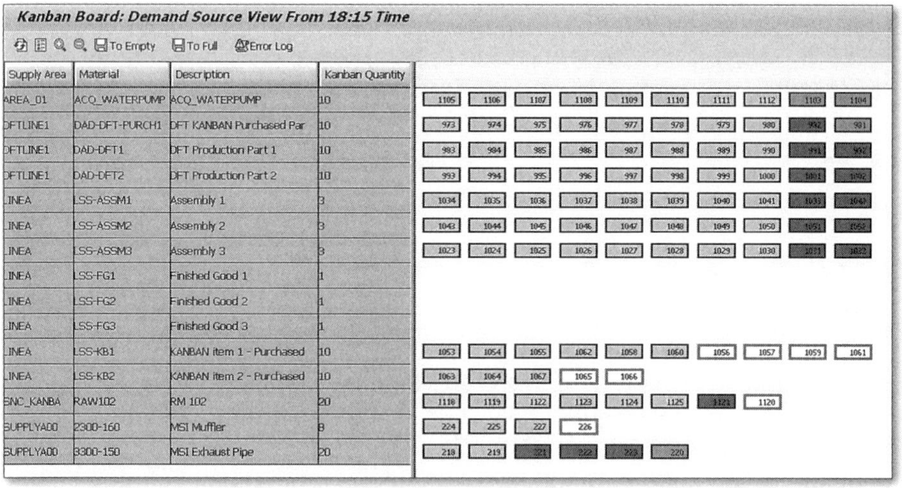

Figure 5.75 Kanban Board: Demand Source View

Here you can select the individual or multiple Kanbans and execute the status change by clicking one of the buttons—To EMPTY or To FULL—depending on the signal needs and triggering predefined replenishment requests or consumption of Kanban quantities. If any of the actions result in error, you can access the error log by clicking on the corresponding button.

If you need more granular level of controls for signals, you can use one of the available transactions for individual signal posting. Table 5.19 lists all relevant Kanban board and signal transactions for your reference.

Transaction	Menu Path
PK13N: Demand-Source View	LOGISTICS • PRODUCTION • KANBAN • CONTROL • KANBAN BOARD • DEMAND-SOURCE VIEW
PK12N: Supply-Source View	LOGISTICS • PRODUCTION • KANBAN • CONTROL • KANBAN BOARD • DEMAND-SOURCE VIEW
PKBC: Bar Code	LOGISTICS • PRODUCTION • KANBAN • CONTROL • KANBAN SIGNAL • BAR CODE
PK21: Manual Entry	LOGISTICS • PRODUCTION • KANBAN • CONTROL • KANBAN SIGNAL • MANUAL ENTRY
PK22: Quantity Signal	LOGISTICS • PRODUCTION • KANBAN • CONTROL • KANBAN SIGNAL • QUANTITY SIGNAL
PK23: Event-Driven Kanban	LOGISTICS • PRODUCTION • KANBAN • CONTROL • KANBAN SIGNAL • EVENT-DRIVEN KANBAN

Table 5.19 Kanban Board and Signal Transaction Codes

5.6 Order Optimizing

SAP Retail was designed to help retail and wholesale operators manage their business processes, which are much different than the standard, especially on the sales and procurement side. SAP ERP 6 now contains the bulk of these transactions. Streamlining the processes and optimizing them are key to achieve a level of profitability in efficiency in this very competitive market. On the procurement side, SAP deploys *order optimizing* as a tool that helps you achieve these goals. Basically, order optimization looks at all open purchase requisitions in the system, combines the requested quantities into collective POs and rounding off the total quantity to the

Retail/wholesale

most cost-effective size matching the defined transportation equipment capacity (truck size, container size, etc.). During this process, the system is also looking at maintained pricing conditions and choosing the best possible price combination.

Optimizing functions

Order optimizing is based on functions that come together during the load building execution and consists of the following:

▶ Investment buying

▶ Load building

▶ Quantity optimizing

▶ Goods receipt capacity check (this is more of the Logistics function, so we'll skip this to focus on key procurement functionality)

The basic principles of optimizing are co-mingled with the regular SAP procurement process as you know from the previous chapters. Due to the large volumes of purchasing data and the amount of data that needs to be evaluated, order optimizing is usually executed in an automated mode and usually in the background.

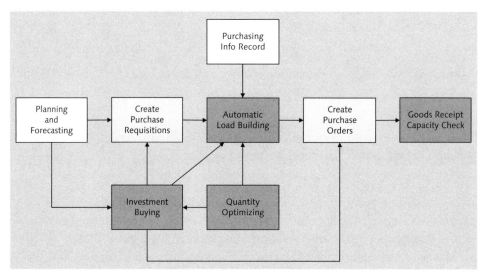

Figure 5.76 Order Optimizing Process Overview

The process overview shown in Figure 5.76 follows these steps:

1. You start with the regular analysis of your demand and forecasts, which then creates procurement proposals as a result of the planning run. The procurement proposals eventually end up in the system as purchase requisitions.

2. Next in the process is the load builder, which can be defined to use the investment buying component (looks at the purchasing info record pricing data) and can result in the PO purchase requisition or PO proposal if the load builder isn't used, and quantity optimizing (looking at the configured rounding profiles, purchasing info records, and material master).

3. Load builder then proposes the makeup of the PO that will be the most cost effective for the transportation method suggested in configuration as well.

4. After you review and correct the proposed order, you can create the PO.

5. And the last step in the process — goods receipt capacity check — enables you to avoid bottlenecks when receiving the shipments of the ordered goods.

Next, we'll cover some of the key transactions related to each of the order optimizing functions.

5.6.1 Investment Buying

Investment buying provides you with tools to analyze current and future price fluctuations to decide if you should make an advance purchase now for future requirements, expecting that the purchase price should go up. Investment buying can create purchase requisitions and POs. Depending on your needs, you can also be integrated with the load builder execution.

Using some of the configuration settings and purchasing info records, the system performs analysis of whether you should be procuring materials ahead of any true requirements showing need in the system, and how much you should buy if the analysis gives you satisfactory results.

Simulation You can perform the simulation using Transaction WLB6 (Investment Buying Simulation) (see Figure 5.77). On the initial screen, you fill in as much info there is available for you. Mandatory fields, however, include VENDOR, PURCHASING ORGANIZATION, MATERIAL, PLANT, LAST DAY BEFORE PRICE CHANGE, and FUTURE PRICE END DATE. This is assuming that your purchasing info record pricing conditions and validity dates have been maintained. If not, you can fill in additional fields, including the expected prices, into the simulation entry screen.

When you're ready, click the EXECUTE button or press F8. The suggested order size, timing, and related ROI data are calculated (see the right side of Figure 5.77 for analysis results).

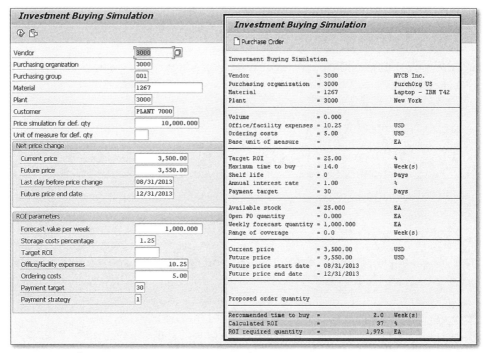

Figure 5.77 Investment Buying Simulation

If the results are what you've expected and you're ready to proceed, you can simply click the PURCHASE ORDER button or press Ctrl + F2 to generate the PO—it will be created with the INVEST. BUY as the created by name (see example in Figure 5.78).

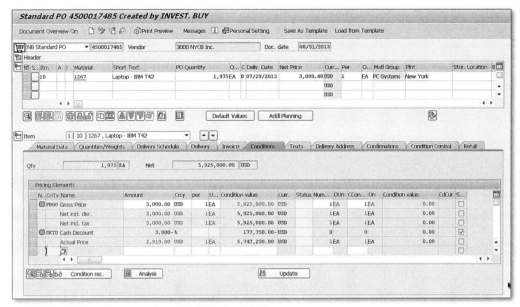

Figure 5.78 Investment Buy Generated Purchase Order

You can find the investment buying transaction codes in Table 5.20 together with the menu path for your reference.

Transaction	Menu Path
WLB1: Determining Requirements for Investment Buying	LOGISTICS • MATERIALS MANAGEMENT • PURCHASING • ENVIRONMENT • ORDER OPTIMIZING • INVESTMENT BUYING • DETERMINING REQUIREMENTS FOR INVESTMENT BUYING
WLB2: Investment Buying Analysis	LOGISTICS • MATERIALS MANAGEMENT • PURCHASING • ENVIRONMENT • ORDER OPTIMIZING • INVESTMENT BUYING • INVESTMENT BUYING ANALYSIS
WLB6: Investment Buying Simulation	LOGISTICS • MATERIALS MANAGEMENT • PURCHASING • ENVIRONMENT • ORDER OPTIMIZING • INVESTMENT BUYING • INVESTMENT BUYING SIMULATION

Table 5.20 Investment Buying Transaction Codes

5.6.2 Quantity Optimizing

Rounding

The quantity optimizing uses configured controls that are applied to round off document quantities accordingly. The rules can apply rounding in either direction—up or down—using the unit of measure groups. You can influence your quantity optimization; for example, you want your POs to round up to cases, cartons, pallets, and container sizes by using the configurable rounding profile, purchasing info record order quantity, or material master rounding value.

Rounding Profile

The rounding profile is defined in configuration and stores threshold values for the rounding procedure. The rounding profile is assigned to the material master, which is the key to access it during the procedure together with the round-off method and the rounding rule. Figure 5.79 shows the configuration detail of the ROUNDING PROFILE.

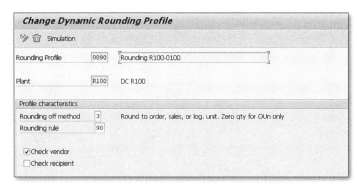

Figure 5.79 Dynamic Rounding Profile: Transaction OWD1

Rounding off method

The rounding off method for rounding up/rounding down items controls the behavior of the rounding profile. You can use one of the following:

▸ No rounding off

▸ Round off to a multiple of the order/sales unit of measure

▸ Round off to absolute threshold values/rounding off values

▶ Round off to a multiple of the order/sales unit of measure and also optimize quantity to complete logistical units of measure

▶ Add or subtract percentage as of a certain threshold value

The rounding rule controls the actual threshold percentage values of rounding up or down for a unit of measure the rule is defined for.

Purchasing Info Record

We've covered this piece of master data extensively in Section 2.7 of Chapter 2. The rounding profile—if different than on the material master—is applied during the purchasing document creation, following the SAP principles of using the most specific information if available.

It works in conjunction with standard order quantities defined in the CONTROL section of the purchasing organization data portion of the purchasing info record (see Figure 5.80). The STANDARD QTY field is used for rounding instead, just like it's applied in building the pricing scales. Also, if the rounding profile is defined, it is used instead.

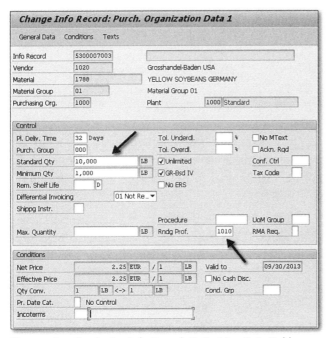

Figure 5.80 Purchasing Info Record: Optimizing Data Fields

Material Master

The material master allows you to store values for rounding off items in the MRP 1 view in the ROUNDING VALUE field of the LOT SIZE data section (see Figure 5.81). You can also apply the rounding profile here, which will be used in the MRP planning procedure as well as in optimizing if used instead of the rounding value.

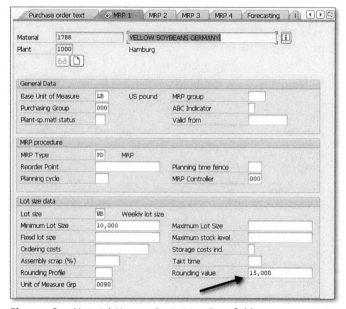

Figure 5.81 Material Master: Optimizing Data fields

You can't use both, however, so choose the method and maintain the fields accordingly. Also, on the PURCHASING view, you have to set the AUTOM. PO flag for the load builder to consider the material during the execution (see Figure 5.82).

> **Note**
>
> If you want to use automatic load building, you should also use forecasting for calculations of the range of coverage.

Figure 5.82 Material Master: Purchasing View

Another critical field in the material master is the unit of measure (UoM) and associated volume data. Load builder uses the defined UoM conversions in the volume calculations.

5.6.3 Load Building

The order optimizing tool uses all of the components we've talked about before in the last set of functions during the load building execution. Load building allows you to look at your demand and evaluate the most cost-effective size of the POs to minimize the following:

Effective PO size

- ▸ Transportation cost
- ▸ Purchase price by ordering large volumes (such as truckloads)
- ▸ Quantity of stock on-hand by ordering as close as possible to lead time

Load builder tries to optimize quantities by converting purchase requisitions to POs destined for the same vendor. If the system finds existing POs for the same vendor, a load under a collective number is proposed. For the vendor to be even considered for the load builder, the vendor master record has to have the restriction profile assigned in the CONDITIONS section of the PURCHASING data view (see Figure 5.83). This profile and its values are set in configuration, including information on the minimum and maximum loading capacity of the means of transport considered for the load builder. Also—just like with the material master—vendor master purchasing data requires the AUTOM. PO flag to be checked. Another requirement is to have the right parameters maintained in your user parameters.

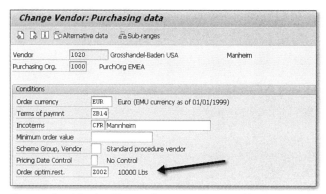

Figure 5.83 Vendor Master: Optimizing Data Fields

Let's take a look at the process steps required to execute the load building from the beginning—evaluation of MRP requirements—to the PO creation. Figure 5.84 shows the transactional steps. We'll cover only the transactions that are most likely executed in real-world situations, so we'll focus on Transactions WLBA, WLB13, and WLB4.

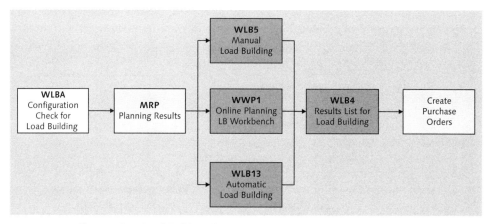

Figure 5.84 Load Building: Process Overview

Configuration Check for Load Building

To make sure all of your supporting configuration and master data are in place to support the load builder execution and avoid errors in the run, you can execute Transaction WLBA (Configuration Check for Load Building). Then follow these steps:

1. On the initial screen, fill in all known information per each of the data sections provided. Always try to be as accurate as possible. Figure 5.85 shows the example for VENDOR NUMBER 1020, PLANT 1000, and MATERIAL NUMBER 1788.

2. When ready, click the EXECUTE button or use the ⌴F7⌴ function key.

3. The system performs a series of analyses to determine areas that need your attention. So the configuration check goes through all nodes related to load builder. The vendor account check, which can be also limited further to the vendor subrange, will verify if all purchasing organization level data and required data settings are correct, such as the AUTOM. PO and restrictions profile assignment.

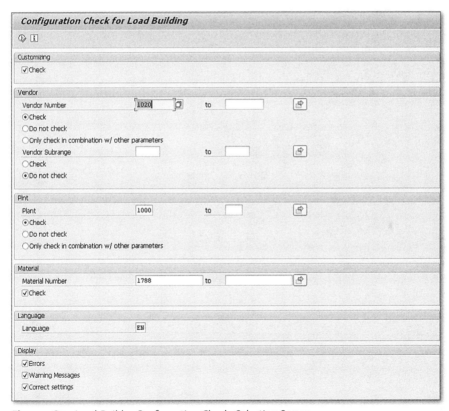

Figure 5.85 Load Builder Configuration Check: Selection Screen

4. On the next screen, you'll get the analysis results sorted by area in scope. You can expand the nodes by clicking on the line and clicking the EXPAND ALL icon or using ⌈Ctrl⌉ + ⌈F9⌉.

5. Repeat the step if you want to display results for each of the individual nodes for PLANT, VENDOR, and MATERIAL. You'll get to the lowest information level, which will now have the columns starting with the traffic lights on the far left indicating the check results (see Figure 5.86). A green light indicates that your check didn't find anything missing, a yellow light indicates that data is incomplete for the entire process to work, and the red light indicates a mandatory data mismatch or missing data altogether.

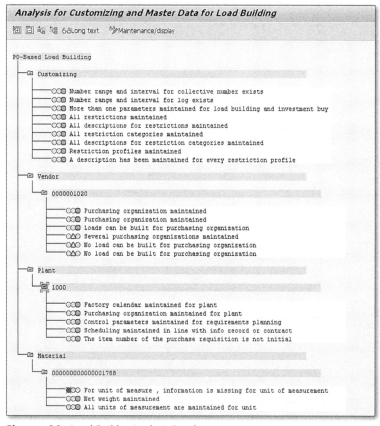

Figure 5.86 Load Builder Analysis Results

6. The line contains the short description of the check results; to see the full message, select the line and use the LONG TEXT button or press F6 .

7. You can also maintain the missing entries directly from this screen by clicking on the red traffic light line and using the MAINTENANCE/DISPLAY button or F5 function key. The relevant maintenance transaction starts — in our example, material 1788 returned an error on the UoM check, so Transaction MM02 (Material Master Change) will be opened.

8. After you review all nodes and verify that all lines are green or yellow (for areas that aren't going to be applicable, such as vendor not fully maintained in purchasing organizations other than the one you're working with), you are ready to start the load building run.

Load Building Run

As we've mentioned before, there are three ways to perform the load build: Methods

▶ Use the dialog mode to interact with the suggested quantities.

▶ Use the automatic load building transaction that will propose the suggested orders based on profiles and other master data objects we've covered earlier.

▶ Save it as a work list that the buyer can review and approve as a result.

This result list review is covered next when we talk about Transaction WLB4. This list includes the existing optimized and non-optimized loads.

So let's walk through the execution of Transaction WLB13 (Automatic Load Building).

On the initial screen, you have four tabs for data selection: Data selection

▶ LOAD BUILDING COMBINATIONS
Allows you to specify the vendor or vendor number range, purchasing organization, vendor subrange (to limit down the load build to desired group of products), and the plant (see Figure 5.87).

▶ REQUIREMENTS ELEMENT RESTRICTION
Allows you to specify that the load built run is to be specific to the purchasing group, materials, material group, or vendor's material number. You can also tighten up the selection by using the purchase

requisition document type, if you have a number of different document types you've defined.

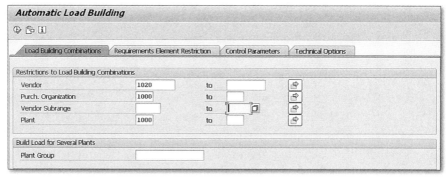

Figure 5.87 Automatic Load Building: Combinations Tab

- CONTROL PARAMETERS
  Contains the set of parameters that influences the load built results. Figure 5.88 shows the settings performing the simulation of a load build, as described here:

  - DOCUMENT CREATION CONTROL
    This field controls whether you generate the true POs and requisitions, or run simulation mode—generating logical not physical loads.

  - RESTRICTION PROFILE
    You can default the restriction profile instead of relying on the system to perform lookups for each of the vendors included in the run.

  - LOAD BUILD PROFILE
    Another one of the profiles we've talked about in the previous sections, this one is defined in configuration and holds a set of parameters used in optimizing to generate full loads.

  - TIME LIMIT FOR PO DATE
    This is the time limit used when determining the earliest possible PO time.

  - INCLUDE PLANNING CYCLE
    Planning cycle will be included in building loads.

  - WITHOUT EXISTING REQ. ELEMENTS
    Loads can be built without existing POs or purchase requisitions being included.

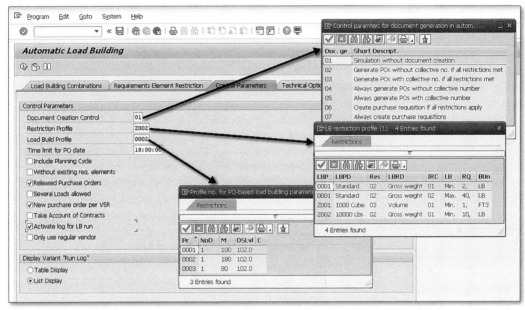

Figure 5.88 Automatic Load Building: Control Parameters Tab

▶ RELEASED PURCHASE ORDERS
Include released POs.

▶ SEVERAL LOADS ALLOWED
Allow more than one load to be created if such a condition occurs.

▶ NEW PURCHASE ORDER PER VSR
Individual loads are generated for materials of the same subrange.

▶ TAKE ACCOUNT OF CONTRACTS
System will look for existing purchasing documents referring to the contract agreements with selected vendor.

▶ ACTIVATE LOG FOR LB RUN
Log file will be created for all activities in the load built run.

▶ ONLY USE REGULAR VENDOR
During the build run, the system will determine if additional quantities of material need to be added. If selected, only those with the regular vendor maintained on the material master matching the vendor in the build run will be considered.

▶ TECHNICAL CONTROL

Allows you to define what should happen if there are program errors, how to maintain parallel processing, and how to split the processing threads most efficiently. This is usually maintained in collaboration with the Basis administration team.

After you're done filling in the selection criteria, follow these steps:

1. Click the EXECUTE button, or press F8 .

2. If you've followed our example, we requested the log file with LIST DISPLAY option (refer to Figure 5.86), and upon completion of the build run, you'll get the summary broken down by status area. Figure 5.89 shows the example of the simulation run results for reference.

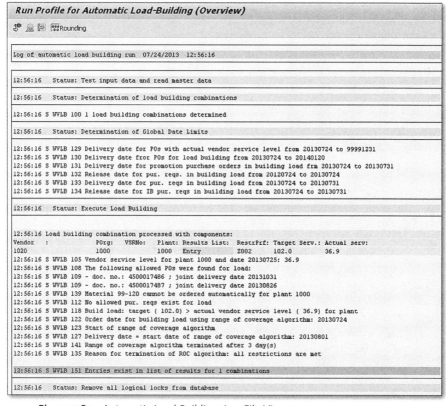

Figure 5.89 Automatic Load Building: Log File View

The simulation run created and populated the data tables (WBO1 for header level data, and WBO2 for items), storing the automatic load builder results for your review and processing using Transaction WLB4. The results entries are deleted after a specified number of days defined in Customizing.

Results List for Load Building

The final step in the process of load building is to review and check the automatic run results, and then convert them to the POs. Execute Transaction WLB4 to access the data created and stored in the automatic load builder run from the step before. On the initial screen, enter your selection criteria (for our example, enter data matching the previous steps) as shown in Figure 5.90. Click the EXECUTE button, or press F8, to run the program. On the follow-up screen, you'll get the list of the proposed and considered document header level data.

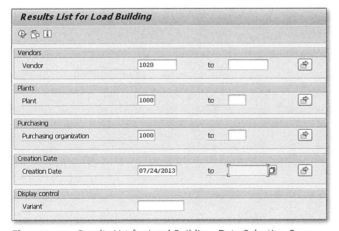

Figure 5.90   Results List for Load Building: Data Selection Screen

The body of the report includes all necessary information that makes up the proposed load. Using the DOUBLE-LINE DISPLAY button, or using Shift + F5, you can display the line level information and other details, such as weight, volume, and pricing (see Figure 5.91).

If you executed the automatic load builder in the simulate mode you can use the DELETE VENDOR FROM LOG button, or press Ctrl + F9, to remove the whole header report lines, with all of items, and rerun the report if needed. You can also delete individual materials from the log and keep the header and other materials by using the DELETE SELECTED ROWS button.

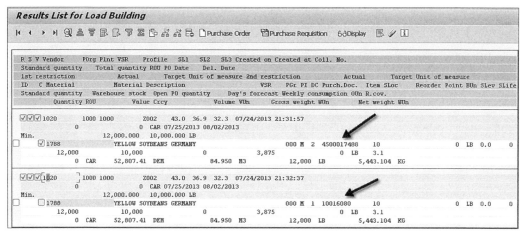

Figure 5.91 Results List for Load Building: Exploded List View

Create PO   Finally, you can create a PO by clicking on the header line you want to process and using the PURCHASE ORDER button. Figure 5.91 shows the PO number 4500017488 in the PURCH. DOC. column. If your procedures require you to create requisitions instead, create your document by using the PURCHASE REQUISITION button instead. The purchase requisition is created and shows up in the same column; see the example with requisition number 10016080 in the PURCH. DOC. column in Figure 5.91.

Display parameters   If you want to display some of the load building parameters that were used in the process, select the header or a line item, and click the DISPLAY button. At the header level, you can view vendor master data and restrictions; at the item level, you can see the stock/requirements list, promotions, material master data, purchasing document created, and pricing information.

Table 5.21 lists some of the transaction codes we covered in this section and menu path information for your reference.

Transaction	Menu Path
WLBA: Configuration Check for Load Building	LOGISTICS • MATERIALS MANAGEMENT • PURCHASING • ENVIRONMENT • ORDER OPTIMIZING • LOAD BUILDING • CONFIGURATION CHECK FOR LOAD BUILDING
WLB13: Automatic Load Building	LOGISTICS • MATERIALS MANAGEMENT • PURCHASING • ENVIRONMENT • ORDER OPTIMIZING • LOAD BUILDING • AUTOMATIC LOAD BUILDING
WLB4: Results List for Load Building	LOGISTICS • MATERIALS MANAGEMENT • PURCHASING • ENVIRONMENT • ORDER OPTIMIZING • LOAD BUILDING • RESULTS LIST FOR LOAD BUILDING
WLB5: Manual Load Building	LOGISTICS • MATERIALS MANAGEMENT • PURCHASING • ENVIRONMENT • ORDER OPTIMIZING • LOAD BUILDING • MANUAL LOAD BUILDING
WWP1: Online Planning in the Planning WB	LOGISTICS • MATERIALS MANAGEMENT • PURCHASING • ENVIRONMENT • ORDER OPTIMIZING • LOAD BUILDING • ONLINE PLANNING IN THE PLANNING WB
WWP3: Order Cancelation in Material Requirements Planning GM	LOGISTICS • MATERIALS MANAGEMENT • PURCHASING • ENVIRONMENT • ORDER OPTIMIZING • LOAD BUILDING • ORDER CANCELATION IN MATERIAL REQUIREMENTS PLANNING GM
WWP4: Load Building in Replenishment Workbench	LOGISTICS • MATERIALS MANAGEMENT • PURCHASING • ENVIRONMENT • ORDER OPTIMIZING • LOAD BUILDING • LOAD BUILDING IN REPLENISHMENT WORKBENCH

Table 5.21 Load Builder Transaction Codes

5.7 Summary

In the previous chapter, we've covered standard procurement procedures that cover about 80% of the usual business requirements. In this chapter, we covered the remaining 20% that require special procurement functions that SAP also provides for even the most demanding process requirements.

You've learned, by example, about subcontracting and third-party order processing, their basic configuration and master data requirements, and what steps you need to execute to take them from generated demand to invoice. You've also learned about STOs, allowing you to move materials between your own facilities using different procedures, and cross-company movements between sister companies that require you to add billing into the mix. We also crossed the functional boundaries and stepped into the Production Planning area to show you how a Kanban procedure is constructed and executed, integrating its steps with procurement functionality we've already covered. And, finally, you've learned about retail procurement heavy hitters—order optimizing.

We walked you through all influencing factors, profiles, master data, and procedures needed to successfully execute investment buying, quantity optimizing, and load builder. All of those special procurement functions covered the procurement of materials. In the next chapter, we'll show you how to manage the procurement of services.

Buying services is something all companies need. Some of these services may be quite complex and require close supervision and constant tracking of deliverables.

6   Procurement of Services

Organizations have many different service requirements—such as cleaning, maintenance, security, or even construction of new sites—where you have to describe very clearly the services to be delivered and the parameters of acceptance. This is where the SAP ERP process of service procurement can help you. The SAP ERP system supports the complete purchasing of services cycle as part of the Purchasing functionality in the Materials Management (MM) component, from raising the requirement to the definition of the tasks needed, bid creation and processing, identification or selection of the vendor, creation of a purchase order (PO) or contract, acceptance of services, invoice processing, and payment. The procurement of service cycle starts with a requirement and ends with the payment to vendor, as shown in Figure 6.1.

The service procurement cycle is completely integrated in SAP ERP MM Purchasing. The same documents that you use to purchase materials support the purchase of services. The service purchase cycle is even possible to integrate with other SAP ERP components such as SAP Plant Maintenance or SAP Project System, which, for example, will issue the requirement for the purchase of a maintenance service for a scheduled machinery repair or to start a new phase of a complex project. This integration allows these other components to create a purchase requisition for the required service automatically previous to the requirement date, and then convert that requisition into a PO or contract release order. Later, as the services are performed, they are registered in a service entry sheet, which has the same function and is equivalent to a goods receipt of materials.

Integration

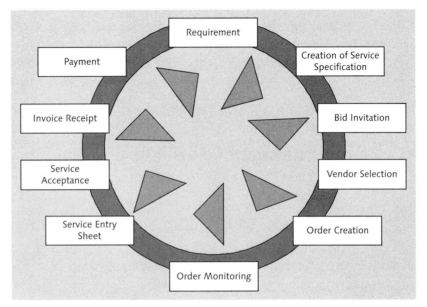

Figure 6.1 The Service Procurement Cycle

In previous chapters, we talked about the master data for services and how to maintain that data in the service master. In this chapter, we describe how to use that master data and create POs or outline agreements to buy services. We'll describe how to monitor their delivery and process the invoice so that your company can produce the payment for the vendor.

Let's start with the first phase of the service procurement cycle: requirements.

6.1   Processing Requirements

Procuring services begins with a requirement. Requirements may be very detailed and allow you to create a service specification in the service master right away, but in many cases, you don't have that detail yet and probably need help from the vendor in getting it. After you have a requirement, you can create a purchase requisition or a request for quotation (RFQ) for unplanned services. Purchasing documents allow you to start the process for either of the cases mentioned.

In Chapter 2, we discussed the creation of service master records, and now you'll see how to use them in a purchasing document. This may be done after you create a purchase requisition for unplanned services with a simple structure and an overall limit. Later, when the vendor comes back with a detailed plan for the execution of all of the project tasks, you can take that plan and create the entries in the service master.

Purchasing document

In the following sections, we'll detail the steps needed to create a purchase requisition or an RFQ. After the information is populated, we'll explain reference documents.

6.1.1 Creating a Purchase Requisition

If you have a specification in the service master, then you can enter the service number in the document to bring all of the details to the document.

To create a purchase requisition, follow these steps:

1. Go to Transaction ME51N (LOGISTICS • MATERIALS MANAGEMENT • PURCHASING • PURCHASE REQUISITION • CREATE).

2. Create a service item by entering an account assignment category (usually "K" for cost center).

3. Enter "D" (for service) in the item category (I) column.

4. Enter a short text, delivery date, material group, and plant for the item.

5. As soon as you press Enter, the system creates two new tabs in the ITEM detail section. In the SERVICES tab, select a service number, a quantity, and a price, if necessary (see Figure 6.2).

6. Press the Enter key.

7. When prompted, enter a General Ledger account and a cost center (see Figure 6.3).

8. Save the document.

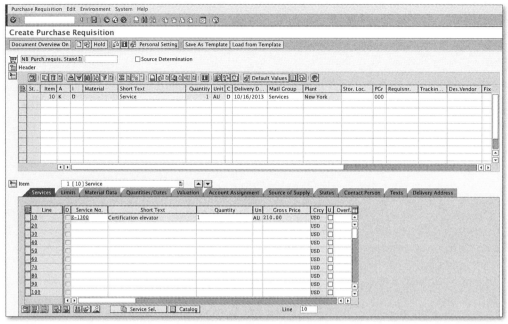

Figure 6.2 Purchase Requisition for a Service

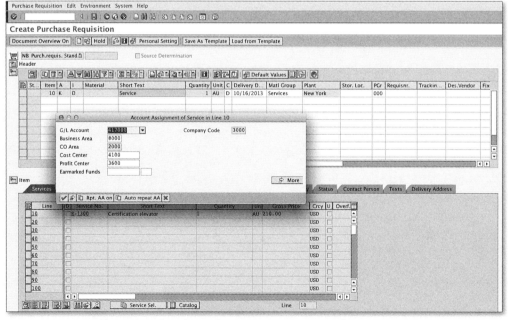

Figure 6.3 Completing the Account Assignment Information

Creating a Requisition without a Specification

If, on the other hand, you don't have a specification and will develop that detail later, you can create the requisition or RFQ by providing a general description of the service and, most importantly, setting a value limit.

You can create this type of requisition for unplanned services, when you buy simple services, one-time services, or when you require the vendor to collaborate with you in defining the detail specification. In some cases, this may happen until the service is delivered or at least until the vendor has developed a plan to execute all of the tasks that are part of the service.

Unplanned serivice

To create a general requisition like the one shown in Figure 6.3, follow these steps:

Create general

1. Go to Transaction ME51N (Logistics • Materials Management • Purchasing • Purchase Requisition • Create).

2. Create a service item by entering an account assignment category (usually "K" for cost center) in column A.

3. Enter "D" (for service) in the item category column (I).

4. Enter a short text, delivery date, material group, and plant for the item.

5. As soon as you press Enter, the system creates two new tabs in the Item detail section. In the Limits tab, enter an overall limit and an expected value.

   The overall limit refers to the maximum allowed value for the order. The expected value is the value you expect the order not to exceed.

6. Press the Enter key.

7. When prompted, enter a General Ledger account and a cost center (see Figure 6.4).

8. Save the document.

With this simple set of data, you have a requisition for unplanned services.

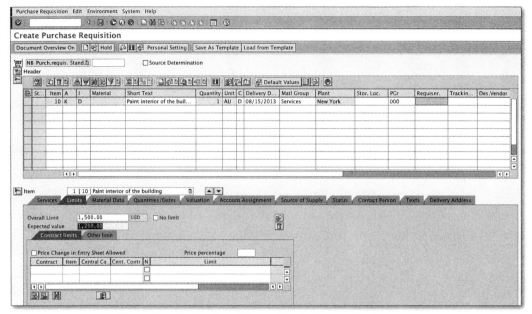

Figure 6.4 Service Requisition without a Service Number

Table 6.1 contains a list of transactions to work with purchase requisitions for services.

Transaction	Menu Path
ME51N: Create	LOGISTICS • MATERIALS MANAGEMENT • PURCHASING • PURCHASE REQUISITION • CREATE
ME52N: Change	LOGISTICS • MATERIALS MANAGEMENT • PURCHASING • PURCHASE REQUISITION • CHANGE
ME53N: Display	LOGISTICS • MATERIALS MANAGEMENT • PURCHASING • PURCHASE REQUISITION • DISPLAY

Table 6.1 Useful Transactions for Purchase Requisitions of Services

6.1.2   Creating an RFQ

RFQs are very useful when you are biding the services among several vendors to obtain the best price or conditions. You can also use them when you don't have an exact idea of how much the services you're buying are going to cost.

In the SAP ERP system, creating an RFQ is very similar to creating a requisition; enter your organizational information in the initial screen of Transaction ME41 (LOGISTICS • MATERIALS MANAGEMENT • PURCHASING • REQUEST FOR QUOTATION • CREATE), and from there, you follow the same steps, except that an RFQ won't require an account assignment for the item.

After you enter the item category for services, the system guides you to a separate screen where you can enter the overall value limit of the order (see Figure 6.5).

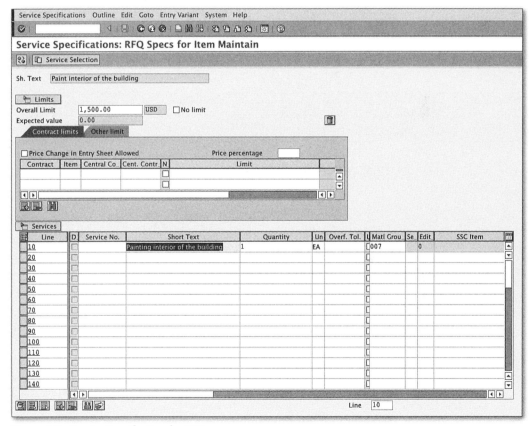

Figure 6.5 Service Specification for RFQ

Service subitem level

From the point of view of the purchasing documents, there is a difference in the document structure between buying materials and buying services. While materials are purchased at the item level, the purchase of services works at a level below the item. This subitem level for services is activated automatically when you enter the item category "D" for services. When you do this, the ITEM detail section of the purchasing document adds two new tabs to enter information about the services: The SERVICES tab allows you to select services from the service master or an unplanned service specification. The LIMITS tab allows you to buy a service without a detailed specification, and you have to enter an overall limit and an expected value.

Statement of Work and Hierarchies

Service document items

Document items for services contain the short description of the service that is being purchased, and then you can include a list of service specifications for this item. This set of specifications is referred to as the statement of work (SOW).

Service specifications

In the example shown earlier in Figure 6.3, we only entered the short description for the service, which was "Paint interior of the building", and we entered an overall limit of $1,500.00. To enter a service specification, double-click on the short text description, and the system takes you to the SERVICE DETAIL screen where you can break this service up by entering a more detailed work delivery plan for the following:

Detailed plan

- Furniture removal
- Installation of protective covers
- Wall preparations
- Painting

Each of these items can have its own quantity and price. There is even an
option to create a specification structure in which you can have a hierarchy of tasks included in the specification, in which there are higher level
items that include lower level items in a parent-child relationship with a
maximum of four levels (see Figure 6.6).

Service outline

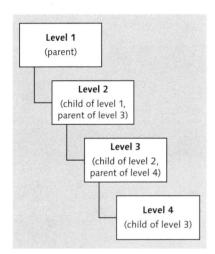

Figure 6.6 Parent-Child Hierarchy

To create this hierarchy, you have to be in the SERVICES full screen, which
you get to by clicking the OVERVIEW icon (mountains and sun icon) at
the bottom of the ITEM section of the document in the SERVICES tab (refer
to Figure 6.5).

Click the OUTLINE ON/OFF icon 🖼, or press the ⌴F6⌴ key (see Figure 6.7).

This parent-child relationship, as shown in Figure 6.7, is called the service
outline, and you can specify up to four outline levels with an unlimited
number of lines per level, such as the following:

Parent-child
relationship

- ▶ Paint interior of the building
  - ▶ Preparation works
  - ▶ Furniture removal
  - ▶ Installation of protective covers
  - ▶ Wall preparations

▶ Painting

▶ Cleanup

▶ Removal of protective covers

▶ Furniture setup

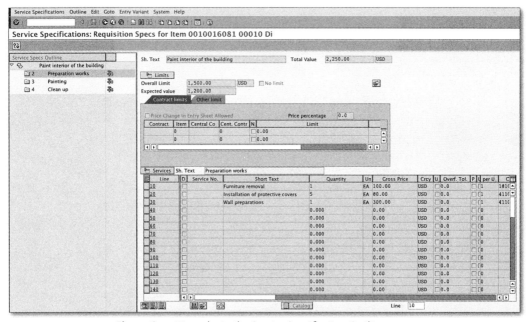

Figure 6.7 Hierarchy in the Service Specification Outline

After the outline is displayed, you can right-click on the top line, which corresponds to the short text you entered in the requisition item, and select CREATE NEW OUTLINE SUBGROUP. As mentioned, you can nest a maximum of four levels.

Enter a unit of measure and a price for each of the tasks that form each level. The services can be expressed in different units of measure; for example, instead of buying one painting service at $150, you can buy painting of 500 square feet at $3.33 per sq. ft. This allows you to post a service entry sheet confirmation for a certain amount (in square feet) that has been painted and is now being invoiced.

Work Breakdown Structure

If your project is large and complex enough and you're following the execution in a project management system, such as Microsoft Project or Oracle Primavera; you can enter the work breakdown structure (WBS) number, or any other number that the vendor uses to identify a particular task, in the task detail of the RFQ using the EXTERNAL SERVICES NUMBER field. This way, you can match the progress of the project to the status of the services in the SAP ERP system. The system allows searches in most service transactions using this number.

Identification

To enter a WBS number, do the following:

1. From the SERVICE outline screen, select EDIT • DETAILS from the top menu bar.

2. In the pop-up window, select the BASIC DATA tab, and enter the WBS number in the SERVICES NUMBER field (see Figure 6.8).

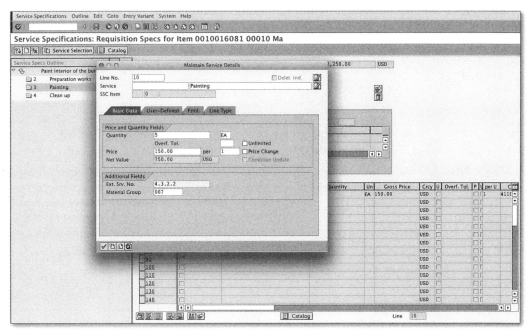

Figure 6.8 Entering an External Service Number

Note

The recommendation to enter the WBS number or a vendor's reference number in the EXTERNAL SERVICE NUMBER field, will help you only when you're entering the service specification directly in the purchasing document, thus creating an order for unplanned services. When you work with services from the service master, there is a field specifically for this purpose: STANDARD SERVICE CATALOG ITEM, which requires you to first create the structure of the reference number in the standard service catalog.

Table 6.2 contains a list of transactions to work with RFQs for services.

Transaction	Menu Path
ME41: Create (RFQ)	LOGISTICS • MATERIALS MANAGEMENT • PURCHASING • RFQ/QUOTATION • REQUEST FOR QUOTATION • CREATE
ME42: Change (RFQ)	LOGISTICS • MATERIALS MANAGEMENT • PURCHASING • RFQ/QUOTATION • REQUEST FOR QUOTATION • CHANGE
ME43: Display (RFQ)	LOGISTICS • MATERIALS MANAGEMENT • PURCHASING • RFQ/QUOTATION • REQUEST FOR QUOTATION • CHANGE

Table 6.2 Useful Transactions for RFQs of Services

6.1.3   Creating a Reference Document from a Purchase Requisition

PO reference After the purchasing document for services is approved, the purchase requisitions for services can be used as the reference document to create either a contract or a PO, and POs can be sent to the vendor. As we've also explained in Chapter 4, you can send the order to the vendor either by email, fax, or Electronic Data Interchange (EDI), depending on your system settings and interface capabilities.

Using a Service Master Record

Using service master records makes purchasing services even easier. Services with very complex specifications and also those bought regularly can be simplified to save you time in data entry in requisitions, POs, or contracts. These services include consulting, maintenance, security, web hosting, and more.

When using the service master, it's also easy to enter various services that go together on the same purchasing document. For example, if your company is building a new storage room, you can buy the floor construction, the walls and windows installation, the plumbing, and the roof construction all in a single document that is sent to a single vendor.

By selecting multiple services from the catalog, you can assemble a more complex service, or you can track the different services that a single vendor—such as an integrator or a construction company that is managing other vendors—is supplying.

To enter a service number in a purchasing document, follow these steps:

1. From the CREATE screen for a specific purchasing document, enter item category "D" for services in the ITEM OVERVIEW section.

2. Enter a short text, a delivery date, and a material group, and then press `Enter`.

3. In the ITEM DETAIL section, select the SERVICES tab.

4. In the SERVICE NUMBER field, enter a service number or use the pull-down search to look up a service.

5. Enter a quantity, unit of measurement, and unit price.

6. Save your work.

6.2   Service Entry and Acceptance

You can closely monitor POs or contract release orders for services, thanks to the ability to confirm the services that have already been performed by the vendor. This confirmation occurs when a service entry sheet is posted.

Service confirmations

Service entry sheets serve two purposes: to confirm that a service or tasks of a complex service have been performed, and to prepare the system for the receipt of a vendor invoice. A vendor invoice is equivalent to a goods receipt for material. The one big difference with receiving materials is that service entry sheets won't post to the clearing account for GR/IR until they are accepted.

Posting the service entry sheet is a two-step process, involving first receiving or acknowledging the services, and then, second, accepting the service entry sheet. In the following sections, we'll go over the steps needed to enter a new service entry sheet and then how to accept a service. Service entry sheets are entered to register the delivery of a service, but they have to be accepted so that an invoice can be posted.

6.2.1 Entering a New Service Entry Sheet

To create a new service entry sheet, follow these steps:

1. Go to Transaction ML81N, or follow the path LOGISTICS • MATERIALS MANAGEMENT • SERVICE ENTRY SHEET • MAINTAIN.

2. On the main screen, click on the NEW button at the top of the screen.

3. Enter a PO, an item number, and a short text to describe the entry sheet.

4. Select the service you're going to receive by selecting from the PO. Choose EDIT • SERVICE SELECTION from the menu bar.

5. In the pop-up window, press the [Enter] key to go to the service outline.

6. Select the service, and then click on the ADOPT SERVICES button (or press [F9]). This takes you back to the service entry sheet.

7. Repeat for all of the services you need to receive and save.

Acceptance When you enter a new service entry sheet, the status is NO ACCEPTANCE with a red traffic light (see top of Figure 6.9). You change the status to ACCEPTANCE by clicking on the green flag icon 🏴 or by opening the tree display on the left side of the screen. This is done by clicking on the icon with the two little color circles 🔳, selecting the new entry sheet at the top of the list with the red traffic light, and right-clicking to open the contextual menu shown in Figure 6.10. With this, the traffic light changes to a status of WILL BE ACCEPTED and shows a yellow traffic light.

Finally, when the entry sheet is saved, the status changes to ACCEPTED, and the traffic light shows green. You can set the status of the entry sheet to ACCEPTANCE using the context menu that appears when you right-click.

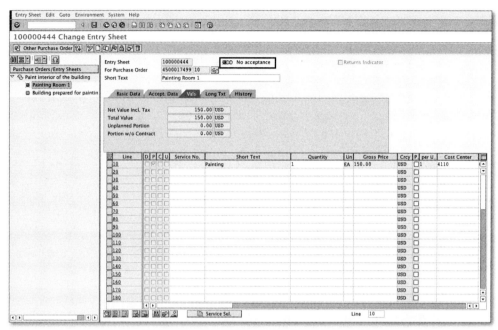

Figure 6.9 Service Entry Sheets

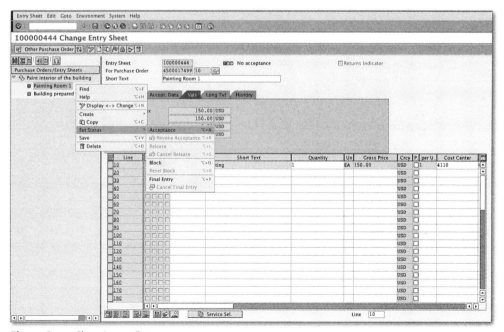

Figure 6.10 Changing an Entry

6.2.2 Accepting a Service

We've now come to the second part of the process: accepting a service. We described earlier that you can accept the service as you enter the entry sheet, but you can prevent the users that enter the sheets from also accepting them by setting the authorizations in the user profile. (This is done by a security analyst and you need to make this requirements probably during the implementation phase.) This way, some users will have authorization to create the entry sheets and other users will have authorization to accept it.

Release strategies
When you need to set the acceptance on a service entry sheet in a separate step that's performed by a different person (normally a manager or supervisor); you need to use release strategies. These approval strategies are setup in Customizing in the same way as the strategies for purchasing documents. This is explained in detail in Chapter 4.

When this is set up, the acceptance is set in Transaction ML85 (Collective Release) instead of doing it inside Transaction ML81N (Maintain Service Entry sheet) (see Figure 6.11). This transaction only lists those entry sheets that are blocked due to a strategy.

In this case, to accept the service, you have to explicitly enter an acceptance for the service entry sheet after you've verified the delivery of the service. You can also create release strategies for service entry sheets in Customizing. You need to describe this need to your functional analyst so that the system can be set up accordingly.

Goods receipt document
After the service entry sheet has been accepted, the system creates a goods receipt document. Both the service entry sheets and the goods receipt documents show up in the PO under the PURCHASE ORDER HISTORY tab. The service entry sheet is labeled as LERF, and the actual goods receipt as WE, just like any receipt for goods, as shown in Figure 6.12.

Revoke acceptance
If you ever mistakenly accept a service you shouldn't have, you can always reverse that action by using the same context menu and selecting SET STATUS • REVOKE ACCEPTANCE.

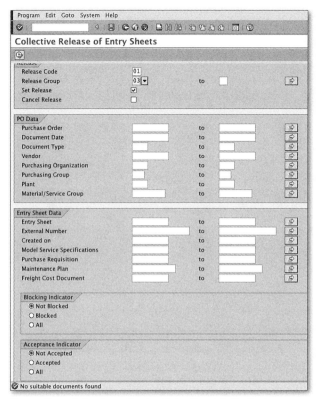

Figure 6.11 Releasing a Service Entry Sheet Collectively

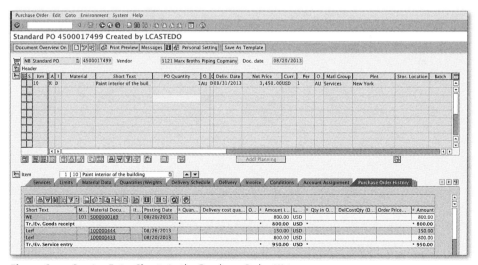

Figure 6.12 Service Entry Sheets in the Purchase Order History

353

GR/IR posting   As mentioned earlier, the service entry sheet also posts to a GR/IR clearing account. This GR/IR account, as shown in Figure 6.13, is cleared after the offsetting invoice is posted into the system by the Invoice Verification component. This way, you get a three-way match for the PO, the service entry sheet, and the invoice. If all match, no differences are posted.

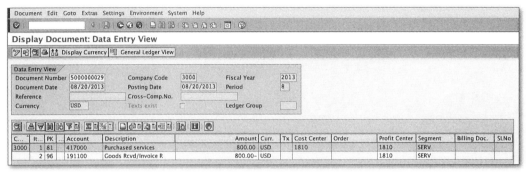

Figure 6.13   Service Entry Sheet Posted to the GR/IR Clearing Account

Through the three-way match for the PO, the service entry sheet, and the invoice, you can verify that the same services that were ordered are being delivered, and then create the invoice.

Table 6.3 contains a list of transactions for purchasing and receiving of services.

Transaction	Menu Path
ME21N: Create	LOGISTICS • MATERIALS MANAGEMENT • PURCHASING • PURCHASE ORDER • CREATE VENDOR / SUPPLYING PLANT KNOWN
ME22N: Change	LOGISTICS • MATERIALS MANAGEMENT • PURCHASING • PURCHASE ORDER • CHANGE
ME23N: Display	LOGISTICS • MATERIALS MANAGEMENT • PURCHASING • PURCHASE ORDER • DISPLAY
ML81N: Maintain Service Entry Sheet	LOGISTICS • MATERIALS MANAGEMENT • PURCHASING • SERVICES • MAINTAIN SERVICE ENTRY SHEET
ML85: Collective Release	LOGISTICS • MATERIALS MANAGEMENT • PURCHASING • SERVICES • COLLECTIVE RELEASE

Table 6.3   Useful Transactions for Purchasing of Services

6.3   Using Outline Agreements for Services

Outline agreements, as discussed in detail in Chapter 4, are long-term contracts between your company and the service vendor, and they can also be used for the procurement of services. This is very useful when you engage in the purchase of repetitive services that will be performed continuously over an extended period of time. These items are identified with an item category "D" for service. Just like in a PO or requisition, as described earlier, you can either enter services selected from the service master or directly enter a detailed service specification manually.

Long-term agreements

In the following sections, we'll go over the steps you'll need to create and release contracts for services.

6.3.1   Creating Contracts for Services

Contracts for services are created in Transaction ME31K, the same as any other material's contracts. To create a contract, follow these steps:

1. Go to Transaction ME31K, or follow the menu path LOGISTICS • MATE-RIALS MANAGEMENT • PURCHASING • OUTLINE AGREEMENT • CREATE.

2. In the initial screen, enter a VENDOR NUMBER, CONTRACT TYPE (QUANTITY or VALUE), PURCHASING ORGANIZATION, and PURCHASING GROUP. Press Enter.

3. In the next screen, you'll see the contract's header information; most of the information has been copied from the vendor's master record (see Figure 6.14). Enter the VALIDITY END date for the contract, and then press Enter.

4. To create a service item, enter "K" (for cost center) in the account assignment category (column A).

5. Enter "D" (for service) in the item category column (I).

6. Enter a short text, material group, and plant for the item.

7. In the contract item, enter the basic data and then proceed to enter the services details (see Figure 6.15).

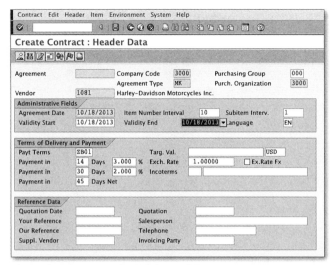

Figure 6.14 Entering the Validity End Date

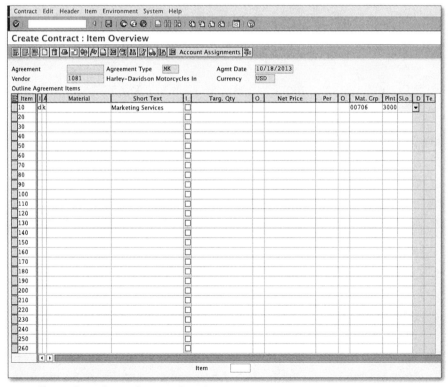

Figure 6.15 Create Contract Overview

8. As soon as you press ⌈Enter⌉, the system takes you to a screen for entering service numbers from the service master or a SHORT TEXT description, a QUANTITY, and GROSS PRICE for each item (see Figure 6.16).

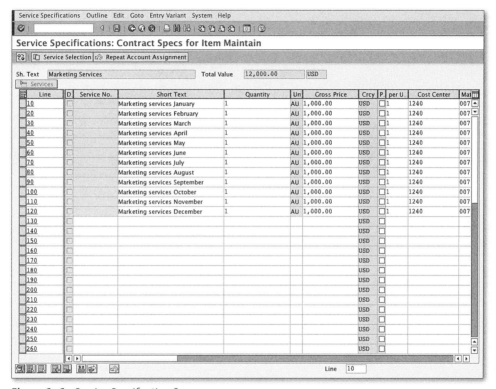

Figure 6.16 Service Specification Screen

9. If you chose to enter a text description instead of a service number, you have to enter a valid General Ledger account and a cost center to charge the purchase to.

6.3.2 Releasing Contracts for Services

When you create contracts for services, you may choose to make them subject to a release strategy; this is done in configuration as discussed in Chapter 4, and the steps to release them are the same as for a contract created to purchase materials.

The subsequent creation of purchase orders created in reference to a contract (release POs) is the same one discussed in Chapter 4 for outline agreements for materials, and the process of entering service entry sheets is the same as discussed earlier in this chapter.

Table 6.4 contains a list of transactions for working with contracts of services.

Transaction	Menu Path
ME31K: Create	LOGISTICS • MATERIALS MANAGEMENT • PURCHASING • OUTLINE AGREEMENT • CREATE
ME32K: Change	LOGISTICS • MATERIALS MANAGEMENT • PURCHASING • OUTLINE AGREEMENT • CHANGE
ME33K: Display	LOGISTICS • MATERIALS MANAGEMENT • PURCHASING • OUTLINE AGREEMENT • DISPLAY

Table 6.4 Useful Transactions for Outline Agreements of Services

6.4 Summary

The procurement of services through the SAP ERP system is simple and flexible. It allows you to have several approval steps during the process to make sure that the services you're buying are bought properly as well as from the right source, and also confirmed and approved to make sure that they were delivered according to the specification—and most of all to your company's expectations.

All of the purchasing documents in the SAP ERP system, except for scheduling agreements, allow you to include services. You can then create service purchase requisitions, RFQs, POs, and outline agreements.

Receiving the services you buy through the use of service entry sheets gives you the same functionality as purchases of goods, where there is a three-way check to make sure that the PO matches the receipt and the invoice in both quantity and price.

In the next chapter, we'll discuss inbound logistics, which is the next logical step after creating a purchase order.

Managing inbound logistics is a balancing act of getting your purchased goods into your facilities as fast and as economically as possible.

7   Inbound Logistics

In previous chapters, we covered many varieties of procurement—from the simple purchase order (PO) to special functions such as subcontracting, third-party orders, and stock transport orders (STOs). They all have common process steps that we haven't covered yet—the goods need to be shipped from the supplier and received in your ordering plant. The goods can be shipped by your vendor, or you can provide the transportation service to do so.

Inbound logistics includes all of the steps you need to perform after you've created a PO. This includes receipt of advance shipping notification (ASN), creating inbound deliveries or a combination with inbound shipment (a potential collection of inbound deliveries), and related packing information, receipt on the dock, verification of materials received, putaway, and an actual goods receipt posting.

Depending on your business situations, you have the options to use a fairly simple process that involves simple inbound delivery, or even inbound shipment to bring the goods in, or a fairly complex process. In this chapter, we'll focus on the activities that allow you to process confirmed vendor shipment quantities using a variety of different methods, such as simple order acknowledgement, inbound delivery, rough receipt, and inbound shipment processing, including shipment cost documents, which are the basic options employed when implementing inbound logistics. First, we'll focus on the key indicator that needs to be set on either the vendor master or purchase info record to steer your system to use the correct method: the confirmation control.

Simple and complex scenarios

7.1 Confirmation Controls

For your POs to be subject to a subsequent logistics processing, you need to let the system know what to do by working with confirmation controls. You have choices to enter a simple vendor order acknowledgement, provide the actual manual confirmation of quantities to be shipped, or create an inbound delivery manually, or via Electronic Data Interchange (EDI) as ASN. These actions can be relevant for material requirements planning (MRP), and you can also tie the goods receipt with reference to the vendor confirmation.

Predelivered options

Figure 7.1 shows an overview of the available predelivered options. These are all definable in Customizing in the CONFIRMATIONS section of the IMG. Usually these settings are maintained by the consulting team; however, it's important for the users to understand the dependencies defined in there.

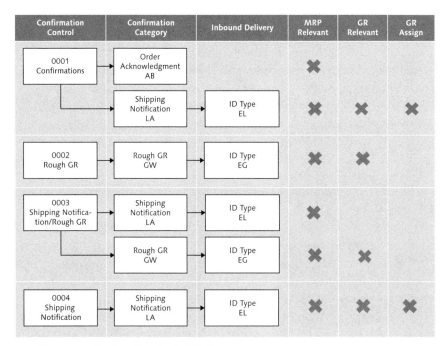

Figure 7.1 Confirmation Control Options

Confirmations provide you with a method of entering the true quantities the vendor will be supplying. Confirmations come in the form of the order acknowledgement, which you usually process manually and update with the quantities and delivery dates upon vendor communication directly into the PO using Transaction ME22N. You can also create the inbound delivery based on received shipping notification, or by using a rough goods receipt with the inbound delivery (we'll talk about these confirmations and how to enter them in detail next). It's possible that you'll have the option to use confirmation control keys that are unique to your business or company, as well.

Vendor
confirmations

7.1.1   Master Data

You can apply the defined confirmation process to default into your POs automatically. During PO creation, the system performs the master data check, looking first at the purchasing info record (combination of the material, plant, and the supplier account number) confirmation control settings, and then if no purchasing info record is found, the system looks at the vendor master confirmation control definition. These are the two master data pieces we've already covered in detail in Chapter 2. Let's look at examples of both in the following subsections.

Default
confirmation
process to PO

Vendor Master

If you want to define a specific confirmation control to the vendor in the specific purchasing organization, you can do so in the vendor master. All subsequent documents will have this setting applied as long as you don't maintain more specific data for individual materials in the info records.

Specific
confirmation
control

To maintain the vendor master record, run Transaction XK02 or Transaction MK02, and follow these steps:

1. Specify the account number and the purchasing organization of choice.

2. Go to the PURCHASING ORGANIZATION DATA section to find the confirmation control setting. The indicator is available for you in the DEFAULT DATA MATERIAL part of the screen (see Figure 7.2).

3. Enter the CONFIRMATION CONTROL key—in our example—we've maintained the 0002 (ROUGH GR). This value defaults automatically into the

PO line at order creation time, and applies to all POs created for this vendor unless purchasing info records are found with more specific assignments.

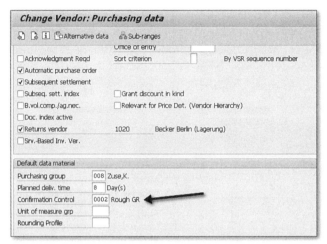

Figure 7.2 Vendor Master: Default Confirmation Control

See Table 7.1 for some of the vendor master maintenance transactions (see Chapter 2 for more details on vendor master).

Transaction	Menu Path
XK02: Change Vendor Centrally	LOGISTICS • MATERIALS MANAGEMENT • PURCHASING • MASTER DATA • VENDOR • CENTRAL • CHANGE
MK02: Change Vendor Purchasing	LOGISTICS • MATERIALS MANAGEMENT • PURCHASING • MASTER DATA • VENDOR • PURCHASING • CHANGE (CURRENT)

Table 7.1 Vendor Master Maintenance Transactions

7.1.2   Purchasing Info Record

The second driver for confirmation control determination is defined on purchasing info records. We've covered the overview and usage of this piece of master data in Chapter 2 in detail. Use Transaction ME12 to maintain the purchasing info record data in the PURCHASING ORGANIZATION DATA 1 screen (see Figure 7.3).

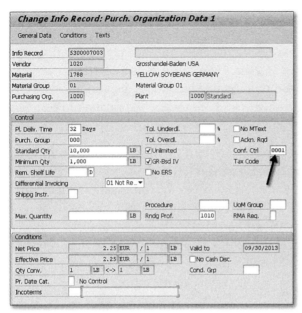

Figure 7.3 Purchasing Info Record: Confirmation Control Assignment

Remember, purchasing info records contain the most specific level of information that will be applied automatically to the PO line data level at the time of order creation. If you require your suppliers to send you the acknowledgement of your POs receipts most of the time, you define it on the vendor master per the previous section. If you need to have a specific confirmations received for a particular purchasing organization, plant, material combination, you can set this in the CONF. CTRL box (see Figure 7.3).

Require acknowledgement

Table 7.2 details the purchasing info record change transactions and menu paths.

Transaction	Menu Path
ME12: Change	LOGISTICS • MATERIALS MANAGEMENT • PURCHASING • MASTER DATA • INFO RECORD • CHANGE
MEMASSIN: Mass Maintenance	LOGISTICS • MATERIALS MANAGEMENT • PURCHASING • MASTER DATA • INFO RECORD • MASS MAINTENANCE

Table 7.2 Purchasing Info Record: Change Transaction Codes

7.2 Order Acknowledgement

In this section, we'll talk about the PO acknowledgement confirmation category. As mentioned before, you can use vendor confirmation to update the quantity and promised delivery date that can be applied to your POs and provide downstream up-to-date information to planning and receiving.

Confirmation options

The PO confirmation options include the order acknowledgement or combinations of confirmation categories, including the acknowledgements. SAP suggests the informative use of confirmations and firmed inbound delivery that carries the dates and quantities all of the way to receiving. The system has the potential to be defined in such a way that order acknowledgement can be receive, as the confirmation category AB and be relevant for MRP, receiving, and assignment at the time of receipt. Figure 7.4 shows the relevancy to GR processing.

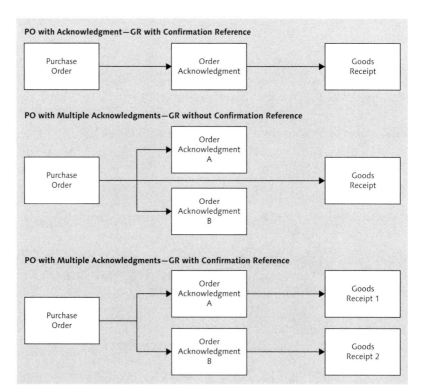

Figure 7.4 Options for Order Acknowledgement Confirmation

7.2.1 Automatic and Manual Confirmation

The confirmation of a specific type can be applied automatically to the Confirm specific type PO lines at the time you create your documents by copying the data from the vendor master or purchasing info records. We covered these two influencing pieces of master data in Section 7.1 (see Transaction XK02 or Transaction MK02).

You can also apply the order acknowledgement entry using an EDI trans- EDI action—message type ORDRSP—and IDoc ORDERS01. Go to the CONFIRMATIONS tab, enter the order acknowledgement on the PO line, and use it as a required entry during goods receipt. At the time of receipt, warehouse personnel need to match the quantity received to the confirmation entry on the PO.

You can have multiple order acknowledgements on your PO (see Figure 7.5). The system also stores information about the acknowledgement origin (EDI, manual, etc.). This can be useful when troubleshooting and determining how and if the acknowledgement was received.

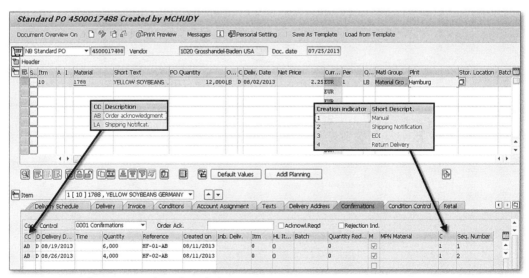

Figure 7.5 Confirmations: Order Acknowledgements Entry

Manual
confirmation

You can also enter the confirmation manually using Transaction ME22N (Purchase Order Change) as shown in Figure 7.5. Note that the confirmation category AB – ORDER ACKNOWLEDGEMENT resides on the PO, and it's not a separate document.

7.2.2 Monitor Confirmations

You can monitor your confirmations to make sure that the promised delivery date by the vendors matches your POs. To do this, you can run a series of reports that show you the status and check if dunning reminders need to be sent to your vendors that failed to send the acknowledgements.

Confirmation
reporting

You can use Transaction ME2A (Monitor Confirmations), which allows you to report on confirmations already received/entered into the system, and drill into them to display PO details. Follow these steps:

1. Run the transaction, and on the initial screen, enter your selection criteria specifying the required confirmation category and any other criteria as shown in Figure 7.6.

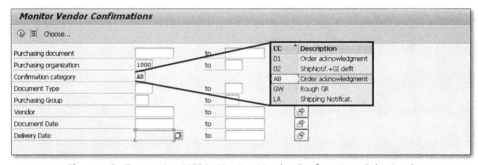

Figure 7.6 Transaction ME2A: Monitor Vendor Confirmations Selection Screen

2. Start the report by clicking the EXECUTE button or use the F8 function key. On the next screen, you'll get the list of POs that received the AB type confirmations (see Figure 7.7).

3. You can display PO data, such as running Transaction ME23N, by double-clicking on the PO number shown in the first column of the report.

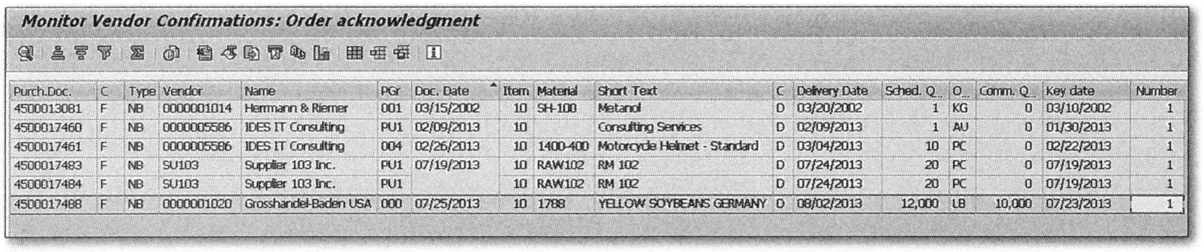

Monitor Vendor Confirmations: Order acknowledgment

Purch.Doc.	C	Type	Vendor	Name	PGr	Doc. Date	Item	Material	Short Text	C	Delivery Date	Sched. Q...	O...	Comm. Q...	Key date	Number
4500013081	F	NB	0000001014	Hermann & Riemer	001	03/15/2002	10	SH-100	Metanol	D	03/20/2002	1	KG	0	03/10/2002	1
4500017460	F	NB	0000005586	IDES IT Consulting	PU1	02/09/2013	10		Consulting Services	D	02/09/2013	1	AU	0	01/30/2013	1
4500017461	F	NB	0000005586	IDES IT Consulting	004	02/26/2013	10	1400-400	Motorcycle Helmet - Standard	D	03/04/2013	10	PC	0	02/22/2013	1
4500017483	F	NB	SU103	Supplier 103 Inc.	PU1	07/19/2013	10	RAW102	RM 102	D	07/24/2013	20	PC	0	07/19/2013	1
4500017484	F	NB	SU103	Supplier 103 Inc.	PU1		10	RAW102	RM 102	D	07/24/2013	20	PC	0	07/19/2013	1
4500017488	F	NB	0000001020	Grosshandel-Baden USA	000	07/25/2013	10	1788	YELLOW SOYBEANS GERMANY	D	08/02/2013	12,000	LB	10,000	07/23/2013	1

Figure 7.7 Monitor Vendor Confirmations: Order Acknowledgements

Table 7.3 lists this and other transactions you can use when using the order acknowledgement confirmation control category.

Transaction	Menu Path
ME22N: PO Change	Logistics • Materials Management • Purchasing • Purchase Order • Change
ME23N: PO Display	Logistics • Materials Management • Purchasing • Purchase Order • Display
ME2A: Monitor Confirmations	Logistics • Materials Management • Purchasing • Purchase Order • Reporting • Monitor Confirmations
ME92F: Monitor Order Acknowledgements	Logistics • Materials Management • Purchasing • Purchase Order • Reporting • Monitor Order Acknowledgements

Table 7.3 Vendor Confirmations Transaction Codes

7.3 Rough Goods Receipt

If you're using SAP ERP 6.0 SAP Retail, the second confirmation category available for you is a rough receipt. Because this isn't a commonly used business scenario, we'll only briefly talk about its usage.

Prepare for goods receipt matching

Rough receipt allows you to prepare for the actual goods receipt matching products and quantities presented on your vendor documentation. Rough receipt can be used standalone or in combination with other confirmation categories such as shipping notification.

Rough receipt basically creates an EG type inbound delivery document—the default SAP-defined document type—with reference to the PO or shipping notification (EL - Inbound delivery type), which can be used to verify incoming materials and check quantities. Also, because this time it's a separate document, you can create and print forms and other documentation to prepare the stage for the actual physical goods receipt. You can have a single rough receipt created for either individual or multiple POs. Figure 7.8 shows possible scenarios.

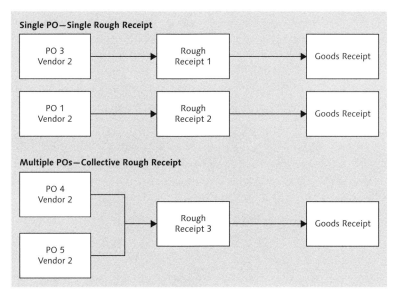

Figure 7.8 Rough Receipt Process Options

Let's walk through this scenario starting from the PO creation.

7.3.1 Create PO

You can create your PO using Transaction ME21N. Enter all of your materials, and specify the quantities and receiving plant—assuming all your supporting master data has been created already. The prerequisite for this scenario is that your PO line item confirmation is set to one of the confirmation controls that include the rough goods receipt confirmation category, which in standard SAP is either 0002 – ROUGH GR or 0003 – SHIPPING NOTIFICATION/ROUGH RECEIPT. In our example, we've set the PO to 0002.

7.3.2 Create Rough Goods Receipt Document

When you receive the confirmation from your vendor of incoming goods shipment, the rough goods receipt document can be created. Execute

Transaction VL41, and specify either the PO number from the step before or inbound delivery number if you use the hybrid confirmation category 0003 mentioned earlier (see Figure 7.9).

Figure 7.9 Rough Goods Receipt: Selection Screen

When you're ready, press Enter to continue. The system pulls all relevant PO information into the rough goods receipt document, and you can now fill in the information, including delivery note number (usually the bill of lading or a packing slip number), the warehouse door that will receive the inbound delivery of goods, transaction ID code, and most importantly, the received quantities of products (see Figure 7.10).

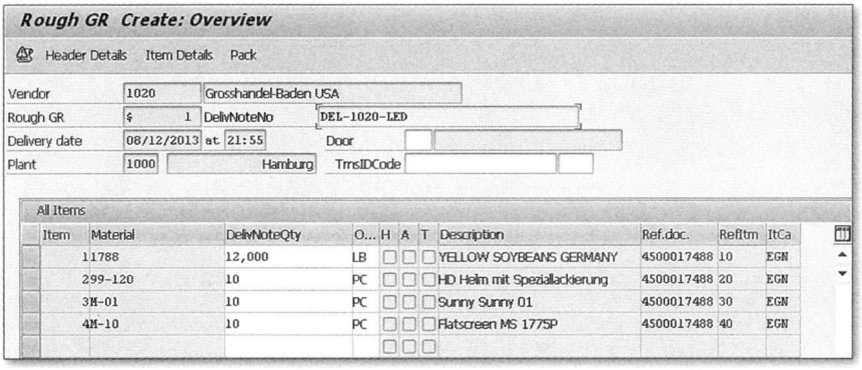

Figure 7.10 Rough GR Create: Overview Detail Screen

369

Save your rough receipt inbound delivery, and the document type EG-ROUGH GR is generated. Your rough goods receipt allows you to process output for check-in forms and labels using standard output conditions, such as CHKL-COUNT LIST and GRPL-PALLET STICKER.

After the physical matching process is complete, you can perform the final step and receive the goods using Transaction MIGO and referencing the inbound delivery rough receipt number generated before.

> **Note**
>
> One final reminder, if you're *not* on SAP Retail, this functionality may not be supported, so make sure you always check before using rough goods receipt as part of your confirmation process. Rough goods receipt in handling unit (HU) managed locations is also discontinued.

Table 7.4 lists some of the rough goods receipt transactions for your reference.

Transaction	Menu Path
VL41: Create Rough GR	RETAILING • MERCHANDISE LOGISTICS • GOODS RECEIPT • ROUGH GR • CREATE
VL42: Change Rough GR	RETAILING • MERCHANDISE LOGISTICS • GOODS RECEIPT • ROUGH GR • CHANGE
VL43: Display Rough GR	RETAILING • MERCHANDISE LOGISTICS • GOODS RECEIPT • ROUGH GR • DISPLAY

Table 7.4 Rough Receipt Transaction Codes

7.4   Inbound Delivery: Shipping Notification

In this section, we walk you through one of the most frequently used confirmation control methods—shipping notification.

EDI vendor confirmation

Shipping notification is a form of vendor confirmation, usually received via EDI transmission, created by a batch job or manually, which contains the information referring to your purchasing document, including materials and quantities shipped and the delivery date. Just like in the rough receipt example we discussed earlier, the shipping notifications create an inbound delivery in the system—SAP default document type EL—with reference to the PO or multiple POs. Figure 7.11 shows the possible combinations of PO, inbound delivery, and subsequent goods receipts needed to complete the transaction.

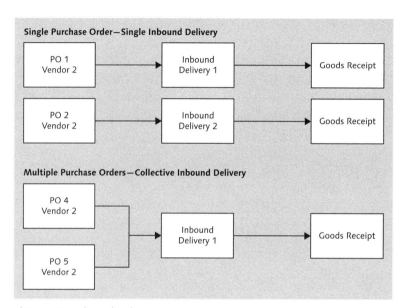

Figure 7.11 Inbound Delivery Process Options

The inbound delivery document allows you to prestage all activities and documents needed to efficiently process incoming shipments of goods, use it for transportation scheduling and monitoring, scheduling of the warehouse check-in process, and preparing for material putaway. If you're using SAP Warehouse Management (SAP WM), you can create transfer orders with reference to the delivery. The putaway quantities will confirm and update the final delivery quantities after confirmation of all transfer orders has been posted. If you have any materials that have differences, you can use the function of updating the delivery quantities to match putaway quantities. This, however, may end up in messages being issued, especially if you maintain over-under tolerances for your POs. Finally, goods receipt can be posted with reference to this document. Again, we'll cover receiving in detail in Chapter 9.

Process

Notifications If you want to use shipping notifications, you need to maintain the confirmation control settings on either the vendor master or purchasing info record, as described in the previous sections. You can start the PO creation using Transaction ME21N, or you can mass-create them using planning functions first and then convert your purchase requisitions into POs (see Chapter 2 for more on planning, and Chapter 4 for more on PO processing details). Just like with the acknowledgments and rough receipts, this confirmation control key can be automatically copied into your PO from the purchase info record or vendor master. This process needs the confirmation control key of 0004 (Shipping Notification) specified in the CONFIRMATIONS data tab of your PO. Figure 7.12 shows the CREATE PURCHASE ORDER screen.

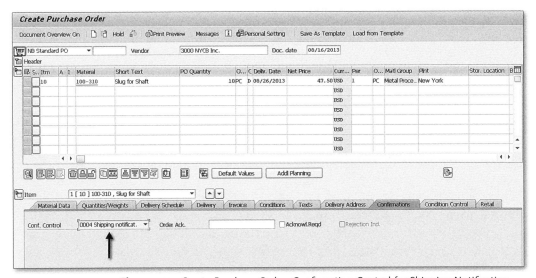

Figure 7.12 Create Purchase Order: Confirmation Control for Shipping Notification

Generated inbound delivery After this information is entered and your PO is saved, your inbound delivery is generated either via incoming ASN communication, a batch job that looks at all open POs requiring creation of the inbound delivery with approaching delivery due date, or manually using Transaction VL31N or en masse using Transaction VL34, which we'll cover in detail in Section 7.4.1.

Table 7.5 lists the transaction codes and menu paths for inbound delivery transactions and reports. We'll be talking about some of them in the next sections, covering standard inbound delivery transactions and an example of extended inbound delivery transactions, which are new with the Logistics–Service Parts Management (LO-SPM) extension of SAP ERP 6.0.

Transaction	Menu Path
VL31N: Create Inbound Delivery Single Documents	LOGISTICS • LOGISTICS EXECUTION • INBOUND PROCESS • GOODS RECEIPT FOR INBOUND DELIVERY • INBOUND DELIVERY • CREATE • SINGLE DOCUMENTS
VL32N: Change Inbound Delivery Single Document	LOGISTICS • LOGISTICS EXECUTION • INBOUND PROCESS • GOODS RECEIPT FOR INBOUND DELIVERY • INBOUND DELIVERY • CHANGE • SINGLE DOCUMENTS
VL33N: Display Inbound Delivery Single Document	LOGISTICS • LOGISTICS EXECUTION • INBOUND PROCESS • GOODS RECEIPT FOR INBOUND DELIVERY • INBOUND DELIVERY • DISPLAY • SINGLE DOCUMENTS
VL34: Collective Processing of Purchase Orders	LOGISTICS • LOGISTICS EXECUTION • INBOUND PROCESS • GOODS RECEIPT FOR INBOUND DELIVERY • INBOUND DELIVERY • CREATE • COLLECTIVE PROCESSING OF PURCHASE ORDERS
VL06I: Inbound Delivery Monitor	LOGISTICS • LOGISTICS EXECUTION • INBOUND PROCESS • GOODS RECEIPT FOR INBOUND DELIVERY • INBOUND DELIVERY • LISTS • INBOUND DELIVERY MONITOR
Extended Inbound Delivery Transactions	
VL60: Process Inbound Delivery	LOGISTICS • LOGISTICS EXECUTION • INBOUND PROCESS • GOODS RECEIPT FOR INBOUND DELIVERY • EXTENDED INBOUND DELIVERY PROCESSING • PROCESS INBOUND DELIVERY
VL60V: Edit Documents	LOGISTICS • LOGISTICS EXECUTION • INBOUND PROCESS • GOODS RECEIPT FOR INBOUND DELIVERY • EXTENDED INBOUND DELIVERY PROCESSING • EDIT DOCUMENTS

Table 7.5 Inbound Delivery Transaction Codes

Transaction	Menu Path
VL60P: Posting	LOGISTICS • LOGISTICS EXECUTION • INBOUND PROCESS • GOODS RECEIPT FOR INBOUND DELIVERY • EXTENDED INBOUND DELIVERY PROCESSING • POSTING
VL64: Generate Inbound Deliveries	LOGISTICS • LOGISTICS EXECUTION • INBOUND PROCESS • GOODS RECEIPT FOR INBOUND DELIVERY • EXTENDED INBOUND DELIVERY PROCESSING • SUBSEQUENT FUNCTIONS • GENERATE INBOUND DELIVERIES

Table 7.5 Inbound Delivery Transaction Codes (Cont.)

7.4.1 Collective Processing of Purchase Orders

Mass-generation of inbound deliveries

To create the inbound deliveries collectively, you need to run Transaction VL34 (Collective Processing of Purchase Orders), which results in mass-generation of inbound deliveries based on the selection criteria on the initial screen. You can also use Transaction VL64 (Generate Inbound Deliveries) instead. We'll cover mass-create steps using Transaction VL34. This transaction looks at all POs for a specific plant, storage location, or other combination of data, that is required to be delivered before the delivery date entered (see Figure 7.13).

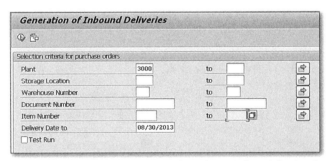

Figure 7.13 Collective Processing of Purchase Orders: Selection Screen

Test mode

You can also execute this transaction in test mode by checking the TEST RUN box. No inbound deliveries will be created, and you'll only get the total of deliveries that the system will create after executing the transaction in live mode. When you're done maintaining the screen, click EXECUTE or press the $\boxed{\text{F8}}$ function key. Your system crunches through all open POs matching your selection criteria and looks for confirmation control settings that require confirmation category LA (Shipping Notification) if you use the SAP standard default configuration setup. The execution results are presented to you in a pop-up window at the end of the run. Figure 7.14 shows an example where two inbound deliveries got created, and an error was displayed due to master data issues with one of the PO materials.

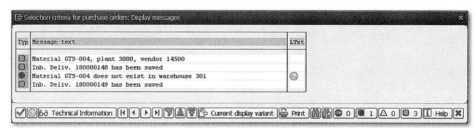

Figure 7.14 Collective Processing: Job Log

The inbound deliveries created didn't include the material, which was not extended to the warehouse location, and it was automatically excluded from the delivery.

7.4.2 Individual Processing of Purchase Orders

When your business has low volumes, no EDI process available, or simply for post-processing or error correction, you can create your inbound deliveries manually. The confirmation control rules are absolutely the same as before, so you must have the confirmation category LA (Shipping Notification) specified in the rule.

Manual

To create the individual inbound delivery, run Transaction VL31N (Single Documents), and then follow these steps:

Create

1. On the initial screen, enter the individual PO number or a series of POs that should be combined into a single document.

2. To select multiple POs, simply click on the PURCHASE ORDERS button or use $\boxed{\text{Shift}}$ + $\boxed{\text{F4}}$ on your keyboard. You'll get to the PURCHASING DOCUMENTS selection screen where you can narrow down your search criteria to relevant POs (see Figure 7.15).

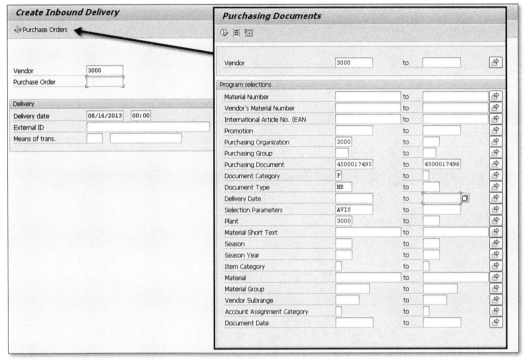

Figure 7.15 Create Inbound Delivery: Purchase Order Selection Screen

3. Click the EXECUTE button or use F8 to continue. On the screen shown in Figure 7.16, you'll get a list of all relevant PO lines that met your search criteria.

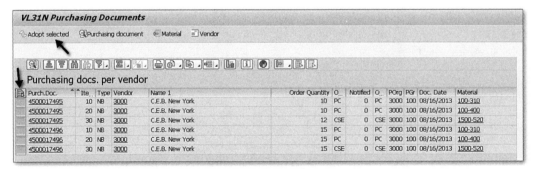

Figure 7.16 Purchasing Documents Selection

4. Click the SELECT ALL button if your selection criteria was limited to a single vendor, or use click individual records and then click ADOPT SELECTED or use [F8] to start delivery creation. On the next screen, you'll see the inbound delivery document in the making (see Figure 7.17).

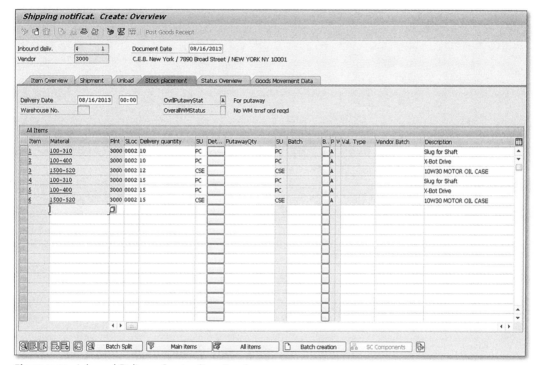

Figure 7.17 Inbound Delivery Create: Overview Screen

5. To check the delivery item reference document—the PO for which the delivery is created—double-click on the line item number.

6. In the ITEM DETAILS screen that appears, click the PREDECESSOR DATA tab. On this tab, you'll find the PO data showing the PO number and line item that the delivery line is created for (see Figure 7.18).

Figure 7.18 Inbound Delivery Item: Predecessor Data Tab

7. Save your delivery and proceed to subsequent functions, such as put-away using the SAP WM process, or pick confirmation if dealing with non-SAP WM structures.

The final step is to post the goods receipt, which we'll cover in detail in Chapter 9.

7.4.3 Monitoring

Now that all of the shipping notifications are created, you need a tool that allows you to monitor them en masse and display them. This is especially important when you have a very granular inbound process using steps such as transportation, putaway, confirmation of putaway transfer orders, posting of goods receipts, or if you also are using decentralized Warehouse Management in your application portfolio. We'll discuss two different tools in the following subsections.

Inbound Delivery Monitor

En masse monitoring

The standard SAP system has a tool that you can use to monitor your shipping notifications at the get-go: the Inbound Delivery Monitor. To check on all of these activities, execute Transaction VL06I (Inbound Delivery Monitor). This transaction is designed to give you the view of the relevant documents based on their respective process status as discussed earlier.

Follow these steps to work with the Inbound Delivery Monitor:

1. Choose the selection type as shown in Figure 7.19, which limits the scope of the processing to documents matching the processing status of your delivery documents. So, if you select the FOR PUTAWAY option, for example, only the deliveries that need to have transfer orders created will be worked on. In our example, we've decided to choose all possible options by clicking the LIST INBOUND DELIVERIES button.

Figure 7.19 Inbound Delivery Monitor: Selection Type

2. On the DATA SELECTION screen, specify the selection criteria that best meets your needs.

3. You can save your selection as a variant if you have repeating queries that need to be executed on a regular basis. Simply click the SAVE button or press [Ctrl] + [S], and proceed with saving your selection data as a variant on the VARIANT ATTRIBUTES screen that appears next.

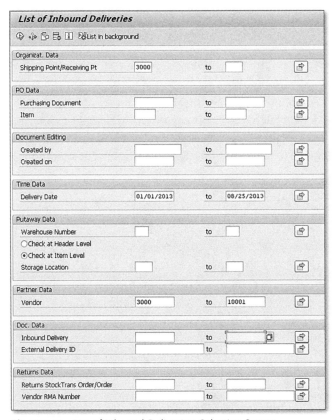

Figure 7.20 List of Inbound Deliveries: Selection Screen

4. Click the EXECUTE button or press the [F8] function key, and you'll see a list of all relevant inbound deliveries that match your selection criteria (see Figure 7.21). The default is set to display the data based on the header level information, so the report will show basic information, including delivery number, date, and vendor account details.

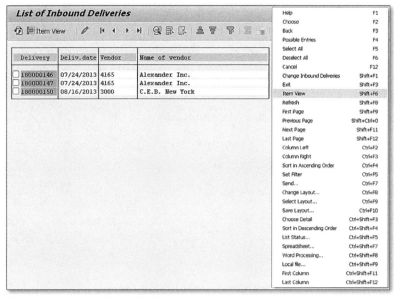

Figure 7.21 List of Inbound Deliveries

Standard reporting tools are available for you in the inbound delivery monitor, including the filtering, sorting, layout modifications, and export options.

Reporting tools

One of the frequently used options is ITEM VIEW, which gives you the ability to switch to the item level data if you want to review the contents of the deliveries being processed. When applied, the standard layout will bring you line item, material, material description, delivery quantity, and UoM. If you're not happy with the default, you can add more fields by clicking the CHANGE LAYOUT button and modifying the contents and sequence of columns displayed. You can access the inbound delivery details, change document data, and proceed with the subsequent functions, such as putaway, update the reference data, or delete the troubled record if need be.

Item View

Processing Documents Using Extended Inbound Delivery Cockpit

Another way of displaying inbound delivery data is through the cockpit mode. This allows you to process the deliveries very efficiently by using one of the new transactions introduced with the SPM extension, LO-SPM, as part of the extended inbound delivery functions.

Cockpit functions Using this cockpit, you can do the following:

▶ Create a shipment (we'll cover this document in Section 7.5)

▶ Assign inbound deliveries to the shipment

▶ Perform any necessary corrections

▶ Initiate the putaway transaction

▶ Post goods receipt

▶ Issue output

▶ Verify log entries if any were recorded along the way

Not only can you initiate transactions, you can also remove deliveries from shipments and yards activities, and delete them altogether if their status allows it. As you can see, this is a very powerful transaction that gives you a lot of functionality from one simple screen, crossing functional boundaries from shipping and transportation, to Inventory Management and SAP Warehouse Management.

Execution

In this section, we'll briefly explain how to process a document with the extended inbound delivery cockpit (you can find more information in Section 7.5). Follow these steps to execute Transaction VL60 (Process Inbound Delivery).

Data display 1. Execute the transaction, and you'll notice that the screen is divided
sections into data display sections.

2. Select different filter criteria to see how they interact. The contents are governed by the filters and managed by the end user, and the profiles are configured in the IMG. The left screen pane contains the lists of deliveries matching the defined criteria per filter settings and the layout defined. See Figure 7.22 for an example of how to access both.

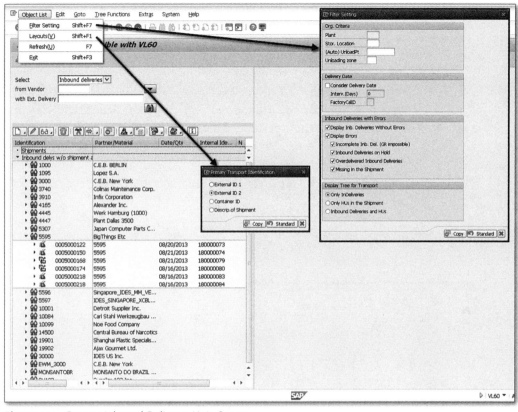

Figure 7.22 Process Inbound Delivery: Main Screen

1. To change your filter criteria for processing documents, use the pull-down menu and choose OBJECT LIST • FILTER SETTINGS, or use `Shift` + `F1` on your keyboard.

2. In the pop-up window, you can select which field will be used as a key field in the IDENTIFICATION column of the LIST pane.

3. You can set the field you want to use for identification to change how your deliveries are identified in the left pane data list. To do that, select the OBJECT LIST • LAYOUTS pulldown menu or press `Shift` + `F7` on your keyboard.

4. To work with the listed inbound delivery documents, select the appropriate function from the available options in the main screen of the transaction (see Figure 7.23). You can invoke the function by using

Edit screen

383

the available buttons, pulldown menus, and function keys. To check what each button does, simply hover your mouse over it to see the description.

For example, if you want to access one of the listed inbound deliveries pulled into the selection screen, you select the VENDOR account in the navigation pane that has a delivery document listed, and click the CHANGE button. This opens the delivery document overview in the right section of the screen, as shown in Figure 7.23. You can choose to execute subsequent functions using buttons located right above the displayed delivery overview. We'll cover this transaction in detail in Section 7.5, coming up next.

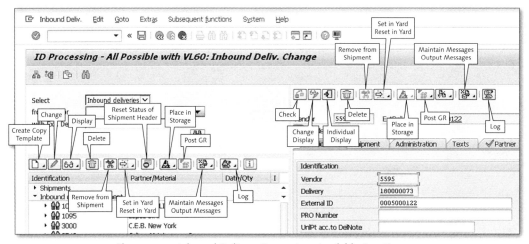

Figure 7.23 Inbound Delivery Processing: Available Functions

We'll cover an example of creating a shipment using Transaction VL60 in the next sections.

7.5   Inbound Shipment

SAP Transportation Management

You now understand how POs work with inbound deliveries or shipping notifications. If your process requires combining inbound deliveries into larger groups, and you need a mechanism to schedule, monitor, track shipment costing, and plan receiving activities for these groups, you can deploy SAP Transportation Management (SAP TM) as part of your Logistics Execution portfolio, which is where the inbound shipment functionalities come into play.

To initiate any of the transportation activities, a consultant needs to define the transportation planning point as part of your enterprise structures. Also, if you're planning to use the shipment costing functionality, you need to link your transportation planning point to the company code.

Shipment document

A *shipment* is an SAP document that allows you to combine deliveries to move them between locations; control transportation activities using planned and actual data; and use routes, stages and connection points for packing and processing of shipment cost documents. In procurement, the inbound shipment document type is used to process incoming goods movements for collection of inbound deliveries, shipped from one or multiple vendors.

Shipment documents are processed by defined transportation planning points. They can represent a physical truck, trailer, train, or ship, for example, which contains either single or multiple inbound deliveries that share a common transportation route. Using this methodology, SAP provides with three different types of shipments:

Shipment types

- **Individual shipment**
  Contains one or more deliveries that go from one point of departure to one point of destination with one mode of transportation.
- **Collective shipment**
  Has several delivery stops at several points carrying multiple deliveries with one mode of transportation.
- **Transportation chain**
  Applicable for scenarios with multiple deliveries that have to deal with several modes of transportation, which is very common for exports.

Using the different types of shipments and matching them to your business process requirements, you can create inbound shipments using multiple levels of relationship to inbound deliveries and originating POs. Figure 7.24 shows examples of individual and collective shipments.

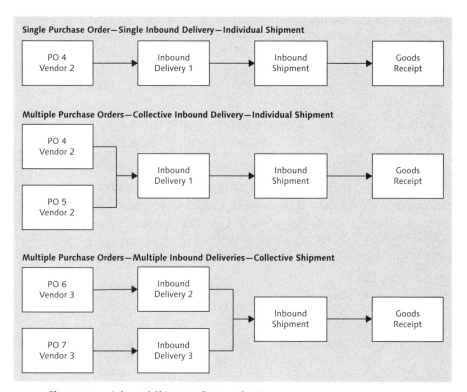

Figure 7.24 Inbound Shipment Process Options

7.5.1 Grouping Shipments

You now know how the inbound deliveries are created, and how they link to the POs. Now let's discuss how you can group them in shipments. For inbound deliveries to be subject for transportation, you need to maintain which of the delivery types, item categories, and routes are relevant for processing in Customizing (IMG menu path LOGISTICS EXECUTION • TRANSPORTATION • SHIPMENTS • MAINTAIN TRANSPORTATION RELEVANCE).

For use in inbound logistics (SAP standard document type EL - Shipping Notification), set this document type as relevant in the basic system. Item category ELN—defined as a default item category for the EL document type—is already set as relevant.

> **Note**
>
> Unlike outbound deliveries, inbound deliveries don't require a route to be specified; only the delivery type and item category must be relevant for transportation to set the delivery transportation planning status.

Armed with all of theoretical knowledge, let's now walk through the example of creating an inbound shipment for each type listed previously. There are a couple of ways to generate the shipments: manually using Transaction VT01N, collectively using Transaction VT04, and via the extended inbound delivery cockpit using Transaction VL60. We'll cover the step-by-step execution examples next.

Table 7.6 provides the relevant inbound shipment transaction codes—some of which we'll cover next.

Transaction	Menu Path
VT01N: Shipment Create Single Documents	Logistics • Logistics Execution • Inbound Process • Goods Receipt for Inbound Delivery • Transportation • Create • Single Documents
VT02N: Shipment Change Single Documents	Logistics • Logistics Execution • Inbound Process • Goods Receipt for Inbound Delivery • Transportation • Change • Single Documents
VT03N: Shipment Display	Logistics • Logistics Execution • Inbound Process • Goods Receipt for Inbound Delivery • Transportation • Display
VT04: Collective Processing	Logistics • Logistics Execution • Inbound Process • Goods Receipt for Inbound Delivery • Transportation • Collective Processing
VL60: Process Inbound Delivery	Logistics • Logistics Execution • Inbound Process • Goods Receipt for Inbound Delivery • Extended Inbound Delivery Processing • Process Inbound Delivery
VT70: Print	Logistics • Logistics Execution • Inbound Process • Goods Receipt for Inbound Delivery • Extended Inbound Delivery Processing • Edit Documents
VT11: Transportation Planning List	Logistics • Logistics Execution • Inbound Process • Goods Receipt for Inbound Delivery • Extended Inbound Delivery Processing • Posting

Table 7.6 Transportation Processing Transaction Codes

7.5.2 Individual Shipment Processing

We'll start with individual shipment creation using Transaction VT01N. The main screen in Transaction VT01N prompts you for the mandatory transportation planning point (TransportPlanningPt) and the Shipment type, as shown in Figure 7.25.

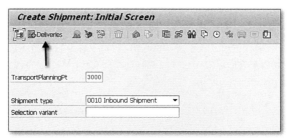

Figure 7.25 Create Shipment: Initial Screen

From there, use the Deliveries button, also shown in Figure 7.25, or press the F6 function key.

Delivery screen options

On the pop-up window, you'll get the list of fields available for you, which helps you add the deliveries you want to include in the shipment. You can filter deliveries using several parameters, including Plant, Delivery Date, Vendor, Route, and several others, as shown in Figure 7.26. The following sections appear on the screen with available options:

▶ Point of departure
You can specify vendor data details such as account number and address information.

▶ Destination
You can provide the destination plant, storage location, and warehouse numbers.

▶ Due date
You can provide the delivery date and scheduling dates.

▶ Transportation planning
You can add the route, forwarding agent shipping type, and special indicators.

▶ DELIVERY STATUS

You can specify what transportation planning status the delivery has to be in to be selected.

▶ WITH REFERENCE TO

You can key in specific documents such as POs, inbound deliveries, or other reference shipments/transports.

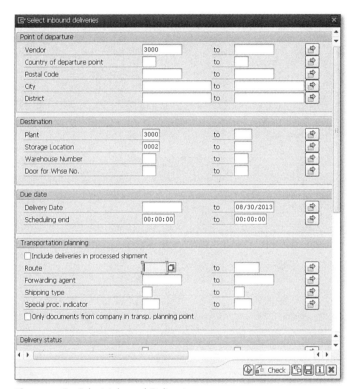

Figure 7.26 Select Inbound Deliveries

You also have other sections such as MEANS OF TRANSPORT, HANDLING UNITS, and DANGEROUS GOODS, if your inbound process uses even more granular selection.

When you're done with your selection, simply click the EXECUTE button or press the F8 function key. On the next screen, the split view shows the in-process shipments and deliveries that matched your selection criteria already assigned (see Figure 7.27).

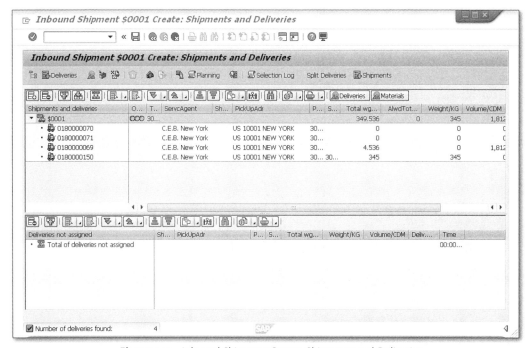

Figure 7.27 Inbound Shipment Create: Shipments and Deliveries

Adjustments
In the SHIPMENTS AND DELIVERIES pane, you'll find buttons to use if you need to adjust the assignments (delete and add shipments, add or remove inbound deliveries, sort, etc.). If you want to look at summary level delivery overview info, for example, you can click the DELIVERIES overview button, or to check the delivery contents, you can click the MATERIALS overview button. When you're ready to continue with your shipment, click on the OVERVIEW OF CURRENT SHIPMENT button or press Shift + F4. The INBOUND SHIPMENT OVERVIEW screen opens with the default PROCESSING tab at the top, and DEADL. data tab on the bottom of the screen (see Figure 7.28).

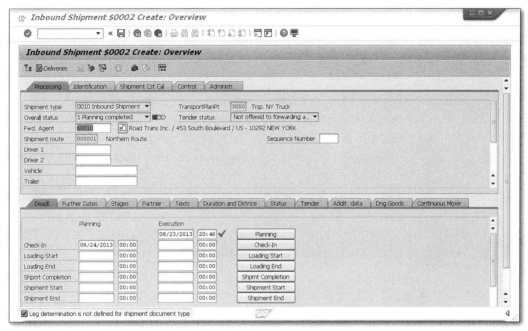

Figure 7.28 Inbound Shipment Create: Overview Screen

In the header data sections, you can maintain partner data, such as the forwarding agent that will be hauling your cargo, drivers, vehicle and trailer types, and equipment identification information. You also define shipment costing relevancy here (covered in the next section in detail).

Maintain partner data

To maintain any scheduling data on the DEADL tab, you need to first click the PLANNING button, which assigns the current date and time to the data line. You can then maintain the following activity dates and times:

▶ CHECK-IN
The truck appointment.

▶ LOADING START
The time the loading activities must start.

▶ LOADING END
The time the loading activities must finish.

▶ SHPMT COMPLETION
The processing is complete and ready for shipment costing.

> ▶ SHIPMENT START
> The truck dispatch time.

> ▶ SHIPMENT END
> Confirmation of destination reached.

Shipment tracking When tracking your shipment status progress, you use the buttons in the EXECUTION section with the relevant date and time stamp. You can fill in the planned data in the PLANNING section and later compare execution deadlines and report deviations to take appropriate corrective actions. When you're done, simply save your data, and the shipment is ready for further processing—such as printing all output forms for example—using Transaction VT70.

7.5.3 Collective Shipment Processing

If you need automation and manual processing isn't an option, you can create shipments in mass mode using collective processing. Let's walk through an example using Transaction VT04 (Collective Processing).

On the selection screen, you need to select your variants that drive the creation of shipment documents. The screen is divided into the following sections, as shown in Figure 7.29:

Variants for
creation
> ▶ DEFAULT SETTINGS
> Select CREATE INBOUND SHIPMENTS.

> ▶ SELECT DELIVERIES
> Choose an existing variant or create the new variant. This will specify the criteria to select the deliveries that will be subject for analysis. You can display or modify variants by clicking on MAINTN to the right of the input field.

> ▶ RULES
> In this section, you can maintain selection variants:

>> ▶ GROUPING CRITERIA
>> This is an optional field. If left blank, all selected deliveries are allocated to one shipment. For example, you might want to group deliveries into a shipment that uses the same shipping point, route, postal code of the destination address, and maximum weight.

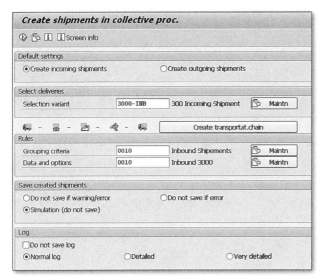

Figure 7.29 Create Incoming Shipments in Collective Processing

▶ DATA AND OPTIONS

This is a required field. Specify additional data such as the transportation planning point, service agent, shipment type, and route, as shown in Figure 7.30.

▶ CREATE TRANSPORTAT.CHAIN

If you want to create an entire transportation chain at once in this collective processing run, click on this button and choose or create new variants for GROUPING CRITERIA and DATA AND OPTIONS. This selection, however, will be relevant for grouping of deliveries in main leg, preliminary, and subsequent leg shipments.

▶ SAVE CREATED SHIPMENTS

You can choose to ignore errors and warnings posted due to route, forwarding agent determination, or weight or volume restriction and create shipment documents anyway. You can also run simulations, which allow you to review the proposed test runs before firming the results.

▶ LOG

Choose whether you want to save the processing log data and at what level of detail.

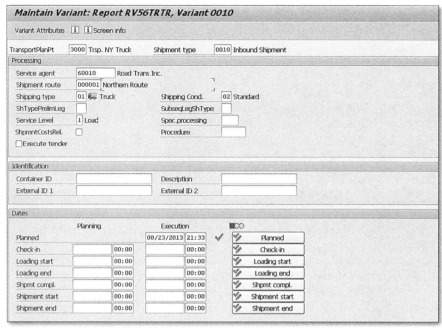

Figure 7.30 Maintain Data and Options Variants

When you're done maintaining your variants, save the data on the main screen as a variant by clicking the SAVE icon or pressing Ctrl + S. Press F8 or click the EXECUTE button to start the process. Upon completion, a new screen will pop up showing the log data. Figure 7.31 shows an example of a successfully executed transaction.

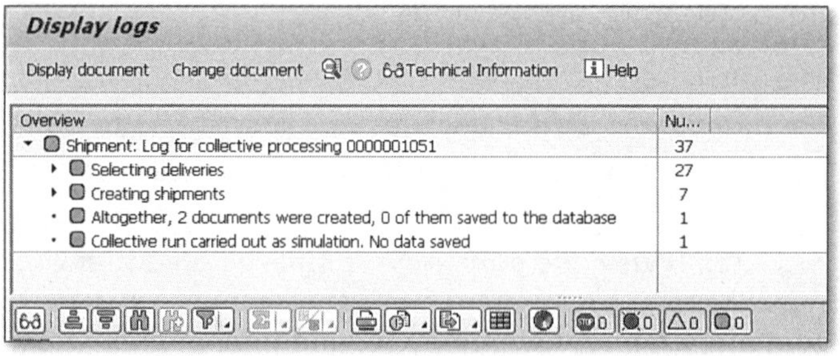

Figure 7.31 Display Log Data

7.5.4 Create Shipment Using Extended Inbound Delivery Processing

If you're using Service Parts Management (SPM) system components in your business process portfolio, you should definitely look at the functions available in the extended inbound delivery processing section we've mentioned in Section 7.4.3. This time, we want to demonstrate how one of the available functions can be applied when creating inbound shipments. Run Transaction VL60 (Process Inbound Delivery), and then follow these steps:

Service Parts Management

1. On the initial screen, expand the INBOUND DELIVERY node in the left pane to see the collection of all possible ready-for-processing inbound deliveries without shipment assignment, grouped by vendor account number.

2. Click on the SHIPMENTS node, and then click the CREATE button to continue (see Figure 7.32).

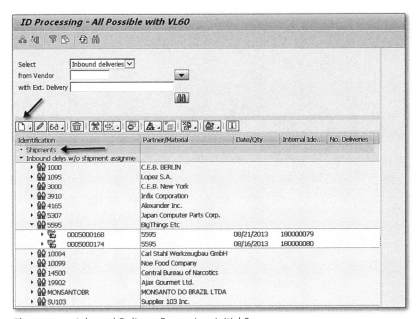

Figure 7.32 Inbound Delivery Processing: Initial Screen

3. On the right pane, the detail shipment data sections are available for processing. In the INBOUND DELIVERIES tab of the OVERVIEW section, enter your relevant inbound delivery number in the DELIVERY column by referencing the INTERNAL ID number in the data pane on the left (see Figure 7.33). Press ⟨Enter⟩ to acknowledge your input.

4. Review the HEADER DATA tabs, and enter all relevant information. This information is stored in the same views we covered when creating the shipment using Transaction VT01N.

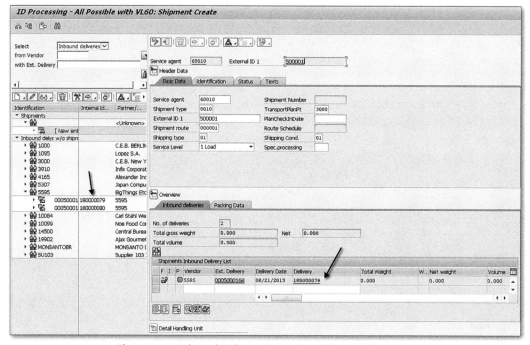

Figure 7.33 Inbound Delivery Processing: Shipment Create

If you're using HU management, you can also add packing information. When you're done, click the SAVE button or press ⟨Ctrl⟩ + ⟨S⟩ to create the shipment and complete the process.

You've now completed the shipment document creation. If you've implemented shipment costing, we have some subsequent steps to cover in the next section.

7.6 Shipment Cost Document

Costing of transportation shipments is available as an optional function in the SAP system and completes the shipment processing together with settlement of the transportation services charges.

Optional function

To enable shipment costing, follow these steps:

1. Maintain the enterprise structure configuration and assign a transportation planning point to the company code, as discussed earlier in Section 7.5.

2. Connect the transportation and procurement processes by assigning purchasing organization structures and plants to the transportation planning point and shipment cost types. This is also done in Customizing using the following menu path: LOGISTICS EXECUTION • TRANSPORTATION • SHIPMENT COSTS • SETTLEMENT • ASSIGN PURCHASING DATA. See Figure 7.34 for a configuration example.

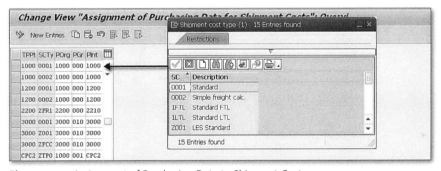

Figure 7.34 Assignment of Purchasing Data to Shipment Costs

> **Note**
>
> Only single plant to transportation planning point and shipment cost type assignment is allowed, so plan your procurement process for these types of services around this limitation. Settlement isn't possible if inbound deliveries in the shipment are for a different plant than the one specified in configuration.

Link invoice to shipments

The shipment costing document enables you to link invoices from your transportation partners to the individual shipment service it was applied to. The shipment cost document is created with reference to the shipment and uses pricing conditions so you can capture freight cost, insurance, fuel surcharges, customs, and so on (your pricing conditions can be fully customized to meet your needs). These costs are calculated based on previously negotiated prices with your transportation partners for each route and transportation mode.

When the shipment cost document is created, it looks up all of the conditions included in the shipment document and uses the data available, such as vendor, distance, weight, volume, route, and so on, to determine the value for pricing conditions and look for defined condition records. If the values are found, they will auto-populate your shipment cost conditions; if none are found, you can maintain them manually during document creation.

Settlement methods

There are two ways to perform settlement of the shipment costs:

▶ Initiate the process using the shipment cost document and automatic creation of the POs at the settlement time—including the automatic creation of the service entry sheet.

▶ Start with the manual PO first, then locate and assign this PO during shipment cost creation instead.

The manual service entry sheet document must be posted as well to acknowledge and approve the charges. Either way, the linked PO is used as a base for AP invoice matching, or automatic credit memo, and the payment. We'll talk briefly about Logistics Invoice Verification covering the AP process in the next chapter.

Table 7.7 lists all relevant transaction codes used during the shipment cost document processing.

Transaction	Menu Path
VI01: Create Shipment Cost Single Document	LOGISTICS • LOGISTICS EXECUTION • TRANSPORTATION • SHIPMENT COSTS • CREATE • SINGLE DOCUMENTS

Table 7.7 Shipment Cost Processing Transaction Codes

Transaction	Menu Path
VI02: Change Shipment Cost Single Document	LOGISTICS • LOGISTICS EXECUTION • TRANSPORTATION • SHIPMENT COSTS • CHANGE • SINGLE DOCUMENTS
VI03: Display Shipping Costs	LOGISTICS • LOGISTICS EXECUTION • TRANSPORTATION • SHIPMENT COSTS • DISPLAY
VI04: Collective Processing	LOGISTICS • LOGISTICS EXECUTION • TRANSPORTATION • SHIPMENT COSTS • CREATE • COLLECTIVE PROCESSING
VI11: Calculation List	LOGISTICS • LOGISTICS EXECUTION • TRANSPORTATION • SHIPMENT COSTS • LISTS AND LOGS • CALCULATION LIST
VI12: Settlement List	LOGISTICS • LOGISTICS EXECUTION • TRANSPORTATION • SHIPMENT COSTS • LISTS AND LOGS • SETTLEMENT LIST
VT11: Transportation Planning List	LOGISTICS • LOGISTICS EXECUTION • INBOUND PROCESS • GOODS RECEIPT FOR INBOUND DELIVERY • EXTENDED INBOUND DELIVERY PROCESSING • POSTING

Table 7.7 Shipment Cost Processing Transaction Codes (Cont.)

Creating an Automatic PO and Service Entry Sheet

Let's walk through an example of a scenario with automatic PO and service entry sheet creation at the shipment cost settlement.

Shipment cost settlement

We'll show you how to create the shipment cost document using Transaction VI01. You can also create the shipment cost document in collective mode using Transaction VI04. Follow these steps:

1. On the initial screen, enter the reference shipment number and specify the type of shipment cost document you're creating. See Figure 7.35 showing SHIP. COST TYPE 0001. Press ⌴Enter⌴ to continue.

2. On the next screen, you'll see an overview of status and items included in the cost document. Note that the status NOT TRANSFERRED on the STATUS tab (see Figure 7.36).

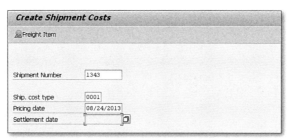

Figure 7.35 Create Shipment Cost: Initial Screen

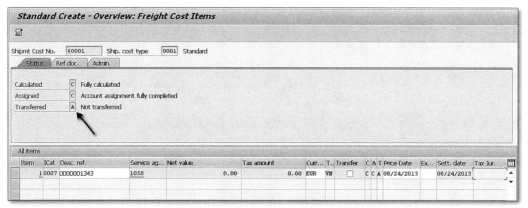

Figure 7.36 Shipment Cost Overview: Freight Cost Item

3. To display line item details, double-click the line item, or select the line, and click on the DISPLAY ITEM DETAILS icon or press F2. Here you can start reviewing all data tabs and verify that all information is correct. The SETTLEMENT tab in Figure 7.37 shows that this document isn't marked for transfer just yet.

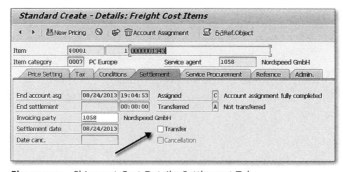

Figure 7.37 Shipment Cost Details: Settlement Tab

If your business process allows for immediate transfer/settlement, you can select the TRANSFER flag while you're in Transaction VI01 (Create). When saved, the subsequent PO and service entry sheet are generated.

Usually, the shipment cost documents are created first, and the actual transfer—or settlement—is performed separately due to separation of duties, or a simple processing step separation, if shipment costs are generated en masse in the collective processing. You can run collective processing in the dialog mode and in the background.

The transfer can be initiated another way besides using Transaction VI01 or Transaction VI02. You can use Transaction VI11, which generates lists of shipment costs based on your selection criteria. Follow these steps:

Shipment cost list

1. Drill into each of the listed shipment cost documents to access the same data tabs as you would when performing the individual document change using Transaction VI02.

2. Access the FREIGHT COST details, and when you're ready to perform the transfer, and select the TRANSFER flag.

3. Save your document to complete the process.

The system creates the PO for the transportation service provided, referencing the invoicing party, partner of the forwarding agent listed on the shipment document. Also the subsequent service entry sheet is created with reference to the PO, such as a goods receipt for services delivered. Both documents are listed on the SERVICE PROCUREMENT data tab of the FREIGHT COST DETAILS and FREIGHT COST ITEMS screens you can access using Transaction VI02, as shown in Figure 7.38.

Figure 7.38 Shipment Cost Details: Service Procurement

You can display the PO by double-clicking on the PO number (see Figure 7.39). Then go to PURCHASE ORDER HISTORY tab to access the service entry sheet data. Instead of using Transaction ML81N, double-click on the document to open it in display mode (see Figure 7.40 showing processed service entry sheet).

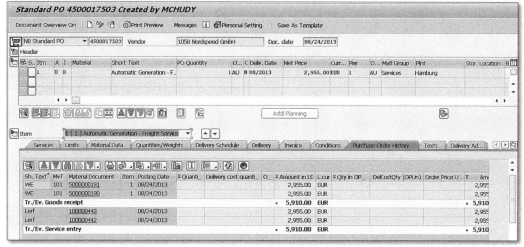

Figure 7.39 Display Purchase Order: Purchase Order History Data Tab

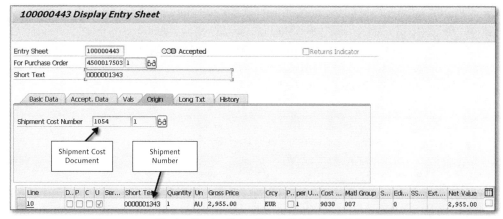

Figure 7.40 Display Service Entry Sheet: Origin Data Tab

The last step in the scenario is to actually process the incoming invoice or credit memo using Transaction MIRO (we'll cover this in Chapter 9).

7.7 Summary

In this chapter, you've learned about multiple methods to handle your inbound logistics processes. Now you should understand how confirmation control settings can help in the processing of shipping notifications and rough receipts, and you understand the differences between them. You also went through the visual tour of inbound delivery processing using different transactions and how to process them together using the shipment document. Finally, you've completed all of the transportation activities to produce a shipment cost document and settle it with procurement via a PO and service entry sheet. Armed with all of this process knowledge, you should be able to make decisions on how to execute or design your inbound logistics processes more efficiently.

In the next chapter, we'll transition to actually taking the transported goods from your supplier and processing the goods receipt and other inventory movements to finally make your stock available for consumption.

Inventory tracking and control is an essential part of any company's operations. Knowing how much stock you have and how much it's worth is the cornerstone of any other activity, including sales and manufacturing.

8   Inventory Management

The SAP ERP system is a very reliable tool that's used to capture all of the different affectations suffered by stock during the day-to-day operations of any company. It's versatile enough to carry many different stock types and categories, including stock in quality inspection, blocked stock, stock from vendor consignment, stock reservations, and others.

Inventory Management is also part of the Materials Management (MM) component of the SAP ERP system. Along with Purchasing, this function enables you to plan and procure materials, and also allows you to perform very accurate inventory control and inventory valuation. By ensuring this accuracy, your company can better execute the core business activities. Sales rely on inventory accuracy to supply customer orders and generate revenue by doing so. Purchasing is in charge to keep a reasonable stock level that will guarantee that supply, while not spending all of the company's budget or overfilling the warehouses.

Control and valuation

In this chapter, we'll give you an overview of the different functions and purposes that encompass Inventory Management. We'll discuss the process of receiving inventory and also working with stock in the SAP ERP system.

8.1   Overview

Inventory Management has a large impact on your system. Production is very dependent on inventory accuracy; missing materials can cause production stoppages that can have very high cost and a very high impact also on customer orders and revenue generation.

Inventory Management, as shown in Figure 8.1, registers every material receipt and issue from the warehouse and creates an auditable set of documents that tells you what kind of material movement was performed, when it was executed, the person responsible for that movement, and also the total value of that movement. The value of the material movement is automatically posted to the General Ledger, affecting predefined accounts according to the characteristics of the material, the valuation area, and the nature of the movement.

Inventory Management is also very good at tracking batches. In industries where this is relevant, you can see the stock and status for each individual batch. Also, thanks to the Batch Management component, you can keep track of manufacturing and expiration dates, total shelf life, and the vendor that supplied it, among many other relevant information.

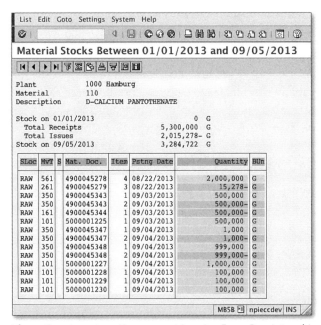

Figure 8.1 Inventory Management Logging Every Receipt and Issue of Material

Stock status

Inventory Management is also capable of distinguishing different material statuses to prevent the incorrect use of materials. The standard SAP ERP system handles the following stock statuses:

▶ **Unrestricted**
For materials that can be sold or used in production.

▶ **Quality control**
For materials that have just been received from a vendor or from the production shop and need to be inspected and approved.

▶ **Blocked**
For materials that are out of spec and need to either be returned to the vendor or destroyed.

These stock categories or statuses apply also for batches, so you can have some batches in unrestricted stock for a given material, others in quality inspection, and others in blocked stock.

Inventory Management is also capable of managing stocks owned by the vendor under a consignment agreement or stocks of materials that you send to subcontractors to perform some transformation and then return them to your warehouse.

Storage location stocks

All this control happens at the storage location level. Storage locations belong to plants, and plants belong to company codes in the enterprise's logistics structure.

The logistics structure, and specifically the storage locations, allows you to segregate materials of different characteristics in different storage locations and still know your total inventory value at the plant level. The system can also summarize all of the plants under the same company code and show you the total inventory value at the corporate level. Figure 8.2 details how the stock for each material is shown for each storage location and for each stock category. For batches, you also know the stock per each individual batch.

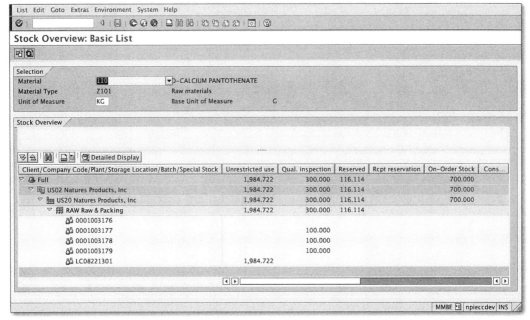

Figure 8.2 Stock Overview List

Now that you understand how Inventory Management works, we'll discuss the details of this function in your daily use.

8.2   Receiving

One of the main activities in Inventory Management is receiving. Depending on your company's activities, you may receive raw materials that will be used for production of goods, and you then receive finished or semifinished goods from production. Or if your company commercializes products manufactured either by another company or another division of your own company, then you'll be receiving what in the SAP ERP system is known as *trading goods*.

Rules   Each of these receipts of materials is different and is subject to different rules. Some materials need to be inspected to make sure they comply with quality requirements; some may need special handling and be put under secured storage or in a refrigerator or a freezer. You can manage these rules in your SAP ERP system with the use of different material types and material groups. And all of them are set in configuration, normally during the original setup of the system in automatic postings and account determination.

The rules are also different when you receive a purchased item, a consignment item, or a manufactured item. The different rules apply also to accounting, where these material types allow you to post to different inventory accounts every time one of these materials is received into stock. You can see the ACCOUNTING view of the material master in Figure 8.3. Each material belongs to only one material type, and the values shown in this view are relevant only to one valuation area.

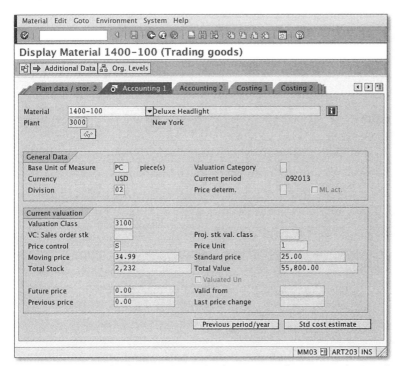

Figure 8.3 Assigned Valuation Class and Valuation Price for a Material's Specific Valuation Area

The rules are based on a combination of different characteristics set in the system:

Rules characteristics

- ▸ **Material type**
  Each material type is assigned a set of accounting codes called *valuation classes*; these valuation classes are used to determine posting rules by movement type.

- ▸ **Material master record**
  Each material in the material master has an ACCOUNTING view, in which you assign a valuation class and register the value of the material either as standard cost or a moving average price.

- ▸ **Movement type**
  The system recognizes different ways of moving stock in, out, and around the warehouse, and for each of them, it has defined a different movement type. Movement types are linked to other accounting keys that, in conjunction with the valuation class, determine an account to post the value of each movement.

- ▸ **Plant**
  The ACCOUNTING view in each material is only relevant for one valuation area. In general, the most common setting in the system is to make a valuation area equivalent to a plant. So the same material can be valuated at different prices in each plant. Normally, the different values correspond to the differences in delivery costs that are involved in getting the material there.

In the following sections, we'll explain the process steps for receiving goods or materials into stock. This process is known in the SAP ERP system as posting goods receipt, or simply PGR. We'll describe how it fits in the Inventory Management component and the role that automatic postings play in the receipt process.

8.2.1 Automatic Postings Role

When you receive a given material into a specific plant with a determined movement type, the system looks into the automatic postings settings and determines which accounts will be affected based on the combination of the previously mentioned elements. The amount to be posted to the General Ledger depends on the quantity being received and the valuation price in the accounting view of the material master. As you can see in Figure 8.4, automatic postings are configured during the system setup and guide all of the accounting postings for Inventory Management.

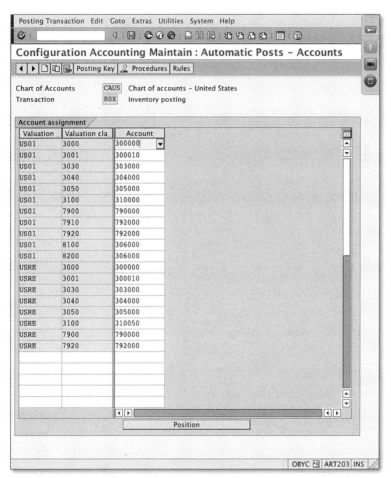

Figure 8.4 Automatic Postings Drive the Postings into the G/L

8.2.2 Posting Goods Receipt with Transaction MIGO

Goods receipts used to be posted in Transaction MB01 for purchase orders, Transaction MB31 for production orders, and Transaction MB1C for other goods receipts, including receipts without POs, without production orders, initial stock entries, and goods receipts for stock transfers between plants and between storage locations.

In more recent versions of the SAP ERP system, SAP developed a central transaction to replace the old MBXX transactions, as part of the Enjoy initiative. From Transaction MIGO, you can post most of the movements of materials (see Figure 8.5).

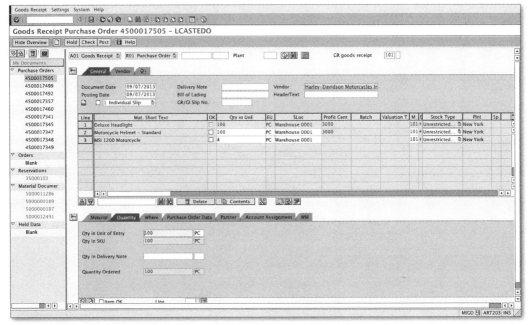

Figure 8.5 Transaction MIGO Screen: Header Data, Item Overview, and Item Detail

Screen Options

As you can see in Figure 8.5, Transaction MIGO integrates everything in a single screen, you don't have to jump from one initial screen to another. It has three sections that also reflect the structure of the material document (you can look at the resemblance in Figure 8.6). The top part is the header, where you can enter important data about the shipment such as the DELIVERY NOTE number, or the BILL OF LADING number. Second, it has an item overview with a list of all of the items from the PO, with the material number and the quantity.

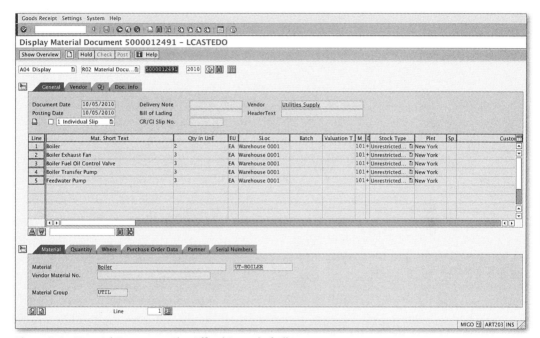

Figure 8.6 Material Document: The Official Record of All Inventory Movements

And third, at the bottom of the screen, there is a collection of tabs where the detailed item information is kept. Here you can change the quantity, enter or change the storage location for the receipt, enter the vendor batch for batch managed materials, enter the manufacturing date, and enter other data such as the number of packages. If you're working with an SAP Warehouse Management (SAP WM) managed location, you can also palletize the quantities using the conversion factors for storage units.

Because Transaction MIGO is multipurpose, you first have to select the type of operation or action that you want to perform; in this case, it's a goods receipt. Then you need to indicate the type of receipt you want to execute by indicating the reference document. The most useful choices in this screen are described in the following list:

▶ PURCHASE ORDERS
You enter a purchase order number, and the system retrieves all of the opened items in that order.

▶ MATERIAL DOCUMENTS
When you enter a material document number, Transaction MIGO copies the items from that document and attempts to create a new document with the same information.

▶ INBOUND DELIVERY
An inbound delivery is a document created based on a shipping notification from a vendor; it might contain all of the items from a purchase order or just a subset of the items. When you enter the inbound delivery number, Transaction MIGO retrieves all of the opened items from that delivery.

▶ OUTBOUND DELIVERY
In the case of intercompany shipments with delivery documents, you can enter the delivery number with which the materials were issued from the supplying plant, and the system copies the opened items from that document.

▶ TRANSPORT
This refers to the number of a stock transport order (STO). This type of PO is created to move stock between plants and can be used instead of the receipt for an outbound delivery.

▶ ORDER
This option allows you to post a goods receipt for a production order.

▶ OTHER
Because this combination of action and reference document won't ask you for a document number, you need to directly enter a movement type. The most common entries are the following:

  ▶ 501: GOODS RECEIPT WITHOUT PO

  ▶ 531: RECEIPT OF BY-PRODUCT

  ▶ 561: RECEIPT OF INITIAL STOCK BALANCE

After you enter a reference document number, the system looks for and retrieves all of the opened items for that document. Opened items are those that have a quantity remaining to be received, so you can only post a goods receipt for these items.

When you are receiving material from a vendor, you have to keep in mind that not all shipments from vendors include all of the items you ordered, the vendor might have shipped whatever items were in hand at that time and will ship other items later, so after the items are displayed, you can choose which ones to receive. From the ones you select, you can also adjust the quantities to match the physical count that is performed upon receipt at the warehouse.

When you're sure that all of the items that arrived to the warehouse have been selected on the screen and the quantities adjusted, the next step is to save the data and post the goods receipt. After you save the document, it's posted in the inventory document as shown in Figure 8.6.

Split orders *(margin note)*

> **Note**
>
> Material documents contain all of the information about a material movement, and like most other SAP documents, they are divided into a header and items. The header contains the information that is valid to all of the items, and each item contains the information to each individual material that was received.
>
> The material document contains information that links it with other documents, including its predecessor, such as a purchase order, and the accounting documents that contain all of the information about the financial results of receiving the material into the warehouse. This information includes the postings to the General Ledger, the affected profit or cost centers, the cost elements, and more.
>
> The process is exactly the same for other types of receipts, such as for production orders or process orders. We won't get into the detail of those receipts because we're just highlighting the receipts for purchase orders, but the steps for posting those other types of receipts are almost identical.

Material document *(margin note)*

Summarizing from the explanation in the previous paragraphs, to receive a purchase order into stock, follow these steps:

Receive PO into stock *(margin note)*

1. Go to Transaction MIGO, or follow the path LOGISTICS • MATERIALS MANAGEMENT • GOODS MOVEMENT • GOODS MOVEMENT.

2. In the ACTION field, select GOODS RECEIPT.

3. In the REFERENCE DOCUMENT field, select PURCHASE ORDER.

4. In the PURCHASING DOCUMENT field, enter your purchase order number.

5. Press Enter and adjust the quantities if necessary.

6. For each item, go to the WHERE tab, and check that the items are being posted into the correct stock category, plant, and storage location.

7. Check the OK box in the lower-left corner for each item after checking them.

8. Save your document.

8.2.3 Accounting Documents as a Result of Inventory Change

If the material movement generated a change in the stock levels, such as a goods issue, goods receipt, scrapping of material, or stock differences found in a physical inventory count, then the system also generates an accounting document. This accounting document contains postings to General Ledger accounts based on the automatic postings configuration; this happens automatically in the background, and you don't need to worry about it. As we've already discussed, the automatic postings are determined based on the combination of plant, material accounting data, and movement type. This accounting document is the journal entry in the General Ledger (see Figure 8.7).

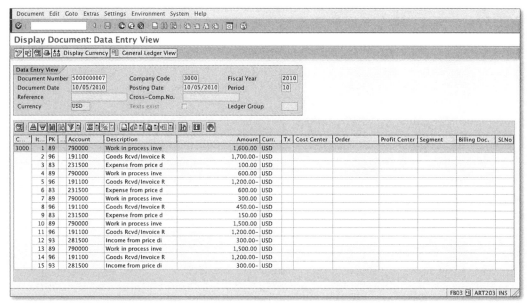

Figure 8.7 Accounting Document: The Journal Entry to the General Ledger for the Corresponding Material Document

8.3   Managing Special Stocks

Special stocks are an important part of the procurement process, and the process relies on Inventory Management to identify and account for these stocks. For example, when your business buys material under a consignment agreement, you'll see an entry in the system for a quantity of that material but with a special stock indicator "K" and a special stock number that is the same as the vendor number. This way, you'll be able to differentiate between your company's owned available stock, owned but unavailable, owned but sent to a vendor, owned by a third party, or in transit—giving you complete visibility of your stock situation.

Visibility

The special stocks are created in the system when you receive purchase orders that require the system to track the materials and their quantities separately, such as a consignment PO. Another example is the receipt of material bought to fulfill a customer order; in that case, the system creates a separate stock for a customer and identifies it with the sales order number. The special stock indicator in this case is "E".

Indicator E

We'll discuss the different special stock situations in the following sections.

8.3.1   Consignment

When a company buys under a consignment agreement, the stocks you receive for those materials have to be identified as property of the vendor. When you use them (e.g., when you issue material to a production order), they change ownership to your company, and at that point a liability is created.

Vendor's property

When you post a goods receipt in the system, as we discussed in the previous section, for a consignment PO, the special stock is automatically created and identified with a "K" and with the vendor's number as the special stock number. All of the necessary information for this stock to be created comes from the purchase order, and the user posting this receipt really just needs to verify that the material quantities are correct (see Figure 8.8).

Indicator K

417

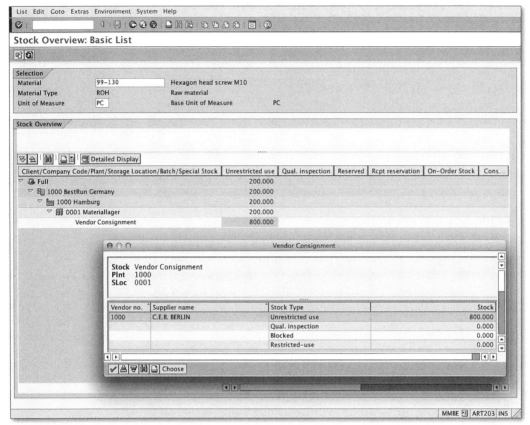

Figure 8.8 Stock Overview Showing the Stock Figures for the Different Types of Stocks

8.3.2 Subcontracting

Send material to vendor

When you send components to a vendor so that some work or transformation is performed on them, the system allows you to see how much of each material is under the vendor's custody.

Indicator L

In Procurement, you create subcontracting POs by using the item category L. The material that you enter in the PO has to be a material that is used as the header of a bill of materials (BOM). The BOM is copied into the PO, and the quantities are adjusted according to the quantity of the main material you require from the vendor. After the PO is created, you can ship the components to the subcontractor using Transaction ME2O. (Subcontracting POs are discussed in detail in Chapter 5.)

When you ship the components to the vendor, they are identified with a special stock indicator "O" or stock provided to vendor and with a special stock number equal to the vendor's number. This is set in the background when you send stock to the vendor, so you don't have to worry about entering any other parameters than the correct vendor number. Every time they send you back the transformed materials, you post a goods receipt for that, and the system automatically discounts the components based on the BOMs included in the PO.

Indicator O

8.3.3 Customer Order Stock

In Sales and Distribution (SD), there are many occasions in which the materials that are being sold to a customer have to be ordered from a vendor because the company doesn't keep stocks of these materials. When these materials are sold, the process in SD triggers the creation of a purchase order for a vendor in Purchasing.

SD processes

When the PO materials are delivered at the warehouse and you post a goods receipt, the system shows this stock under a special stock indicator "E" and a special stock number equal to the sales order to the customer. This way they won't be sold to another customer.

Indicator E

8.3.4 Stock in Transit

As a buyer in charge of sourcing material, sometimes you'll source materials from other plants of your company. This is done in Purchasing by creating a type of order called stock transport orders (STOs), which are discussed in detail in Chapter 5. When you post a goods issue for an STO, the stock leaves the supplying plant's unrestricted stock and is put into stock in the receiving plant as stock in transit. When this is done, and you check the stock in the stock overview Transaction MMBE, you can see the inventory in a separate column for stock in transit and no longer in unrestricted stock. The stock changes ownership with the goods issue and remains in transit until the goods receipt is posted at the receiving plant. At that moment, the stock moves from *in transit* to *unrestricted* in the receiving plant.

Same company code

When the stock is moved between your storage locations or even between plants of the same company code, you have the option of not using an STO. This is convenient when the physical movement of the goods doesn't imply loading trucks and moving great distances. Normally, these types of movements are recommended only when the plants or storage locations are located in the same geographic area, and when there is no intercompany billing involved.

Creating a Stock Transfer without an STO

To create a transfer of stock without an STO, follow these steps (see Figure 8.9):

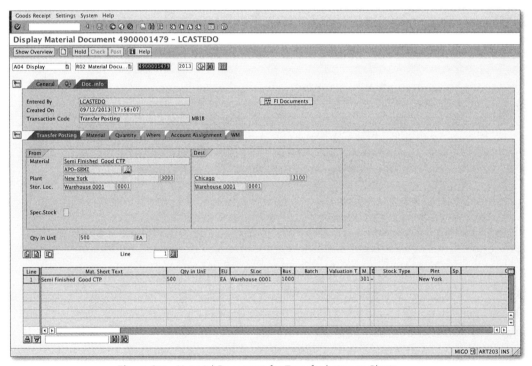

Figure 8.9 Material Document for Transfer between Plants

1. Go to Transaction MIGO, or follow the menu path LOGISTICS • MATERIALS MANAGEMENT • INVENTORY MANAGEMENT • GOODS MOVEMENT • GOODS MOVEMENT.

2. Select the TRANSFER POSTING action and the OTHER reference document. Because this combination of action and reference document won't ask you for a document number, you need to directly enter a movement type. See Table 8.1 for a list of frequently used movement types.

3. Enter the material to be transferred, the plant, and the storage location.

4. Enter the quantity.

5. Enter the batch number if applicable.

6. Review your data, and save the document.

Movement Type	Description
301	Transfer posting plant to plant (one-step)
303	Transfer posting plant to plant—remove from storage (two-step)
305	Transfer posting plant to plant—place in storage (two-step)
311	Transfer posting storage location (one-step)
313	Transfer posting storage location to storage location—remove from storage (two-step)
315	Transfer posting storage location to storage location—place in storage (two-step)

Table 8.1 Frequently Used Movement Types for Stock Transfers

Depending on the movement type you select, the transfers can be done in one or two steps. One-step movements move the stock immediately from one plant or storage location to another, whereas with two-step movements, you can post the issue from one and the receipt at the other one. If the valuation level of your system is the plant, then there is a possibility that the same material is valuated at a different price in different plants. If this is true for one of the materials that you're transferring, then the system generates a General Ledger posting to show that difference in the value of the inventory. That difference may be a gain or a loss from inventory transfer (see Figure 8.10).

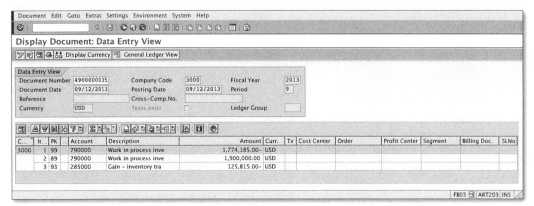

Figure 8.10 Valuation Price Differences Resulting in Posting to Gain/Loss for an Inventory Transfer

8.4 Transfer Postings

Change

Transfer postings differ from stock transfers, in that transfer postings aren't connected with a physical goods movement. They usually involve a change in stock type, batch number, or material number. With transfer postings, you can move stock between the different stock statuses or types—unrestricted, quality inspection, and blocked—allowing you to move damaged material into blocked stock, or quality released material into unrestricted.

Create

To create a transfer posting, follow these steps (refer to Figure 8.9):

1. Go to Transaction MIGO, or follow the path LOGISTICS • MATERIALS MANAGEMENT • INVENTORY MANAGEMENT • GOODS MOVEMENT • GOODS MOVEMENT.

2. Select TRANSFER POSTING as the action and OTHER as the reference document.

3. Because this combination of action and reference document won't ask you for a document number, you need to directly enter a movement type. See Table 8.2 for a list of frequently used movement types.

4. Enter the material on which you'll apply the transfer, the plant, and the storage location. You may need to enter this information on both

the issuing and receiving material, plant, and storage location, depending on the movement type.

5. Enter the quantity.

6. Enter the batch number if applicable.

7. Review your data, and save the document.

Movement Type	Description
309	Transfer posting material to material (also used for batch to batch)
321	Transfer posting quality inspection to unrestricted
322	Transfer posting quality inspection to unrestricted— reversal (used to move from unrestricted to QI)
343	Transfer posting blocked stock to unrestricted-use stock
344	Transfer posting blocked stock to unrestricted-use stock—reversal reversal (used to move from unrestricted to blocked)

Table 8.2 Frequently Used Movement Types for Transfer Postings

You can also reflect the transformation that some materials suffer with time in the system; for example, wine turning into vinegar are two completely different materials that have to be valuated differently, but if wine goes bad your company may not throw it away, but sell it as vinegar.

Transformations

To post a transformation like this, use the steps listed previously to create a transfer posting. Select movement type 309, which allows you to post stock from one material or batch into another (see Figure 8.11).

These types of movements, or transformations, automatically post differences resulting from revaluation into the General Ledger. In the material document, you'll see one issue from one material's stock and the receipt into the other material's stock. In accounting, you'll also see one stock value being removed, another being added, and a loss/gain from stock transfer (see Figure 8.12).

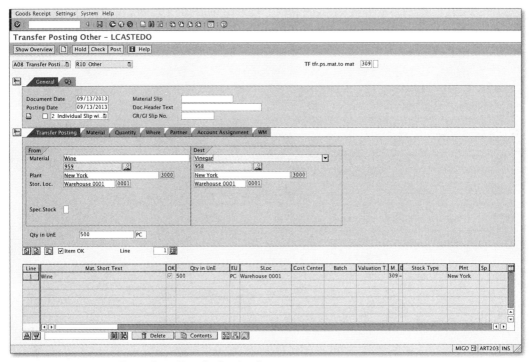

Figure 8.11 Transfer Posting Screen

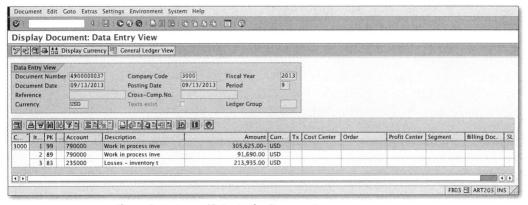

Figure 8.12 Losses/Gains in the Document

8.5 Summary

Each time there is a goods receipt/issue or a change in stock type or stock category, the system generates a material document that is the official record for movements in the warehouse. At the same time, if the movement caused a change in the stock levels, then it also automatically generates an accounting journal entry to the General Ledger, which is logged into an accounting document. This way, your company can track every detail of the movement of stocks and the value of those movements.

Up to now, we've described how to purchase materials and services, how to receive them into stock, and how those postings affect the accounting registries. In the last chapter, we'll discuss how to receive an invoice for the goods and services provided by vendors.

Procurement of goods and services ends with activities of processing incoming invoices and issue of payment. This is the crossing point between procurement and finance.

9   Logistics Invoice Verification

In previous chapters, we've walked through many ways of procuring goods and services, both planned and unplanned. We also talked about getting these goods into your facilities using inbound logistics and performing goods receipt for these deliveries. The last step in the procurement process is to post incoming invoices into the SAP system with reference to the purchase orders (POs) and forwarding these invoices to accounting for payments. This is done using the Logistics Invoice Verification functionality of Materials Management (MM).

Logistics Invoice Verification (LIV) allows you to process incoming vendor invoices, verify their content with reference purchasing documents if they exist, compare prices, and, if approved, process relevant information to financials for payment. Invoice receipts and credit memos can be created with reference to PO, service entry, and goods receipt, or without reference documents by posting the invoices directly to the SAP General Ledger accounts or material accounts. Credit memos can also be processed either as invoice reversals or in reference to return deliveries.

Process invoices

Invoices can be posted into your system in multiple ways. Depending on the communication methods, SAP has a way to handle the invoices:

Posting invoice methods

▶ **Manual entry**
By keying in the invoice into the system.

▶ **Background processing**
Electronic Data Interchange (EDI) invoices received are matched against the reference documents, and if no errors are recorded, posting is automatic.

▶ **Automatic settlement**

If you use invoicing plans, consignment or pipeline settlement, or evaluated receipt settlement (ERS), this method applies.

During LIV, you create an MM invoice document and Financial Accounting (FI) invoice document. Because the Invoice Verification processes closely integrate with FI, usually process ownership is assigned to that group. In this chapter, we'll cover only the process steps that should be highlighted due to their procurement origin. We'll walk through some selected invoice creation methods and discuss making corrections using subsequent credits, debits, and reversals. We'll also cover the process of blocking, and parking invoices.

As with all other processes in procurement that we've discussed so far, the verification process requires certain information for the invoicing to take place. Transactional data that drives the process from the PO is usually derived from the purchasing info record, vendor master, and configuration. Master data drives the frequency and method of payment and the type of verification that should be used when processing invoices. You can find more details in Chapter 2, where we talked about the vendor master and purchasing info records in more detail.

In this chapter, we'll walk through different ways of creating the invoices and several transactions that we'll discuss in more detail.

9.1 Invoice Processing

In this section, we'll explain some of the different ways in which you work with invoices. We'll discuss the methods to create an invoice, both manually and automatically and then go over how to block, release, and park an invoice.

9.1.1 Create Invoice: Manual Entry

To manually create the invoice, execute Transaction MIRO (Enter Invoice). The transaction interface of the entry screen is divided on functional areas (see Figure 9.1). The screen has the following areas:

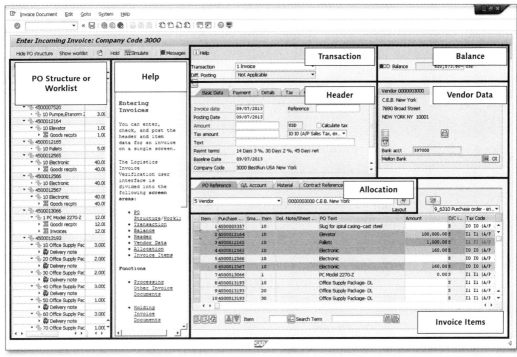

Figure 9.1 Create Invoice Interface

▶ PO STRUCTURE

Screen areas

Displays the list of PO items and their relevant document flow history. You can show/hide this part of the screen using the corresponding buttons.

▶ WORKLIST

Can be used in place of the PO structure. The worklist has buckets for held, parked, and ready for posting documents. The worklist can be switched on or off by using the SHOW/HIDE WORKLIST button.

▶ HELP

Enabled when the HELP button is clicked; additional information about the transaction can be accessed.

▶ TRANSACTION

Specify what type of transaction you'll be processing (e.g., incoming invoice, credit memo, etc.).

▶ HEADER

Enter all of the details related to the entire document at the header level, such as invoice date, payment amount, tax info, and notes.

▶ BALANCE

In this calculated field, the system shows you the balance for all selected PO lines, for example, for invoice entry.

▶ ALLOCATION

Allocate the invoice for the PO transaction, and the system will propose the relevant items for processing — for example, a vendor account (all relevant POs are proposed), PO, or scheduling agreement — and will narrow down your entry to an individual document selected, and so on.

▶ VENDOR DATA

System shows you the vendor master snapshot summary information and access to display more account details, or send email directly by using the EMAIL icon, for example.

▶ INVOICE ITEMS

List of proposed items specified by your allocation option is shown here. You can choose the lines you want to process, use sort and search tools if needed, and change the display layout.

Invoice entry with PO reference

Let's walk through an invoice entry with a PO reference, so you can see what role the screen section areas play during invoice entry. Follow these steps:

1. On the initial transaction screen, choose INVOICE in the TRANSACTION field (see Figure 9.2, ❶).

2. Populate the INVOICE DATE from the received vendor document in the header screen area ❷.

3. Allocate the invoice, and choose from PURCHASE ORDER/SCHEDULING AGREEMENT ❸ in the PO REFERENCE tab.

4. In the adjacent purchase order action text box ❹, enter the PO number — "4500017465" from our subcontracting scenario covered in Chapter 5 — the subcontracting order for assembly of a finished good with provision of two other components. You can see the details and the history related to this PO in the PO STRUCTURE pane on the left side of the screen.

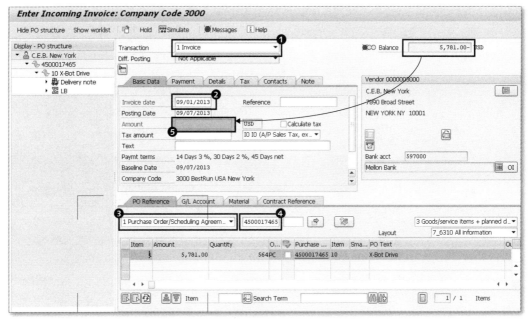

Figure 9.2 Entering the Incoming Invoice with Reference to the Purchase Order

5. When you press ⎡Enter⎤, the system displays the relevant PO items and vendor master data matching the allocation. The BALANCE field shows you the total amount the system will consider for payment and what should match the incoming invoice amount. This number, assuming there are no differences, goes into the AMOUNT field ❺. When you confirm the entry and press ⎡Enter⎤, the messages light and the traffic light by the BALANCE field change to green, and BALANCE is updated to show zero.

If you have tax amounts that need to be maintained, you also enter the values into the corresponding fields, and maintain any other header section tabs per your company business process requirements. After all information is entered, click the SAVE button or press ⎡Ctrl⎤ + ⎡S⎤ to complete the process. The invoice number is displayed on the message bar at the bottom of the screen. You've successfully created the invoice document.

Next, we'll show you how to perform the same function automatically.

9.1.2   Create Invoice: Automatically

In instances where massive amounts of data need to be processed, and you have no need to check items individually, you can use Transaction MIRA (Enter Invoices for Invoice Verification in the Background). Here you can schedule unprocessed invoices, and then a subsequent execution of the program RMBABG00 (Logistics Invoice Verification in Background) attempts to verify and post the actual documents.

> **Note**
>
> You can also run Transaction MRBP instead of program RMBABG00; bear in mind that this transaction isn't on the standard SAP menu path.

If some of your proposed invoices failed to post automatically, and manual intervention is necessary, another step in this process may be needed. The Transaction MIR6 report gives you the ability to review, complete processing, or delete the proposed invoice documents.

Let's start with Transaction MIRA. Follow these steps:

1. In the initial screen, choose INVOICE as the document type in the TRANSACTION field as shown in Figure 9.3 ❶.

2. Specify the INVOICE DATE ❷.

3. Allocate the proposed invoice to vendor ❸. Other choices include PURCHASE ORDER/SCHEDULING AGREEMENT, DELIVERY NOTE, BILL OF LADING, SERVICE ENTRY SHEET, and so on.

4. Specify either the subsequent documents or a vendor account ❹.

5. You can also choose what item types you want to process from goods/ service items to planned delivery costs, or all of them combined ❺. Each of the options chosen may give you additional selection criteria option to further narrow down the scope. For example, the vendor allocation opens up additional selection by plant, and we've entered PLNT "3000" ❻ to process some of the example POs generated in the earlier chapters.

6. Enter the invoice amount ❼, the currency, and the tax amount if you're anticipating any.

7. When ready, click the SAVE button or use ⎡Ctrl⎤ + ⎡S⎤ to save your
data.

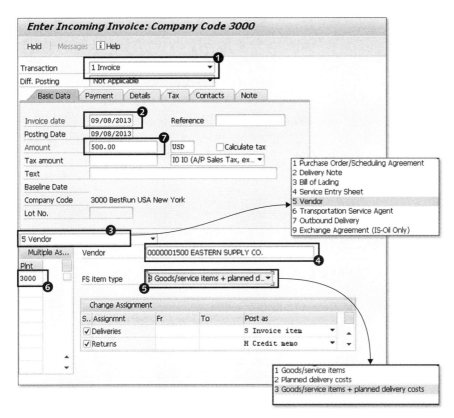

Figure 9.3 Entering Incoming Invoices in the Background: Data Entry Screen

This allocation criteria you've just entered will be used to determine the
item list when the job, or Transaction MRBP, is executed, and verification of the invoices is performed in the background. The invoice number
will be generated, and you can find it on the bottom left of the screen.

You can display these invoices queued up for background verification using
report MIR6 (Invoice Overview). See Figure 9.4 for an example of the
invoice generated by batch run before the verification program execution.

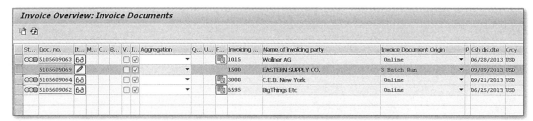

Figure 9.4　Invoice Overview: Batch Run Records

Next, you can run Transaction MRBP or set up a background job for program RMBABG00 to start the automated background verification process. The entry screen gives you options to specify the selection criteria that allows you to pick up all documents generated in the previous steps (see Figure 9.5).

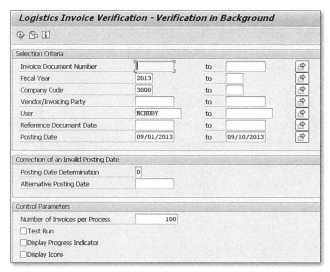

Figure 9.5　Invoice Verification Background Job Selection Screen

The program calculates the net total from the item list and performs the totals to what we've entered in Transaction MIRA. If the *Net Total = (Gross Amount Invoiced – Tax Amount) ± Tolerance*, then the system posts the invoice in the background, completing the process. Figure 9.6 shows a successfully processed verification.

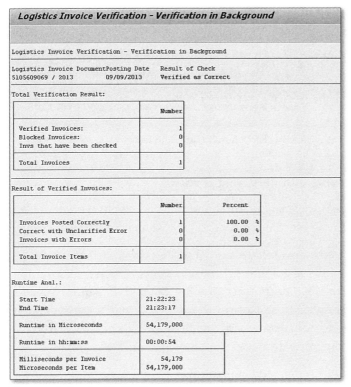

Figure 9.6 Invoice Verification Background Job Results

If the *Net Total ≠ (Gross Amount Invoiced – Tax Amount) ± Tolerance*, the invoice won't be posted in the background. The system will save the document, which needs to be processed manually. If your job posted any errors in the Invoice Verification in the background, simply run the MIR6 report again, using the selection criteria shown previously.

In our example, the body of the report lists invoices successfully posted and those that posted with errors. The system allows you to access the error log using the MESSAGE LOG 🖼 icon, access the invoice document change mode using the CHANGE INVOICE ✏ icon, and maintain the proposed header data, invoice amount, and reschedule the invoice for the next background job using the SCHEDULE BACKGROUND JOB 🖳 icon. You can also display FI documents using the FOLLOW-ON DOCS icon 📑 , as shown in Figure 9.7. Your Invoice Verification process will be processed again to try a second time for a clean and successful verification posting.

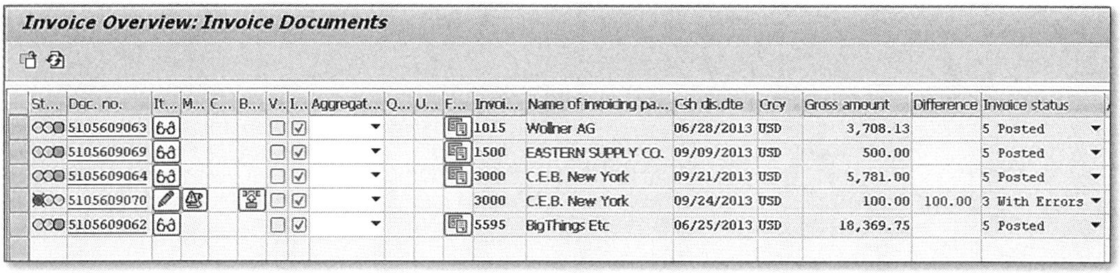

St...	Doc. no.	It...	M...	C...	B...	V..	I...	Aggregat...	Q...	U...	F...	Invoi...	Name of invoicing pa...	Csh dis.dte	Crcy	Gross amount	Difference	Invoice status	
○○◙	5105609063	6∂				☐	☑	▼				1015	Wolner AG	06/28/2013	USD	3,708.13		5 Posted	▼
○○◙	5105609069	6∂				☐	☑	▼				1500	EASTERN SUPPLY CO.	09/09/2013	USD	500.00		5 Posted	▼
○○◙	5105609064	6∂				☐	☑	▼				3000	C.E.B. New York	09/21/2013	USD	5,781.00		5 Posted	▼
◙○○	5105609070	✎	⚠		☒	☐	☑	▼				3000	C.E.B. New York	09/24/2013	USD	100.00	100.00	3 With Errors	▼
○○◙	5105609062	6∂				☐	☑	▼				5595	BigThings Etc	06/25/2013	USD	18,369.75		5 Posted	▼

Invoice Overview: Invoice Documents

Figure 9.7 Invoice Overview: Batch Run Records with Errors

9.1.3 Blocking and Releasing Invoices

If there are variances that call for FI to stop payment on an invoice, there is a mechanism to block these documents manually or automatically.

When you enter an invoice, the system suggests the values that it expects on the invoice as a result of the three-way match. If you find any differences between these documents, you can block the invoice while you research and resolve the variance by checking with your internal partners, the buyer, and your supplier. The invoice can be blocked for payment for the following reasons:

Reasons
- Variances in the item and item amount
- Manual payment block
- Stochastic blocking

Usually you don't investigate all differences because it's not cost effective and it's time-consuming. You can control which documents should be investigated by setting up configurable tolerance limits. If the variances are within these limits, you can automatically post the document, but if the limits are exceeded, the system messages are issued, and the invoice is automatically blocked for payment.

> **Note**
>
> If the invoice is blocked, all of the document items are blocked, even if only one of the items triggered the block.

Manual or automatic release
All blocked invoices are subject to release, and you can release them manually or automatically using Transaction MRBR (Release Blocked

436

Invoices) or using program RM08RELEASE scheduled as a background job. On the initial screen, enter your selection criteria for blocked invoices as shown in Figure 9.8.

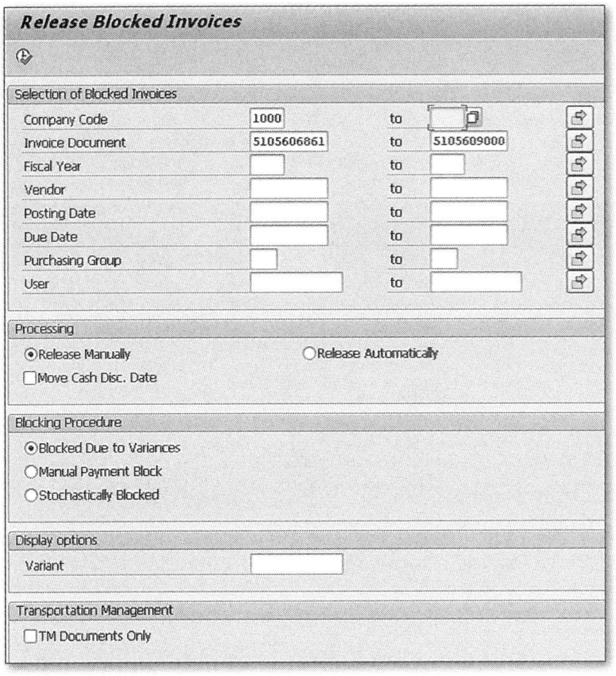

Figure 9.8 Release Blocked Invoices: Selection Screen

The SELECTION OF BLOCKED INVOICES section allows you to use a combination of invoice header data fields, from COMPANY CODE, INVOICE DOCUMENT numbers, VENDOR accounts, USER names, and POSTING DATE and DUE DATE.

In the PROCESSING section, you can choose whether you want release blocked invoices manually or automatically. Also, just like with the ERS procedure, you can choose to select TM DOCUMENTS ONLY from the TRANSPORTATION MANAGEMENT section. On executing, the list of blocked invoices matching your selection criteria is displayed, as shown in Figure 9.9.

The invoice list displays a lot of information using a standard ALV grid, and you can modify the layout to your needs and save it as a variant. To

Delete block methods

release any of the invoices listed, select the line, and click on the RELEASE INVOICE icon ![icon] or use F9 on your keyboard. The STATUS column is updated by showing the RELEASE INVOICE flag icon for the lines processed (see Figure 9.9).

Release Blocked Invoices

Sta	Doc. No.	Year	Crcy	Exchange rate	L.cur	O	Q	P	Q	I	D	M	T	CoCd	Invoicing Pty	Name	Amount	Purch.Doc.	Item
⚑	5105606861	20..	EUR	1.00000							✖		RE	1000	T-K515A29	Sapsota Company Limited	5,000.00	4151516129	20
⚑	5105606862	20..	EUR	1.00000					✖		✖		RE	1000	T-K515A29	Sapsota Company Limited	5,000.00	4151516229	10
	5105606863	20..	EUR	1.00000							✖		RE	1000	T-K515A30	Sapsota Company Limited	5,000.00	4151503130	20
	5105606864	20..	EUR	1.00000							✖		RE	1000	T-K515A30	Sapsota Company Limited	500.00	4151509230	10
	5105606864	20..	EUR	1.00000							✖		RE	1000	T-K515A30	Sapsota Company Limited	5,000.00	4151509230	20
	5105606865	20..	EUR	1.00000					✖		✖		RE	1000	T-K515A30	Sapsota Company Limited	200.00	4151509330	10
	5105606865	20..	EUR	1.00000							✖		RE	1000	T-K515A30	Sapsota Company Limited	400.00	4151509330	20
	5105606865	20..	EUR	1.00000							✖		RE	1000	T-K515A30	Sapsota Company Limited	600.00	4151509330	30
	5105606866	20..	EUR	1.00000							✖		RE	1000	T-K515A30	Sapsota Company Limited	500.00	4151510130	10
	5105606866	20..	EUR	1.00000							✖		RE	1000	T-K515A30	Sapsota Company Limited	5,000.00	4151510130	20
	5105606867	20..	EUR	1.00000			✖				✖		RE	1000	T-K515A30	Sapsota Company Limited	100.00	4151512130	10
	5105606867	20..	EUR	1.00000			✖				✖		RE	1000	T-K515A30	Sapsota Company Limited	1,000.00	4151512130	20
	5105606867	20..	EUR	1.00000							✖		RE	1000	T-K515A30	Sapsota Company Limited	600.00	4151512130	30
	5105606867	20..	EUR	1.00000			✖	✖			✖		RE	1000	T-K515A30	Sapsota Company Limited	240.00	4151512130	40
	5105606868	20..	EUR	1.00000							✖		RE	1000	T-K515B30	Abbot Supplies Inc.	5,000.00	4151514330	20
	5105606869	20..	EUR	1.00000							✖		RE	1000	T-K515B30	Abbot Supplies Inc.	2,400.00	4151514330	30
	5105606870	20..	EUR	1.00000							✖		RE	1000	T-K515A30	Sapsota Company Limited	5,000.00	4151516130	20
⚑	5105606871	20..	EUR	1.00000					🗑		🗑		RE	1000	T-K515A30	Sapsota Company Limited	5,000.00	4151516230	10
	5105608744	20..	EUR	1.00000				✖					RE	1000	1101	ABC Dienstleistungs GmbH	4.00	4500017191	10
	5105608992	20..	EUR	1.00000			🗑						RE	1000	15	Tiedemeier Entsorgung ...	56.70	4500017368	10

Figure 9.9 Release Blocked Invoices: Processing list

Another way of releasing is by deleting blocking reasons in the blocking reason columns, which are identified by the ![icon] icon. You can delete these reasons by placing your cursor on a blocking reason and clicking on the BLOCKING REASON button or using F8 on your keyboard. Some of the blocking reasons will be removed automatically depending on the subsequent business scenarios. The blocking reasons or applied releases are set and ready to go, but you still need to click the SAVE button to apply your changes. You'll get the informational message on the bottom of the screen confirming that the release of the invoices has been done.

9.1.4 Parking Invoices

When entering a large amount of invoices manually, and when your work is often multitasking that gets in the way of completing the work in one session, you can use the parking functionality when entering invoices. *Parking* allows you to create a DRAFT version of the invoice that can be processed later by the same or a different user and posted as a final invoice to finance.

> **Tips & Tricks**
>
> Another way of saving the incomplete invoices is to put the document on hold while in create mode using the Hold button where available (see Transactions MIRO and MIRA).

You can park an invoice or credit memo; save the document, add, remove, and correct the data; and not post the invoice until all of the information and data entry is complete. When you're done with all data maintenance of the parked document, you can post it, and the system saves the final credit memo or invoice.

You can also use the parking functionality to split the document pro-cessing by function. You can have one employee simply enter and park the invoices, and another review the entered data and approve them by posting the actual invoice or credit memo.

Split processing

To park your invoice or credit memo, run Transaction MIR7 (Park Invoice). Note that the entry screen looks and behaves exactly the same as in Transaction MIRO that we covered earlier (see Figure 9.10).

Steps

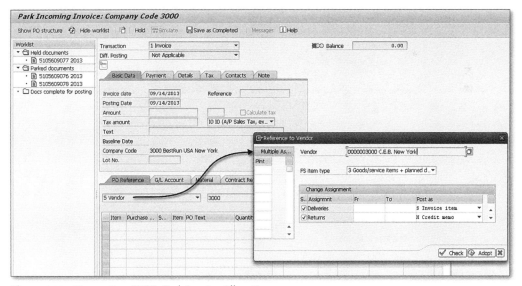

Figure 9.10 Transaction MIR7: Park Invoice Allocation

Now follow these steps:

1. In this example, you used the allocation type VENDOR, and in the popup window, you can further specify if you want to narrow down your document selection per plant and if you want to look at deliveries and returns. To continue, click the ADOPT button.

2. The invoice item list displays all matching POs, and those that can be processed are automatically selected and highlighted (see Figure 9.11). You can select only the lines you want to process, you can ignore the totals and error or warning messages.

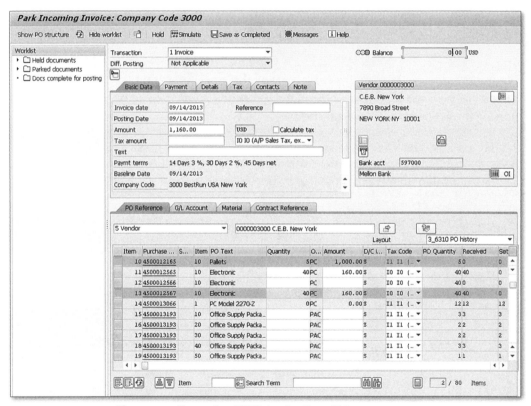

Figure 9.11 Transaction MIR7: Invoice Items List

3. Click on the SAVE button or use [Ctrl] + [S] to park the document. All of your parked and held documents are shown on the left side of the screen in the WORKLIST pane, as shown in Figure 9.12.

Figure 9.12 Parked and Held Documents in the Worklist Pane

4. Access these documents for further processing by double-clicking the document in the WORKLIST section.

5. You can make changes such as completing the invoice data, updating the allocation, simulating the posting, saving them as complete, deleting, and finally posting.

You can also perform the same function from Transaction MIR6 (Invoice Overview), which we've also covered earlier. This transaction allows you to select the documents in the parked and held status and process them directly from the report by clicking on the CHANGE icon ✎ (see an example in Figure 9.13).

St...	Doc. no.	It...	M...	C...	B...	V...	I...	Invoice status	Q...	U...	F...	Invoicing ...	Name of invoicin...	P	Csh dis.dte	Crcy	Gross amount	Difference
○○	5105609070	✎	♨		☑	☐☑	3	With Errors				3000	C.E.B. New York		09/24/2013	USD	100.00	100.00
	5105609075	✎				☐☑	1	Defined for bac...				3000	C.E.B. New York		09/13/2013	USD	20,000.00	
	5105609076	✎				☐☑	A	Parked					3000	C.E.B. New York		09/28/2013	USD	21.00	0.00
	5105609077	✎				☐☑	D	Entered and held				3000	C.E.B. New York		09/28/2013	USD	160.00	0.00
	5105609078	✎				☐☑	A	Parked					3000	C.E.B. New York		09/28/2013	USD	128,160.00	0.00
	5105609079	✎				☐☑	A	Parked					3000	C.E.B. New York		09/28/2013	USD	1,160.00	0.00

Figure 9.13 Transaction MIR6: Invoice Overview of Parked/Held Invoices

A list of invoice processing transactions covered in this section is provided in Table 9.1, showing transaction codes and their menu paths.

Transaction	Menu Path
MIRO: Enter Invoice	LOGISTICS • MATERIALS MANAGEMENT • LOGISTICS INVOICE VERIFICATION • DOCUMENT ENTRY • ENTER INVOICE
MIRA: Enter Invoice for Invoice Verification in Background	LOGISTICS • MATERIALS MANAGEMENT • LOGISTICS INVOICE VERIFICATION • DOCUMENT ENTRY • ENTER INVOICE FOR INVOICE VERIFICATION IN BACKGROUND
MIR4: Display Invoice Document	LOGISTICS • MATERIALS MANAGEMENT • LOGISTICS INVOICE VERIFICATION • FURTHER PROCESSING • DISPLAY INVOICE DOCUMENT
MRBR: Release Blocked Invoices	LOGISTICS • MATERIALS MANAGEMENT • LOGISTICS INVOICE VERIFICATION • FURTHER PROCESSING • RELEASE BLOCKED INVOICES
MIR5: Display List of Invoice Documents	LOGISTICS • MATERIALS MANAGEMENT • LOGISTICS INVOICE VERIFICATION • FURTHER PROCESSING • DISPLAY LIST OF INVOICE DOCUMENTS
MIR6: Invoice Overview	LOGISTICS • MATERIALS MANAGEMENT • LOGISTICS INVOICE VERIFICATION • FURTHER PROCESSING • INVOICE OVERVIEW
MR90: Output Messages	LOGISTICS • MATERIALS MANAGEMENT • LOGISTICS INVOICE VERIFICATION • FURTHER PROCESSING • OUTPUT MESSAGE

Table 9.1 Invoice Processing Transaction Codes

9.2 Automatic Settlement

If you have a good relationship with your suppliers, you can implement automatic settlement, called *evaluated receipt settlement* (ERS), to reduce the amount of paperwork and eliminate data entry errors. With this process, you don't need to get a copy of invoice documents from your vendor. In ERS, your POs and related goods receipts are settled directly without paper copy of the vendor invoice. The system creates a message record at the time of settlement, which allows you to send the vendor a letter about the settlement.

For this procedure to work, you need to have your master data defined to default into your POs. ERS relevancy is set on the vendor master and purchasing info records (refer to Chapter 2).

The other method of automation is to actually process the invoice via
EDI message sent by your supplier instead; again no paper documents
are required for processing. We'll discuss these processes in the following sections.

9.2.1 Evaluated Receipt Settlement

Assuming you've set up some of your vendors for the ERS procedure
and that you actually have POs that have been either fully or partially
received, you can proceed to settle the transactions using Transaction
MRRL (Evaluated Receipt Settlement [ERS]). The PO items should be
flagged for GR-BSD IV (goods receipt-based Invoice Verification) and
ERS, as shown in Figure 9.14.

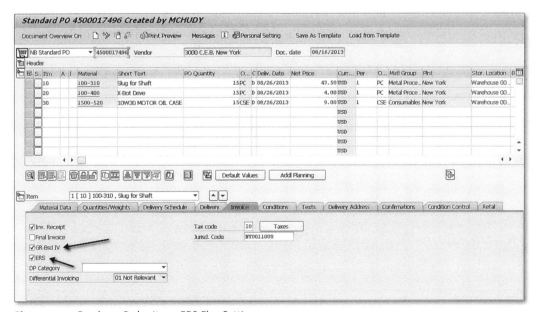

Figure 9.14 Purchase Order Item: ERS Flag Setting

When you execute the transaction, follow these steps:

1. On the initial screen, enter the COMPANY CODE number and PLANT, and then narrow down the selection criteria by populating data in some of the following fields (see Figure 9.15):

   ▶ GOODS RECEIPT POSTING DATE

   ▶ GOODS RECEIPT DOCUMENT (basically the material document number)

   ▶ FISCAL YEAR OF GOODS RECEIPT

   ▶ VENDOR account number

   ▶ PURCHASING DOCUMENT

   ▶ ITEM (the PO line item)

2. In the PROCESSING OPTIONS section, you can specify how you want to process the candidate document with the following options in the DOC. SELECTION field:

   ▶ 1 DOCUMENT SELECTION PER VENDOR

   ▶ 2 DOCUMENT SELECTION PER PURCHASE ORDER

   ▶ 3 DOCUMENT SELECTION PER ORDER ITEM

   ▶ 4 DOCUMENT SELECTION PER DELIVERY DOCUMENT/ SERVICE ENTRY

3. Address the two other options in the PROCESSING OPTIONS section as well:

   ▶ TEST RUN
   Choose the option to execute this report in test mode.

   ▶ SETTLE GOODS ITEMS + PLANNED DELIVERY COSTS
   This option is available only for non-GR related data selection.

Note

You can't use ERS to settle *only* the delivery costs portion of relevant purchasing documents.

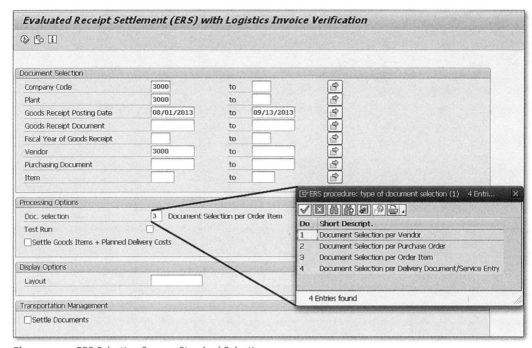

Figure 9.15 ERS Selection Screen: Standard Selection

4. If you want to process the SAP Transportation Management-related POs generated by shipment cost documents for shipments that used this document in the process, you can choose the SETTLE DOCUMENTS option at the bottom of the screen. This will change the selection screen to content that is relevant to a shipment processing document, as shown in Figure 9.16. (We covered shipment costing in detail in Chapter 7, so refer there to see how to create POs for transportation services.)

5. After you finish with your selection criteria entry, you can save it as a variant to allow you to run this job periodically for the pool of partners with ERS enabled. In our example, we'll be running the settlement in the foreground.

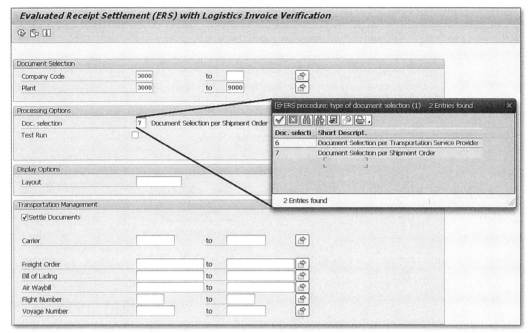

Figure 9.16 ERS Selection Screen: Travel Management Extended Selection

After you execute, the system attempts to post invoices and the list is displayed, classifying the documents that can and can't be settled. The items that settled successfully get the invoice number, as shown in Figure 9.17. You can also drill into the documents listed to access the display mode for POs, invoices, material documents, and display of long texts if information messages include more details. If the invoiced quantity is greater than the delivered quantity (for example, due to returns), the settlement run will create credit memos.

	Pstable	Vendor	Ref. Doc.	FYrRef	Rflt	Purch.Doc.	Item	Reference	Inv. Doc. No.	Year	InfoText	FI Doc.	DC	B/Lading	Smart No.
X	3000	5000000192	2013	1	4500017496	10		5105609071	2013		5100000009			
	3000	5000000192	2013	2	4500017496	20		5105609072	2013		5100000010			
	3000	5000000192	2013	3	4500017496	30		5105609073	2013		5100000011			

Figure 9.17 ERS: Completed Documents List

The lines that couldn't be processed are identified as not posted, and also get the error log message in the INFORMATION TEXT column. You can select such records and click the SAVE icon or press `Ctrl` + `S` to exclude them from the next ERS scheduled run.

Similar automated settlement procedures are applicable for consignment and pipeline materials using Transaction MRKO (Consignment and Pipeline Settlement).

9.2.2 EDI Processing

Many of your business partners are probably using the Electronic Data Interchange (EDI) communication for both inbound and outbound exchange of documents (sales orders, POs, confirmations, etc.). You can transmit invoices electronically using message type INVOIC with basic type INVOICE01. This gives you the advantage of replacing the paper invoice and eliminating data entry errors.

Upon receipt, the system tries to post the transaction and performs determination of the items, quantities, and values based on the PO reference provided in the transmitted IDoc. To enable and deploy this functionality, you'll need the assistance of the Basis team, ABAP developer, and a functional consultant.

> **Note**
>
> Automated settlement uses item data for processing. Invoice processing in the background, in contrast, uses the header data.

During incoming invoice processing, if the EDI invoice data matches the reference PO items proposed, the system posts the invoice. If the invoice has either quantity or value variances, you can post it with the variances, reduce it, or hold it for manual processing.

> **Note**
>
> Subsequent debits/credits and delivery costs can't be settled via EDI.

A list of automatic settlement transactions is provided in Table 9.2, which lists transaction codes and their menu paths.

Transaction	Menu Path
MRRL: Evaluated Receipt Settlement (ERS)	LOGISTICS • MATERIALS MANAGEMENT • LOGISTICS INVOICE VERIFICATION • AUTOMATIC SETTLEMENT • EVALUATED RECEIPT SETTLEMENT (ERS)
MRDC: Automatic Delivery Cost Settlement	LOGISTICS • MATERIALS MANAGEMENT • LOGISTICS INVOICE VERIFICATION • AUTOMATIC SETTLEMENT • AUTOMATIC DELIVERY COST SETTLEMENT
MRKO: Consignment and Pipeline Settlement	LOGISTICS • MATERIALS MANAGEMENT • LOGISTICS INVOICE VERIFICATION • AUTOMATIC SETTLEMENT • CONSIGNMENT AND PIPELINE SETTLEMENT
MRIS: Invoicing Plan Settlement	LOGISTICS • MATERIALS MANAGEMENT • LOGISTICS INVOICE VERIFICATION • AUTOMATIC SETTLEMENT • INVOICING PLAN SETTLEMENT
MRNB: Revaluation	LOGISTICS • MATERIALS MANAGEMENT • LOGISTICS INVOICE VERIFICATION • AUTOMATIC SETTLEMENT • REVALUATION

Table 9.2 Invoice Automatic Settlement Transaction Codes

9.3   Processing Subsequent Debits and Credits

You'll definitely find yourself in situations where an additional invoice or credit memo is received from your vendor for a transaction that has already been processed, invoiced, and paid for. You need to post a subsequent debit/credit for the PO involved, and the posting will update the transaction value, but the invoiced quantity remains the same.

Lower/higher price   If a vendor invoiced you at a lower price, and you've already processed it, and then the vendor realized the error and sent a second invoice for the difference, a new invoice must be entered as a subsequent debit for the initial invoice quantity and a difference value.

If the vendor invoiced you at a higher price and you've processed it, and the vendor again realizes the error and sends the credit memo for the difference, you need to enter the credit memo as a subsequent credit for the initial invoice quantity and a difference value.

> **Note**
>
> The subsequent postings can't be created with reference to another invoice; they are always done with reference to the original PO with the invoice already posted. The subsequent debit/credit quantity has to match the quantity already invoiced.

Let's walk through an example of posting a subsequent debit for an existing invoice for a PO created earlier in our scenarios. Execute Transaction MIRO (Enter Invoice). Follow these steps:

Debit for existing invoice

1. On the now-familiar initial screen, specify the transaction type by choosing SUBSEQUENT DEBIT.

2. Provide the typical pieces of the header data such as INVOICE DATE, for example, and then choose PURCHASE ORDER/SCHEDULING AGREEMENT in the allocation section of the screen.

3. Enter the PURCHASE ORDER number and press [Enter] to continue. The invoice ITEM list or individual item is displayed. As shown in Figure 9.18, we have a single material, so the quantity of the PO item is provided.

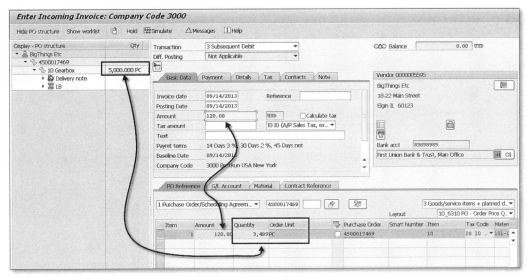

Figure 9.18 Entering an Incoming Invoice: Subsequent Debit

4. Provide the difference amount you need to apply to the original and already invoiced amount. Note the quantity on the original PO was 5000 pc, but the QUANTITY proposed in the invoice line details shows 3499 PC, which matches the initial goods receipt and invoice receipt quantity. Press ⟨Enter⟩ again.

5. In the HEADER DATA section, populate the AMOUNT field matching the AMOUNT of the line entry.

6. When done, click SAVE or press ⟨Ctrl⟩ + ⟨S⟩ to post your subsequent debit document.

Block posting   Depending on the configuration settings and tolerances defined, your subsequent posting can be blocked immediately for payment and will require review and approval to post the document (see Section 9.1.3 for details on how to perform the release of blocked invoices). And, finally, the subsequent adjustments post to the PO history, as shown in Figure 9.19.

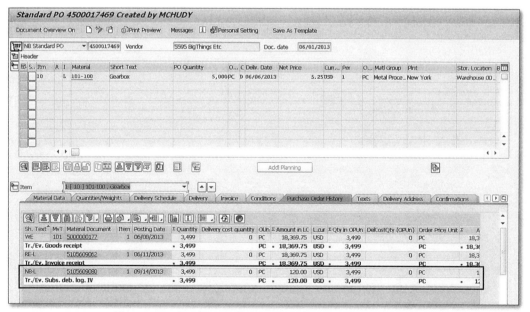

Figure 9.19 Purchase Order History: Subsequent Debit

9.4 Cancelling Invoice Document

Invoices can also be cancelled due to many different reasons. The reasons for reversals are defined in configuration and control whether an alternative posting date is allowed and whether generation of negative postings is allowed. These values give your system responses when you try to reverse/cancel the invoices already posted in the system.

Follow these steps to execute the cancellation/reversal:

1. Execute Transaction MR8M (Cancel Invoice Document) or use the menu path in Table 9.3.

2. On the initial screen, provide the original invoice document number you're cancelling and a fiscal year.

3. Fill in the REVERSAL REASON field and, if needed, populate the POSTING DATE for the transaction using one of the preconfigured entries, as shown in Figure 9.20.

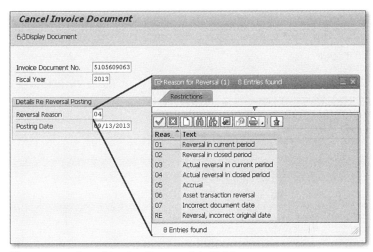

Figure 9.20 Cancel Invoice Document: Initial Screen

4. Review your data and click on the REVERSE button or use Ctrl + S on your keyboard to complete the cancellation.

If everything goes well, you'll get a confirmation message that the invoice document has been cancelled; otherwise, you may receive error messages related to the allowed combinations of reason codes and posting dates.

Transaction	Menu Path
MR8M: Cancel Invoice Document	LOGISTICS • MATERIALS MANAGEMENT • LOGISTICS INVOICE VERIFICATION • FURTHER PROCESSING • CANCEL INVOICE DOCUMENT

Table 9.3 Invoice Processing Transaction Codes: Cancellation

9.5   Summary

In this chapter, you've learned about finishing your procurement process with invoice processing. Now you should be able to process incoming invoices, process credit memos, and post subsequent debit/credit adjustments. You've also learned about the automatic invoice processing and evaluated receipt settlement (ERS), which can be used to simplify the process and eliminate data entry errors. Now you also know how to process blocked invoices, how to park or hold them, and how to release for further processing.

Now that you've finished this chapter, you've concluded your journey through the plethora of procurement processes.

Appendices

A   Procurement Tables

This appendix illustrates some of the most important procurement tables used in Materials Management and beyond. You can use this information when searching for needed data beyond standard reporting transactions using Transaction SE16N.

A.1   Material Master

Table	Description
MAEX	Material Master: Legal Control
MAKT	Material Descriptions
MALG	Assignment of Layout Modules to Materials
MAMT	Material Master Texts per Unit of Measure and Text ID
MAPE	Material Master: Export Control File
MARA	General Material Data
MARC	Plant Data for Material
MARD	Storage Location Data for Material
MARE	Reference Fields of Material for Change Documents
MARM	Units of Measure for Material
MARV	Material Control Record
MAW1	Material Master: Default Fields and Special Retail Fields
MBEW	Material Valuation
MFHM	Production Resource Tool (PRT) Fields in the Material Master
MKAL	Production Versions of Material
MLAN	Tax Classification for Material
MLGN	Material Data for Each Warehouse Number
MLGT	Material Data for Each Storage Type
MKOL	Special Stocks from Vendor

Table A.1 Material Master Tables

Table	Description
MKOP	Consignment Price Segment
MPOP	Forecast Parameters
MPRP	Forecast Profiles
MSKA	Sales Order Stock
MSKU	Special Stocks with Customer
MSLB	Special Stocks with Vendor
MSTA	Material Master Status
MVER	Material Consumption
MVKE	Sales Data for Material
MWLI	Listing (Retail)

Table A.1 Material Master Tables (Cont.)

A.2 Vendor Master

Table	Description
LFA1	Vendor Master (General Section)
LFAS	Vendor Master (VAT Registration Numbers General Section)
LFAT	Vendor Master Record (Tax Groupings)
LFB1	Vendor Master (Company Code)
LFB5	Vendor Master (Dunning Data)
LFBK	Vendor Master (Bank Details)
LFBW	Vendor Master Record (Withholding Tax Types) X
LFC1	Vendor Master (Transaction Figures)
LFC3	Vendor Master (Special G/L Transaction Figures)
LFEI	Vendor Master: Preference for Import and Export
LFLR	Vendor Master Record: Supply Regions
LFM1	Vendor Master Record Purchasing Organization Data
LFM2	Vendor Master Record: Purchasing Data

Table A.2 Vendor Master Tables

Table	Description
LFMH	Vendor Hierarchy
LFZA	Permitted Alternative Payee
WYT1	Vendor Subrange
WYT1T	Vendor Sub-Range Description
WYT3	Partner Functions

Table A.2 Vendor Master Tables (Cont.)

A.3 Purchasing Sourcing Information

Table	Description
EINA	Purchasing Info Record: General Data
EINE	Purchasing Info Record: Purchasing Organization Data
EIPA	Order Price History: Info Record
KOMG	Allowed Fields for Condition Structures
KOMK	Communication Header for Pricing
KOMP	Communication Item for Pricing
EORD	Purchasing Source List
EQUK	Quota File: Header
EQUP	Quota File: Item

Table A.3 Purchasing Sourcing Data Tables

A.4 Planning and Forecasting

Table	Description
MDKP	Header Data for MRP Document
MDRV	Generated Table for View
MDVM	Entry in MRP File
MKAL	Production Versions of Material
PLAF	Planned Order

Table A.4 Planning Tables

Table	Description
PBED	Independent Requirements Data
PBHI	Independent Requirements History
PBIM	Independent Requirements for Material

Table A.4 Planning Tables (Cont.)

Table	Description
PROF	Forecast Errors
PRON	Post-Processing of Forecast Errors and Exception Messages
PROP	Forecast Parameters
PROW	Forecast Values

Table A.5 Forecasting Tables

A.5   Investment Buy and Load Building

Table	Description
WBO1	Log Header File for Simulative List for Load Building
WBO2	Log item File for Simulative List for Load Building
WBO3	Log File for Investment Buy
WBO4	Log, Load Building, Restriction Profile Used
WBO5	Calculated Actual Vendor Service Level

Table A.6 Load Building and Investment Buy Tables

A.6   Purchasing Documents

Table	Description
EBAN	Purchase Requisition
EBKN	Purchase Requisition Account Assignment
EBUB	Index for Stock Transport Requisitions for Material
EINA	Purchasing Info Record: General Data

Table A.7 Purchasing Documents Tables

Table	Description
EINE	Purchasing Info Record: Purchasing Organization Data
EIPA	Order Price History: Info Record
EKAB	Release Documentation
EKAN	Vendor Address: Purchasing Document
EKBE	History per Purchasing Document
EKEH	Scheduling Agreement Release Documentation
EKEK	Header Data for Scheduling Agreement Releases
EKES	Vendor Confirmations
EKET	Scheduling Agreement Schedule Lines
EKKN	Account Assignment in Purchasing Document
EKKO	Purchasing Document Header
EKPA	Partner Roles in Purchasing
EKPB	"Material Provided" Item in Purchasing Document
EKPO	Purchasing Document Item
EKPV	Shipping Data For Stock Transfer of Purchasing Document Item
EKRS	ERS Procedure: Goods (Merchandise) Move to be Invoiced
EKRSDC	ERS Procedure: Planned Delivery Costs to be Invoiced
EKUB	Index for Stock Transport Orders for Material

Table A.7 Purchasing Documents Tables (Cont.)

A.7 Shipping

Table	Description
LIKP	SD Document: Delivery Header Data
LIPS	SD Document: Delivery: Item Data
SHP_IDX_CRED	Outbound Deliveries in Credit Check: Blocked and Released
SHP_IDX_EXIB	Inbound Delivery: External Identification

Table A.8 Shipping Tables

Table	Description
SHP_IDX_EXOB	Outbound Delivery: External Identification
SHP_IDX_GDRC	Inbound Deliveries: Not Posted for Goods Receipt
SHP_IDX_GDSI	Outbound Deliveries: Not Posted for Goods Issue
SHP_IDX_PICK	Outbound Deliveries: Not Picked
SHP_IDX_PUTA	Inbound Deliveries: Not Putaway
SHP_IDX_ROGR	Rough Goods Receipts for Vendor
SHP_IDX_UNCH	Outbound Deliveries: Unchecked
VBFS	Error Log for Collective Processing

Table A.8 Shipping Tables (Cont.)

Table	Description
VFKK	Shipment Costs: Header Data
VFKN	Account Determination in Shipment Costs Item
VFKONV	(Freight) Conditions
VFKONX	Conditions: Dimension-Dependent Data
VFKP	Shipment Costs: Item Data
VFPA	Partner for Shipment Costs
VFSCAH	Scale Header
VFSCAHT	Descriptions for Scales
VFSCAID	Scale Item: Gross Weight
VFSCAIF	Scale Item: Gross Volume
VFSCAIFO	Scale Item: Measuring
VFSCAILO	Scale Item: Postal Code
VFSCAIL2	Scale Item: Tariff Zone
VFSCAIL4	Scale Item: Transportation Zone
VFSCAIL6	Scale Item: Region
VFSCAIR	Scale Item: Distance

Table A.9 Shipment Costing Tables

Table	Description
VFSCAIS	Scale Item: Number of Shipping Units
VFSCAIS0	Key Item: Shipping Material
VFSCAIS1	Scale Item: Length of Loading Platform (Shipping Unit)
VFSCAIT0	Scale Item: Duration (Idle Time, Travel Time, and so on)
VFSCAR1	Freight Rates (One-Dimensional)
VFSCAR2	Freight Rates (Two-Dimensional)
VFSCAR3	Freight Rates (Three-Dimensional)
VFSI	Shipment Costs: Sub-Item Data
VFZP	Correct Original Assignment of Conditions

Table A.9 Shipment Costing Tables (Cont.)

A.8   Transportation

Table	Description
VTDST	Status of Deliveries within Transportation Planning
VTFA	Shipment Document Flow
VTPA	Shipping Partner
VTRDI	Shipment Planning Index
VTSP	Stage of Transport/Item Allocation
VTTK	Shipment Header
VTTP	Shipment Item
VTTS	Stage of Shipment
TVKN	Routes: Transportation Connection Points
TVKNT	Routes: Transportation Connection Points: Texts
TVRAB	Route Stages
TVRO	Routes
TVROT	Routes: Texts
TVRSZ	Routes: Legs for Each Route
TVSR	Routes: Legs

Table A.10 Transportation Tables

A.9   External Services

Table	Description
ASMD	Service Master: Basic Data
ASMDT	Service Short Texts
ESKL	Account Assignment Specification: Service Line
ESKN	Account Assignment in Service Package
ESLA	Service Type Editions
ESLB	Service Type Header of Standard Service Catalog
ESLH	Service Package Header Data
ESLL	Lines of Service Package
ESLP	Service Item
ESLT	Service Item Short Texts
ESLZ	Service Type Lines
ESSR	Service Entry Sheet Header Data
ESST	Service Item Short Texts
ESUC	Ext. Services Management: Unplanned Limits on Contract Item
ESUH	Ext. Services Management: Unplanned. Service Limits: Header Data
ESUP	Ext. Services Management: Unplanned Limits on Service Package
ESUS	Services Management: Unplanned Limits on Service Types

Table A.11   External Services Tables

A.10   Inventory Management

Table	Description
CHVW	Table CHVW for Batch Where-Used List
IKPF	Header: Physical Inventory Document

Table A.12   Inventory Management Tables

Table	Description
ISEG	Physical Inventory Document Items
MCH1	Batches (if Batch Management Cross-Plant)
MCHA	Batches
MCHB	Batch Stocks
MKPF	Header: Material Document
MSEG	Document Segment: Material
RESB	Reservation/Dependent Requirements
RKPF	Document Header: Reservation

Table A.12 Inventory Management Tables (Cont.)

A.11 Invoice Verification

Table	Description
RBCO	Document Item, Incoming Invoice, Account Assignment
RBKP	Document Header: Invoice Receipt
RBKP_BLOCKED	Logistics Invoice Verification: Blocked Invoices
RBMA	Document Item: Incoming Invoice for Material
RBTX	Taxes: Incoming Invoice
RBVD	Invoice Document: Aggregation Data
RBVDMAT	Invoice Verification: Aggregation Data, Material
RBVS	Invoice Verification: Split Invoice Amount
RBWS	Withholding Tax Data, Incoming Invoice
RBWT	Withholding Tax Data, Incoming Invoice
RKWA	Consignment Withdrawals
RSEG	Document Item: Incoming Invoice

Table A.13 Invoice Verification Tables

B   Working with Procurement Documents: Quick Reference Guide

We hope the quick reference guides we selected to create in this section are very useful to you. Even seasoned users don't create all types of documents in their everyday work, and some details may escape them. Additionally, novice users can benefit from these guides because they are easy to follow, and yet robust enough that anyone can use them.

B.1   Create Info Record

To quickly create an info record, follow these steps:

1. Use Transaction ME11 or follow menu path LOGISTICS • MATERIALS MANAGEMENT • PURCHASING • MASTER DATA • INFO RECORD • CREATE.

2. From the initial screen, enter the following values:

Field Name	Description	User Action and Values
VENDOR	Number of the vendor supplying this material	Required.
MATERIAL	Material number for the item you want to purchase from this vendor	Required.
PURCHASING ORG.	Purchasing organization for which you plan to purchase this item	Required. (Each info record requires a purchasing organization to save prices and conditions.)
PLANT	The plant where the material will be used	Optional. (If you enter the plant, the price will only be valid for that plant. However, if you leave the plant blank, the price is valid for all plants within the purchasing organization.)
INFO CATEGORY	How the data will be used when creating a PO	STANDARD, for normal purchasing; SUBCONTRACTING for MM subcontract purchasing.

3. In GENERAL DATA: VENDOR MAT. NO, optionally enter the vendor's material number if known.

4. In PURCH.ORGANIZATION DATA 1, enter the following values and press Enter :

Field Name	User Action and Values
PLND DELY TIME	Enter the delivery time from the vendor (if you entered a plant on the initial screen, this will populate from the material master).
PURCH. GROUP	Enter the purchasing group (if you entered a plant on the initial screen, this will populate from the material master).
STANDARD QTY	Enter "1".
NET PRICE	Enter the price.
PRICE UNIT	Enter the price unit (i.e., the net price per XX units).
TAX CODE	Enter "I1".

5. To enter more pricing details, choose CONDITIONS.

6. In CONDITION SUPPLEMENTS, select the PRICE LINE.

7. To enter scale prices, choose SCALES.

8. Select the SCALES button.

9. Enter SCALE PRICING as necessary:

   ▶ In SCALE QUANTITY, enter the quantity at which the price applies. Leave the first SCALE QUANTITY blank, and then every quantity from zero up to the next SCALE QUANTITY will have the first price.

   ▶ In AMOUNT, enter the scale amount.

B.2   Create Source List

To create a source list, follow these steps:

1. Use Transaction ME01 or use the path LOGISTICS • MATERIALS MANAGEMENT • PURCHASING • MASTER DATA • SOURCE LIST • MAINTAIN.

2. On the MAINTAIN SOURCE LIST screen, make the following entries:

Field Name	User Action and Values
MATERIAL	Enter a material number.
PLANT	Enter a plant number.

3. Choose [Enter].

4. On the MAINTAIN SOURCE LIST: OVERVIEW screen make the following entries:

Field Name	User Action and Values	Comment
VALID FROM	Usually, enter the current date.	
VALID TO	Enter the validity end date.	
VENDOR	Enter the vendor number.	Enter the same vendor from the info record.
PURCHASE ORGANIZATION	Enter your purchase organization.	Enter the same purchasing organization from the info record.
AGREEMENT NUMBER		Enter the agreement number if you have one.
ITEM	1	Enter the agreement item number.
MRP	2	Use in MRP.

5. Save your entries.

B.3   Convert Purchase Requisition into Purchase Order

To convert a purchase requisition into a purchase order, follow these steps:

1. Use Transaction ME58 or use the path LOGISTICS • MATERIALS MANAGEMENT • PURCHASING • PURCHASE REQUISITION • FOLLOW-ON FUNCTIONS • CREATE PURCHASE ORDER • VIA ASSIGNMENT LIST.

2. On the ASSIGN AND PROCESS PURCHASE REQUISITIONS screen, make the following entries and then choose EXECUTE:

Field Name	User Action and Values	Comment
PURCHASING GROUP	Enter your purchasing group.	
PURCHASING ORGANIZATION	Enter the purchasing organization for which you are executing this function.	
VENDOR	Enter a vendor number.	You can leave wide open or enter a single value or a vendor range.
PLANT	Enter a plant number.	Choose the plant you have planned before.
SCOPE OF LIST	A	

3. Click EXECUTE.

4. From the OVERVIEW OF ASSIGNMENTS screen, choose the assignment for one of the vendors by clicking with the mouse.

5. Click the PROCESS ASSIGNMENTS button.

6. In the new pop-up window, enter the following:

Field Name	User Action and Values	Comment
DOCUMENT TYPE	NB	For standard PO document type.
PURCHASE ORDER DATE	Enter the date for the PO that is about to be created.	Usually, the current date.
PURCHASE ORDER	Leave blank.	The system will assign a number.
PURCHASING GROUP	Confirm your purchasing group.	
PURCHASING ORGANIZATION	Confirm the purchasing organization.	

7. Press ⌶Enter⌷.

8. In the CREATE PO screen, the requisitions are listed on the side bar on the left-hand side.

9. Drag each requisition to the shopping cart on the top-left corner of the main screen.

10. Save the PO.

B.4   Create Purchase Order (Stock Material)

To create a purchase order for stock material, follow these steps:

1. Use Transaction ME21N or follow the path: LOGISTICS • MATERIALS MANAGEMENT • PURCHASING • PURCHASE ORDER • CREATE • VENDOR/ SUPPLYING PLANT KNOWN.

2. On the CREATE PURCHASE ORDER screen, make the following entries:

Field Name	User Action and Values	Comment
ORDER TYPE	NB	Standard PO.
VENDOR	Enter a vendor number.	
ORG. DATA tab	Choose	
PURCHASING ORG.	Enter the purchasing organization.	Purchasing organization.
PURCHASING GROUP	Enter your purchasing group.	
COMPANY CODE	Enter the company to which the plant belongs.	
EXPAND ITEM OVERVIEW	Expand.	If ITEM OVERVIEW window is not visible.
ITEM CATEGORY	Leave blank.	For stock materials.
MATERIAL	Enter a material number.	
ORDER QUANTITY	Enter a quantity.	
DELIVERY DATE	Any, in future.	
NET PRICE	Enter the purchase price of the material.	This is not necessary if you have an info record.
CURRENCY	Enter the currency for the purchase.	Normally the currency of the vendor, comes from the info record.
PER	Enter how many units the price is valid for.	This is not necessary if you have an info record.

Field Name	User Action and Values	Comment
PRICE UNIT	Enter the unit of measure that qualifies the price.	This is not necessary if you have an info record.
PLANT	Enter the plant where the material will be delivered.	
STORAGE LOCATION	Enter the storage location where the material will be delivered.	Target storage location.

3. Save the changes.

B.5 Create Purchase Order (Subcontracting)

To create a purchase order for subcontracting, follow these steps:

1. Use Transaction ME21N or follow the path LOGISTICS • MATERIALS MANAGEMENT • PURCHASING • PURCHASE ORDER • CREATE • VENDOR/ SUPPLYING PLANT KNOWN.

2. On the CREATE PURCHASE ORDER screen, make the following entries:

Field Name	User Action and Values	Comment
ORDER TYPE	NB	Standard PO.
VENDOR	Enter a vendor number.	
ORG. DATA TAB	Choose	
PURCHASING ORG.	Enter the purchasing organization.	Purchasing organization.
PURCHASING GROUP	Enter your purchasing group.	
COMPANY CODE	Enter the company to which the plant belongs.	
EXPAND ITEM OVERVIEW	Expand.	If ITEM OVERVIEW window is not visible.
ITEM CATEGORY	L	For subcontracting items.
MATERIAL	Enter a material number.	
ORDER QUANTITY	Enter a quantity.	

Field Name	User Action and Values	Comment
DELIVERY DATE	Any, in future.	
NET PRICE	Enter the purchase price of the material.	This is not necessary if you have an info record.
CURRENCY	Enter the currency for the purchase.	Usually, the currency of the vendor, comes from the info record.
PER	Enter how many units the price is valid for.	This is not necessary if you have an info record.
PRICE UNIT	Enter the unit of measure that qualifies the price.	This is not necessary if you have an info record.
PLANT	Enter the plant where the material will be delivered.	
STORAGE LOCATION	Enter the storage location where the material will be delivered.	Target storage location.
ITEM DETAIL SECTION	Expand.	If item detail window is not visible.
SELECT THE MATERIAL DATA TAB	Click the BOM button, and enter or verify the components.	If the material entered in the item overview has a BOM (PP master data), it will be automatically copied.
SELECT THE SHIPPING TAB	Make sure the tab exists and the shipping data is complete.	

3. Save the changes.

B.6   Create Purchase Order (Consignment)

To create a purchase order for subcontracting, follow these steps:

1. Use Transaction ME21N or follow the path LOGISTICS • MATERIALS MANAGEMENT • PURCHASING • PURCHASE ORDER • CREATE • VENDOR/ SUPPLYING PLANT KNOWN.

2. On the CREATE PURCHASE ORDER screen, make the following entries:

Field Name	User Action and Values	Comment
ORDER TYPE	NB	Standard PO.
VENDOR	Enter a vendor number.	
ORG. DATA TAB	Choose	
PURCHASING ORG.	Enter the purchasing organization.	Purchasing organization.
PURCHASING GROUP	Enter your purchasing group.	
COMPANY CODE	Enter the company to which the plant belongs.	
EXPAND ITEM OVERVIEW	Expand.	If ITEM OVERVIEW window is not visible.
ITEM CATEGORY	K	For consignment items.
MATERIAL	Enter a material number.	
ORDER QUANTITY	Enter a quantity.	
DELIVERY DATE	Any, in future.	
NET PRICE	Field not available for entry.	A consignment info record is mandatory to create a consignment PO.
CURRENCY	Field not available for entry.	
PER	Field not available for entry.	
PRICE UNIT	Field not available for entry.	
PLANT	Enter the plant where the material will be delivered.	
STORAGE LOCATION	Enter the storage location where the material will be delivered.	Target storage location.

3. Save the changes.

B.7   Create Purchase Order (Expensed Items)

To create a purchase order for expensed items, follow these steps:

1. Use Transaction ME21N or follow the menu path Logistics • Materials Management • Purchasing • Purchase Order • Create • Vendor/ Supplying Plant Known.

2. On the Initial screen, make the following entries and choose Enter :

Field Name	User Action and Values	Comment
PO Type	NB	Standard PO.
Purchasing Organization (Org. Data)	Enter a purchasing organization.	
Purchasing Group (Org. Data)	Enter your purchasing group.	
Company Code (Org. Data)	Enter the company code for the plant making the purchase.	
Vendor	Enter a vendor number.	

3. On the Item Overview line, make the following entries:

Field Name	User Action and Values	Comment
Account Assignment Category	▸ K for cost center. ▸ F for internal order.	If you choose K, you should enter a cost center and a GL account.
Short text	Enter description of item.	Short description for what you are buying.
Quantity	For example, 100.	Enter a quantity.
OUn	EA	Enter order unit.
Net price	For example, 10 USD.	Enter a net price.
Currency	Enter the currency.	Enter purchase currency.
Per	Enter how many units the price is valid for.	This is not necessary if you have an info record.
OPu	EA	Enter order price unit.
Material Group	Select a material group.	
Plant	Enter a plant number.	Enter relevant plant.

4. Choose `Enter`.

5. On the ACCOUNT ASSIGNMENT tab, when prompted, enter COST CENTER, if the ACCOUNT ASSIGNMENT CATEGORY is entered as K. Or enter the internal order via `F4` Help if ACCOUNT ASSIGNMENT CATEGORY is entered as F.

6. If it is not already selected, select the GOODS RECEIPT checkbox on the DELIVERY tab.

7. Choose SAVE.

C   Additional Resources

For further reference in any of the subjects we covered in this book, we suggest that you consult the following references and materials:

- SAP Help: Available on the web at *http://help.sap.com/*

- SAP Developers Network: Available on the web at *http://www.sdn.sap.com/*

- Hoppe, Marc and Ferenc Gulyássy. *Materials Planning with SAP*. Boston: SAP PRESS, 2009.

- Murray, Martin. *100 Things You Should Know About Materials Management in SAP ERP*. Boston: SAP PRESS, 2013.

- Murray, Martin. *Materials Management with SAP ERP: Functionality and Technical Configuration*. 3rd Ed. Boston: SAP PRESS, 2010.

D   The Authors

Matt Chudy is an independent SAP Logistics consulting lead. He has more than 15 years of experience in SD, MM, and Logistics, spanning project administration, design, gap-analysis, testing, implementation, and supporting and training. He has been a strong team leader and covered several SAP project lifecycles. His specialties include Logistics Execution System, Transportation Management, Sales and Distribution, Inventory and Warehouse Management, Materials Management, and Production Planning. He currently lives in the greater Chicago area.

Luis Castedo is an independent systems and business consultant with more than 20 years of experience. For the past 16 years, he has been focused on SAP implementations. He has experience working with Fortune 500 companies and on multisite projects. He is a certified SAP MM consultant, and his specialties include Sales and Distribution, Materials Management, Inventory and Warehouse Management, Shipping, and Transportation. He currently lives in the Mexico City area.

Together, Matt and Luis have written the bestselling SAP PRESS books *Sales and Distribution in SAP ERP—Practical Guide* and *100 Things You Should Know About Sales and Distribution in SAP*.

Index

Interested in reading more?

Please visit our website for all new
book and e-book releases from SAP PRESS.

www.sap-press.com